D0363445

Bernard Spilsbury

Bernard Spilsbury

His Life and Cases

DOUGLAS G. BROWNE
and
TOM TULLETT

With a Foreword by
PROFESSOR KEITH SIMPSON C.B.E.

HARRAP LONDON

First published in Great Britain 1951
by GEORGE G. HARRAP & CO. LTD
182 High Holborn, London WC1V 7AX

Reprinted: 1951 (*twice*); 1952 (*three times*); 1954
Reissued: 1980
Reprinted: 1981 *(twice)*

ISBN 0 245 53586 1

Printed in Great Britain by
Biddles Ltd, Guildford, Surrey

FOREWORD

THE twentieth century has seen a number of famous detectives—Wensley, Dew of Crippen fame, Savage, Burt, Greeno, Cornish, to mention a few—and one medical man who in crime investigation stood head and shoulders above his fellows. This was Bernard Spilsbury, tall, aloof, good-looking, professional; always well dressed, he shouldered the Crown's medical responsibilities in every notable case for nearly forty years without either assistant or secretary—and with very indifferent laboratory support. "Call Sir Bernard" was, any counsel knew, a body blow to his opponents in court. A positive hush would descend as the great man made his way through to give his evidence: calm, assertive, brushing aside criticism as one might a troublesome fly, his word shut the door on many a good-enough-looking defence. An utterly confident, transparently honest-looking man, he would marshal the facts he had observed at autopsy in carefully chosen words, and then calmly wait for a cross-examination that was seldom more than perfunctory. It seemed hopeless to oppose this quietly confident man, and among his fellows only the redoubtable Sydney Smith and a shaky Brontë ever did . . . both to no avail. Indeed, in the Merritt case in Scotland, leading counsel so lost his nerve as to address the great man as "*St* Bernard". Judges of the quality of Travers Humphreys, well versed in criminal-trial procedure, would even compliment him in open court.

Could Sir Bernard repeat his performances in Crippen, Seddon, Armstrong, Thorne, Fox and similar cases to-day? Or would the testings of less awed lawyers and the opposition of well-trained contemporaries—which Sir Bernard so seldom met—moderate the great man's attitudes? I doubt it, for he was never caught doing a job at the scene or in the mortuary writing a report, or giving evidence, with any but the most painstaking thoroughness; opposition might have irritated him, but he would have shown no trace of it. He really was a fine witness, and Browne and Tullett's absorbing account of his many exploits is well worth reading again—and again. This fine biography contains innumerable lessons in crime-detection fundamentals—maybe only comparatively little science, for it was then in its infancy—but much to show the percipience, care and logical deduction that made Sir Bernard such a respected figure in his day.

These pages teem with famous—and not so famous—crime cases which this great man either "solved" or clarified for both Scotland Yard and the County Police Forces who put their confidence in him. He rose to prominence in the Crippen case, largely by the calm authority with which he gave his evidence, and in continuous stream there followed Armstrong, Seddon, the "Brides in the Bath" case, Voisin, Mahon (the Crumbles dismemberment), the Thorne case at Crowborough, Vaquier, the Brighton trunk murder, Fox, Rouse, Vera Page, Merritt, Casserley, the assassination of Sir Michael O'Dwyer, Antiquis—crimes of colour and importance which his biographers recount with a sure journalist's touch. It was no surprise the book became an instant best-seller when first published, and everyone with an interest in forensic science will welcome its reappearance.

London, 1980 K.S.

ACKNOWLEDGMENTS

The close and friendly co-operation of Lady Spilsbury and her daughter, Mrs Evelyn Steel, has been an essential factor in the writing of this book, and Mr Richard Spilsbury has supplied valuable reminiscences of his father. The exclusive material which they have furnished renders this book an authoritative account of Sir Bernard Spilsbury's life.

The most cordial thanks are also due to Sir Harold Scott, K.C.B., K.B.E., Commissioner of Police of the Metropolis, for permission to use certain official photographs and for granting other facilities at New Scotland Yard; to Mr Ronald Howe, C.V.O., M.C., Assistant Commissioner, Criminal Investigation Department; to Mr R. L. Jackson, the Secretary, New Scotland Yard; to Mr F. E. Heron and the staff of the New Scotland Yard Reference Library, who have been of the greatest assistance in preparing and checking data; and to a number of senior officers of the Metropolitan Police who have willingly given time and thought to recording their recollections—in particular, Chief Superintendent G. Hatherill, M.B.E., Chief Superintendent H. W. Hawkyard, M.B.E., Chief Superintendent F. R. Cherrill, M.B.E., Superintendent C. R. M. Cuthbert, and Chief Inspector P. G. Law.

Mr G. R. Paling, C.B.E., Deputy Director of Public Prosecutions, has been very helpful indeed; and acknowledgment should be made of the courtesy and interest shown by M. Népote, of the Secrétariat Général, Commission Internationale de Police Criminelle, and M. J. Ledoux, Secrétaire Général du Parquet, Palais de Justice, Paris.

A particular debt of gratitude is owing to the Right Hon. Sir Travers Humphreys, Sir Archibald Bodkin, K.C.B., Lord Alness, Mr W. Bentley Purchase, C.B.E., M.C., and the late Dr Eric Gardner, who have gone to considerable trouble to supply information, written and oral; to Mr Robert Churchill, the authority on firearms, who read the chapter on shooting cases and was in other ways helpful; and to Mr. G. Grafton Green for his enthusiasm and encouragement.

Among others to whom thanks are due are Sir Norman Kendal, K.B.E., Sir Patrick Hastings, K.C., Dr J. H. Ryffel, Dr John Taylor, Miss F. Tennyson Jesse, Mr Ernest Goddard, Dr P. H. Willcox, Mr

Alan St H. Brock, and the late Mr Ivor Back; all those whose names have been mentioned in the text in connexion with information supplied; and many more whose anecdotes and recollections have been incorporated.

Messrs William Hodge and Co., Ltd, of Edinburgh, have most kindly granted permission for very free use of their series of Notable British Trials, without constant reference to which no book of this kind can be written.

CONTENTS

PART ONE: EARLY YEARS (1877–1910)

PART TWO: THE INCOMPARABLE WITNESS (1910–25)

PART THREE: SPILSBURY AS OTHERS SAW HIM

PART FOUR: THE FULLEST YEARS (1926–39)

PART FIVE: THE LAST PHASE (1939–47)

ILLUSTRATIONS

(between pages 220-221)

Part One

EARLY YEARS (1877–1910)

Chapter 1: CASE HISTORY

TOWARDS the close of the eighteenth century the little village of Leamington Priors, two miles from Warwick, and as near as need be the geographical centre of England, began to be known beyond the bounds of the county as what was then called a 'spaw.' It must have seemed a very primitive place to those familiar with the ancient splendours of Bath and the growing amenities of Cheltenham, for when William Abbotts built the first public baths in 1789 two indifferent inns, the Dog and the Bowling Green, and rooms in a few of the cleaner cottages, provided the only lodgings for invalids who came to drink or to bathe in the waters. But Leamington grew with remarkable speed; within some twenty-five years it had become a flourishing and even elegant spa.

It was about this time that a typical rural family, scattered over Warwickshire and Worcestershire, and later to be associated with a Leamington which would have astonished Mr Abbotts, also made a break with tradition. For a couple of centuries there had been Spilsburys holding Midland and West Country livings. Against occasional deviations into Dissent could be set a Master of Pembroke and Bishop of Bristol. From about 1670 onward, however, a new spirit of enterprise fired this conventional race to launch out into trade, medicine, and the arts. Spilsburys could be found pursuing these diverse careers not only in London, but in Asia Minor and in India. The most unorthodox of them all was Francis Spilsbury, who at his house in Mount Row, on the Surrey side of Westminster Bridge, dispensed anti-scorbutic pills, drops, and other medicaments of his own concocting, doing very well out of them, apparently, but never refusing, as he says, even when he had to raise his prices, "compliance to the folicitations of the poor." He was, in fact, something of a philanthropist, and the term 'quack' applied to him seems to be a misnomer. He does not figure among those medical humbugs listed as flourishing in London in his day. He was able to retire in his old age to the village of Hampstead, where he died in 1793.

In view of the origins of his most renowned descendant, the subject of this book, it would be pleasant to think of Francis purveying his pills in the rising spa in those Midlands from which his family came; but he died before Dr Lambe's analysis of the Leamington waters began to attract there the fashionable and wealthy. Perhaps he is primarily of interest now because his "Dispensary" in Mount Row was the forerunner of a laboratory which that descendant was to make famous.

In the meantime, among other Spilsburys breaking new ground, one became Mayor of Worcester, a second was a linen-draper, and a third a goldsmith. With this last, and with yet one more who was a printer, the family began to show that bent for craftsmanship and the artistic which, after the bishop, was its chief claim to fame before the name of Bernard Spilsbury grew to be a household word. Round about 1800 John and Jonathan were winning reputations as etchers and engravers. Maria, variously described as the daughter of either,[1] was a capable painter. A spurious "Inigo" Spilsbury was probably John. Two threads in the racial make-up were combined in a doctor who exhibited at the Royal Academy, and in J. B. Spilsbury, who wrote and illustrated a book on the Holy Land while on a cruise in the Levant. Doctoring, again, was carried on by the direct line of the empirical Francis, and George Green Spilsbury, Physician-General on the Royal Establishment, died in India in the year of the Mutiny.

There were Spilsburys, however, who remained at home in the Midlands. One, a corn merchant in Stafford, supplied hay to Dr Palmer of Rugeley, and among Bernard Spilsbury's papers is a letter from Palmer to Ann Brookes, or Thornton, his future wife and victim, in which he speaks of sending medicine and pills to her mother, whom he also poisoned. With another Spilsbury, who was to prove not the least restless, the family annals begin a new chapter in Leamington. It was a Leamington very different from Dr Lambe's in which, twenty years after the Mutiny, James Spilsbury, analytical and manufacturing chemist (the scientific strain had reached Warwickshire), made the first of his numerous homes. His son Bernard, if his interest in antiquities was of early growth, may have smiled over Mr W. Field's description of the town as it had been little more than fifty years before. "And now," wrote this author in the year of Waterloo,

> how changed the scene! The busy hum of men succeeds to the lowing of the kine; and where, so late, the plough cut its furrowed way, or the

[1] The *Dictionary of National Biography* says that Maria was the daughter of Jonathan.

> sweeping scythe laid its waving treasure low—the walls of human habitations ascend!—an extensive and beautiful town appears!—a street is formed, and others are forming!

Among the streets then formed or forming was Bath Street, terminated by a theatre built "of Roman cement, finished in a pleasing style of simple elegance." The scene was even more radically changed by the 1870's, when James Spilsbury took a human habitation in Bath Street, having his business premises on the first floor and living with his young wife in no fewer than twelve rooms above.

James made a success of his wholesale business, and it became the most prosperous of its kind in the town, which was full of retail chemists. But he was a dissatisfied man. His father, one of the Dissenting Spilsburys, a small landowner, well-to-do, with a house in Stafford, was in sympathy with his son's desire to follow one family tradition and become a doctor; but the young man's strong-minded mother held other views. Mrs Spilsbury saw no future in medicine. James must go into trade. And into trade, reluctantly, James had gone. But he had a will of his own; he chose a medical trade; and, having married Marion Joy, of Stafford, and set up in business for himself in Leamington, away from the rather overpowering influence of his mother, he made a far-reaching decision about the future. If he had a son, that son should be a doctor.

2

The son was born in 1877, in January, in the house in Bath Street. He was christened Bernard Henry. A sister and a brother, Constance and Leonard, followed at intervals of a few years. Bernard, in the meantime, was growing out of childhood in a dying age—that age of moral earnestness, at its most fervid, outside Scotland, in the Nonconformist Midlands, which, for all its narrowness, proved so powerful an agent in the formation of character. It produced great men, and James Spilsbury's eldest son, by the time he reached middle age, had seen the passing of a whole generation of remarkable figures in the world of science—Lister, Kelvin, Crookes, and many more. He was himself to carry on the great tradition. But though, in the austere side of his nature, in his devotion to morality and justice, a flavour of the Victorian seems to linger, boyhood, in his case, was never hedged about, as too often it still was, by vetoes and conventions. His father was something of a disciplinarian, and his mother a churchwoman, and on Sundays the small Bernard had to go twice to church, which he probably endured with the placid gravity that seldom was to desert him. He did not inherit the paternal restlessness. James Spilsbury, however, was an individualist and an intelligent man, who never forgot his own frustrations, and was determined that his children should not suffer in a like way. It was a happy family that lived in the house in Bath Street.

No less important, perhaps, was the environment of their first home. Leamington was far indeed from being a typical Midland town. It was a modern growth, artificial, smart, and even gay. From all England people came there for the waters, and to be amused while they took them. There were few industries, and those small. Even Bernard Spilsbury's self-reliant and decided character must, in these formative years, have been influenced by his surroundings; and while, in Stafford and Birmingham, his grandmother and her kind clung to their belief that success meant money, and that work for its own sake—still more for that of others—was thriftless folly, the boy was broadening his mind, and perhaps already looking forward to far wider horizons and less selfish ends.

Perhaps—for, in fact, there is no evidence that in those Leamington days, or for some time after, he looked forward at all. He seems to have been a thoroughly normal youth, living for the present. There are the usual cherished photographs of him at successive ages—wearing the long hair and unsuitable clothes of 1880, when little boys were indistinguishable from little girls; in a neat, dark knickerbocker suit with an Eton collar; and in tweeds beside his younger brother and sisters, for a second girl, Gertrude, had been born before he was ten. He might have been spoiled, for he was the eldest, and he had the extreme good looks which he retained all his life—a short nose, a clean-cut face, grey eyes, light-brown hair, and great height (he grew to be six feet two) without weediness. Though rather quiet, he was always cheerful and good-tempered. Moreover, until his tenth year he was educated by a tutor at home. No young man, however, can have been less affected by this sometimes dangerous experiment, or by these gifts of looks and charm. There was a steel-like core in Bernard Spilsbury which few can have suspected who saw the well-mannered, handsome, easily contented boy watching his father in his laboratory, or mingling with the smart, alien crowd in the tree-lined streets of Leamington.

He had, of course, every reason to be cheerful and contented. His is not the trite story of the poor boy struggling through adversity to fame. Dr Smiles, whose *Self-help* was still popular, would have drawn no moral from it. James Spilsbury was in comfortable circumstances.

His children's reasonable wishes could be fulfilled. The eldest's choice of a career, if he yet thought about it, coincided with that made for him before his birth, and there was no one to cavil at his pursuing it. Or only one. His paternal grandmother was still alive to remind him of what his own case illustrated, that there was a good deal to be said for trade; and now, for a time, from his eleventh year, she was to have more frequent opportunities of doing so.

For James Spilsbury was on the move. He was tired of the wholesale business, and perhaps he was tired of Leamington. In 1888 he accepted the position of consulting chemist to several large firms in London and the provinces, and decided to make his home in the capital. While he looked for a house there his family was transferred to that of his parents at Stafford.

Bernard had just gone to his first school, Leamington College, the headmaster of which was that Dr Wood who was later headmaster of Tonbridge and Harrow. With the family dispersed, the boy became a boarder, spending his holidays with his grandparents, his mother, and the younger children in the large house on the outskirts of Stafford. It stood virtually in the country, which then stretched unspoilt to the southward to Cannock Chase and Lichfield. Beyond water-meadows flowed the river Sowe, where Bernard learnt to fish with his grandfather's rod. There were attics in the big house, and stabling and a tiled courtyard to play in, and a favourite bedroom outside which grew an espalier pear. And there was his grandmother, asking what he intended to do with life, and pointing the moral of his father's success in trade.

This interlude did not last long. James Spilsbury found a house in Crouch End, in North London, and Bernard left Leamington College with a report in terms that were to be typical. He was satisfactory, but could do better. Now, for another year, he was at University College School, then in Bloomsbury, but soon to move to Frognal, in Hampstead. There were some relatives named Hetherington among the artists of St John's Wood, with whom their young Warwickshire cousin struck up a lasting friendship. From this period, perhaps, dates Spilsbury's affection for Hampstead, where Francis, the maker of nostrums, had died a century before, and where he himself was to be living, in Frognal, within a few hundred yards of his old school, at the time of his death.

He saw the last of it, for the time being, in the winter of 1890–91. James Spilsbury, with his natural abilities, and the substantial profit from the sale of the Leamington business in the bank, was in the happy position of being able to gratify his bent for change. Since he was judicious as well as enterprising, each change was financially for the better; but Mrs Spilsbury, who had just learnt her way about London, may have heard with mixed feelings that she had got to pack up again and leave Crouch End for Manchester, where her husband was joining an important firm of wholesale chemists. The children probably thought it all rather fun. From their third home, in Higher Broughton, Bernard went to his third school in four years. It was Manchester Grammar School, and here he continued his adequate but unspectacular way, showing no promise of joining the company of eminent men the school had already produced. He was still exasperatingly normal, and his father, knowing that the boy had brains, could not understand his inability to win prizes, or his apparent indifference to them. His grandmother could not understand it either. There were reproaches and lectures, sometimes before the younger son, Leonard, who resented and remembered them, unlike the culprit himself, who no doubt smiled charmingly, said little, and soon dismissed them from his mind. In fact, while it seems most unlikely that at fifteen Bernard had any real notion of his capabilities, certain qualities, to become very marked in later life, were already developed. Whatever he did he would do in his own way, and he would not be hurried.

In 1893, having reached the Matriculation form, he left the Grammar School for Owens College. Here he played Rugby football and other games, but without distinction. Like prizes, they were unessentials. He was thought rather a solitary being, given to taking long walks by himself, and he was fond of skating, which he could also do alone. An accident about this time left him with a shortened index finger on his right hand, and it may have been the temporary disability that led him to practise the use of his left—so thoroughly (which was typical) that for the rest of his life he was ambidextrous, though he usually worked with his left hand.

He was soon free from his father's affectionate, if sometimes irritable, inquisitions, for that mutable man took the rest of his long-suffering family back to London again. For the first time in his life Bernard was alone; and perhaps, during those long walks, he was making up his mind, in his own unhurried and methodical way, about what he really intended to do. It was agreed, except by his grandmother, that he was to be a doctor. His ambition had still risen no higher than general practice, preferably in the country, where he could have the horse and trap which he had once said were the attraction of medicine as a profession. He was realizing, however, that biology and bacteriology, and above all surgery, most appealed to him. He was reading treatises by Dr Almroth Wright, and dissecting small animals. In January 1895 he sat for the London University Matriculation, taking preliminary science, chemistry, and biology; and, having passed, he secured admission to Magdalen College.

Before, in the following year, he went up to Oxford, his grandmother, more determined than ever in her old age, made a final endeavour to turn him from his unprofitable course. If he would be articled to Brookfield's, the big drapers in Stafford, and show the diligence he had hitherto, in her opinion, failed signally to display, she would buy him a partnership. From everything that is known of the later Bernard Spilsbury his reaction to the first, and probably the last, attempt to bribe him can be imagined. No doubt he kept his thoughts to himself; and the final word, in a sense, was with his father, who took a firm line with the old lady; but, whatever line had been taken, the son, it is safe to say, would never have been a draper.

Chapter 2: OXFORD AND ST MARY'S

SPILSBURY was at Magdalen for three years. He came down at the end of Trinity Term, 1899, having taken his B.A. degree, prepared to enter St Mary's Hospital Medical School with a University Exhibition worth £26 5*s.* per annum. He was in his twenty-third year, and older than the average graduate. If his retarded start on a career was due to no fault of his, but to his piecemeal schooling with its final two years at Owens College, it must have seemed at the time typical of an easygoing young man who would not hurry, and of whom one Oxford contemporary said, "I regarded him as a nice, very ordinary individual, and certainly never expected him to do anything brilliant."

In fact, he made little mark at Oxford. He had some distant relatives in the town, and only they, and the small circle of friends who used to visit his rooms overlooking the Deer Park, realized that his life there, as one of them put it, "was one long grind of work." As he seldom talked about himself, and enjoyed robust health, his capacity for work went generally unnoticed, the more so because when he relaxed he was as normal and 'ordinary' as ever. He had looks and natural charm, and the rather formal fastidiousness which he retained all his life; and another lifelong habit, that of dressing well, was already formed. He liked children, and was liked by them, and he went in for mild horse-play, and for giving people nicknames. That of "Buggins," which he applied to himself, was one which few would think of calling him to his face in later years.

He left Oxford, and Oxford thought no more about him. It is probable that at this time he would have agreed with his tutors and friends that looks, manners, and kindliness would get him as far as intellect and application. General practice was still his immediate goal. And as a general practitioner, or, at most, as a specialist among many others, he might have ended his career, if good fortune had not opened a door to the outstanding abilities which as yet, in all likelihood, were hidden even from himself.

He was fortunate because he went to a particular hospital at a particular time. St Mary's, in Praed Street, Paddington, was distinguished at the turn of the century by having on its staff three remarkable men who are the founders of modern forensic medicine—Dr A. P. Luff, Dr William Willcox, and (perhaps the greatest of the three) Dr A. J. Pepper. To many in the profession, who spoke of pure medicine as an art, the study of morbid anatomy and pathology was still "a beastly science." In particular, in its application as forensic medicine to the work of criminal and coroners' courts, this science had been under a cloud for forty years. In 1859 Dr Thomas Smethurst was charged with murdering Isabella Bankes by administering an irritant poison. Before the magistrates a leading toxicologist, Dr Alfred Taylor, testified that he had found traces of arsenic in the body. At the trial he admitted that the arsenic came from an imperfection in the apparatus he used in his analysis, while he and two more medical witnesses for the prosecution contradicted each other, in the words of the *British Medical Journal*, "in matters where there could be no possibility of doubt." Dr Smethurst, nevertheless, was convicted. There was an outcry, papers such as the *Lancet* and *The Times* criticizing the expert evidence severely; a group of eminent medical men, in a letter to the Home Secretary, asserted that there was no chemical proof whatever that any irritant poison was feloniously administered; and Dr Smethurst made history by having his case referred to yet another medical authority and being granted a free pardon. It was a sad muddle; and in a spirit of prophecy the *Dublin Medical Journal* wrote of Dr Taylor that he had "brought an amount of disrepute upon his branch of the profession that years will not remove."

For so it proved. By the time that Spilsbury was beginning his professional career the labours of his immediate predecessors in the "beastly science," especially the trio at St Mary's, were at last mastering public suspicion of medical evidence; but another ten years went by before the work of the pathologists in the Crippen case, and not least Spilsbury's own decisive contribution, finally established forensic medicine in the firm position which it now holds.

If it was the inspiration of Luff and Pepper, and, later, of Willcox, who was nearer Spilsbury's age, that was to crystallize the latter's bent for pathology, his father played his part when he gave the young student a better microscope than he had ever used before. Armed with an instrument that opened new worlds to him, Bernard Spilsbury came to London in the autumn of 1899, took rooms at 25 Cambridge Terrace, Paddington, within a few minutes' walk of St Mary's, and on October 2 reported to Dr Caley, the Dean of the Medical School.

2

With general practice in view, Spilsbury had taken the norma subjects for his degree, among them physiology, biology, chemistry, anatomy, histology, and pharmacology. Surgery followed at St Mary's, and then bacteriology; but it was the new microscope, and the immediate influence of Luff and Pepper, which awakened an interest that became absorbing in the still-struggling science of pathology and the work of the post-mortem room. Like other students, he followed the forbidden practice of taking home small specimens for examination with his own instrument. Luff and Pepper, soon detecting in the latest convert to their "beastly science" unusual qualities of energy, thoroughness, and perception, encouraged his enthusiasm for microscopy, and Pepper urged him to make a special study of scar tissues—advice which was to bear remarkable fruit ten years later, when master and pupil appeared together at the trial of Crippen. Through his two seniors at St Mary's Spilsbury was introduced to Almroth Wright, whose work he had known since his days at Owen's College. Wright, then a man of forty, who was to die in the same year as Spilsbury himself, was so impressed by the latter's abilities that he made him an honorary member of the group of young men specializing in bacteriology—one of them was Alexander Fleming, later of penicillin fame—who were known as "Wright's Circus."

A maturity of outlook, and a growing sense of his capabilities—both unsuspected by such as his grandmother—attracted Spilsbury to the society of older men, particularly those from whom he could learn. He had his acquaintances among his fellow-students, but no close friends. His marked "aloofness"—the term so often used of him in later life—was noticeable in his twenties, and extended to physical aversions. He shrank from obtrusiveness, and the cheerful back-slapper would be dashed by a chilling "Don't touch me, please!" The rather lonely furrow of pathology which he had chosen helped to isolate him from the mass of his contemporaries at St Mary's, and, as most of these played as hard as they worked, his habit of almost unremitting study drew him further apart. This, again, would have surprised his grandmother.

The fact was that he had found his *métier*, and things outside it were among the unessentials. But he had his recreations, reduced to what he considered rational usage. A growing love of classical music took him to concerts, and a more light-hearted streak to music-halls. He is found playing Rugby football for the hospital, for the last time in

1903, without distinction and merely as a name in the team. His younger brother, Leonard, was by now at Cambridge, and for several years the pair went together to the University Rugby match, then played at Queen's Club. They had a wager on the result, the loser paying for a dinner and seats at the Empire or the Oxford with the two fifteens. It recalls an era as remote as the Middle Ages to learn that they usually dined at "Le Gourmet," for there a plate of soup then cost twopence, and a vol-au-vent sixpence. A twopenny cup of coffee and another twopence for the waiter rounded off an adequate meal for a shilling.

Like most young men, Spilsbury had decided views. Unlike many, he changed few of them in later life. Some might be called prejudices, for they were part of his inheritance and make-up; others were the result of reflection, and this with him was always a careful and logical process. If it seemed a slow one it was because he never answered a question without giving it thought. It was not by chance that one of his sons became a lecturer in philosophy and logic. Of interest to-day is a rather stilted editorial written by the father fifty years ago for the *St Mary's Hospital Gazette*, controverting an article in the *National Review* which disparaged the voluntary hospital system and advocated nationalization. At an age when so many embrace Utopias, Spilsbury, an individualist like his father, used this word of such a scheme. He never altered his early opinion that it could not be a success in a free country. He did not mean that it could not be made to work. Success, in his view, had a wider connotation than that.

There were milestones, professional and domestic, in his career as a student. In 1901 he was appointed Student Demonstrator of Physiology, and for two years in succession (1903–4 and 1904–5) he was Joint Assistant Demonstrator of Pathology, under Pepper. His colleague in this post being more devoted to bacteriology, Spilsbury did most of the work, keeping such long hours that he had neither time nor interest for competitive examinations, those unessentials, which might have brought him prizes and distinction. It seemed more serious that this appointment, compliment and portent though it was, together with the long hours dedicated voluntarily to research in all branches of morbid anatomy, interfered with normal study for his medical degree. While he remained a student many who had entered the school after him had qualified and become his professional seniors. The opinions of those who thought him a mere plodder appeared to be confirmed. It was not until the end of 1904, when he had been a student far longer than modern standards allow, that he passed his finals with the Conjoint Board. He had to wait another six months for his university degree. He was getting on for twenty-eight when the Oxford Pass Lists included the name of Spilsbury (B. H.), M.B., B.Ch.

Nobody, least of all the newly qualified doctor himself, could foresee that within another six years that name would be on the way to becoming a household word. There can be little doubt, however, that Spilsbury himself knew very well what he was doing. If he gave so much of his time to pathology it was with the encouragement of such men as Luff and Pepper and Willcox, of whom the latter was appointed Dean of Pathology at St Mary's in Spilsbury's second year. There was only some five years' difference between this pair, and they were to be closely associated in the future, not only as professional colleagues, but as friends. Since the retirement of Sir Thomas Stevenson in 1900 Willcox and Luff had been joint toxicologists to the Home Office, a post which Willcox was to hold alone, as senior analyst, for a decade after Luff in turn retired. Pepper, throughout this period, was Home Office Pathologist. These three men, in short, were by far the most prominent and influential figures in forensic medicine. Their presence on the staff of St Mary's had given that hospital and its school a lead in the progressive, if beastly, science which was to be maintained for many years. A protégé of theirs was likely to go far.

It was advisable to look ahead, for in the meantime other circumstances were altering. The Spilsbury family had been pursuing its usual roving course. The second stay in London lasted little longer than the first one, for while Bernard was at Magdalen his father became a partner in a firm of manufacturing chemists in Birmingham, and this entailed fresh moves, first to Stafford and then to Moseley. It was in this suburb of Birmingham, in 1900, that the young medical student met Edith Horton, the future Lady Spilsbury; and while during the next few years their friendship ripened slowly, chiefly at meetings on the tennis-courts in the summer vacation, the enterprising James Spilsbury was meditating an entirely new departure. Always interested in the experimental side of chemistry, and foreseeing the future of the internal-combustion engine (though he did not own a car, the stables of the house he built at Moseley included a garage), he turned his mind to the problems of synthetic rubber. To make time for research, he dissolved his partnership in Blackwell, Hayes, and Spilsbury in 1904, taking instead the less onerous duties of directorships on various companies. Research, however, required money, and there were still children to be educated; and the eldest, having qualified, should now be in a position to take care of himself. Bernard was in entire agreement with this view, and since, in that same year, he became engaged to Edith Horton, he had every reason in the world to make the utmost of those gifts of which he was increasingly conscious.

Chapter 3: CHANGE OF DIRECTION

If a protégé of Luff, Pepper, and Willcox was likely to go far, the direction he would take was as clearly indicated. Spilsbury's almost daily association, while still a student, with the triumvirate retained by the Home Office as expert medical advisers in certain classes of criminal proceedings not only intensified his addiction to pathology, but roused his interest in its application, as forensic medicine, to problems of crime. The prospect of general practice began to lose its charm. Other related events were building up the background against which he was to appear as the first great medical detective.

With the establishment throughout England and Wales of regular police forces, all under the supervision of the Home Office, more and more criminal cases of difficulty or importance came to be referred to that department, where they were handled by the Treasury Solicitor. The Prosecution of Offences Act of 1879 set up an officer called the Director of Public Prosecutions. There was no separate branch of that name, and the new Director did not initiate criminal proceedings, as in certain cases his successor can to-day, but acted merely as adviser to the Treasury Solicitor. In 1884 the office lapsed; and it was not until 1908, when Spilsbury was definitely being groomed for the part he was so soon to play, that a fresh Prosecution of Offences Act established a Department of Public Prosecutions, with a Director possessing extensive powers of his own, under the superintendence of the Attorney-General. But the machinery had long been there, controlled by the Treasury Solicitor, who called in medical experts and others as occasion required, and Spilsbury must have become well acquainted with its working during his early years with the famous trio at St Mary's.

In theory this machinery still only initiates; "the detection and investigation of crime in England and Wales," to quote from Sir John Moylan's *Scotland Yard,*[1] "rests with the police, and so does its prosecution." In practice the Department of Public Prosecutions

[1] Sir John Moylan, *Scotland Yard and the Metropolitan Police* (Putnam, 1929; 2nd ed., 1934).

works hand in hand with the C.I.D., and in Spilsbury's second year as a student an appointment had been made at Scotland Yard which also was to have its bearing on his future. Mr Edward Henry became Assistant Commissioner (Crime). Soon to be Commissioner of Police of the Metropolis and Sir Edward Henry, Bart., he is best known to the public as the inaugurator of the fingerprint system in this country, but of his influence in general Moylan writes: "During the seventeen years that he was the presiding genius the force underwent a very rapid development and attained a high standard of efficiency." Henry's Commissionership coincided with Spilsbury's rise to fame and the beginning of his intimate association with the C.I.D. No one can have appreciated more fully than he did the increase in the Force's efficiency. Its expansion made necessary the duplication of Norman Shaw's original New Scotland Yard by the erection, beside it, of Scotland House, and in Spilsbury's lifetime more buildings were to arise, or were to be taken over. In all of them, as in the old home of the Department of Public Prosecutions in Richmond Terrace, Whitehall, and in its later quarters in Devonshire House, he was to become a very well-known figure indeed. During a generation officials and policemen came and went, including half a dozen Commissioners at Scotland Yard and nearly as many Directors of Public Prosecutions, but in all that time there was only one Honorary Pathologist to the Home Office.

Many years, however, were to pass before the development of which Spilsbury himself was naturally the warmest advocate was seriously taken in hand. In writing of Scotland Yard no excuse is needed for continuing to make free use of Sir John Moylan, who as late as 1934 could say of the scientific branch of the C.I.D.:

> Where Scotland Yard has not led the way is in regard to laboratory work. Police laboratories have long been established at Vienna, Prague, Berlin, Paris, New York, and other foreign police headquarters, and in this country small laboratories are now adjuncts to some provincial police forces. . . . Scotland Yard has in the past had no laboratory of its own.

For this neglect Moylan seems to give two reasons which are rather contradictory. "In the staff of the Government Chemist and the Home Office pathologists and analysts," he goes on, "it had at hand expert assistance of the highest order." Yet a little later he says: "English judges and juries are inclined to be distrustful of laboratory evidence." This makes somewhat strange reading for 1934, and even stranger for 1929, when the first edition of the book was published, and when echoes of the outcry about Spilsbury's reputation with judges and juries for infallibility were still to be heard. The author may have been thinking less of medical evidence than of "the latest refinements as regards, say, poroscopy, or the analysis of professional and occupational dusts and muds," of which he speaks.

Such refinements were indeed far in the future when young Mr Spilsbury, an assistant demonstrator of pathology, but not yet a qualified doctor, used to listen (he was always a good listener) to Luff or Pepper or Willcox talking in 1903 of the Moat Farm murder, or, two years later, of Devereux, who put his wife's body in a trunk—prototypes of crimes which Spilsbury himself was to investigate. Of the quartette, he and Willcox were to see the police laboratory founded at Hendon in 1934, and he was to know it in its present home in the newest and biggest and ugliest of the three buildings on the Embankment.

He was no doubt warned that there was not much money in giving evidence in criminal cases, and that in this country murders do not occur every day. In the London area they average normally twenty or thirty a year, which explains, as Sir John Moylan says, why Scotland Yard has no homicide bureau. But the incidence of sudden death from disease or accident is everywhere on an altogether different scale. The coroners' courts are always busy. Moreover, in Spilsbury's second year as assistant demonstrator in his chosen subject another timely innovation offered new scope to those who wished to make that subject their career. The London County Council requested all general hospitals in its area to appoint two qualified pathologists to perform post-mortem examinations in cases of sudden death. There was to be a fee of two guineas for each autopsy. At St Mary's, the birthplace of modern forensic medicine, where the senior pathologist was Pepper, who had great faith in Spilsbury, the latter could now look forward to a useful source of income, including a salary, once he had taken his degree. In October 1905, three months after his name appeared in the Oxford Pass Lists, he was appointed Resident Assistant Pathologist under Pepper, at a salary of £200 per annum.

A qualified medical man since the beginning of the year, he had performed his first post-mortem in January, entering the details in the first of his long series of little black notebooks. When, in later years, for the purposes of the text-book he was going to write, but never did, he began to summarize selected cases on filing-cards, he preserved three from these first twelve months. They deal with a death from pulmonary embolism after an operation for acute appendicitis, and two suicides, one by poison and the second by a leap from a window after the victim had stabbed himself. If Spilsbury also preserved all his life that first notebook it was not from sentiment. He threw few of these fuller records away. In the end they contained the details of 25,000 post-mortems.

Since 1903 he had been joint secretary of the hospital medical society, and so in a position to encourage frequent discussion of medico-legal matters. Two outside events in the same year were to further general interest in the subject, and were to prove of importance in his own later career. The Medico-Legal Society was formed to promote the study of forensic medicine, Pepper being a foundation member. Spilsbury was to be elected in 1908, and thereafter until a year or two before his death was a regular attendant at meetings. These were always crowded when he was to read a paper. He became a member of the council, and was in turn honorary secretary, president, and treasurer.

Almost simultaneously with the Medico-Legal Society was born another social body which had some affinity with it, but more convivial habits and a more varied membership—the dining club of criminologists called "Our Society," or, popularly, the Crimes Club. It grew out of an evening party at the house of H. B. Irving, the actor, and it was to include judges, counsel, coroners, doctors, writers, actors, and others interested in crime. Papers were read, as in the more austere *milieu* of the Medico-Legal Society. Like the latter, "Our Society" flourishes to-day. From 1928 onward one of its most prominent members was Dr Pepper's Resident Assistant of 1905, who was to address it on crimes present and past, from those in the investigation of which he had taken part to the murder of Sir Edmund Berry Godfrey in 1678.

2

In the first decade of this century it was still possible for a newly qualified medical man to think of marriage on £200 a year and an uncertain additional income from coroners' fees. The sands were running out; but few who talked of the political landslide of January 1906 as the end of their world can have realized how right they were. Spilsbury, in every sense a conservative all his life, may have had misgivings, but he was the last man to exaggerate, and even his habit of clear thinking can scarcely have forewarned him how rapidly, with the last Liberal Governments, the struggle with the Lords, the armament race with Germany, and the strikes and other troubles of the next few years, the new world of upheavals, slaughter, and impoverishment was coming into sight. Besides, he had happier preoccupations. At twenty-nine, a rather late starter, he was on the threshold of a chosen career. If, in his quiet way, he was ambitious and confident, he was as unhurried and methodical as ever, and he proposed to spend the next two years establishing his position. Then he would get married.

Miss Horton acquiescing in this sensible plan, he remained in his rooms in Paddington, passed his days in the pathological laboratory at St Mary's, and saved money. Money, it should be said, was always a secondary consideration with Spilsbury, except for such special purposes as marriage and its consequences. He spent very little on himself; clothes were probably his only personal extravagance, and he took care of them. He was a smoker, but in the early 1900's tobacco was cheap. He drank little, and was not particularly interested in food. As he grew older he cultivated a sense of what was due to his position, but his own requirements were always modest. Throughout his life he showed that quality of generosity which goes with comparative indifference to money. When he received his first coroner's fee of two guineas he gave the mortuary-keeper ten shillings. A customary tip in these days, when fees and tips are higher, it was a big one nearly fifty years ago. Spilsbury never gave less.

In writing the summaries on his case-cards it was his habit (until in later years he could not spare time even for this) to add to his medical findings brief histories of the cases. The history behind his first post-mortem performed outside the hospital—it was at Fulham, in March 1906—is recorded by a newspaper cutting pasted on the back of the card. Spilsbury's name is spelt wrongly, with two 'l's.' A little natural pride at seeing it in print was soon suppressed, and the card in this respect is unique.

His second outside case began when in May that year a woman was admitted to St Mary's suffering from the effects of criminal abortion. She died three days later, and Spilsbury's evidence at the inquest resulted in a verdict of murder against some person unknown. He notes on his card that a certain woman was suspected. There was no type of case about which he felt more strongly. While working for his degree he gained practical knowledge of midwifery in the poorer quarters of Paddington, and he had been profoundly moved and angered by the extent to which abortion was practised there, not always by unqualified persons, at grave risk to life. He never forgot this experience. With every sympathy for desperate women driven to perilous measures, his detestation of the practice was not based solely on medical grounds. It was abhorrent to the sense of morality he inherited from religious Midland forbears, and in his pursuit of abortioners there was an element of the crusade. Nor did this attitude ever change. Late in his life a friend of long standing tried to argue that non-therapeutic circumstances could justify abortion if performed by qualified men under suitable supervision. "My dear ——!" said Spilsbury. "How can you talk like that?"

Holding these views, he was merciless towards culprits of his own profession. Before the year 1906 was out—his first year as a fully fledged doctor—his testimony at the inquest on a young woman at St Pancras Coroner's Court, before Mr Walter Schröder, brought about the professional ruin of a much older medical colleague, who was sent to prison. As experience increased, and the records in the filing cabinet multiplied, Spilsbury took to noting on his cards the names of doctors questionably involved in cases of death from abortion; and system and memory sometimes combined to produce remarkable consequences. The most striking example was when his habit of referring periodically to his records led him to detect certain similarities in a series of these fatalities. The upshot was the sentencing of the medical man concerned to seven years' penal servitude. How yet another long career of professional malpractice was ended by the same methodical watchfulness will be told later. It is said that by then Spilsbury's reputation inspired so much alarm that there was a marked decline in such cases during his lifetime. Unqualified abortioners had less to lose, and many years afterwards, in his presidential address to the Medico-Legal Society in 1933, he said that their evil business was still on the increase.

The year 1907, his second as a qualified doctor and assistant pathologist at St Mary's, found him giving evidence in ten coroners' courts in the London area. As he became more in demand experience developed that simple style of explaining scientific detail which before long was to impress and persuade judges and juries. As a lecturer, his flat, matter-of-fact delivery was not inspiring, but if the attention of his hearers wandered it was realized that a rather tedious manner concealed a great deal of valuable matter, and copies of his lectures were sought for private study. When he was demonstrating in the post-mortem room there was no flagging of interest. He was already winning a name for sureness and rapidity as an operator, and for an eye for morbid changes as good as a microscope; and there was the added fascination of watching him use his ambidexterity, by constant practice now made second nature, to increase his speed of execution by shifting instruments from hand to hand as convenience dictated.

It is said that there were moments when he doubted his wisdom in devoting his powers to pathology, still generally regarded as an eccentricity on his part. But such doubts must have been rare. His heart was in his work, and the work was multiplying. The qualities that made him an ideal demonstrator caused coroners to make more and more frequent calls upon him, and by the summer of 1908 he was really busy outside the hospital. His salary was doubled by coroners' fees. He was getting known elsewhere, being elected this year to the Medico-Legal Society, where he took part in a discussion on the law and punishment of infanticide. This was another subject about which he had learnt and thought much during his work in the Paddington slums, and he spoke of the importance of proving that the child had had a separate existence, and that the accused mother knew it—a point that he was often to emphasize in his own practice, in order to give some unhappy woman the benefit of the doubt.

In July that year he received his M.A. degree from Oxford, and in August, in his thirty-second year, he married Edith Horton at Moseley.

Chapter 4: PRELUDE TO CRIPPEN

FOR the first four years of their married life the Bernard Spilsburys lived at Harrow-on-the-Hill, in a small modern house in Hindes Road, a turning off the road from Harrow Station to Wealdstone, at the foot of the hill itself. In 1908 North-west London came to an end at Willesden and Hampstead, though at Golders Green, beyond the cross-roads where there was only a tree, the streets of the new Garden Suburb were being laid out across the fields. Hendon was a village, Wembley a few houses set in meadows and coppices, and Harrow a small country town dominated by the tall school buildings and by the prominent spire of which Charles II had said, during a discussion by bishops about the Visible Church, that this must be the parish church of Harrow, for it could be seen everywhere. It can still be seen rising above the flood of bricks and plumbing, undreamt of when the Spilsburys made their home there, which has engulfed Hindes Road and obliterated whole square miles of Middlesex.

Spilsbury travelled to Paddington every morning by the Metropolitan Railway, only recently electrified. He still had the normal working man's leisure, and could get home in the evenings and be free at week-ends to see something of his wife and the first of their four children, the only one to be born in Hindes Road. There were summer holidays in that West Country to which he returned, whenever he could, throughout his life, though future pressure of work was foreshadowed in 1910, when at the last moment Mrs Spilsbury and the child had to go to Minehead without him.

The world was all before him, but it was a less happy world than Milton's Eden. There were troubles in Europe, and troubles at home—the death of King Edward VII during a political deadlock, and two elections within a year, followed by the Parliament Bill. Passion no doubt ran high even in Harrow. Of uncontroversial domestic events, among those of particular interest to a rising young pathologist, with his eye on work for the Home Office, the establishment of the Department of Public Prosecutions has been mentioned. One of the powers of the new Director which was to keep Spilsbury very busily employed was that of applying to the Home Office for authority to order exhumations—a power invested in the Home Office itself by the Act of 1857, and possessed from ancient times by coroners, as it still is. About the same date, in 1907, the Court of Criminal Appeal came into being. With these innovations, coinciding with Spilsbury's emergence on the medico-legal scene, and the Criminal Evidence Act of 1898, the machinery of criminal procedure into which he was to fit had assumed its present form.

2

Only two years were to pass between Spilsbury's marriage and his introduction to the case which was to lift him from relative obscurity to the status of a coming man. He was already, in 1908, something of a figure in the medical world, and he became a more prominent one in the following July, when he succeeded Pepper, on the latter's retirement, as Pathologist at St Mary's. This did not mean the end of the association between the pair; though Pepper now preferred an easier life, he remained on the staff of the hospital as a consultant, and he had not severed his connexion with the Home Office, a fact that was to be of importance to his favourite pupil a year later.

Spilsbury's work in the coroners' courts continued to increase, and his growing reputation led to his being invited to St Bartholomew's in March 1909, to perform a post-mortem in a case of anæsthetic death. Three months afterwards he was describing himself by his new title in the Kensington Coroner's Court in the course of a far more unusual case, that of a woman of twenty-nine who died while having her hair shampooed at a store. The process entailed applying a lotion containing tetrachloride of carbon. An electric fan was required to disperse the fumes, which had been known to cause slight cases of fainting, but Spilsbury, who performed what the *Morning Post*, in its old-fashioned way, called the necropsy, said that in a perfectly healthy subject there was no danger to life. The victim suffered from status lymphaticus. Though the store was censured for employing an unskilled operator, it was otherwise exonerated; but soap and water must for a time have regained their popularity with hairdressers.

The consequences of human folly are frequently illustrated in Spilsbury's records, as they are in those of all medical men, and within a few months at this time he had three cases of death of which he wrote, "accelerated by neglect. Christian Science case," and a fourth victim hastened her end by swallowing bladder-wrack, thyroid proteid, liquorice, phytolacca, and cascara made up into witches' brews, compressed into pills and tablets, and sold in fancy bottles as a 'safe' reducing treatment. Another common foible, from which doctors are among the worst sufferers, is a disinclination to pay bills, and though Spilsbury was to have so little time for private work that his experience of this weakness was small, he had an early lesson. His first professional journey far out of London was to Yorkshire, where a man had died, or so his family thought, as the result of a tram accident in Italy. Spilsbury's opinion was sought to support a claim against the Italian Government. His case-card notes that his fee of £13 13*s.* was not paid.

Three cases involving medical men, of varying qualifications, occur among the cards for 1910. In the first days of January a doctor, or his dispenser, mistakenly mixed strychnine in a prescription with fatal results, and later that month an early use of radium as a cure for cancer is mentioned, the patient, who died under the anæsthetic before the radium was administered, being himself a doctor. A week later Dr Hawley Harvey Crippen was buying hyoscine, and a card of September records what he did with it.

Part Two

THE INCOMPARABLE WITNESS (1910–25)

Chapter 1: THE CRIPPEN CASE

IN the autumn of 1910 Bernard Spilsbury was thirty-three. During that year the earth passed through the tail of Halley's Comet, and King Edward VII died. An aeroplane rose to 3000 feet at Mourmelon-le-Grand, and another flew from London to Manchester. The Suffragettes added their activities to the other political troubles of the time, and Spilsbury's old mentor, now Sir Almroth Wright, roused them to fury by pointing the physiological moral in letters to *The Times*. The Charing Cross Bank failed, and capital crime was well represented by the Slough murder and the killing of Mr Nesbit in a train by Dickman, by a second trial and acquittal in connexion with the Gorse Hall assassination of the previous year, by another mystery which officially has remained unsolved (the death of Atherstone the actor in an empty Battersea flat), and by the Crippen case. This, the first of the long series of sensational trials for murder in which Spilsbury was to play a leading part, was now to make him known to the general public as what Lord Darling called "that incomparable witness."

At a casual reading of the transcript of evidence it may be difficult to understand why the junior pathologist of the quartette called by the prosecution created the remarkable impression which undoubtedly he did. Closer study of the brief but vital examination and cross-examination of Spilsbury will show how half a dozen questions and answers made it plain that in the small, specialized world of forensic medicine a new force had arisen. More generally, the case was important to that world because, as has been seen, it was still fighting scepticism and prejudice. The trial of the little American doctor, with its strangely appropriate echo of the Smethurst controversy, was a landmark in the history of forensic medicine, as well as in Spilsbury's own career.

The story of the Crippen case, often though it has been told, will always find readers. It would seem that Spilsbury himself felt the spell. Though the case was indeed the turning-point of his career, this scarcely accounts for the fact that, of all his volumes of the "Notable British Trials" series, *The Trial of H. H. Crippen* was the one most often and most carefully read. The book was published ten years after the event, when his own position had been long established. Yet the spine is broken by frequent handling, pages are loose, and scores of paragraphs in Filson Young's introduction and in the report of the evidence are marked in the margin or underlined.

2

Hawley Harvey Crippen was born in Michigan, U.S.A., in 1862. When he was twenty-one he came to England "to pick up some medical knowledge," according to Mr Young, who goes on to say, "His education had followed the ordinary course of studies for the medical profession in America." There is nothing to show that this is irony, and there is a reference to Crippen's attendance at the Homœopathic Hospital at Cleveland, Ohio. Here he obtained a diploma. It was endorsed by the Faculty of the Medical College of Philadelphia, and in 1885 Crippen acquired another diploma, as an eye and ear specialist, from the Ophthalmic Hospital in New York. These qualifications might not then, or now, satisfy the General Medical Council, but they dispose of the assumption by Bechofer Roberts, in his life of Sir Travers Humphreys, that all the little doctor possessed was "an obscure American degree, doubtless obtained through the post." Crippen was entitled to describe himself as a doctor, though he could not openly practise as one in the British Isles.

Spilsbury's views on this point appear to have been what would be expected. On the card upon which he set down the essential facts he merely wrote cautiously: "American medical qualifications. Called Dr." But in his copy of *The Trial of H. H. Crippen* he has underlined the words "the ordinary course of studies," in the introduction, and has put a query in the margin.

After Crippen's first visit to England he wandered about the United States, practising in a number of the larger cities. In Utah, in 1890 or 1891, his wife died, and he sent his boy of three to live with her mother in California. During one of his stays in New York he married again. His second wife was a girl of seventeen whom he knew as Cora Turner; her real name was Kunigunde Mackamotski, and she was half American-German and half Polish-Jew. According to Crippen's story, she had been the mistress of a stove manufacturer. There were more wanderings—to St Louis, to New York once more, to Philadelphia, with a few months across the Canadian frontier in Toronto. Crippen was now employed by the Munyon Company, which dealt in patent medicines. Mrs Crippen, whose small gifts as a singer deluded her into thinking that she had the voice for grand opera, went to New York for a time to have it trained.

In 1900 Crippen was in England again, and, except for one short interval, for good. He came as manager at Munyon's offices in Shaftesbury Avenue, and later in the year his wife joined him in rooms in South Crescent, off Tottenham Court Road. At one period, it is said, he took the grave risk of practising as a dentist and a woman's consultant. In 1902 Munyon's recalled him for six months to Philadelphia. Mrs Crippen had been seeking work on the music-hall stage, with slight success; during her husband's absence she obtained a few engagements at smoking concerts, in the course of which she met an American music-hall performer named Bruce Miller, who was to be a witness at the Old Bailey. She was living at this time in Guilford Street, which in those days had an unsavoury reputation; and, if this part of Crippen's story is to be believed, she saw a good deal too much of Mr Miller.

When Crippen returned to London for the last time the pair stayed for some years in Store Street, Bloomsbury, at Nos. 34 and 37. The little doctor forsook Munyon's for a variety of jobs with dubious concerns vaguely connected with medicine. Several of them failed, and presently he was back with Munyon's, now in Albion House, New Oxford Street. In Albion House, when Munyon's business began to decline, he was also in partnership with another firm, the Yale Tooth Specialists, and here he was employing as his typist Ethel le Neve, whom he had met when she was working for one of his failures, the Drouet Institute. Finally he took over Munyon's branch as an agency, on commission, but still it did not pay. Everything was going wrong. On January 31, 1910, his sixteen years' connexion with the firm terminated.

In the meantime the Crippens had moved into a house of their own in Camden Town, No. 39 Hilldrop Crescent of sensational memory. A gloomy-looking house built of London stock, in a gloomy street in a gloomy neighbourhood, it was larger than they needed—large, indeed, by present-day standards, for the rent of £58 10*s*. a year. The new tenants did not use the first-floor rooms. Though by some accounts they lived rather squalidly, chiefly in the kitchen, they often entertained, at home or at restaurants. They kept no maid. As Crippen's salary, while he earned one, was £3 a week, plus what little he drew from his somewhat shady side-lines, it seems remarkable that they could have lived as they did, that Mrs Crippen could have ermine and fox furs and good jewellery and dresses, and that they could still put money away. At the end of January 1910 Crippen was overdrawn at the bank by a few pounds, but there was £600 on deposit, more than half of it in his wife's name. Those, however, were the days when whisky was 3*s.* 6*d.* a bottle, when ermine coats could be bought for £34, and when an income tax of a shilling or so was thought extortionate.

Mrs Crippen, under the name of Belle Elmore, continued for a time to try her luck on the music-hall stage. She obtained only a few engagements in suburban or provincial halls, but she became well-known and popular in certain theatrical circles. For two years before her death she was honorary treasurer of the Music Hall Ladies Guild, which hired a room in Albion House. She was described as vivacious and pleasant, fond of dress and display, with a New York accent and dark hair, which she dyed auburn. A Roman Catholic, she converted her husband to that faith. If she was seventeen when she married Crippen she lived to be thirty-four or thirty-five—not thirty-seven, as often stated.

Crippen himself, like those other poisoners Palmer, Armstrong, and Smethurst (who, however, should perhaps be given the benefit of the doubt), was a very small man. He appeared to be mildness itself, an almost insignificant figure, dapper in dress, with a high, bald forehead, a heavy, sandy moustache, and rather prominent eyes behind gold-rimmed spectacles. Witnesses, without exception, described him as kindly, gentle, and naturally well-mannered. He was forty-eight at the time of his trial.

At the earlier proceedings at Bow Street Police Court another figure, in black, heavily veiled, sat beside him in the dock. Ethel le Neve moves through the tragedy like a ghost. She never seems to come to life, as both Cora Crippen, with her cheerful vulgarity and vitality, and Crippen himself, by his very lack of conspicuous qualities, quite recognizably do. Crippen had known her for eight years, and for the last three she had been his mistress. After office hours they used to meet furtively in obscure hotel bedrooms. She took over the household at 39 Hilldrop Crescent, lived there with Crippen as his wife, and imported a French maid. But there is no real clue to what she thought, or knew, or suspected, during those months between the vanishing of Mrs Crippen and her own flight with her lover, disguised as a boy, to Antwerp and the s.s. *Montrose*. She is a completely baffling character, who glides from the scene without leaving trace or impression. Only this can be said: either there was nothing in her or there was a great deal.

For many years the former negative opinion might have been held of Crippen. But if his common, pleasure-loving, rather slatternly wife often showed another side to her husband when friends were not present, and sometimes when they were, events were to show that he too had another side. During those years he endured her domination. He let her hold the purse and choose his suits and ties. He did much of the domestic work. For a time paying guests, as Mrs Crippen preferred to call them, who were always men, were taken in at No. 39; the money was not needed then, but she liked company. It was the little doctor who took up their breakfasts and cleaned their boots. It was one of these lodgers who described him as always pale, quiet, and imperturbable during the worst of his wife's excitable outbursts of temper. "Restraint," said another witness, "was the one and only evidence of firmness in his character." In Spilsbury's copy of *The Trial* he has underlined these words; and, indeed, something more than restraint was there. If Cora Crippen's theatrical bent ever led her to read Shakespeare she should have remembered Cassius, who thought too much. "Such men are dangerous."

Crippen must have been thinking dangerous thoughts for some time before he made up his mind to act. The crisis came in December 1909. His wife was tired of him, and she knew about Ethel le Neve. His story that she was threatening to leave him may be believed. Nothing would have suited him better, but for one fact: she was taking with her their joint savings, which she claimed to be hers. On the 15th of the month she gave notice of withdrawal to the bank. A month later Crippen ordered five grains of hyoscin hydrobromide at Lewis and Burrows' shop in New Oxford Street. It was so large an amount that it had to be ordered from the wholesalers. He collected it on January 19.

Since he intended to conceal his wife's body, he could have employed any other lethal means. But poison would seem to be the small man's weapon—not only, perhaps, because small men are not given to violence, but also because they often suffer from a sense of inferiority. The remote and generally prolonged action of poison gives them a feeling of power. They can sit back, like gods, and watch it at work. This may be true even of Crippen, who undoubtedly had been tyrannized by his wife; for though she must have died soon after the dinner-party with the Martinettis, she did not die at once.

It is worth while to consider the effect upon Bernard Spilsbury, still young enough to be impressionable, of his introduction, in his first big case, to his first poisoner. He was himself an upright man of genuine goodness of heart. To the end of his life he would go out of his way to help others. His behaviour to all reflected innate kindliness.

A sensitive nature remained unhardened by years of experience, and was revealed in a reserve that was not diffidence—in his work he was self-confidence itself—but that nevertheless amounted to shyness. That self-confidence, however, was based on moral strength; and out of this grew an element of sternness which, combined with his terse, unemotional manner and the intense concentration he applied to the business in hand, made him seem in his professional capacity an inflexible machine. It is very likely that to some extent this public front was protective. Even to a pathologist one dead body is not just like another: one lies in the mortuary because of accident or disease, the next, perhaps, through brutal violence; and a sensitive man who comes to be associated with victims of brutality may be expected to acquire two characteristics—a protective mechanism of detachment and a detestation of brutes. The crusading quality in Spilsbury, possibly an inheritance from his Nonconformist stock, has already been referred to. Of all murderers poisoners are the worst; and it is not far-fetched to assume that his first encounter with one, in No. 1 Court at the Old Bailey, made a considerable impression on him. Ten years later, indeed, his invaluable copy of *The Trial of H. H. Crippen* was made the vehicle of his opinion on this point too. Filson Young makes the surprising remark that Crippen was "always considerate—even in the weapon he used to kill his wife." Spilsbury's comment on this is enlightening and sufficient. He underlined the words "always considerate," and put one of his queries in the margin.

3

In July of that year, 1910, Spilsbury was going with his wife and small child to Minehead. He had never heard of Dr Crippen, though he may have read in the newspapers of the 10th and 11th a few lines about the disappearance of a woman of that name from her home in Camden Town. A day or two later, however, his holiday plans were upset, and Mrs Spilsbury and the baby went to Minehead without him. Cora Crippen had been found, and the medical side of the inquiry into her death was in the hands of a team from St Mary's. It was natural, but none the less a compliment, that Drs Willcox, Pepper, and Luff should call on the young Demonstrator of Pathology whose painstaking work was known to them all, and who had succeeded Pepper himself. But Spilsbury's reputation at large was growing rapidly, and it is said that R. D. Muir, who was in charge of the case, applied for him. With Muir was Travers Humphreys, who had to hurry back from Filey, his holiday also spoiled. Muir never wasted a minute. A link between the lawyers and the doctors was supplied by Mr Ingleby Oddie, a qualified medical man as well as a barrister.

At this stage Crippen's whereabouts were unknown, and the enormous public interest the crime was to arouse, largely because of the pursuit across the Atlantic and the use of wireless, was not yet foreseen. Had it been, no doubt one of the Law Officers would have led for the Crown. It is unusual for a sensational trial for murder by poisoning to be left in the hands of two members of the Junior Bar. The development of the case, under the forceful direction of Muir, was to mean four months of increasingly hard work for all concerned. Its conclusion was to find the newcomer, Spilsbury, established as a coming man.

To this climax the events of half a year had been darkly leading. On the evening of the last day of January there were two guests to dinner at 39 Hilldrop Crescent. They were a retired music-hall performer named Martinetti and his wife. Mr Martinetti was in poor health, and Crippen, with what ulterior thoughts no one can say, pressed him to come because a game of whist would cheer him up. Dinner was served in what was called the breakfast-room, in the half-basement. Next to it was the kitchen, where Mrs Martinetti helped her hostess to dish up. On the same floor was a coal-cellar. Afterwards the quartette played whist in the parlour, on the floor above. It was 1.30 in the morning when the Martinettis left, the Crippens saying good-bye to them at the head of the steps leading to the front door. "Don't come down, Belle," said Mrs Martinetti. "You will catch a cold." It was a scene which the departing guests must have remembered to the end of their lives—the dark, deserted street, the bare trees in the small front gardens, the gas lamps burning yellow, and, silhouetted against the light from the open door, the two figures at the head of the steps waving good-bye. Belle was to catch something worse than a cold that night.

Within a few hours, about midday on that 1st of February, Crippen, quite at ease, was calling in his considerate way at the Martinettis' flat in Shaftesbury Avenue to see if Mr Martinetti had been cheered up. To a friendly inquiry about his wife he replied, "Oh, she's all right," and promised to convey Mrs Martinetti's love to her. The next day he was pawning a diamond ring and earrings for £80, and that night Ethel le Neve slept at Hilldrop Crescent. On the morning of the 3rd two letters signed "Belle Elmore" and dated the 2nd were received by the Secretary of the Music Hall Ladies Guild. Mrs Crippen was resigning her honorary treasurership, the illness of a near relative having summoned her at a moment's notice to America. The letters were not in her handwriting. Mrs Martinetti, hearing the news in a roundabout way, reproached Crippen when they next met for not telling her. He had been so busy, he said, and all the night before his wife's departure they had been packing. "Packing and crying, I suppose?" said Mrs Martinetti. "Oh, we have got past that," said Crippen.

He had by now pawned more rings and a brooch for £115. On the 20th he took Ethel le Neve to the ball of the Music Hall Ladies Benevolent Fund, and Miss le Neve was wearing another brooch which, it was not disputed, had been Mrs Crippen's. On March 12 the girl threw up her situation and went to live at Hilldrop Crescent. Soon after this Crippen gave his landlord a quarter's notice, subsequently having this extended to the end of September. He was not to require the extension. Just before Easter, which fell early that year, he told Mrs Martinetti and other friends that his wife was dangerously ill in America and not expected to live. If she died he would take a week's holiday in France. On March 24, the day before Good Friday, a telegram came for Mrs Martinetti: "Belle died yesterday at six o'clock." It had been sent from Victoria Station, before Crippen and Ethel le Neve set off for Dieppe. While they were away notice of Mrs Crippen's death was published in the *Era*.

This sequence of rather curious proceedings caused a good deal of talk among Belle Elmore's friends. Crippen, on his return from France, while apparently frank and circumstantial on the subject of his wife's sudden death, contrived to parry almost all attempts to send tokens of remembrance. Mrs Crippen had died at Los Angeles, at the home of his relations, among them his son, who was by his stepmother's side when she passed away: the ashes were coming to England, and letters of condolence and everlasting wreaths would arrive too late. Everything was neatly explained, and the little doctor showed no marked signs of strain, still less of fluster or alarm. He was his usual self, quiet, pale, and controlled. He led his normal life, visiting the Martinettis and others, leaving Hilldrop Crescent daily for Albion House, where he was still acting as physician for the Yale Tooth Specialists. Ethel le Neve was now openly wearing Mrs Crippen's furs and jewellery, which was considered to be in somewhat poor taste.

A month went by, in the course of which one of these friends of Cora Crippen's, a Mr Nash, paid a short visit to the United States, where he tried unsuccessfully to get news of her last days. As soon as he was back in England he called upon the doctor with some awkward questions. Whether Nash was a conscientious seeker after truth or merely a busybody, he was left thoroughly dissatisfied; and he took his story to Scotland Yard. With that he disappears from the scene, but he had done his work. He had set the ball rolling; and he had frightened Crippen.

At no time, however, did the latter show greater powers of self-control and dissimulation. He certainly deceived Chief Inspector Dew, when that experienced officer, after a week's inquiries, called at Albion House. Crippen at once admitted that he had been telling lies: his wife, as far as he knew, was alive. On February 1 she had left him, as she had often threatened to do. His belief was that she had gone to Chicago to join her friend of the Guilford Street days, Bruce Miller. His own fabrications were designed to shield her, and to shield himself from scandal. Dew, with a search warrant, then went with the doctor to Hilldrop Crescent. (When, later, there was talk of renaming the street alternatives suggested were Dewdrop Crescent and Filleted Place.) The Chief Inspector went through every room, and down into the coal-cellar. But though, that evening, he circulated a description of the missing woman, he had almost been persuaded that Crippen's new story was the truth.

Had Crippen realized this, and stood fast, he might have been safe. But he was shaken, he had already made his plans, and the next day he and Ethel le Neve were on their way to Antwerp, the girl in boy's clothes. They had not even been watched. It was merely to verify a date that Dew sought out Crippen two days later, and found him gone.

Now the hunt was up. While every police officer in the kingdom was memorizing descriptions of Crippen and his companion—the modern equivalent of the old hue and cry—Dew and his men took possession of the dreary, deserted house in Hilldrop Crescent. Every room was ransacked. The garden was dug up. The coal-cellar was searched with the rest. Except for Mrs Crippen's jewellery, which the little doctor had willingly produced, and three baskets and a large trunk full of her clothes, nothing to confirm suspicion was found until the third day. Then, armed with a poker, Dew was once more in the cellar, where there was a little coal, some chips and rubbish, and an old chandelier. He began to probe the brick floor. Bricks came up; and below, buried in lime, were the remains of Belle Elmore.

4

The gist of all this is to be found written by Spilsbury on his card of the case—or, rather, cards, for they are the ordinary small, oblong pieces of pasteboard used for filing, and he needed three. Of Crippen he wrote: "Skill in evisceration—acquisition of hyoscine—access to textbooks." And of the one-time Kunigunde Mackamotski: "American. 35. Vivacious—good company—attractive—dressed well—jewellery—fast life. Private: very overbearing—bad temper." Then, after a summary of the events already related, and a reference to the pursuit across the Atlantic and the arrest in the St Lawrence, he comes to the discovery in the cellar:

> Human remains found July 13. . . . Medical organs of chest and abdomen removed in one mass. Four large pieces of skin and muscle, one from lower abdomen with old operation scar. 4 in. long—broader at lower end. Impossible to identify sex. Hyoscine found 2.7 grains. Hair in Hinde's curler—roots present. Hair 6 in. long. Man's pyjama jacket, Jones Bros., Holloway, and odd pair of pyjama trousers.

"Remains," in this case, was the right word. There was no head, there were no bones, and all the limbs were missing, except what might have been parts of a thigh. Upon the residue the four doctors now set to work. Willcox and Luff analysed the various organs, while Spilsbury assisted Pepper, at the latter's request, with the pieces of skin. One of these, that with the scar, was to prove of paramount importance.

With this laboratory work in the summer of 1910 Spilsbury entered upon that domain which he was to make almost his own. He had got a foothold in the small inner ring of the medico-legal fraternity, and there he would stay. His unobtrusive self-confidence must have stood him in good stead. He was now to work with a team of public men of marked character, vested with wide responsibilities. His fellow-pathologists he knew well; but he cannot then have been closely acquainted with Muir, twenty years his senior, or with Travers Humphreys, who was forty-three. The work itself, in the fuller sense of team work, he must have found intensely interesting. The powers of Treasury Counsel, when given charge of a case, are very large. It was Muir who now directed the police investigation. A great criminal lawyer, Muir was a driver, with the thoroughness of the Scot, and he was in the prime of his energy. By the time the case was ended every member of the team was thoroughly tired of it—except himself, and perhaps Spilsbury, the youngest, to whom it was a novel experience.

Muir was gravely dissatisfied with the police work. Crippen should have been watched and arrested the moment he tried to get away, if not before. With Travers Humphreys, Muir went to Hilldrop Crescent, and both lawyers were astonished to find Mrs Crippen's furs still there, when they should have been held as exhibits. For if the lady was unlikely to leave her jewels behind it was equally improbable that she would set off on a transatlantic voyage in February without her ermine coat and muff. After Chief Inspector Dew's newspaper triumph, on his return with his prisoners from Canada, he seemed so completely to lose interest in the case that Muir said he must be suffering from sleepy sickness. Again, it was Muir who drove the police into resuming their abandoned efforts to trace the date of purchase of the pyjamas found with the remains in the cellar. This date was one of the decisive factors which convicted Crippen. Muir's thoroughness must have appealed to Spilsbury, as the same quality in him no doubt appealed to Muir. The latter was as formidable in court as he was careful in preparing a case, and Crippen's doleful words, if hardly those of an innocent man, are a tribute to the great advocate's reputation: "It is most unfortunate that he is against me. I wish it had been anyone else but him. I fear the worst."

A little later, when Spilsbury's own reputation was fully established, many criminals must have echoed those sentiments when they learnt that he was to give evidence against them. The result of this, his first big case, was to hinge on the medical evidence. The purchase of hyoscine and the positive identification of the operational scar by himself and Pepper, together with the inability of the defence to produce any news of Mrs Crippen after the small hours of February 1, would no doubt have been enough for the jury; the pyjama jacket merely made assurance doubly sure. It was to raise, however, one of the only two points in the case of real interest to lawyers. The first was disposed of when it was decided to try Crippen and Ethel le Neve separately. With regard to the jacket, Muir's insistence that the date of purchase could and must be traced was not rewarded until the trial had begun. The defence knew nothing of this fresh and damning piece of evidence. It could not fairly be produced without warning, but so late had it come to hand that twenty-four hours' notice was the most that could be given. Crippen's counsel, Mr Tobin, might then apply for a postponement of the trial, which the prosecution could scarcely oppose. It will be shown how Muir got round this difficulty.

On the medical side there was a matter of tactics which must have caused Spilsbury and his colleagues to feel resentment and regret. Crippen's solicitor was Arthur Newton, one of the most astute of criminal lawyers. In a few years' time he was to be too clever, and go to gaol. Crippen had no money, and Newton's fees were paid by a newspaper, which expected some return for them. He took little part in the early proceedings; he was saving his ammunition for the trial, and for the doctors. Perhaps he remembered the Smethurst case. He induced two distinguished medical men to give hasty and erroneous opinions—in the case of one of them on the distinct understanding that he would not be called as a witness. The unfortunate man did not know Arthur Newton. It has been suggested that this sharp practice was based on jealousy felt by the staffs of certain hospitals of the success of the School of Pathology at St Mary's. Sir Travers Humphreys, with his inside knowledge of the case, writes of the possibility "that there were doctors, not St Mary's men, who would not be sorry to catch out in a mistake that young pathologist who was making such a name for himself, Dr Spilsbury."

Newton wished to brief F. E. Smith (later Lord Birkenhead) for the defence of Crippen. Smith, however, advised that, as the two accused were to be tried separately, separate counsel would be necessary, and he elected to defend Ethel le Neve. Marshall Hall denied the story that Newton approached him, and that he declined the brief.

5

The trial opened on October 18 before the Lord Chief Justice, Lord Alverstone. A coroner's jury having returned a verdict of wilful murder against Crippen, the remains buried in the cellar in Hilldrop Crescent had been reburied in Finchley Cemetery, the week before, as those of Cora Crippen. This would seem to be a prejudgment of the case. For the defence at the trial, the only possible defence if manslaughter was ruled out, was that the remains were not even demonstrably those of a woman, still less those of Cora Crippen, and that they had been buried without Crippen's knowledge, probably before he took possession of the house.

The prosecution argued on the familiar lines of circumstantial evidence. No one could be produced who had seen Mrs Crippen since the early hours of February 1, nine months before. If she had gone to the United States or elsewhere she had gone without money, clothes, or jewellery. The remains, meagre as they were, answered to her description in two respects. On a piece of skin from the lower part of the abdomen there was an operational scar; just before her marriage to Crippen she had undergone such an operation. A tuft of dark hair was found, six inches long, bleached gold or auburn, indicating that it was a woman's; Mrs Crippen was a brunette, who bleached her hair. Of less importance was a woman's undervest, similar to those worn by her.

Hyoscine was found in the remains, and Crippen had purchased hyoscine a few weeks before his wife's disappearance. There was no trace of his having acquired this drug at any other time during his ten years in England. Filson Young, apparently quoting Hall, says that the little doctor learnt of the use of hyoscine as a sexual depressant during his experience in lunatic asylums. Spilsbury has queried this statement, for which the only authority seems to be Crippen's reference in his evidence to a visit or visits to the Royal Bethlehem Hospital. Among the objects that were found in the grave in the cellar were portions of a pyjama jacket, including the collar on which was the retailer's label. Crippen was found to possess two identical pyjama suits, the jackets similarly labelled, and the trousers only of a third suit. Finally, from the day after his wife was last seen Crippen had acted as though he knew she would neither return nor need her belongings; he pawned some of her jewels, gave the rest, with her furs and clothes, to Ethel le Neve, and established the latter in the house.

The trial lasted five days. Crippen was defended by A. A. Tobin, K.C., later a judge, with whom were Mr Huntly Jenkins and Mr Roome. Crown witnesses on the first day included Mrs Martinetti, other acquaintances of the Crippens', some of the doctor's associates in business, and Bruce Miller and Cora Crippen's sister, both from America. On the second day Chief Inspector Dew gave evidence, and read a long statement by Crippen. In the afternoon Dr Pepper was called, and the vital controversial testimony began.

Pepper described the piece of skin on which was the mark which in his opinion was the scar of an abdominal operation. The exhibit, preserved in formalin in a dish, was handed about the court. The evisceration of the body, the pathologist went on to say, was the work of a person skilled in dissection. The remains were those of an adult, young or middle-aged, but there was no certain anatomical indication of sex. When he first examined them in July they had been buried from four to eight months. Burial had taken place shortly after death. Asked by Muir if it could possibly have occurred before September 21, 1905—the date when Crippen became tenant of the house—the witness replied, "Oh, no, absolutely impossible." During a long technical cross-examination by Mr Tobin, covering the effect of lime and clay on putrefaction, and going on to suggest that the so-called scar was really a fold caused after death, Pepper was asked whether he had cut a piece across the area of the scar and handed it to Dr Spilsbury. He said that his instructions were that it should be done that way.

Spilsbury himself was the first witness called next morning, that of the 20th. He was in the box for about a seventh of the time taken up by Pepper's evidence, which he was there to confirm. It was the way he did this that deeply impressed those professionally interested who had not heard him testify in public before. Tall, handsome, well-dressed, a red carnation in his buttonhole, his bearing in his first capital case was as detached, imperturbable, and confident as it was when he was at the height of his fame. In cold, unemotional tones he described his examination of the piece of skin and its adherent flesh as a whole, and then of the section handed to him by Pepper for microscopical scrutiny. This section was one and a half inches in length, and nearly half an inch in width. It included a portion of the mark asserted to be a scar. At each end of this minute fragment he found glands, but there were none in the centre, proving that, in fact, the mark was a scar, and not a fold. The presence and arrangement of certain muscles proved further that the specimen came from the lower part of the wall of the abdomen. He had formed his opinion about the scar before microscopical examination; this had merely corroborated it.

In cross-examination Mr Tobin asked Spilsbury how long he had been associated with Pepper, and whether he had heard, before his examination of the piece of skin, that Mrs Crippen had undergone an abdominal operation. Muir, who no doubt knew his man, must have welcomed the opportunity these tendentious questions gave him when he rose to re-examine. They gave Spilsbury his opportunity too. He replied to Muir:

> "The fact that I have acted with Mr Pepper has absolutely no influence upon the opinion that I have expressed here. The fact that I had read in the papers that there had been an operation on Belle Elmore had no effect at all upon the opinion I have expressed. I have no doubt that this is a scar."

A little later the Lord Chief Justice was moved to carry the point further, with what intention is not known. In his book of *Recollections* he covers the trial in a few lines, without mentioning the pathologists. It is possible, however, that Lord Alverstone, sitting aloft in scarlet, under the Sword of Justice, the embodiment of the Crown and the Law, was a little astonished when the same quiet, authoritative voice addressed him.

"I have an independent position of my own," said Spilsbury, "and I am responsible for my own opinion, which has been formed on my own scientific knowledge, and not in any way influenced by any supposed connexion with Mr Pepper." And then he said again, "I have absolutely no doubt in my own mind as regards the scar. . . . I have my microscopic slides here, and I shall send for a microscope in case it should be wanted."

Here was a new, dominating voice in the courts of justice. Its moderation failed to hide what was, in fact, a rebuke of the implication, if such was intended, that the witness could be influenced by any but scientific considerations. If there was no sensation in court, in the accepted sense, there was a stir. Muir must have smiled to himself; and many others were profoundly impressed. Among them was one who was to become Spilsbury's lifelong friend, and who, as coroner for St Pancras, was to conduct the inquiry into his death. By an odd chance young Mr Bentley Purchase, who was a student of law in 1910, was coaching at the house in Store Street where Crippen for a time had his office. He remembers how people were saying, as Spilsbury left the witness-box, "There is a coming man."

Spilsbury's part in the trial was not yet ended. Having said he would send for his microscope, he obtained it; and in an adjoining room he was presently demonstrating to the jury, by means of the slides, the existence of the scar. He was to attend another conference on the fourth day, after he had again been in the witness-box to carry out a rather painful task.

His evidence was followed, when less important witnesses had come and gone, by that of Willcox and Luff. Willcox described the strangely assorted contents of five jars received from the coroner's office—a small portion of liver, one kidney, a pair of combinations, hair in a curler, and three fragments of a pyjama jacket. The importance of the pyjama jacket was then scarcely realized, except by Muir. Willcox later examined other parts of the remains, including the piece of skin bearing the scar. He agreed that it was a scar, but his main contribution to the case against the accused was his discovery of hyoscine in the organs. In this he had the help of the St Mary's cat. Having established the presence of an alkaloid by a patient process lasting a fortnight, Willcox let fall a drop of the resulting solution into the cat's eye. The eye dilated, proving that the alkaloid was mydriatic, and therefore vegetable. Further tests showed it to be hyoscine.

Luff corroborated Willcox, and a few more witnesses closed the case for the Crown, except for one further piece of evidence, to be forthcoming next day. The rest of that third afternoon was taken up by Mr Tobin's opening speech for the defence, and by the examination of Crippen by Mr Huntly Jenkins.

Crippen was again in the witness-box, being cross-examined by Muir, for most of the fourth day. Of this terrible ordeal, under which his replies became more and more evasive and confused, only one passage need be recalled. Muir was now in possession of the facts about the purchase of the pyjama suit connected with the remains in the cellar. He wished to bring out these facts by forcing Crippen to commit himself to a date for the purchase. Crippen fell into the trap: he swore that the pyjamas had been bought by him as far back as 1905 or 1906. He was warned that this statement might be disproved, and when he persisted in it the Lord Chief Justice ruled that his evidence made the date of sale important and admissible.

Crippen was followed by the medical evidence for the defence. Dr Hubert Maitland Turnbull, Director of the Pathological Institute at the London Hospital, had been at Magdalen with Spilsbury, and they had kept up their acquaintance. Spilsbury told a friend how Turnbull was asked by Arthur Newton at a bridge party if he would examine the all-important piece of skin "as a matter of interest." Having done this, rather perfunctorily, Turnbull was so foolish as to sign a report to the effect that the skin came from the thigh, not the abdomen, and that the supposed scar was a fold. After further examination, and a study of Pepper's and Spilsbury's depositions, he began to feel doubts about his first opinion. Horrified to learn that he had been tricked into giving evidence at the trial, he telephoned Spilsbury for advice. Spilsbury recommended him to withdraw the report. Finally, however, Turnbull determined to stand by it. Muir cross-examined him, and asked the judge to allow Spilsbury to point out a certain tendon which the witness said he had not seen. Spilsbury took his forceps into the witness-box and indicated the tendon. Turnbull was still reluctant to admit his mistake, and at length the Lord Chief Justice said to him, "Please answer this one way or the other; it is most important. Do you find that tendon there or not?"

"Yes," said Turnbull.

Later in his evidence Pepper joined him in the witness-box to point out another feature in the exhibit. At one stage the harassed Turnbull made a remark about persons unaccustomed to the microscope, and Muir pulled him up sharply:

"We are not talking about people unaccustomed to the microscope. We are talking about people like Mr Spilsbury."

Turnbull was followed by Dr Wall, also of the London Hospital, who admitted that he too had changed his first opinion, and that the piece of skin probably came from the abdomen.

A third medical man, Dr Blyth, was called by the defence to controvert Willcox's evidence as to the presence of hyoscine in the remains. He made an equally poor impression. This *débâcle* of the specialists, painfully reminiscent of the Smethurst case, but differing from that because there was now, on the other side, a team of doctors who really knew what they were talking about, is summed up by Sir Travers Humphreys as a "painful sight."

At the close of the medical evidence for the defence Muir played the missing ace. He made an application to rebut Crippen's statement about the date of purchase of the pyjamas. The application was allowed. A buyer for Jones Brothers of Holloway was able to prove that the pyjama material was not acquired by his firm until the end of 1908, and that three suits made of it were supplied to 39 Hilldrop Crescent in January 1909. As Muir put it in his final speech, who alone during the next twelve months could have buried the jacket in that house? "Who was missing who could be buried in it? Nobody but Belle Elmore."

The jury took this view. They were out less than half an hour. On November 5 Crippen's appeal against his conviction was dismissed by the Court of Criminal Appeal. In the meantime Ethel le Neve had been on trial as accessory after the fact, and had been acquitted. A report of her death in Australia has lately appeared in the Press. By other accounts she died some years ago.

Two days before Crippen's execution he wrote Miss le Neve a long letter in which he criticized the Crown's evidence in the matter of the scar. He complained that this point had been omitted from a statement already made for publication in a newspaper. Without mentioning Spilsbury by name, he attacked his evidence. Spilsbury had said:

> "In a surgical operation when the edges of the skin are brought into contact it is common for at least one side to turn in a little, and, as the scar forms, some of the surface stuff covering the skin may become enclosed in the scar and embedded in it. I found such a piece of included epidermis in this mark which I say is a scar, and having found that I think there is no room for doubt as to its being a scar."

Crippen's comment on this was that such a turning under in sewing up a wound was "a most unlikely thing to have been done by skilled surgeons, who especially avoid such an occurrence in abdominal operations." In the next paragraph he tried to show that Pepper was wrong in asserting that the scars of abdominal operations are widest at the lower end. In Spilsbury's much marked and worn copy of *The Trial of H. H. Crippen* he has put a pencil-stroke against this passage. It should be remembered that this letter of Crippen's, like his previous statement, was intended for publication.

Two last words on the case deserve quotation. The final line of Spilsbury's card reads: "Summary. No direct evidence." And Muir, after Crippen's execution, made the cryptic remark, "Full justice has not yet been done."

Chapter 2: SEDDON—THE MEAN MURDERER

THE Crippen trial was a great individual triumph for Spilsbury. The Press of the whole country had given enormous prominence to the case, and the personality and good looks of the young pathologist, his precise and extremely lucid manner of giving evidence, and his refusal to be awed by anybody captured the popular fancy. At thirty-three he was not indifferent to all this; but if he could feel the thrill of becoming a national figure, and could carry home the papers which would show his wife that his name was making headlines, he was never in the slightest danger of putting too high a value on notoriety of such a kind. His self-confidence never approached egoism. Far more important and flattering than publicity was another outcome of his sudden rise. Pepper, his old teacher and chief, his associate in the long-drawn investigation which culminated in those October days at the Central Criminal Court, now decided to give up public work. In terminating his Home Office appointment Pepper recommended Spilsbury as assistant to Willcox, now senior Home Office Pathologist. Willcox warmly supported this recommendation. Such sponsors would no doubt have secured Spilsbury the post in any case, but the Crippen trial had already placed him in the direct line of succession. Thus began a connexion with the Home Office and Scotland Yard which was to last for thirty-seven years.

It was a good start to 1911; but otherwise the first months of the new year found Spilsbury busy with his usual lectures and demonstrations at St Mary's, and with routine post-mortems there and at coroners' mortuaries. His evidence in an abortion case resulted in two doctors being struck off the Medical Register. He first appeared at a trial for murder as pathologist for the Crown in Rex *v*. Pateman, a case which will be referred to farther on.

The year 1911 was a notable one at the Finchley mortuary, where Spilsbury had examined the body of Pateman's victim in April. He was twice there in November in cases of murder, one being that of Lord George Sanger, known all over Europe for his circuses, and the other that of a middle-aged woman whose exhumation was to ring up the curtain on the second of Spilsbury's great criminal trials.

A fortnight before Sanger's death Spilsbury and Willcox had gone together to Finchley for the former's post-mortem on the remains of Eliza Mary Barrow, aged forty-nine. Before the year was out they knew that they would be giving evidence at the trial of Frederick Henry Seddon and his wife for the murder of Miss Barrow.

2

From Hilldrop Crescent in Camden Town a walk of less than a mile, north-east along Camden and Parkhurst Roads, past Holloway Prison, and then across Holloway Road into the network of dreary streets reaching to Finsbury Park, brings one to a thoroughfare called Tollington Park. Here, at No. 63, Miss Eliza Mary Barrow died on September 14, 1911. Two days later she was buried in Islington Borough Cemetery, at Finchley, where, eleven months earlier, the remains of Cora Crippen had been interred.

Four days before Crippen's trial opened the resident owner of 63 Tollington Park, Frederick Henry Seddon, made the first move in a financial project which was to bring him, in turn, into the dock at the Old Bailey. Seddon was employed by the London and Manchester Industrial Assurance Company as superintendent of collectors and canvassers in North London, and he was entitled to secure business on his own account; and though Islington is the second largest of the London boroughs, it is impossible not to wonder whether coincidence went so far as on some occasion to bring him and Crippen together. He must, at any rate, have taken the keenest interest in the pursuit and trial of the little American doctor who had lived only twenty minutes' walk away. At some time in the next ten months he began to consider the last, irrevocable step in his own cold-blooded scheme; and the fate of Crippen did not deter him.

When Spilsbury went to Islington Cemetery for the exhumation of Miss Barrow's body, two months after the burial, he must have known something about the events which led the Home Office to authorize this action. When he had conducted the post-mortem he probably felt fairly certain that suspicion was justified. To confirm it was the business of Willcox, who was Senior Analyst to the Home Office, besides doing most of the forensic pathology until Spilsbury's appointment relieved him of this work, and at some of his tests for arsenic Spilsbury was present. By that time he had learnt a great deal more about the case.

Miss Barrow was a middle-aged woman of unpleasant habits who had quarrelled with most of her relatives. Her habits and character were not the sole cause of dissension: she possessed property amounting to some £4000, and when she said her relations were unkind to her she really meant that in her opinion they were interested only in her money. No doubt they felt curiosity about its disposal. This group —Miss Barrow, the Seddons, and the Vonderahes—belonged to that class which through upbringing and circumstances thinks and talks a good deal about money. Miss Barrow, selfish and mean, as well as common and ignorant, carried this trait to extremes; and in Frederick Seddon she must have been delighted to find a kindred avaricious spirit.

In July 1910 she had been living for more than a year within a few hundred yards of Tollington Park, in the house of Mr Vonderahe, her cousin. A long series of squabbles coming to a head, she made the last of her frequent moves, taking Seddon's second floor, unfurnished, at a rent of 12*s*. a week. Seddon, like Crippen, had a house too large for his needs, and besides letting this floor he found quarters for his father and used a basement room as an office, for which he charged his employers 5*s*. weekly. He owned the house, and had other residential property. When Miss Barrow moved in she brought with her a retinue comprising an engine-driver named Hook, his wife, and his nephew, aged ten. The Hooks had known Miss Barrow for some years, and the nephew, Ernest Grant, had been more or less adopted by her.

Within a fortnight a curious incident followed. The Hooks were handed a note from Miss Barrow, telling them to go. Though she lived on the same floor, they did not see her again; the whole affair was managed by Seddon, whose version of it was that the Hooks and Miss Barrow had been quarrelling, and he gave them all notice, afterwards relenting in the case of Miss Barrow and her protégé, the boy, Grant. It was typical of the man that he gave a quasi-legal touch to the ejectment by tacking to Hook's door a notice to quit signed "F. Seddon, landlord and owner." Wherever the truth lies, the upshot of this sordid domestic crisis was that the poor couple were turned out, and the well-to-do lodger remained. It is evident that within a fortnight Seddon had begun to acquire that influence over Miss Barrow which was to end in her undoing, and his.

Two months went by, during which there were no doubt many agreeable talks about money between landlord and tenant. Miss Barrow was perturbed by the Lloyd George Budget, and by October she had decided, or had been persuaded, to transfer to Seddon her India stock, worth £1600, receiving from him in return an annuity and the remission of her rent. No written agreement was ever found in respect of this transaction. Apparently it never occurred to Miss Barrow that this casual method of doing business was surprising in a very business-like man, who was, moreover, employed by a concern which dealt in annuities. She seems to have been an extremely stupid woman; the doctor who attended her in her last illness said of her that he did not think her mental condition was ever good. But in view of her grasping and miserly character this casual arrangement with Seddon is a proof of how greatly his hold over her had increased in these two months.

It went on increasing. She owned some leasehold property, and in January this was assigned to Seddon, who then raised her annuity to about £3 a week, which he paid until just before her death. Finally, in June, alarmed by the Birkbeck crash, she withdrew in coin upward of £200 which she had on deposit at a Savings Bank. It was said by Vonderahe and Hook that she always kept a considerable sum in gold and notes in a cash-box—£400 in gold was mentioned—and she also had some jewellery. Now, therefore, in June, the whole of her £4000 was either in Seddon's hands or in his house.

Early in August Miss Barrow went with the Seddons for a few days to Southend. On the 26th of that month, according to Walter Thorley, a chemist with a shop in Crouch Hill, Seddon's daughter Maggie purchased from him a threepenny packet of fly-papers, stated on the label to contain arsenic and prominently marked "Poison." On September 1 Miss Barrow was taken ill. Her own doctor being unavailable, the Seddons' medical man, Dr Sworn, was called in. He saw the invalid almost daily until she died, diagnosing her complaint as epidemic diarrhoea, which was prevalent at that time. She was a heavy woman, and subject to asthma, and as in her state of exhaustion there was a danger of heart failure, the doctor warned Mrs Seddon that she should not be allowed to get out of bed. The conditions of her illness, and her sluttish habits, made the sick-room a revolting place: Dr Sworn said he had never seen so many flies. He did not notice the fly-papers which, according to the Seddons, were in saucers on the mantelpiece. To this squalid scene on the second floor a final disgusting touch was added when Miss Barrow did get out of bed—driven from her room by the flies, said Mrs Seddon—and, ill as she was, went to share the bed of the boy Grant in the room next door.

At midnight on the 13th Miss Barrow was heard to cry out, "I'm dying." She was still alive when Seddon returned from a music-hall: in his wife's words, "He did not go up immediately—he was talking to my sister-in-law about a man doing him out of sixpence or something at a theatre." Later, while Mrs Seddon attended to Miss Barrow, who was, in fact, dying, he stayed outside the room, smoking and reading a newspaper. At half-past six in the morning Miss Barrow was dead.

Dr Sworn had not been summoned. Later that day, without seeing the body, he gave Seddon a certificate. Arrangements were made for the burial in a common grave, though it was known to Seddon that Miss Barrow's family had a vault at Highgate. In the evening Mrs Seddon and her sister-in-law sought rest and recreation at a music-hall.

3

A manual for murderers would include two strongly worded sections on the dangers of being too greedy, and of antagonizing the victim's relatives and friends. Again and again well-laid schemes have gone wrong through neglect of one or both of these elementary principles.

Had Seddon put himself out a little to conciliate the Vonderahes, and had he been content with the India stock and the leasehold property and left Miss Barrow's cash-box alone, doubts as to the manner of her death might never have arisen. Since she left the Vonderahes' house this couple had moved, but they were still within a few minutes' walk of Tollington Park. If the letter of which Seddon kept a carbon copy was really sent it never reached them, and he made no other attempt to convey the news. Miss Barrow had been buried several days before her cousin heard that she was dead. When the Vonderahes did see Seddon it was to receive other surprising information, together with a few lies. The four or five hundred pounds in gold and notes which Miss Barrow was believed to have possessed, and the £200 recently withdrawn from the Savings Bank, had alike vanished. Ten pounds, said Seddon, was all he found in her room. A statement he drew up, accounting for his expenditure of this sum on the funeral and on Ernest Grant's keep and clothing, seemed to show that he was £1 1*s.* 10½*d.* out of pocket. Another statement dealt with the transfer of stock and house property. Seddon was always ready with documents of this kind: he could explain anything on paper. There was even a will, drawn up by him for Miss Barrow only three days before her death. Witnessed by his wife and father, it appointed him sole executor and trustee for young Grant and his sister, to whom were left the testator's personal belongings. As these were valued at the rather derisory sum of £16, the Vonderahes went away from the interview profoundly dissatisfied. Having talked things over, they communicated their misgivings to the police.

A few days afterwards instructions were issued for the exhumation of Miss Barrow's body. In this investigation, as in many more to come, Spilsbury and Willcox worked hand in hand; and just as presently the former was to assist at his senior's laboratory tests, so now Willcox accompanied him to the cemetery, and attended at the post-mortem. According to Dr Sworn's certificate, Miss Barrow died of heart failure resulting from epidemic diarrhoea. Similar symptoms would be produced by arsenical poisoning. Arsenic acts as a preservative, and the description on Spilsbury's case-card of the condition of the internal organs begins: "Extremely well preserved." A few lines below he writes: "No disease apparent." These findings are repeated under the heading "Conclusions." Willcox's discovery of arsenic in the organs and tissues, combined with the behaviour of Seddon, as already referred to, justified the remark made by Marshall Hall when he had read his brief for the defence: "This is the blackest case I have ever been in."

Conflicting views, however, have always been held about it. Did Miss Barrow die of acute or chronic poisoning? Why was Mrs Seddon, who was arrested some time after her husband, and charged with him, let off so lightly? Was Seddon's guilt ever really proved? What convicted him—the evidence or his own showing in the witness-box? To Filson Young, who sat through the trial, "It appeared as if, in fact, Seddon was convicted not because the Crown succeeded in proving his guilt, but because he failed to prove his innocence." Marshall Hall himself had no faith in his client—a rare occurrence in the career of that great advocate—but he thought the Crown's case a weak one. There was a good deal of criticism of the means employed by the police to connect Maggie Seddon with the purchase of fly-papers, and of certain aspects of the judge's summing-up. On the other hand, Sir Travers Humphreys, who was one of the Treasury counsel at the trial, had no doubts about the matter. "The case was referred to at the time," he writes, "as an instance of the accused being convicted as the result of his own evidence. I think that is a mistake. There was always a strong case against the Seddons."

4

Seddon was arrested on December 4, his wife not until the middle of January. Both were committed for trial. This time the Law Officers did not neglect the usual custom, that one of them should appear in a poison case, and the Attorney-General, the then Sir Rufus Isaacs, was to lead for the Crown. Mr Gervais Rentoul appeared for Mrs Seddon. The trial began at the Old Bailey on March 4, before

Mr Justice Bucknill; among the longest of modern capital trials, it was to last ten days. It is agreed that the outstanding features were Seddon's behaviour in the witness-box and the medical testimony of Willcox and Spilsbury. These two were in the box for most of the fourth and part of the fifth day, and on the eighth day Willcox was recalled.

The first three days were taken up with the story of Miss Barrow's life in the house in Tollington Park, her financial transactions with Seddon, and her illness and death; with Seddon's possession of a large sum in gold, estimated at £200, a few hours after she died, and the curious business, very damaging to the accused, of the thirty-three £5 notes, admittedly Miss Barrow's, which Mrs Seddon changed at shops and banks, at the former giving a false name and address; and with the various purchases of fly-papers that played so important, if unsatisfactory, a part in the case. Whether or no the police suspected the use of fly-papers from the start, it was Seddon himself who concentrated attention on this source of arsenic. After his arrest he suggested to his solicitor, Mr Saint, that Miss Barrow had drunk water in which such papers had been soaked. "You can't buy poisonous things like that, can you, at an ordinary chemist's?" asked the innocent Mr Saint, who cannot have been troubled by flies, and who had forgotten the Flanagan and Higgins case, and that of Mrs Maybrick, in the 1880's. "Oh, can't you!" said Seddon; and his daughter Maggie, who was believed to have bought some in August, was sent out to buy some more. It was explained by Willcox in evidence that a single sheet of fly-paper could contain a fatal dose of arsenic; but that Seddon's most improbable theory was put forward, and by him, raises a doubt as to whether this was, in fact, the means by which the poison was obtained. Willcox himself did not think it was.

Obtained, however, it had been, and administered to Miss Barrow in one or more lethal doses very shortly before she died. The evidence of the two pathologists from St Mary's placed this beyond question, in spite of a very clever attempt by Marshall Hall—to be touched upon later—to discredit Willcox's chain of reasoning. Spilsbury, going first into the witness-box, laid the foundation of the Crown's case when he described the results of the post-mortem. He was examined by Rufus Isaacs, and questioned by the judge, and both Marshall Hall and his junior, Mr Dunstan, cross-examined him. His replies are notable for their characteristic brevity. After his opening statement he seldom used more than a dozen words.

In reply to an early question he said that with the exception of the stomach and intestines he found no disease in any of the organs sufficient to account for death. The stomach was a little dilated, and a black substance was present on its inner surface. In the upper part of the small intestine the inner surface was red. If the man and woman in the dock, watching and listening intently, derived any encouragement from this rather negative opening they must have been dashed when Spilsbury continued:

> "The body was very well preserved, internally and externally, apart from some post-mortem staining externally. Taking into account that the death took place in September 1911, the state of preservation in which I found the body was very abnormal. I was not able to account for it at the time the post-mortem examination was made, but since the analysis which has been made by Dr Willcox I think the preservation was due to the presence of arsenic in the body."

Under cross-examination by Mr Dunstan, Spilsbury repeated what he had said about the absence of evidence of disease except in the stomach and intestines. The small intestine showed reddening, and Mr Dunstan asked:

"Apart from that reddening, there was no sign of any disease at all?"

"None at all," Spilsbury agreed.

"And death might have been due to syncope or heart failure?"

"Certainly, apart from the reddening, so far as I could see."

This reddening, he agreed further, and the absence of disease in other organs, would be equally consistent with death from epidemic diarrhoea. But he added: "With the one exception of the condition of the preservation of the body."

Mr Dunstan here introduced the arsenic-eating Styrian peasants, who crop up in almost every case of arsenical poisoning, and whose bodies after death are well preserved. With the assistance of the judge, he then went into the question of a skin rash and watery affection of the eyes. Spilsbury said that a rash would not necessarily result from less than a fortnight's administration of arsenic. Miss Barrow was ill for under a fortnight. He did not think the eyes would be affected at all in such a case. These symptoms, again, are those of chronic poisoning; not of "fairly large doses," in Mr Dunstan's words. At the police-court proceedings Willcox had defined "a moderately large fatal dose" as one of five grains and upward, and Mr Dunstan went on:

"At what time would a dose of that class prove fatal?"

"It would not be likely to prove fatal—a single dose, of course—in less than three days, probably, and it might be longer."

When the Attorney-General, as tall and as good-looking in his dark way as the witness who was standing in the box, rose to re-examine, Spilsbury repeated that he would distinguish a chronic case by a running from the eyes, and by a rash on the skin, which would tend to disappear after death. On internal examination of the body he had not found fatty degeneration of the liver or the heart walls, which might have been present; but the preservation of the body was more consistent with acute arsenical poisoning than with epidemic diarrhoea. In the case of a patient who had died two months before examination, in that period of heat, from the latter complaint, he would have expected to find advanced putrefaction. Arsenic, he told the judge, acted as a preservative of any part of the body to which it gained access.

The amount of arsenic found in the body was discussed. It certainly indicated, Spilsbury said, that more than three-quarters of a grain had been taken. Having agreed that he had great experience of post-mortem examinations, including cases of acute arsenical poisoning, and that he was familiar with the works on the subject, he was further cross-examined by Marshall Hall.

The line to be taken by the defence was already apparent. It was that Miss Barrow had suffered from chronic, not acute, arsenical poisoning. Marshall Hall used the phrase "chronic arsenical taking," as by the useful Styrian peasants, and by more sophisticated persons (like Mrs Maybrick) for their complexion. In other words, Miss Barrow had somehow been absorbing the poison over a long period of time, but it did not cause her death. Her own doctor had denied ever prescribing for her a medicine in which there was arsenic, but Hall instanced drugs obtainable of any chemist containing up to one-twentieth of a grain. He went on to ask Spilsbury:

"The taking of what are known as medicinal doses for a long period of time would not necessarily develop symptoms of arsenical poisoning?"

"Yes, that is so," was the reply.

Finally, Marshall Hall put forward as "a scientific fact" a theory of which Spilsbury said he had never heard—that poison in a body at the time of burial, and particularly arsenic, tends to gravitate to the organs on the left side.

A few more questions, and a brief re-examination by Rufus Isaacs, ended Spilsbury's evidence. He had been in the witness-box a little over three hours.

Willcox went into the box, and remained there for the rest of that day. What was to become a duel with Marshall Hall of absorbing interest, not only to the medico-legal fraternity, but to every one in court, began quietly with the Attorney-General's examination. After commenting on the state of preservation of the body when exhumed Willcox went on to give the result of his analyses of certain organs, fluid, muscle, hair, and nails. In the liver and intestines he found ·63 of a grain of arsenic. Since arsenic spreads rapidly through the body, this indicated a much larger dose. By the Marsh–Berzelius test Willcox estimated that in the whole body, at the time of exhumation, there were 2·01 grains. Two grains can be a fatal dose. But arsenic is expelled from the system almost as rapidly as it spreads, and such a residue, Willcox said, implied that at least five grains had been administered to Miss Barrow shortly before her death. Rufus Isaacs' last question at this stage was:

"Now, taking the result of your various analyses, tests, and examinations, what do you say was the cause of Miss Barrow's death?"

"Acute arsenical poisoning."

Though Marshall Hall might have doubted his client's innocence, he threw into this case, as he always did, all his energy and forensic skill. His cross-examination was masterly: towards the end of the day he drove Willcox into admitting an oversight, and immediately afterwards, in Willcox's own words, again very nearly tied him up. The Marsh test, of which everybody has now heard, had never before this date been employed in a court of law for quantitative purposes, but only to establish the presence of arsenic. It had been thought impossible to weigh, in every part of the body, a substance so minutely distributed. Willcox, to arrive at his figure of 2·01 grains, used the test quantitatively. The experiment is carried out by extracting arsenic in the form of a gas, which is then deposited on a tube called a 'mirror.' To quote Willcox himself: "A series of standard mirrors prepared from known amounts of arsenic enable the test to be used quantitatively, since the arsenical mirror from a solution containing an unknown amount of arsenic may be matched against one of the standard mirrors." He admitted that as the specimens were microscopical, and the calculations involved extremely delicate, an initial error in the test might be multiplied hundreds or thousands of times. This was the point towards which Marshall Hall had been working. Processes of decay had reduced the weight of Miss Barrow's body from ten stone to four, the reduction being chiefly brought about by the evaporation of water. There is a great deal of water in the bones and muscles—50 per cent. and 77 per cent. respectively—and these accordingly lose weight far more rapidly after death than other parts of a corpse. Yet two months after Miss Barrow's burial Willcox estimated the muscles alone at two-fifths of the weight of the whole body.

"I am sure," said Marshall Hall at this point, "it was an oversight; I mean—I may be wrong—but in making this calculation you have made no allowance whatever for the loss of water?"

Willcox agreed that he had not. It was a good point; and, having driven it home, no doubt with some of his expressive glances at the jury, Marshall Hall at once went on to make what seemed an even more effective one. He asked Willcox if he was still convinced that this was a case of acute arsenical poisoning, and again Willcox replied that he had no doubt about it. Hall's next question was about the hair, in which arsenic had been found, even in the distal end, farthest away from the roots. A few years before a Royal Commission had inquired into the causes of arsenical poisoning due to beer-drinking; Marshall Hall now quoted the Commission's report, which stated that arsenic did not reach the proximal hair (nearest the scalp) until after some weeks, and that for it to reach the distal end would take months, and perhaps years. Hair grows at a rate of five or six inches a year; Miss Barrow's was twelve inches long; and it would appear that a simple calculation must show roughly when the arsenic found in it was first administered. Hall hammered away at this point, and got Willcox to admit that the poison discovered in the distal end, though only three-thousandths of a millimetre, might mean that it had been taken more than a year before.

Hall was still at it, speaking of metabolic changes in the hair and quoting Dixon Mann, when the true answer to the problem occurred to the analyst. The hair, while in the coffin, had become soaked in the bloodstained fluid from the body. Analysis of hair removed by the undertaker at the time of burial showed a much lower arsenic content. Marshall Hall professed to be scornful of such second thoughts, but Willcox took the first opportunity of proving their correctness. Hair from a patient at St Mary's was soaked in fluid from Miss Barrow's coffin. Analysed by Dr Webster, it was found to be impregnated with arsenic.

Three days later Willcox was recalled to give the result of this analysis. Before the main part of his testimony ended, early in the morning of the fifth day, he reiterated, to the Attorney-General and to the judge, his opinion as to the cause of Miss Barrow's death. It was in no way altered because of arsenic found in the hair.

"There cannot be the slightest doubt," were his words, "as to this being a case of acute arsenical poisoning."

Spilsbury must have listened with the keenest interest, and perhaps with profit, to these vital exchanges between Willcox and Marshall Hall. If ever he needed a lesson in the importance of taking nothing for granted he was given one now, as he watched a layman—though, indeed, a very brilliant one, and the son of a doctor—twice nearly trip up his friend and colleague.

Though, of course, the medical evidence was discussed at length in counsels' speeches, and by the judge in summing up, the second half of this long trial was dominated by the human element. After Marshall Hall had vainly submitted that there was no case against Seddon, and Mr Rentoul had made a similar fruitless plea on behalf of Mrs Seddon, Seddon himself left the dock for the witness-box. He was there for the greater part of three days—one of the longest of such ordeals ever faced by the accused in a murder trial. His wife followed him; but in spite of her very questionable actions, and her inadequate explanations of them, there was always an air of unreality about the proceedings against her. Two of her replies to the Attorney-General have the ring of truth, and no doubt influenced a jury already predisposed in her favour. Her husband, she said, speaking of business matters, never took any notice when she said anything to him; he always had other things to think of. And, again, of the £5 notes she had changed: "I never mentioned it to my husband; I didn't tell my husband everything I did. . . . He never told me everything he did."

Why the jury, and other persons concerned, should have been so predisposed does not appear from the evidence. This, on the contrary, Sir Travers Humphreys observes, "pointed to Mrs Seddon as the actual administrator." But he goes on to add that "no Jury would convict her if they could find a way out, and our evidence left out, necessarily, the comparison of the two individuals which could only be made by a Jury which had seen and heard them both." Juries must have been more squeamish then than in Edith Thompson's day. The comparison, at any rate, was made; Mrs Seddon was acquitted because she was regarded as "a weak and probably ill-treated creature"; and Seddon condemned himself out of his own mouth. No account of this remarkable case is complete which does not indicate how he did so.

5

There was no motive for me to commit such a crime, I would have to be a greedy inhuman monster, or be suffering from a degenerate or deranged mind, as I was in a good financial circumstances, 21 years in one employ, a good position, a good home with every comfort, a wife, 5

> children & aged Father (73) depending on me, my income just on £15 per week to pay the deceased the small annuity of £2.8.0. weekly and out of this my daughter received 7*s*. weekly and on death of the deceased I [had] to keep & clothe the boy which is equal to 13*s*. weekly. So I should only gain 28*s*. weekly by the death of the deceased. Surely an insufficient motive for one in my circumstances in life.

It was indeed. This ill-written document was composed at a time when slipshod construction was excusable, but it shows the ruling passion for pounds, shillings, and pence prevailing to the very end, and it poses, in the convicted murderer's own words, the real problem of the Seddon case. It is a case almost in a class by itself—one of those rare murders committed for unneeded gain. It is a mystery of the human mind. Frederick Seddon's was certainly degenerate, but it was very far from being deranged. "He was," said Marshall Hall, "the ablest man I ever defended on the capital charge." Seddon was, in fact, just what he denied being—greedy and inhuman. His extraordinary insensitiveness, which was so damaging to him in the witness-box, is revealed in another letter, written to his wife on the eve of his execution. "I am still cheerful," he says, and so he appears to have been. He could even make jokes, and he included what he called a chapter of incidents to prove that the number thirteen is unlucky. "Strange but true," he adds tritely. Cold, callous, and calculating to the last, this was the man who gave a pauper's burial to the woman whose murder brought him several thousand pounds, who took a commission of 12*s*. 6*d*. from the undertaker, and who carried cynical hypocrisy so far that he caused the following doggerel to be printed on the memorial cards:

> A dear one is missing and with us no more,
> That voice so much loved we hear not again,
> Yet we think of you now the same as of yore,
> And know you are free from trouble and pain.

"What a terrible charge—wilful murder!" he cried when he was arrested, adding, almost incredibly, "It is the first of our family that has ever been charged with such a crime." When he was under cross-examination by Rufus Isaacs, and was being questioned about his rebate from the undertaker, he replied, "If an agent for a Singer's sewing-machine buys one himself he gets a commission. . . . I was under commission if I introduced him business." Twice—the second time with apparent indignation—he denied counting the dead woman's hoard of sovereigns in the presence of two of his agents; and both times he marred the effect by adding, with the air of being clever, "I would have had all day to count the money."

Cleverness was his undoing. So strong in him was the conceit characteristic of murderers that he was positively anxious to pit his wits against those of Rufus Isaacs, an ordeal from which the most self-sufficient might have shrunk. He insisted on going into the witness-box, and there, for long hours, so far as verbal exchanges were concerned, he held his own with one of the most brilliant legal minds of the day. But the result, to quote Travers Humphreys once more, "was to turn what was always a strongish case into a conclusive one." Seddon was too clever and cool, and showed too plainly that braggart hardness and lack of decent feeling which dismayed his advisers.

Granting all this, the human problem remains. Murderers for gain, one and all, except Seddon, have been in need of the money to obtain which they killed. Some, like Crippen, have been influenced by subsidiary motives. Seddon was in no need, and had no motive but financial gain. Though avaricious and unpopular, by his diligence and honesty he had worked his way up to a good position. His income, from all sources, was nearly £400 a year, he was only forty, and he could look forward to further promotion and a comfortable old age. He had a wife and children for whom he seems to have felt as much affection as his love of money left over, and he was completely master in his own home. All this he threw away, and his life with it, because he could not withstand the temptation to add to his already adequate means. The lasting fascination of this case, to the lay public, lies in the puzzle of such a mind as his.

And not only to the lay public: the lawyers concerned felt the fascination, and among others Spilsbury must have felt it too. It is a specious and dishonest way of treating a biography to assume that the subject of it was interested in this or that when there is no direct evidence that he was; but he said after the trial that it was Seddon's conduct in court which prompted him to make a study of murderers and their vanity. He was convinced that the famous masonic signal to the judge, and the accused's final remarks, were of a piece with his constant turning towards the windows so that Press photographers could photograph him to the best advantage—symptoms of overweening conceit. It was Spilsbury's first encounter with a type with which he was to become only too familiar—the cunning killer who treats murder as a business. It must have strengthened his interest in the human element, for there are indications that he was among those who considered that Seddon convicted himself—or, at any rate, what comes to the same thing, that the Crown's case was weak. In his copy of *The Trial of the Seddons*, in the well-known series which he used to refresh his memory of past cases, he has marked two passages in Marshall Hall's opening speech for the defence. The first is where Hall said, "The whole of the evidence in this case is totally different from the evidence in any other case of which we have any record. It is entirely constructive evidence; it is entirely argumentative evidence." Farther on Spilsbury has pencilled heavily the following lines:

> If the Crown, with all their resources, with the whole of Scotland Yard and the detective force at their command, with unlimited money to spend, with the facility of making any inquiry they choose—if that is the best evidence of the purchase of fly-papers that there is against these people, it shows how very weak their case must be; because if that is the link in the chain—and no chain is stronger than its weakest link—how weak that link is. I should be sorry to have to rest, if I were prosecuting a person upon any indictment, upon a chain of which that link formed a small component.

Whatever was weak in the Crown's case, it was not the medical evidence. Seddon having been convicted, and his wife acquitted, he appealed against his sentence. In delivering the judgment of the Court of Criminal Appeal Mr Justice Darling swept aside in a few words Marshall Hall's first point for the appellant—that the pathologists were wrong, and that there was not sufficient evidence that Miss Barrow died of acute arsenical poisoning. "In the opinion of the Court," said Darling, "there was ample, and, in fact, conclusive, evidence that she did die from that cause." The appeal was dismissed, and Seddon was hanged, showing to the end his own virtue of stoicism and his preoccupation with money. He would talk only about the sale of his property. "That's finished it," he said, when he heard of the poor prices fetched at auction.

A last strange light was thrown upon the strange characters of this human, or inhuman, drama by the subsequent actions of Mrs Seddon. Within a few days of her husband's execution she married again. Then she sold to a newspaper a "confession" that she had seen Seddon poison Miss Barrow, and had kept silence because he threatened her with his revolver. Another journal soon induced her to repudiate this fiction.

Chapter 3: THE BRIDES IN THE BATHS

WITHIN less than five years of his marriage Spilsbury's work had so greatly increased, and was often prolonged to so late an hour, that a home in London became a necessity. The Harrow house, moreover, was too small: towards the end of 1912 his wife was expecting the birth of a second child, and he was feeling the need of more room himself. He wanted to have his own laboratory. During that year, accordingly, the family moved to a large, semi-detached house in St John's Wood—No. 31 Marlborough Hill, which runs parallel to Finchley Road between Lord's and Swiss Cottage. In a back room on the top floor Spilsbury began to equip the laboratory that was to become so well-known to all, whether doctors, lawyers, or policemen, concerned with medical jurisprudence. Here were held innumerable conferences, and from here, long after the rest of the household was asleep, he would go down to his study on the ground floor to write up his notes.

From this growing array of black notebooks Spilsbury had already begun to file a selection of cases the details of which he thought worth preserving. These case-cards eventually reached a total of six thousand. The great majority are of purely medical interest, but those which have an appeal for the general reader are not always concerned with crime.

The abnormal and bizarre cropped up, for instance, in October 1912, when Eric Hugh Trevanion, a well-to-do young man of twenty-eight, died of veronal poisoning at Hove. A friend who shared his flat applied for permission to have the body cremated. Trevanion's queer habits were no doubt known to the Sussex police; the request was refused, and the body was interred in the family vault at Norwood. Inquiries went on, and early that October Chief Inspector Ward was at the Home Office, applying for an exhumation. Two days later Spilsbury and Willcox were at the Norwood cemetery. Inside a double coffin and a leaden shell, hermetically sealed, the body lay covered with cotton-wool and a sprinkling of flowers. It was clothed in a silk nightgown, to the front of which was pinned a curious umbrella-shaped brooch of gun-metal. There were two bangles on the right wrist, and under that hand three women's handkerchiefs; there was an incision on the wrist over the radial artery. Spilsbury's post-mortem, and Willcox's analysis, confirmed the original diagnosis of death from an overdose of veronal—at least 150 grains, in Willcox's opinion, 50 grains being a fatal dose—but there was nothing to show how it had been administered. The family had an unfortunate history. A grandfather, a navvy, made a huge fortune in Australia during the gold rush, and his descendants inherited more money than sense. Spilsbury's card does not indicate his view of the case, but there is little doubt that the perverted young man committed suicide. Willcox's notes on the case add a serio-comic touch. At a second inquest in the new year, which failed to clear up the matter, the coroner criticized Trevanion's doctor for neglect. To some remark by Willcox, the doctor retorted, "I thank you. I was there, and you were not." Willcox's last note, written a week later, reads: "Dr X objectionable. Postcard. Sent same to Sir C. Mathews." Sir Charles Mathews was then Director of Public Prosecutions. What was on the postcard, and what action Sir Charles took, if any, is not recorded.

A month after the Trevanion exhumation Spilsbury was examining at the Marylebone mortuary a victim of what was then a novel cure for rheumatism, electrical treatment in a bath. A guide lamp broke, and the patient was all too thoroughly shocked. It was Spilsbury's first experience of death in a bath; three years later he was to investigate a whole series, including the most sensational trio of all. The year 1912 ended with a case of shooting in Holborn, where a man named Trix was found dead with two bullet-wounds in his chest and one in his back. All had been fired from a distance. The murderer was never found.

2

The Spilsburys' second child, Alan, was born in the third week of March 1913. The previous six weeks had been terribly worrying for both parents. Early in February Mrs Spilsbury had to undergo a sudden operation for appendicitis. A specialist from St Mary's hurried to Marlborough Hill; the operation was successful, Mrs Spilsbury making a complete recovery, but as a result of her illness the child was delicate from birth, and was to die relatively young. The fact that on the day of the operation her husband was performing a post-mortem in a case of death during a similar one cannot have conduced to his peace of mind. A ruptured muscle had, in fact, been mistaken for acute appendicitis, and the patient died under the anæsthetic of a diseased heart.

The year 1913 had opened in what was becoming a normal atmosphere of trouble. An event of immediate interest to Spilsbury, who had not changed his early views on State medical services, was the new Health Insurance Act. It had come into force the previous July, but title to medical benefits, and the accompanying business of stamp-licking, began with the new year. A large part of the medical profession had been hostile to the Act, but the resistance of general practitioners, to whom certain concessions were made, had weakened in the previous six months. Spilsbury, scarcely affected by the scheme, was opposed to it on principle as the first step towards more thorough State control; since it had come, however, the duty of the profession, as he saw it, was to make the new machinery work. March saw the end of his year of office as president of St Mary's Medical Society, and in his final presidential address he dealt with the question of medical education, which in his opinion would need reform to meet fresh demands.

On the day of his address to the hospital medical society one of his rare private cases had taken him and Willcox to Iver, in Buckinghamshire, where, a year before, Lieutenant-Colonel Charles Meeking had been buried at the age of seventy-two. It was an interesting case, arising out of the scarcely concealed suspicions of members of the Colonel's family that he had not died of natural causes.

The fact that a great deal of money was involved may conceivably have sharpened these suspicions. The Colonel had inherited more than a million pounds from his father, the founder of the drapery business which afterwards became Thomas Wallis and Co.; he had been High Sheriff of Buckinghamshire, and in addition to a mansion at Iver he had his London home in Belgrave Square. He had married a French lady considerably younger than himself. In view of his age there must have seemed to be strong reasons for granting the application to have his body exhumed. The form which rumours took, if not to whom they pointed, is indicated by Willcox's report that he made special tests for arsenic and other irritant poisons.

His finding, which Spilsbury's post-mortem confirmed, was that death was due to acute dilation of the heart, brought on by natural causes, probably intestinal colic. One of the executors, still unsatisfied, argued that Colonel Meeking had never suffered from heart trouble. Willcox replied that the condition would have developed only a few hours before death. The executor had later to deny statements attributed to him, and there was a further sequel in May, when the family solicitors, Lewis and Lewis, published in the *Daily Telegraph* a letter quoting in full the report signed by Willcox and Spilsbury, and pointing out that Mrs Meeking, the widow, had readily consented to the exhumation. All concerned in raising this unhappy and unnecessary scandal must have wished by then that they had let the Colonel lie.

It is pleasant to record that for the post-mortem, less difficult than many he performed for a few guineas in coroners' courts, Spilsbury's fee was £125—the highest he was ever paid.

He was still worried about the health of his wife and baby. It was his busiest time that year; he preserved more of his case-cards for April than for any other month, and two of them show him helping to prepare charges of murder.

3

Towards the end of 1913 there had been a fatal affray in Tottenham Court Road. A demented Armenian named Titus shot and killed the manageress of the Horseshoe Hotel and wounded a barmaid. He fired again as people in the street cut off his escape, and one of these, John Starchfield, who had a newspaper pitch close by, was shot in the abdomen. Titus went to Broadmoor; Starchfield was indemnified by a grant of £50 and a weekly allowance of £1 from the Carnegie Fund.

On January 9, 1914, Spilsbury was called to Shoreditch, where Starchfield's son Willie, aged five, had been found strangled under the seat of a railway carriage. In addition to marks of a ligature round the neck, the dead child's head was bruised. There was nothing to show how the body came to be in the train, which was on its way from Chalk Farm to Broad Street. The boy lived in the former neighbourhood with his mother, who was separated from her husband. The latter, however, bore an excellent reputation, and as he had become something of a hero since the affair in Tottenham Court Road, there was talk of raising a fund on his behalf. His admirers were considerably dashed when a coroner's jury brought in a verdict of wilful murder against him, and he was arrested on the coroner's warrant. The officer in charge of the case described the conduct of the inquest as loose and irregular, and his own task as a thankless one, for the evidence against Starchfield was very weak. At the trial which followed Mr Justice Atkin took an even stronger view. Calling the inquiry "an entire mockery and abuse," he stopped the case and directed the jury to return a verdict of "Not guilty." The mystery of Willie Starchfield's death was never cleared up. John Starchfield died two years afterwards from the effects of his bullet-wound.

There had recently been much criticism, both among professional bodies and in the Press, of that very ancient institution the coroner's court. In other notorious cases coroners had presumed upon the wide latitude allowed them, and few in country districts were both lawyers and medical men, as was by then customary in the London area. No one, except coroners themselves, knew more about the workings of this system than Spilsbury, and it can scarcely have been by chance that an article attributed to him appeared in the *St Mary's Hospital Gazette* while the Starchfield case was still in the public mind. The writer's arguments, which will be quoted in a later chapter, strongly defended the general usefulness of coroners' courts.

Spilsbury was also expressing his views in public at this time on a medical subject in which he was profoundly interested all his life. Invited to take the chair at a laboratory meeting of the Royal Society of Medicine, held at St Mary's, he spoke about tumours of the brain. He emphasized the urgent need of classifying tumours, and mentioned the effects of blows, direct or *contre-coup*, as original factors in cases of cerebral growths. Later in life he developed his theories about the results of blows on the head, and his general interest in the brain was to lead him to make a special study of it. After he began to do post-mortem work on executed criminals he sometimes took portions of the brain for microsopic examination.

His ruling passion was amusingly illustrated in the late summer of that year, memorable now as the last summer of a passing age. He went with Mrs Spilsbury and the children to Bude, where he boated and fished, and indulged in mild antiquarian researches with the aid of R. S. Hawker's *Footprints of Former Men in Far Cornwall.* On the fly-leaf, under the heading "Medico-legal Notes," are such references as these:

P.60 Retention of articles in the hands of shipwrecked men.
P.72 Floating of corpses of the drowned.
P.74 Tatooing of seamen.
P.84 Live burial.
P.79 Black John. ?Rachitic dwarf.

A section in the appendix to the book deals with the other end of the human scale, the famous Cornish giant of the Civil War period, Anthony Payne. Huge bones, believed to be Payne's, had been found in 1887 in a tomb in Stratton churchyard. A thigh-bone measured 2 feet 9 inches. "This," wrote Spilsbury in a marginal note, "would give as stature of the body to which the bones belonged approximately ten feet."

These diversions coincided with the visit of the Archduke Franz Ferdinand to Sarajevo; and within a month the country was at war.

4

That August Spilsbury was thirty-seven. His reputation was made; he stood, with Willcox, at the head of his profession, and he was nearing the unique position he was to hold for the last third of his life. He was finding his medico-legal work ever more absorbing and exacting, and besides cherishing ambitions natural in any man of outstanding ability, he had by now a well-justified sense of his value in his own sphere. It was characteristic, however, that he at once offered his services to the War Office, in any capacity. To do so would seem to him a matter of course. When the offer was declined, on the ground that he was more useful where he was, it is said that he was greatly annoyed, which would also be in character. He may have felt some slight envy of his friend Willcox, who contrived to overcome similar official objections. While Willcox was taking a prominent part in the reorganization of the Indian Medical Service in Mesopotamia, Spilsbury remained at home, doing three men's work.

Three cards in October 1915 record fatal casualties from the first Zeppelin raid on London. This marked a change in Spilsbury's mode of life; his family was now dispatched to Malvern, and the house in Marlborough Hill saw him only when he slept there and ate scratch meals in the intervals of working in his now well-equipped laboratory on the top floor on specimens brought from mortuaries or from the post-mortem room at St Mary's.

5

The work of a Home Office Pathologist may take him anywhere in England and Wales, though never officially to Scotland, which has its own judiciary and system of law, and where there are no coroners. Spilsbury's two professional visits to that country were made as witness for the defence. Accustomed as he was to setting off on a journey at a few hours' notice, the one journey was usually enough. Once, however, in a case unique even in his unexampled experience, and in its way unique in the history of capital crime in these islands, he covered enough ground for three. In just over a fortnight in February 1915 he went first to the Finchley mortuary, then took train for Blackpool, and finally travelled to Herne Bay, to conduct at each place a post-mortem on one of the victims of George Joseph Smith.

A month earlier Mr Charles Burnham, a fruit-grower living at Aston Clinton, in Buckinghamshire, had read a newspaper account of the drowning of a woman in her bath at Highgate. His thoughts went back to the similar death of his daughter at Blackpool almost exactly two years before. Alice Burnham had then recently married a man named Smith. Her father, on the only occasion when he met Smith, took a strong dislike to him, a dislike accentuated by his son-in-law's behaviour over a matter of money, and by an extremely vulgar reply (on a postcard) to an inquiry about his antecedents. Five weeks after the marriage a telegram from Smith announced that Alice had died at Blackpool. Her mother and brother at once left home for the north, to find on arrival that a coroner's jury had already brought in a verdict of accidental death. Almost at that moment Mr Burnham was receiving a letter from Smith stating that the inquest would not be held until the following week. Though these and other circumstances aroused deep misgivings, Mr Burnham took no further steps at the time.

Now, two years afterwards, he was reading the story of another death in a bath. It duplicated in several respects the case of his daughter. Suspicions were revived, and through his solicitor Mr Burnham conveyed them to the Aylesbury police.

Within a day or two a Mr Crossley, having also read an account of the drowning at Highgate, was writing to the Criminal Investigation Department at New Scotland Yard. When Alice Burnham died at Blackpool, Crossley had been living in the house.

One of the most widespread police investigations ever undertaken now began. Inquiries were to be made in over forty towns, and statements taken from more than 150 persons, 112 of whom appeared as witnesses at the subsequent trial. Before this patient spade-work was far advanced the police were turning their attention to a third and earlier case of drowning in a bath, again of a newly married woman, and this time at Herne Bay. Its circumstances were very similar to those now made familiar by the deaths at Blackpool and Highgate, the most important common factor being the 'husband.' For everything went to show that in all three cases he was one and the same man, though only to Alice Burnham and her family did he give his right name.

For nearly a month after the inquiries were begun Smith remained at liberty, but under constant watch, of which apparently he was quite unaware. The time came when it was necessary to have him available for identification. The evidence against him did not yet justify a charge of murder, and when he was arrested, on February 4, it was for causing a false entry to be made at his bigamous marriage to his third victim at Bath. That night he was identified by Mr Burnham and others. He was remanded at Bow Street, and after nearly two months' detention was further charged with the wilful murder of Beatrice Mundy, Alice Burnham, and Margaret Lofty.

On the day of Smith's arrest Spilsbury was at the Finchley Cemetery, supervising the exhumation of Miss Lofty's body. Six days afterwards he was at Blackpool, at the grave of Alice Burnham. A week later again, on the 18th of that month, his cousin Garfield Williams called late in the evening to see him at Marlborough Hill. The two men sat talking until one in the morning, when Spilsbury remarked that he would be leaving in a few hours for Herne Bay in connexion with what was already known as "The Brides in the Bath" case. He asked Williams to say nothing about this, as reporters were haunting Marlborough Hill. The reporters had other sources of information, for that morning's papers had the news that Spilsbury was on his way to attend the disinterment of Beatrice Mundy, the earliest of Smith's known victims.

During the next few weeks, while the murderer remained on remand on the minor charge, long hours in the laboratory at St Mary's, and perhaps in the smaller one in Spilsbury's home, went to build up the case which, by March 23, was so far completed that Smith could be charged with his three most abominable crimes.

6

It is difficult, in retrospect, to realize that only two years separate the murder of Belle Elmore in Camden Town, and only one year that of Miss Barrow in Islington, from the drowning of Beatrice Mundy at Herne Bay. The crimes of Crippen and Seddon have the charm, if it may be put that way, of a period piece; they belong to a vanished world; with George Joseph Smith, whose last victim perished during the upheaval of a tremendous war, we are definitely in modern times.

A more repellent criminal than Smith has never stood in the dock; and here lies the real interest and mystery of his career. How did this vulgar and all but illiterate ruffian contrive to induce a whole series of women, some of whom by nature and upbringing should have shrunk from him at sight, to give themselves to him body and soul, and often within a few days? It has been suggested that his own claim to military service, if true, might account for the clean and passable exterior of his later years. But this had by then become part of his stock-in-trade, and was perhaps merely the outcome of experience. He had found that it paid him, in every sense, to wear a top-hat and frock coat, even on the esplanade at Weston-super-Mare. And the cleanliness seems to have been superficial; Miss Pegler could recall his having only one bath in all their years of intermittent association. He had other uses for baths.

Like Dougal of the Moat Farm, he had some quality which instantly appealed to women of a certain type, and he had the gift of recognizing that type at sight. When all allowance has been made for feminine repressions and inhibitions it still seems probable that he possessed some hypnotic power. Spilsbury did not believe this, but both Marshall Hall and Montague Shearman, who were briefed for the defence at the trial, spoke of the extraordinary effect of his eyes. "He had a horrible way of looking at me," Shearman said; and Marshall Hall was convinced of Smith's hypnotic power, and argued seriously that he employed it to induce his victims to drown themselves, though scientific opinion is against such a theory.

The story of Smith's early life can be told briefly. He was born in 1872, at Bethnal Green or Bow, the son of an insurance agent. Precocious criminal tendencies sent him at the tender age of nine to what was called a reformatory, the sort of place where the birch and cane were freely used. To-day a children's court would deal differently with such a case, though whether the methods of 1881 helped to shape the future of young George Smith is highly questionable. Murderers of his type are surely born, not made. Further misdemeanours, culminating in one which earned him a six months' sentence, brought him to his nineteenth year, when, by his own account, he enlisted in the Northamptonshire Regiment. He is next heard of in 1896, serving another sentence of twelve months hard labour under the name of George Baker. He had already begun his most lucrative and congenial business—the exploitation of women for profit.

His technique, with artistic variations, was always the same, until he elaborated it too far. Having picked out, with his almost unerring skill, some simple and impressionable girl, usually (but by no means always) of the servant class, he would ascertain the amount of her savings and induce her to hand them over to him. Sometimes he had to go to the expense of a marriage licence. Then would come a walk in a public park, or at some place of entertainment or instruction, such as the White City or the National Gallery. Smith would make an excuse to leave his victim, hurry to her rooms to collect her belongings, and then vanish. It will never be known how many women he deluded and fleeced in this way: it is reasonable to suppose that those who were later traced by the police were in the minority, for almost entirely by these means he made a livelihood for some fifteen years.

From restlessness, or with the idea of concealing his traces, Smith was always on his travels. He turns up at Brighton, Southampton, Margate, Southend, Bournemouth, Bristol, and other places. His predilection for seaside resorts is significant; in such towns, instinct or experience taught him, he would most readily meet lonely women no longer young, but still craving for what they thought of as romance. It was during his first known stay in Bristol, where he opened a junk-shop, that Miss Edith Pegler went to him as housekeeper. Edith Pegler was the exception to Smith's rule of life; apparently she had nothing to offer him but her attractions and a remarkably faithful heart; nevertheless he went through the familiar form of marriage with her, giving his correct name, and for the next seven years she was to remain his constant and long-suffering friend. He was more often away from her than with her, sometimes leaving her without money. When he wrote to her it was from an accommodation address. But at least he did write to her, and return to her, and at these reunions he would give her clothing which he said he had bought second-hand, but which he had, in fact, acquired by methods already referred to. It would seem that even this inhuman man felt the need of a homely base and a welcome in the intervals of his travels and labours.

He had been on one of these journeys, a three weeks' absence, just before Christmas 1914. The period covered the death of Miss Lofty at Highgate. A day or two after Christmas Miss Pegler was about to have a bath, and Smith, who so seldom had one, made a curious remark which events soon to follow gave her cause to remember. "I should not have much to do with those things. Women have been known to die in baths through having fainting-fits or weak hearts." Within a month, when he was away again on one of his mysterious jaunts, Miss Pegler heard of his arrest.

It was two and a half years since he had first proved that one of "those things" could be very dangerous to women. He was then forty, and hitherto had dealt only in petty knavery. When and why did "this cheap *accapareur de femmes*," to quote Mr Eric Watson, develop his system to the pitch of murder? The answer to 'why,' no doubt, is Miss Mundy's money. She was far better off than the general run of his victims, and he could not touch her capital while she lived. And, once done, the thing became easy the second and third time. But that first step was an enormous and daunting one; and the fascinating if insoluble question to all who, like Bernard Spilsbury himself, strive to comprehend the working of the human mind is how such a man first envisaged it, and faced it, and accustomed his thoughts to it.

Smith met Beatrice Mundy at Clifton in the summer of 1910. The daughter of a bank manager, she was thirty-three. She had a small fortune of some £2500 in gilt-edged stock. Upon this young woman, presumably unused to making sudden friendships with men of greatly inferior social standing to her own, Smith's extraordinary powers wrought with their usual rapidity. Within a few days the couple were engaged; a few more, and at Weymouth, under the alias of Williams, Smith had added another to his growing list of marriages.

His flair had not failed him; but he was disgusted to learn, immediately after the marriage, that his Bessie's family had summed her up long before. Foolish and weak-minded, "she did not," said her uncle, "understand money matters at all." The family lawyer agreeing that she was incapable of managing her financial affairs, her interest under her father's will had been transferred in trust to that uncle and her brother. She received only the income of her £2500. As this exceeded the monthly allowance paid to her, a sum of about £130 had accumulated in the trustee's hands. "Mr Williams" at once took steps to obtain these arrears, and then absconded, leaving Miss Mundy "penniless and almost without clothing." That same day he wrote her an atrocious letter, accusing her of infecting him with disease.

He returned to Miss Pegler at Bristol, and it should have seemed to Bessie Mundy that she was well rid of him. She resumed the shiftless life she was accustomed to lead, drifting from boarding-house to boarding-house at seaside resorts, or staying with friends. In the meantime Smith and Miss Pegler were also on the move, opening more junk-shops at Southampton and elsewhere. From time to time Smith would go off on his own travels. Early in 1912 they were once more at Bristol.

Funds were running low, and Smith was talking of selling a house at Southend which he had purchased through a building society with £260 stolen from the woman whom he had abandoned among the Old Masters at the National Gallery. He was soon, however, to have the means to acquire other such properties. In March he told the faithful and gullible Miss Pegler that "he would go round the country for a little while," to do some dealing. He went to Weston-super-Mare, a suitable place for the sort of deals he had in mind. But he was not to be put to the trouble of seeking new dupes. By a most unhappy chance —for chance it seems to have been—Bessie Mundy had drifted to Weston. Going out one morning, she met the man she believed to be her husband, of whom she had heard nothing for eighteen months, "looking over the sea."

At this romantic coincidence sense and reason again deserted the foolish and ill-starred woman. All was instantly forgiven—even the abominable letter. A few days later the vulgarian who boasted of his "marked love of poetry and the fine arts" was writing to Bessie's brother and trustee, "I know not how I shall offend in dedicating my unpolished lines to you," and going on about Time, the great healer, and peace and goodwill keeping the past at bay. Miss Mundy sent her uncle a photograph of herself and "Mr Williams." He stands beside her, clean-shaven, in his top-hat and frock coat, carrying an umbrella and gloves—a conspicuous *ensemble* at the seaside. A casual reference to solicitors in his letter to her brother does not seem to have perturbed the family unduly. Bessie had been left to roam for a long time, and her capital was safely tied up. They did not know George Joseph Smith.

But this was not the Smith of eighteen months ago. Something had roused the tiger in him since he deserted Miss Mundy at Weymouth. For he clung to her now. Her allowance was no larger than it had been, and the trust fund was still a trust fund; yet for ten weeks the reunited pair, at his restless will, wandered from place to place, from the Bristol Channel to the mouth of the Thames, before they settled at Herne Bay. Why Herne Bay? One town, of course, was as good as another for Smith's normal routine. But that routine was now to be drastically varied, and in connexion with Herne Bay there was an ominous precedent. Devereux, who killed his wife and put her in a trunk, had lived there not long before.

Smith, at any rate, was finding that his Bessie's £8 a month did not go far. He was pressing for arrears owed to her, and for a balance due for the Southend house. And at Herne Bay, instead of going into rooms, as usual, he took a small house in the High Street, paying a month's rent in advance. He made a very poor impression on Miss Carrie Rapley, who acted as secretary to the owner of the property. With a little money which had come in, including £33 of Bessie Mundy's, furniture was bought. A brass plate was fixed on the front door describing Mr Williams as an "Art Dealer."

It was now the end of May. Perhaps Smith still hoped to find an alternative to murder. In the middle of June "Mr and Mrs Williams" called on a solicitor, bringing drafts of two wills and a copy of the voluntary settlement in respect of Miss Mundy's capital. "Mrs Williams" said, or was made to say, that she wanted the trust revoked, so that she and her husband could have the use of the money. The solicitor suggested getting counsel's opinion on this point. In *The*

Trial of George Joseph Smith, in the "Notable British Trials" series, Mr Eric Watson sums up the situation as follows:

> The trustees were very unlikely to consent to a revocation of the settlement in the circumstances; if the wife died intestate, her estate would go to the next of kin under the Statute of Distributions, and the husband would get nothing; but if she, with £2500, left a will in his favour, and he, without a shilling, executed a similar will in her favour, and she died? Counsel's opinion came back on July 2nd: it was Bessie Mundy's death warrant.

Smith, indeed, wasted no more time. On July 8 mutual wills were executed. On the 9th Smith acquired a bath, a cheap and simple affair without taps. He got the price reduced by half a crown, but he never paid it. The bath was returned a week later, the thrifty purchaser having no further use for it. Another twenty-four hours, and he was taking Bessie Mundy to a doctor, with a story about her having had a fit. She did not remember being ill, but both she and the doctor took her "husband's" word for it. On the 12th the doctor was summoned to the house in the High Street; he found the patient in bed, showing no particular symptoms of anything. As before, a sedative was prescribed. That night Miss Mundy wrote to her uncle, obediently describing her "fit," lauding her husband's goodness, and referring to "the best medical men in the town" who were constantly giving her treatment. The actions of all Smith's victims are beyond rational explanation; the single doctor who saw her, Dr French, was, in fact, the most recently qualified of the dozen then practising at Herne Bay.

The next day was Saturday. The superstitious may note that it was July 13; but chance did not enter into these carefully planned affairs. All Smith's three 'brides' died on a Friday night or a Saturday morning, for reasons that will appear. At 8 A.M. on that Saturday Dr French received a note: "Can you come at once? I am afraid my wife is dead." The doctor found "Mrs Williams" lying in the bath. She was on her back, her head under water, her right hand clutching a piece of soap. Artificial respiration was tried in vain.

On the death being reported to the coroner the latter arranged for the inquest to be held on the Monday afternoon. Smith, in the meantime, had sent telegrams to Bessie Mundy's uncle and brother, who lived respectively in Wiltshire and Dorset. The brother wrote two letters in reply to the news of his sister's death, one to the coroner, and in both demanded a post-mortem. The only result was that the coroner, a lawyer without medical knowledge, made "Mr Williams" sign a deposition. The inquest was soon over, the only witnesses being the bereaved husband and Dr French. The verdict of the jury was death by drowning caused by an epileptic seizure—in other words, by misadventure.

The burial of Bessie Mundy on the following day, the 16th, rounded off these summary proceedings. Only a week had gone by since the execution of the mutual wills. Smith, like Seddon, economized with a common grave. The date of the funeral was unknown to the Mundy family until it was too late for them to attend; neither uncle nor brother, however, seems to have thought of making the journey, even for the inquest. The swift sequence of events and the intervening week-end left them, it is true, little time. Smith's calculations had worked out to a nicety, and the success of this week-end procedure encouraged him to repeat it in the future.

Smith's system of murder, which the Crown was to call so many witnesses to prove, has now been illustrated, and the last two and a half years of his life can be briefly summarized. Two more murders are replicas of the first, with minor variations. In this connexion, however, one incident is notable, as seeming to show, not only that murder was now always in his mind, but how soon his thoughts were bent to the need of slight changes of method.

From Herne Bay, in July or August of that year, 1913, Smith went to Margate. Here Miss Pegler joined him. Soon on their travels again, they remained together for a whole year. It says much for Smith's callousness that the autumn of 1913 found them at Weston-super-Mare, with its memories of Bessie Mundy. Perhaps he thought it a propitious spot, and, in fact, "Mr and Mrs Smith" here got to know a young woman, a governess, upon whom he tried out one of those variations of his system which he had been pondering. Smith suggested to her that he should insure her life. Details of this curious affair, of which even Miss Pegler disapproved, are lacking; but provisional arrangements were made for a policy of £500, Smith paying the premium. The policy was cancelled, and the governess, fortunately, no doubt, for her, disappears from the scene. In this episode, however, the workings of Smith's thoughts are disclosed. He could not often hope to meet Bessie Mundys, with small fortunes; but there were other ways of making less wealthy victims profitable.

By October 1913 the tiger was becoming restless, or in need. Miss Pegler was left with her mother at Bristol while Smith went off once more alone. This time he tried Southsea, and there he met Alice Burnham, it is said at a chapel she attended. Miss Burnham was a robust girl of twenty-five, engaged in nursing, and possessed of a little money of her own. There was the usual prompt and brief engagement, the visit to Aston Clinton already referred to, and a marriage at Portsmouth on November 4. It was after this that Smith sent Mr Burnham a postcard:

> Sir—In answer to your applications regarding my parentage, etc. My mother was a Bus horse, my father a Cab-driver, my sister a rough-rider over the arctic regions—my brothers were all gallant sailors on a steam-roller. . . .

The writer had already applied for the repayment of a loan made by Miss Burnham to her father. The latter, thoroughly distrusting Smith, delayed sending a cheque, and more acrimonious letters and post-cards followed, some from the daughter, who in her infatuation turned against her parents. The loan was repaid at the end of November. A fortnight later an insurance of £500 on "Mrs Smith's" life was effected. The same week she made a will in her husband's favour. Apart from the insurance money, all she had to leave was about £140, and some jewellery.

The stage was now set once more, and Smith, his speedy methods improving with practice, made an end of things, and of poor Alice Burnham, in another four days. He had decided to break fresh ground in the North of England, and less than forty-eight hours after the completion of the will he was taking her to Blackpool for what, no doubt, she believed to be their honeymoon. He was gaining confidence too; instead of the seclusion of an empty house, he took rooms with a Mrs Crossley. Other lodgings had proved unsuitable because there was no bathroom. Mrs Crossley had one.

It was now December 10. The next, and penultimate step, common to all these crimes, was taken that same evening. "Mrs Smith" consulted a doctor about her headaches. As she was a nurse of some experience, unlikely to be persuaded that she had a non-existent ailment, the theory has been held that Smith gave her something to produce one. Perhaps hypnotic suggestion would explain the case. All his 'brides' believed so much that he told them, and lied freely at his behest.

The honeymoon lasted one more full day. On the afternoon of the 12th Mrs Crossley's daughter was asked to prepare a bath for eight o'clock. At that hour the new lodgers went upstairs together. The Crossley family, including Joseph Crossley, who a year later was to write to Scotland Yard, were together in the kitchen, beneath the bathroom. Presently a small patch of water appeared on the kitchen ceiling. Smith then came down, talked for a few minutes, and went upstairs again. He was heard calling out. Alice Burnham had died as Bessie Mundy died.

It was a Friday. Again a week-end was at hand. Again inquest and funeral followed with convenient haste—the former on the Saturday, the burial on Monday. Again Smith ordered a common grave—"what they put anyone in." "When they're dead they're dead," he said to Joseph Crossley. It nowhere appears that he was much given to drink, but that Saturday afternoon he got through a bottle of whisky. He also played the piano for some time; what he played on this occasion is not stated.

Back once more at Bristol at the end of the year, Smith announced that "he would have a run round again before Christmas with a young fellow he had met in Clifton." His companion in this "run round" was, in fact, Margaret Elizabeth Lofty. She was a woman of thirty-eight. Her father, a clergyman, had been dead for many years, and at Bristol, where she lived with a younger sister and a mother of eighty, she led the sort of existence which is proverbially to be commiserated: having little money and no real occupation, she acted from time to time as companion to elderly women in better circumstances than her own. An unhappy love affair had recently unsettled her, and no doubt Smith found her particularly easy game. She went to Bath, where on the 17th she was married to Mr John Lloyd, a land agent. "Mr and Mrs Lloyd" went straight from the registrar's office to the station, and so to London, and that night, from Bismarck Road, Highgate, Miss Lofty broke the news to her family of her marriage to "a thorough Christian man."

She had already insured her life for £700, and without more ado Smith's famous system, with its dreadful stereotyped sequence, was put in hand. Only the order of events was this third time slightly varied. The visit to the doctor came first, on that same evening of the 17th. The call on the lawyer followed the next day, and "Mrs Lloyd" made her will, bequeathing everything—£19 and expectations under the insurance policy—to her husband. Back at Bismarck Road, a bath was ordered for that night. Just after 7.30 the landlady, ironing in her kitchen, heard splashing in the bathroom upstairs, and a sound as of wet hands being drawn down the side of the bath, and then a sigh. A few minutes afterwards the harmonium in her sitting-room boomed out. "Mr Lloyd" was playing *Nearer, my God, to Thee.*

7

The case of "The Brides in the Baths" was the third big occasion in which Spilsbury was associated with his friend and one-time teacher at St Mary's, William Willcox. It marked the third big step forward in his own progress as a public figure. It was now he who seemed to play the leading part. He had conducted the exhumation of the three bodies, and the subsequent post-mortems; at the trial his evidence preceded that of Willcox, who did little more than corroborate it. The cross-examination of the latter takes up in print only a third of the space occupied by Marshall Hall's endeavours to shake Spilsbury's assured and monosyllabic replies. As between these two eminent men such comparisons have no significance; the point is made merely to show how and why, in popular estimation, Spilsbury now took his place on a level with his distinguished chief.

The two were to spend between them the equivalent of a whole day in the witness-box, because the course adopted by the prosecution involved a good deal of make-believe. Smith was originally charged with three murders; when he came to be tried, for reasons never openly stated, it was on one charge only, and that the most remote in point of time, and, therefore, it would seem, the least susceptible of proof—the three-years-old drowning of Bessie Mundy at Herne Bay. Though evidence as to the other connected deaths was adduced in order to prove system, they were no longer referred to as murders. For weeks, however, in spite of the war news, the Press had found space for columns about the "brides in the baths," and every man and woman in the country, including the jury, must have felt convinced that if Smith had murdered any one of the three he had murdered them all. The judge's attempt to define the distinctions involved was not, and perhaps could not be, easily comprehensible to the lay mind. He told the jury:

> "If you find an accident which benefits a person, and you find that the person has been sufficiently fortunate to have that accident happen to him a number of times, benefiting each time, you draw a very strong, frequently an irresistible, inference that the occurrence of so many accidents benefiting him is such a coincidence that it cannot have happened unless it is design. And it is for that purpose that the prosecution invite you to consider the circumstances of the deaths of Alice Burnham and Margaret Lofty."

Then, however, Mr Justice Scrutton went on to say that there was one purpose for which the jury must not consider such circumstances. He quoted Lord Herschell:

> "It is not competent for the prosecution to adduce evidence tending to show that the accused has been guilty of criminal acts, other than those covered by the indictment, for the purpose of leading up to the conclusion that the accused is a person likely from his criminal conduct or character to have committed the offence for which he is being tried."

But since the prosecution had been calling such evidence for several days, to tell the jury, as Mr Justice Scrutton proceeded to do, that they must not allow it to influence them was surely asking an impossibility.

Marshall Hall, whose task in defending Smith was his most forlorn hope, of course protested against this procedure. It was a matter of form; he must have known that his protest would be overruled. Once it was, and after a hundred witnesses had been examined about the events at Herne Bay, Blackpool, and Highgate, Spilsbury and Willcox were called to prove to the satisfaction of the jury what the latter must already have firmly grasped—that the three deaths showed similar symptoms, and that these symptoms were those of drowning. But to the end a pretence had to be kept up that only one murder, as such, was on the agenda. A reasonable possibility was gravely assumed that all three 'brides' might have died through mischance; and in respect of each case the distinguished medical witnesses were cross-examined at length as to the effect on a person in a bath of epilepsy, faintness, influenza, or shock.

This unreal atmosphere, and the consequent dragging on of the trial to the end of the eighth day, must have brought home to many present the triviality of these long proceedings when contrasted with other events of that year, which saw the battle of Neuve-Chapelle, the Dogger Bank action, and the sinking of the *Lusitania* and the *Cressys*. But the machinery of the law was not to be thrown out of gear or hastened by any world upheaval, though its workings, against so tremendous a background, could sometimes produce a curious mingling of the sublime and the ridiculous. On the day when the *Lusitania* sank with a loss of 1200 lives the Lord Chief Justice and two other judges were solemnly pronouncing that a winkle was a fish.

June that year was very hot, with shade temperatures in London of over 80°. Throughout the trial the packed court at the Old Bailey contained twice as many women as men, though in consequence of disgraceful scenes at Bow Street the police had instructions to keep women out if possible. It was not possible. According to a Press account, some hung their heads when the grosser portions of Smith's letter to Bessie Mundy were being read. The same reporter, however, said of the accused that he looked thoughtful and intelligent, giving an impression of power. Photographs do not bear out this view, and Smith's behaviour was the reverse of intelligent. His counsel dared not put him in the witness-box, but towards the end of the trial he kept breaking out into abuse of witnesses, as he had done during the police-court proceedings. Mrs Crossley was a lunatic; Inspector Neil a scoundrel, who should have been in the dock. When Montague Shearman, who was with Marshall Hall and Grattan Bushe for the defence, remonstrated with his client he was shouted down. "I don't care what you say," Smith cried, banging the dock with his fist. He repeatedly interrupted the judge's summing up with such outbursts as "You may as well hang me at once, the way you're going on," and "It's a disgrace to a Christian country, this is. I am not a murderer, though I may be a bit peculiar." Under increasing strain the craven nature revealed itself; terror of the death he had meted out to three foolish but trusting women broke Smith's nerve; and on being sentenced he all but collapsed.

Such was the man, with his narrow forehead, his harsh, bony features, his thin lips hidden by the straggling moustache he now wore, his dark, bright eyes whose stare repelled his own counsel, against whom Spilsbury was to give damning evidence, which began on the evening of the sixth day of the trial, June 28, and was carried on into the next afternoon.

Examined by Archibald Bodkin, Spilsbury began his testimony by describing the results of his post-mortems on the three bodies, starting with that of "Constance Annie Williams," otherwise Bessie Mundy, with whose murder the prisoner was charged. It was in an advanced stage of decomposition, but there was no ascertainable trace of disease. A condition of the skin known as goose-skin "occurs," said Spilsbury, "in some cases of sudden death, and perhaps more frequently in sudden death from drowning."

The remains of Alice Burnham, or "Alice Smith," were even more decomposed, though her death had occurred a year later. A slight thickening of the mitral valve, which allows the blood to pass in one direction only through the cavities of the heart, should not have affected her health in any way. Such a case of thickening, Spilsbury added, was almost an everyday occurrence in post-mortems. He could find nothing else wrong with her.

In the case of Miss Lofty, or "Mrs Lloyd," the last of the three to die, though her body was the first exhumed, the heart and other organs were healthy. There were in this instance slight bruises on the left arm, which in Spilsbury's opinion had been caused before death. The brain, the only one of the three in a condition to permit of thorough examination, showed signs of congestion, a symptom of death by suffocation.

Spilsbury next turned to the means of death, the three baths, particularly in connexion with the theory of an epileptic fit put forward by the defence in the case of Miss Mundy. Slight commotions, to use Bodkin's word, had already been caused by these baths being brought into court and placed at the end of the solicitors' table. A juryman, supported by Marshall Hall, wished some one to be placed in the Herne Bay bath; but experiments in public were limited to measurements taken by Hall with a foot-rule, and a later demonstration with the Blackpool bath by the doctor called in after Alice Burnham's death. Spilsbury had already covered this ground in his depositions upon which the case for the prosecution was based, and instead of following his evidence at this point it will be convenient to quote from these earlier statements. Many of his observations forestalled questions which were to be put to him in cross-examination.

"I have seen the three baths. If a woman of the stature of Miss Mundy were in the bath Ex. 140 [the Herne Bay bath] the first onset of an epileptic fit would stiffen and extend the body. In view of her height, 5 feet 7 inches, and the length of the bath, 5 feet, I do not think her head would be submerged during that stage of the fit. The head end of this bath is sloping, and if her feet were against the narrow end when the body was rigid, it would tend to thrust the head up out of the bath. The second stage of an epileptic fit involves contraction, and therefore movements of the legs and arms. In the ordinary form of epileptic seizure the legs and arms are drawn up and then extended again rapidly. I do not think such a woman would get her head submerged during the second stage of an epileptic seizure, because the trunk, especially the lower part, would be resting on the bottom of the bath, and the body would therefore not be likely to move as a whole down towards the foot end. After the seizure has passed the state of the body is that of relaxation. The body would probably be limp and unconscious. Bearing in mind the length of the body and the size of the bath, I do not think she would be likely to be immersed during the stage of relaxation, because the sloping part at the head and bottom of the bath would support the upper part of the trunk and head.

"Dr French has described the legs straight out from the hips and the feet up against the end of the bath, out of the water. I cannot give any explanation of how a woman—assuming she has had an epileptic seizure—could get into that position by herself. *If the feet at the narrow end were lifted out of the water that might allow the trunk and head to slide down the bath.*[1]

[1] The original is not italicized.

"The result of sudden immersion of a living person might be severe shock and even loss of consciousness from the rush of water passing up the nose during the act of immersion. Unconsciousness might supervene immediately or within a very few seconds after immersion; in some cases the period would be longer, perhaps up to a minute, when the person would be liable to move and struggle. If the submersion were complete the person would not make any sound. With the legs out of the water she would not be in a position to offer much resistance.

"I should expect to find the brain congested in a case of death by drowning suffocation. Supposing the immersion were unexpected owing to a sudden lifting of the legs and pressure upon the body, the loss of consciousness would probably be more rapid. That would be due in part to fright.

"In the case of a person taking a bath sitting in the ordinary position and having a faint, the body, becoming limp, would fall back against the sloping back of the bath. If water were then taken in through the mouth or nose *it would have a marked stimulating effect and would probably recover the person.*[1]

"There is no position in which a person could easily become submerged in fainting. A person standing or kneeling while taking a bath might fall forward on the face and then might easily be drowned. *Then the body would be lying face downwards in the water.*"[1]

This concise and comprehensive statement also covers, in essentials, what Spilsbury had to say of the other two baths during an examination and cross-examination which take up thirty-three pages of print. The passages italicized are of particular importance. Taking the last first, it was stated that all three women were found lying on their backs. (Smith's statement that Miss Lofty was lying on her side may be disregarded, if only because of the size of the bath.) The importance of the stimulating action of water taken through the mouth or nose by an unconscious or semi-conscious person needs no stressing. "It would have a very powerful smarting effect," said Spilsbury in evidence, and all who have undergone the experience will agree. These two points went far to demolish the theory, to call it that, of epileptic or fainting fits. But it was the first passage italicized, that dealing with the effect of suddenly lifting the feet of the person in a bath, which must have most impressed the jury. For they had been taken out of court to witness an experiment that ended in a startling and convincing manner. A nurse in bathing costume got into the bath. Inspector Neil grasped her feet and pulled her head under water. She immediately showed signs of distress, and, when hastily pulled out,

[1] No italics in original.

had to be revived by artificial respiration. It has been said that Spilsbury helped in this, but he always denied being present, and is believed to have discouraged the experiment.

The gist of his depositions is to be found in even briefer form in a document by Willcox. Spilsbury's own findings at the three post-mortems were discussed at a series of conferences, some of them attended by Archibald Bodkin. The opinion of the medical men is summed up in rough notes made by Willcox after a conference on May 8.

> *Q.* Was drowning accidental—*e.g.*, fit or syncope followed by asphyxia?
>
> *A.* From evidence we think "No."
>
> *Q.* Was death suicide?
>
> *A.* No evidence of suicidal tendencies in these cases, nor of mental disease.
>
> *Q.* Was death homicidal?

The answer to this was an explanation of how the deaths had probably been brought about:

> Right hand on head of woman. Left forearm of assailant beneath both knees. Left forearm of assailant raised suddenly while right hand is pressed on head of woman. Then the trunk of body slides down towards foot end of bath, the head being submerged in water.

No one can have known better than Marshall Hall, when he began his cross-examination, that the result of the trial was already a foregone conclusion. In Spilsbury's reply to the first routine question presence and calm assurance must have lent peculiar force to what was a mere statement of fact.

"I am a recognized authority upon health, and I am invariably called in by the Treasury for the purpose of all matters of this kind."

In the turning and returning of old ground that followed—the possibility of epilepsy or fainting, the amount of water in the baths, the displacement caused by a body—only two points are worth noting. Marshall Hall tried to get the witness to say that the clutching of a piece of soap lent support to the theory of epilepsy.

"It is not impossible," was as far as Spilsbury would go. "It is not very likely."

The other question concerned a case of drowning in a bath which had occurred earlier in that month of June. The victim was a man named Vicar; Spilsbury performed the post-mortem, and his card indicates that there were peculiar features in the case. It is headed: "? ? Drowning. Not sufficient evidence to show how drowning occurred." At the inquest an open verdict was returned, and Spilsbury informed Mr Eric Watson that it might be a case of accident or suicide. Marshall Hall raised the point because there were bruises on Vicar's body, as there were on Miss Lofty's.

Bodkin's closing speech for the Crown was brief, and Marshall Hall's for the defence little longer. He had called no witnesses, and there was really nothing he could say for his wretched client. Rhetoric was not enough; and after the summing up the jury was out for only twenty minutes. Before Mr Justice Scrutton sentenced the prisoner to death he observed that he would spare him the usual exhortation to repent. He felt that such an exhortation would be wasted on George Joseph Smith.

Chapter 4: 1916–18: THE VOISIN CASE AND OTHERS

OTHER cases during the war years took Spilsbury all over England, from Maidstone to the Midlands, to Cheshire, to Middlesbrough and Stockton-on-Tees, and south again to Wiltshire. The Middlesbrough death and the murder in Wiltshire were cases of shooting. The former is an instance of the uncertainty common to so many of these cases, a feature which will be considered in another part of this book. A woman was thought to have shot herself with her husband's revolver, and Spilsbury's case-card shows his interest in aspects beyond the purely medical. He writes of the wound: "Most unusual position and direction for self-inflicted." And of the evidence of another doctor and a gunsmith called in:

> If this [the weapon] discharged a foot away barely possible for self-infliction. How could there have been blackening of thumb? Was that and the bruise caused by blue colouring of muscles showing through skin? Had revolver been placed in hand after death? Why was it in her hand at all, as she survived for some time?

In the Wiltshire case Spilsbury was called in to assist the local police and the military. On a night in January 1918, soon after "Lights Out," a shot was heard in a camp of the Canadian Corps near Warminster. A Corporal Dunkin was found dead in his bed, the bed-clothes drawn up to his shoulders, his arms hanging down to the floor, on which lay a ·303 long Lee-Enfield rifle. His hands, which were perfectly clean, did not touch the weapon. The breech of this was open, and one cartridge had been ejected. Dunkin had been shot through the head, the bullet entering in front of the left ear and emerging behind the right one; it had then travelled through his bedding, his kitbag, and the wall of the hut, at an angle of 35 degrees downward from the horizontal, burying itself in the ground outside.

The police were unable to decide whether it was a case of suicide or murder. Spilsbury estimated the distance at which the rifle had been fired at five inches or more, and, having measured Dunkin's arms, which were exceptionally short for his height of 5 feet 7¼ inches, he showed that while the corporal was lying at full length in bed he could have reached the trigger only if the muzzle was close against his cheek. Suicide was therefore out of the question. A private named Asser was convicted of murdering Dunkin while the latter was alone in the hut and asleep.

Early in 1915 a unique case came from the battlefields of Flanders. The body of a young soldier of eighteen, killed in action in the first weeks of the War and hastily buried, was disinterred and conveyed to England for cremation. Called in to perform the necessary post-mortem, Spilsbury found the body fully clothed in uniform. The young man had died of a sabre-wound in the back which penetrated to a lung.

Doctors' innocent errors in diagnosis figure occasionally in the records of these years, and a few medical men of a different sort were reaping a furtive harvest from the conditions of the time. The medical department of the War Office noted that a certain area in London produced a high proportion of men rejected as unfit for military service. Some of them, it was suspected, had been drugged, and, the matter being passed to the Home Office, Spilsbury was called upon to investigate these cases. As a result a doctor was convicted of introducing into a malingerer's nose a swab soaked in a harmless drug which temporarily lowered the pulse-rate. In the same month, in a different connexion, there is an ominous reference to another doctor. It has been mentioned that Spilsbury's method of periodically going through his notebooks more than once led him to observe that a series of deaths due to abortion had similar features. The most significant common factor was the medical man in attendance. A card dated May 1917 is headed, "Dr Starkie's patient." It was not the first, or the last. The sands were running out for Dr Starkie, and it is interesting to conjecture whether, before it was too late, he began to reflect that a relentless eye and memory might be checking his misdeeds.

Spilsbury can scarcely be said to have had any domestic life during this period, except when he was able to pay flying visits to his family at Malvern, and for a few months in the latter half of 1917, when his wife and children came to Marlborough Hill. A second son, Peter Bernard, as healthy a child as Alan was delicate, had been born in May 1915. Work now encroached on Sundays, but when Spilsbury could make time he indulged in the exercise which he enjoyed most, next to walking, on the tennis-courts of the Hampstead Cricket Club. The pressure of work, indeed, and too many short nights, began to affect even his robust constitution: early in 1917 he became thoroughly run down, and after performing a post-mortem on a badly diseased body he suffered from an infection of his left arm. Twenty years later he was to contract a similar disease in the same way. He was now advised to rest, but though for a time he stayed away from mortuaries, nothing would tear him from his laboratory. It was from this 'rest,' in the early hours of a morning when, in fact, he had not been to bed, that he was called out in connexion with the curious Varenhorst case, the curtain-raiser, as it were, to a sequence of sensational crimes which, on the home front, diversified the last eighteen months of the War.

2

The attempted double murder by Gerrit Hendrick Varenhorst is of little interest from the medico-legal aspect. In a study of Spilsbury's career it is chiefly remarkable because he was called in at all, and so promptly that he accompanied and assisted the police in their investigation of the victims' house. It would seem that by this time the value of his services as a detective, as well as a pathologist, had come to be recognized.

The motive of the attempt to murder Mr and Mrs de Leerch is obscure. They lived at 63 Warren Street, off Tottenham Court Road, only a short distance away from the scene of the abominable crime committed later in the year by Louis Voisin and Berthe Roche. Of their two rooms on the ground floor they were using only the front one when early one morning in March 1917 Mrs de Leerch awoke, feeling ill and breathing with difficulty. She smelt gas, and heard a hissing sound coming from the empty back room. Another noise, as of some one moving furniture, roused her husband. When he went to the door leading to the front hall it was held against him. He hastily locked it, while his wife opened the window and screamed "Murder."

It was about 4 A.M. when Spilsbury, having just left his laboratory to go to bed, was summoned to Warren Street. A police car took him there so quickly that he was in time to give medical attention to Mr and Mrs de Leerch. With the police he then examined the two rooms, to find a singular state of affairs. The door from the unused back room into the passage had been forced. From a second door, communicating with the front room, a chest of drawers had been moved; a hole had then been pierced through the door at a point where it was concealed by a wardrobe on the other side. A gas-fire in the back room was disconnected, and a length of more than seven feet of ¾-inch rubber tube was fitted to the gas main, passed over a chair, and squeezed into the hole in the door. It was this forcing process, Spilsbury suggested, that caused the hissing noise heard by Mrs de Leerch.

When her cries brought a constable to the house gas was escaping, and both rooms reeked of it.

The originator of this ingenious but too complicated device had no doubt intended to return in an hour or so, when his victims were dead, to restore order. As it was, he had only just got away from the house in time, and he was soon run to earth, in a basement in the same street. He was another Dutchman, Gerrit Hendrick Varenhorst. In his possession were a key to the front door of No. 63, a piece of tubing of which the recently cut end fitted the length found in the back room, and chips of wood from the hole cut in the door. Tried and convicted, Varenhorst heard his sentence of penal servitude in the same silence he had maintained throughout.

Spilsbury must have found it a welcome change to be called in before it was too late; and this same March had seen him take part in the winding up of a far more extraordinary affair, also unravelled before harm was done—if, indeed, the unbalanced people who plotted to murder Mr Lloyd George and Mr Arthur Henderson would ever have had the nerve or wit to carry their schemes through.

For a good many months Military Intelligence and the police had been watching Mrs Wheeldon and her family. This consisted of an elder daughter, living with her mother at Derby, and a younger girl and her husband, a chemist named Mason in business at Southampton. These four, or, at any rate, Mason and his mother-in-law, were born malcontents; they were against everything, including war, and their associates were typical Adullamites—conscientious objectors, half-baked cranks, the disgruntled and disillusioned, and downright crooks. Like almost all political plotters in English history, they were thoroughly incompetent, and no judges whatever of character. They admitted to their counsels one of those mysterious 'agents' that Governments employ in times of emergency, a certain "Gordon," who had come upon traces of the conspiracy in its early stages. He was initiated into the usual hocus-pocus, including a code based on the refrain "We'll hang Lloyd George on a sour apple-tree." To this group the Prime Minister was the current source of all evil, and the formula "Lloyd George must die" was constantly on their lips.

Political assassination, by Englishmen, is almost unknown in this country. The shooting of Spencer Perceval by Bellingham was the act of a distraught mind, and the fanaticism which led Felton to stab Buckingham to death was born of personal grievances. It is probable that at first no one took the Wheeldon group very seriously; but Gordon's report caused Major Melville Lee, in charge of the anti-subversive branch of Military Intelligence, to send a second agent, Herbert Booth, to seek further information at Derby. Booth was an intelligent and resourceful man who had worked for criminal lawyers, and it was as easy for him as it had been for Gordon to ingratiate himself with the gullible conspirators. They thought so well of him, indeed, that he was soon promoted to the leading rôle. He was given an air-gun and pellets and darts dipped in curare, and, so armed, was instructed to lie in wait for the Prime Minister at Walton Heath, when Mr Lloyd George was playing golf, or at some other convenient spot.

This news, and the information that Mrs Wheeldon was expecting her son-in-law, the Southampton chemist, to send her a parcel of other poisons, decided the authorities to act. When the parcel arrived, and was found by Booth to contain, in Mrs Wheeldon's words, "all the incriminating evidence," she and her daughter were arrested. Mason and his wife were taken into custody the same day.

The contents of the parcel, the pellets, and the darts were handed to Spilsbury for examination. Mason had sent two tubes of strychnine, containing nearly nine grains—a quarter of a grain can be a fatal dose—bottles of vermin-killer, and other medical preparations in which strychnine was present, and another two tubes full of curare. A favourite with novelists, this poison had not before figured in a criminal case, but under its correct name of *wurali* it has been known to science for a hundred and fifty years. Spilsbury's case-card quotes, as an authority on its action, Waterton's *Wanderings in South America*, a book published in 1825. Mixed with water, curare becomes a sticky substance which will adhere to an arrow or other projectile. It can be swallowed without ill-effect, but can be fatal if introduced into a wound, when it paralyses first the motor nerve endings of the spinal muscles and then the respiratory system, causing asphyxia. There was enough of it in Mason's two tubes to kill several persons. In Spilsbury's lifetime a curare alkaloid was to be employed in anæsthesia, but its use, says his old opponent in the Merrett case, Professor Glaister, "is not without danger."

With regard to the strychnine, Spilsbury's card contains a note on various simple ways of administering this with evil intent—in pills, as by Palmer; in sweets, as by Neill Cream; in cocoa, chocolate, or sugar icing, or spread on bread and butter. In a few years' time, in the Armstrong case, he was to demonstrate how another poison, arsenic, could be dispensed by hospitable methods.

The trial of the Wheeldons and Masons was unique in its mingling of scientific evidence, medievalism, and fantastic stories and accusations by the accused. An arrow tipped with curare was handed about the court carefully wrapped in blotting-paper, though Spilsbury pointed out that hardly any poison was left on the barb. The defence put forward was a denial of any intent to injure the Prime Minister or anybody else; the design of the plotters was to rescue conscientious objectors from prison, and the quantity of poison—sufficient to kill the whole jury—was wanted merely to silence dogs alleged to be used as guards. The code was a means of communicating with an objector in hiding. Crown witnesses were attacked; Booth was a liar, and Gordon was not produced because he was Steenie Morrison, then serving a life sentence for the murder of Leon Beron. The Attorney-General, Sir Frederick Smith (later Lord Birkenhead), who led for the prosecution, disposed of these fantasies in his best style, and three of the accused were found guilty. Mrs Wheeldon's elder daughter, apparently an innocent go-between, was acquitted. Her mother was sentenced to ten years penal servitude, Mason to seven, and his wife to five.

Mr Lloyd George, who seems to have treated the conspiracy with the contempt it probably deserved, soon after procured Mrs Wheeldon's release. The other two were later allowed to leave prison before their sentences were completed.

3

Spilsbury was a prodigious collector, but only in the interests of science. He was really the creator of the pathological museum at St Mary's, to which he sent hundreds of specimens for teaching purposes. In this connexion he once performed a remarkable feat of memory. Press of work during the First World War left him no time for the catalogue he alone could compile, and in the meantime the collection of objects pickled in bottles continued to increase. When the War was over he went round the museum one day with a colleague and recounted the history of every specimen. Had his acquisitive instincts been less altruistic he could have formed a fascinating little collection of his own, a minor edition of Scotland Yard's "Black Museum." Of the macabre or curious relics of his 25,000 cases all he cherished, apparently by chance, were a few odds and ends, such as a leg-bone, with a bullet in it, in a tall glass jar, and a couple of small cardboard boxes, some of the contents of which are *outré* in the extreme. Not all are connected with crime, but this is notably represented by a smaller cardboard box, such as chemists use for tablets or powders, in which is a scrap of faded, rust-coloured material. The rust colour is dried blood, and the fragment was cut from a hearthrug that once lay in the shambles of a basement kitchen of a tenement house in Charlotte Street, W.1.

The postal address suggests Mayfair, but it includes the northern extension of Soho, with its foreign population. Nearly a mile east of Charlotte Street, across Tottenham Court Road, is Regent Square, in Bloomsbury; and it was here, in the early hours of Friday, November 2, 1917, that a roadman known as Jack the Sweeper noticed that a bundle done up in sacking had been dropped over the railings of the central garden, which it was his duty to keep in order. He was then on his way to breakfast; on his return he untied the bundle, to find inside, wrapped in a bloodstained sheet, the trunk and arms of a woman, sans head, legs, and hands. Jack the Sweeper ran as fast as his own trembling limbs would carry him to find a policeman.

The ensuing investigation, in its early stages, was directed by Divisional Detective Inspector Ashley, of Bow Street, with the police of "E" Division. Further search in the garden of Regent Square discovered the missing legs, in a paper parcel, but not the head or hands. The sacking in which the torso was wrapped was, in fact, a meat-sack, stencilled with the horribly appropriate trade-name "Argentina La Plata Cold Storage." On the bloodstained sheet was sewn in red cotton the laundry-mark "II H." With the remains were some pieces of coarse muslin, silk and lace underclothes, and a scrap of brown paper on which the words "Blodie Belgiam" were roughly scrawled.

Within twenty-four hours the laundry-mark led the police to 50 Munster Square, in the decaying neighbourhood east of Regent's Park. A Frenchwoman, Émilienne Gerard, whose husband, a chef, was then in the French Army, occupied two rooms in the house. She had been missing for three days. On the night of October 31 there was an air-raid, and Mme Gerard left the house soon after eleven to shelter in a Tube station. Her failure to return roused no particular curiosity; in such a district live and let live is a rule of conduct; Mme Gerard, who was only thirty-two, had a lover, and, besides, she was often away in France, it was believed on missions for the British Government. She seems, in fact, to have been permitted to cross the Channel from time to time, ostensibly to see her husband.

By this time, early on the Saturday, Scotland Yard had been called in, for "E" Division, always busy, was overworked and undermanned during those war years. When Chief Inspector Wensley took over the case the only evidence that the remains found in Regent Square were those of Mme Gerard was the laundry-mark. But examination of her rooms disclosed a number of small bloodstains in both kitchen and bedroom. On a table was an I.O.U. for £50 signed by Louis Voisin, said to be her lover, whose portrait hung over the mantelpiece. In the opinion of the police surgeon the mutilation of the nameless body had been performed by some one with a knowledge of anatomy, possibly a butcher; and Voisin was a butcher. When to these pointers were added the meat-sack and the pieces of muslin, of a coarse type used by butchers to wrap carcases, the desirability of questioning M. Voisin was obvious.

He lived in the basement of 101 Charlotte Street, less than half a mile from Munster Square, and twice that distance from Regent Square. Lines connecting the three points form an acute-angled triangle with its apex in Regent Square, and along the short base and one long side of this triangle Voisin had made two memorable journeys in the day and night following the air-raid of October 31. When Superintendent McCarthy and other officers arrived at No. 101 on the evening of this Saturday, November 3, the butcher was sitting in his kitchen with a woman named Berthe Roche. The state of the kitchen was enough to deepen suspicion. Except that neighbours had heard the voices of more than one woman in the basement on the night of the 31st, nothing had yet emerged to connect Berthe Roche with the crime, but she was taken to Bow Street with Voisin for interrogation. A number of other witnesses were waiting to be questioned, but McCarthy and Wensley decided that these latest arrivals should be interviewed first.

Both, like Mme Gerard, were French. Voisin, who spoke broken English, was a very powerful man—short and thick-set, with a heavy jaw, eyes sunken in his fleshy face, and dark upturned moustaches. Berthe Roche (who was also known as Martin) had little or no English, and Wensley, when he interrogated the pair, had the help of an officer who spoke French. Voisin's first story was that he knew nothing of any crime. He had been friendly with Mme Gerard for eighteen months; during part of the time she had been his housekeeper. He had last seen her on the afternoon of October 31, when she was with a girl named Marguerite. This pair were going to France together, by way of Southampton, and Mme Gerard had asked him to go to her rooms daily to feed her cat. This he had done, and that was all he knew about her movements.

Voisin and Roche were detained at Bow Street that night. It was quite certain that Mme Gerard had not gone to Southampton on the 31st; she had been at Munster Square when the air-raid began. A man named Evrart had met her in Charlotte Street earlier that evening, and dined with her at an Italian restaurant near Soho Square. She had said nothing about leaving London. Moreover, news was coming in of the state of things in Voisin's basement. On the Sunday morning Wensley resumed his interrogation of the couple with a test which was to be one of the grounds of the subsequent appeal. He asked Voisin if he had any objection to writing the words "Bloody Belgium." The butcher hesitated, and then agreed. In his illiterate hand he spelt the two words as they were spelt on the piece of brown paper found with the body—"Blodie Belgiam." Wensley made him do it again—five times in all. Each time there was the same mis-spelling, and the handwriting closely resembled that of the original. Wensley then charged Voisin and the woman with the murder of Émilienne Gerard. When the charge was translated to Berthe Roche she broke out into abuse of her companion. Voisin, who seldom lost his air of rather stupid impassiveness, merely muttered with a shrug that it was all most unfortunate.

This was an understatement, for during these hours incriminating evidence had been pouring in. The rent of Mme Gerard's rooms in Munster Square was paid by Voisin, who had a key to them; he had called there, as he had said, on November 2, to feed the cat, but while explaining to the landlord that Mme Gerard would be away for a week or two he had added that she was expecting a sack of potatoes, which she wished placed in the kitchen. It was not potatoes that would have been in the sack. Voisin's own kitchen was stained and splashed with blood, and caught in a bloodstained towel was an earring, identified as Mme Gerard's. Finally, among keys taken from him was that of a low, barrel-vaulted coal-cellar beneath the pavement of Charlotte Street; and here, in a cask, resting on sawdust and covered with powdered alum, were the missing head and hands.

Confronted with these discoveries, Voisin told a second story, of a familiar type. On an earlier visit to Munster Square, on November 1, he found Mme Gerard's door unlocked. Her kitchen was spattered with blood, and her head and hands, wrapped in a flannel jacket, were on the table. The rest of the body was missing. There was no one in the house, but instead of summoning the police Voisin fell into a panic, tried to clean up the blood, got some on his clothes, and fled back to Charlotte Street. He returned later, to fetch the head and hands. A trap had been laid for him, and his only thought was to escape from it. His third visit to Munster Square, next day, and his story of Mme Gerard's absence and the sack of potatoes were expedients to gain time while he got in touch with her husband.

Voisin had the chivalry to insist throughout that Mme Martin, as he called Berthe Roche, knew nothing of all this, and the lady herself added her own violent and abusive denials. But every circumstance told a different story. She and Voisin together had committed a crime as brutal in execution as their attempts to conceal it were horrible and clumsy. The police worked fast to get at the truth within forty-eight hours, but their task was simplified by the criminals' stupidity; and for those who look beyond the details of shocking barbarity the interest of the case lies in the questions, how, where, and by whom was Émilienne Gerard killed?

4

Spilsbury was called in early on that October week-end. He examined at the mortuary the remains found in Regent Square, and later the head and hands from the cellar in Charlotte Street, which fitted the mutilated torso. He was now to be associated once more with R. D. Muir (by then Sir Richard), and, hardened though the latter was to horrors, he was so affected by these shattered and dismembered fragments that he could not get the thought of them out of his mind for days. Spilsbury's notes of what he found form a dreadful record. Five case-cards are filled in, on both sides, very largely with the injuries inflicted, before and after death, on Mme Gerard. From these, and from visits to Charlotte Street and Munster Square, Spilsbury reconstructed a crime that in every sense was butchery. In this country only the significant case of Mrs Pearcey has really comparable features.

Émilienne Gerard had been struck by violent and repeated blows on the head and face—at least eight, Spilsbury stated, after enumerating twelve separate injuries. These blows had not killed her, though her head was a pulp; she survived them for half an hour or more. They were followed, as was proved by the condition of her heart, by an attempt at strangulation, for which purpose, and perhaps to muffle her cries, Spilsbury deduced the use of the towel to which her earring was found attached, for there were no marks of manual handling on the neck.

Spilsbury, even more positively than the police surgeon, pronounced that dismemberment of the body had been performed by a butcher, with a butcher's knife. It was at least a workmanlike job, with none of the mangling often found in such cases, and in strong contrast to the heedless ferocity of the first blows on Mme Gerard's head. The contrast is of importance in distributing the guilt between the two accused.

As soon as Spilsbury had inspected the dead woman's rooms in

Munster Square he was able to assert that this was not the scene of the crime. There were bloodstains on the oilcloth covering the kitchen table, where Voisin said he found the head and hands, on the wall above this, on the door and door-post near the handle. In the bedroom were more spots and smears—on the counterpane of the bed, on the wash-hand stand, the rim of the basin, and the neck of the water-jug. A bucket was two-thirds full of dirty water tinged a reddish colour. To the Benzidrine test all these specimens gave the reaction for blood, and further tests proved that blood to be human. But their amount and distribution, in Spilsbury's words, was not such as was to be expected if murder had been done there.

The basement of 101 Charlotte Street told another story to the pathologist. In the squalid back room, mingled with traces of animal blood, there was human blood everywhere. Chiefly it lay in lines and splashes on the floor and wall round a door leading into a back-yard, and on the door itself, and even on the ceiling above. There was a spot on the wall of the yard outside. There were more stains on the sink and draining-board, and on a gas-stove; but Spilsbury's conclusion was that the attack on Mme Gerard began near the back door, which was open at the time, and through which, perhaps, the poor terrified woman was trying to escape.

He tested a number of bloodstained articles collected by the police —a man's shirt and woollen jacket, a towel, and three pieces of cloth, all from the cellar; a butcher's overall from the back-yard; and from the kitchen two most sinister objects—a chopping-board and a butcher's knife. At the rear of the yard was a stable, used by Voisin for his horse and trap, and here, soaked through with blood, with hairs on it resembling Mme Gerard's, was the hearthrug of which Spilsbury kept a fragment in his cardboard box.

As in the recent Malcolm case, and in others going back to his impressive debut at the Crippen trial, he and Muir worked hand in hand. Muir went with him to the Charlotte Street basement and to Mme Gerard's rooms; and in consultation with Wensley and other police officers this formidable pair—the younger man then at the height of his vigour and good looks, Muir white-haired and a little ponderous, but at sixty as compelling and thorough as ever—pieced together, from fact and inference, the story of that night when Zeppelins were over London and two women met, it is believed for the first time, in Voisin's sordid kitchen. Inference had to play a large part in this reconstruction, for Voisin held to his own improbable version to the end, and Berthe Roche would say nothing.

It is the dramatic circumstances of this crime that single it out from a hundred cases intrinsically far more interesting. The raid in progress on that final night of October was all but the last on London; but no one was to know that. Most of the mixed population of Soho had fled to the Tubes. Whether or no Mme Gerard did likewise, it would seem that she soon decided to seek shelter with Voisin, in the basement she knew well. Not the least tragical inference in the dark story concerns the motive that sent her there. There, at any rate, she hurried, hugging the walls, through the empty streets and the noise and the flickering lights; and there, in the basement with her lover, she found Berthe Roche. She may have heard of Berthe Roche, if the pair had not met; Berthe certainly had heard of her, and knew of her relations with Voisin. Both women were Latins, excitable, and under great strain, and little imagination is needed to conjure a picture of the quarrel that must instantly have flared up. Of the two Mme Gerard had known Voisin much the longer, and from what emerges of his character it is likely enough, as Muir believed, that she had some hold over him, and threatened him with exposure if he did not order her supplanter out of the house. She little knew Berthe Roche. The latter's rapid decline into insanity suggests that she was always unbalanced. In her, at any rate, as in Mrs Pearcey, there was a tigress.

For in Spilsbury's opinion, with which Muir and Wensley agreed, it was the woman, not the man, who seized some weighty, blunt instrument like a poker, and struck the first frenzied blows. Shocking though the wounds were, the skull was not fractured, and Voisin, with his great strength, and accustomed as he was to pole-axing cattle, could have shattered it with one stroke. It was when the victim cried out that he gripped her from behind, smothering her screams with the towel, while his frenzied companion, to the accompaniment, now unheeded, of bomb explosions and gunfire, continued to rain down her savage blows.

The raiders passed and the guns ceased firing; voices were heard in the dark streets as the braver came home from their shelters; and in the reeking, blood-splashed kitchen, where Mme Gerard lay dying on the floor, the wretched couple came to their senses. The body must be disposed of, and for ease of transport cut in pieces—work, to a butcher, presenting none of the usual difficulties. The pieces were wrapped in the hearthrug. An attempt was made to clean up the blood; earlier than she was wont on a cold morning, Berthe Roche was in the yard, drawing water from a tap, and volunteering to a neighbour the information that Voisin had killed a calf, and bloodied his clothes. In the butcher's own story to the police, at the first interview, it was a bullock that he cut up at Surbiton. But many of the tell-tale stains were left, from laziness or mere stupidity; neither of the pair seems to have known that human and animal blood are distinguishable.

During that morning of November 1 they evolved the plan of conveying the remains to Mme Gerard's rooms, and in the afternoon Voisin was preparing the ground with his story of the sack of potatoes. It was then, presumably, that he smeared about the kitchen and bedroom at Munster Square the blood he had somehow brought with him, and took away a sheet from the bed. Scarcely was this done, however, when the folly of the scheme must have occurred to one or the other of the pair, and a simpler means of disposal was substituted. It was, of course, too late; Voisin had now drawn attention to himself. That night, however, he got out his horse and trap. With intent to mystify, the scrap of paper with the words "Blodie Belgiam" was included in the parcel made of the body, and this and the legs were put in the trap. Voisin drove off through the silent streets, across Tottenham Court Road and Gower Street, through the quiet Bloomsbury squares to one of the smallest of them, Regent Square, with its church and garden. He was so insensitive a man that his jolting burden may have wrung not so much as a shudder from him; but that drive ranks high, almost as high as Mrs Pearcey's demented travels with a perambulator across St John's Wood to Kilburn, among journeys of horror.

To postpone identification of the remains was an element in this new plan. Mme Gerard's battered head was still recognizable, and so, the murderers must have thought, were her hands, for pending removal elsewhere head and hands were hidden in the cask in the coal-cellar, where mice nibbled at the fingers. The pair still had before them the best part of a day of freedom, but they seem to have made no use of it. The blood in the kitchen in Charlotte Street was left to tell its story. Probably they thought that the hasty trail laid in Munster Square would deceive the police. It is not likely that it would have done so for long, and Spilsbury saw through it at once.

Six weeks after their arrest Voisin and Roche stood together in the dock at the Old Bailey, and when Spilsbury had given his evidence it must have been as clear to Mr Justice Darling as it was to every one else that the woman had struck the first blows, and that in apportioning the guilt there was nothing to choose between the two. The judge, however, felt compelled to direct the jury that Roche could not be convicted of wilful murder. She was remanded, to be charged at the next sessions as accessory after the fact. The trial of Voisin continued. Spilsbury explained how, in his opinion, the murder had been committed, and where. Everything had to be interpreted to the prisoner, and the judge delivered the inevitable sentence of death in French. An appeal was dismissed, and Voisin was hanged, outwardly insensitive to the end.

The day before his execution his accomplice again appeared in the dock, before Mr Justice Avory. Again proceedings were interpreted into French. On this occasion the prosecution relied upon Spilsbury to a far greater degree than in the case of Voisin. *Where* the latter murdered Mme Gerard was almost immaterial, since he possessed her head and hands; but in order to convict Berthe Roche it was necessary to prove that the crime was committed in Charlotte Street, where she admitted spending the night of October 31, and not in Munster Square or anywhere else, where she could not have been. Spilsbury repeated his evidence. The bloodstained door of Voisin's kitchen was produced in court. The judge then informed the jury that they would be taken to see the room.

"Dr Spilsbury," he went on, "will accompany you. He will point out the bloodstains, but he will not speak. You must not allow anyone to speak, as a single word might render this trial abortive."

In that dreadful basement, accordingly, Spilsbury demonstrated in dumb show how the killing had been done. The jury returned to the Old Bailey to find Berthe Roche guilty. She was sentenced to seven years penal servitude. Within a few months she went mad, and in two years she was dead.

Chapter 5: TRAGEDIES OF THE WAR

Among Spilsbury's cases of the war years three very tragic ones stand in a class by themselves, because all three (though one did not occur until after the War was ended) were attributable, or were attributed, to the conditions of the time.

The cases of Douglas Malcolm and David Greenwood illustrate a popular tendency to veer irrationally between sentiment and sentimentality. Malcolm was a young officer who had joined the colours at the outbreak of war. His character was exemplary, and he was married to a girl whom he loved passionately. While he was overseas his wife became infatuated with Anton Baumberg, a Russian, who called himself Count Anthony de Borch, and who was known to the police in connexion with the white-slave traffic. He was also thought to be a spy in German pay. Mrs Malcolm went to live with him, and was with him in a cottage in the country when her husband came home on leave in the spring of 1917. Malcolm thrashed Baumberg into unconsciousness, and later wrote twice to challenge the Russian to a duel. As he received no reply, he seems to have returned to the front somewhat reassured; but within a month his wife was writing to say that she would not give up her lover, and demanding a divorce.

From Malcolm's talk of duels it will appear that he had an antique sense of honour quite out of touch with the progressive spirit of the age. Having replied to his wife, promising Baumberg another thrashing, and adding, "I may shoot him if he has a gun," he applied for compassionate leave; and on August 16, the day after landing in England, he was calling at Baumberg's rooms in Porchester Place. He may have heard something of the Russian's disreputable activities, for he got in by calling himself an inspector from Scotland Yard. He carried a riding-whip, and a ·32 revolver.

There were sounds of a quarrel, and five shots were heard. Malcolm then walked out of the house and gave himself up to a policeman, saying, "I have shot a man. When I saw the cur you can understand what my feelings were, and what I did was on the impulse of the moment." Baumberg was found dead on his bed, smothered in blood.

When Malcolm was charged he said, "Very well, charge me with what you like. I did it for my honour."

Later that day Spilsbury was at Porchester Place. He took measurements of Baumberg's position on the bed, and traced the passage of five wounds through the Russian's head, neck, chest, and arm into the floor. Any one of the wounds, except that in the arm, would have been fatal. From the distribution of powder-grains round those in the forehead and neck Spilsbury calculated that these two shots had been fired at close range—between three and six inches. There was a chest-of-drawers in the room, one of the drawers being half open, and in this, in a holster, was an automatic pistol loaded in four chambers.

Spilsbury's findings, and the presence of the pistol in the open drawer, were consistent with the theory put forward by the defence at Malcolm's trial. The latter had not fired until after a struggle in which Baumberg reached for his own weapon. The trial itself was remarkable; not only was public sympathy entirely with the accused, but Sir Richard Muir consented to prosecute only after a personal appeal from the Director of Public Prosecutions, and when the jury had delivered their verdict he was one of the first to congratulate Malcolm as the latter left the dock. "I should be less than human," Muir said in his closing speech, "if I did not sympathize with all my manhood with the prisoner. I have had as hard a task as any advocate for the Crown ever had." He had told a friend that a verdict of murder was out of the question. Sir John Simon, for the defence, thought his case so strong that he would not agree even to a plea of manslaughter, which Muir himself suggested. Simon refused to allow Malcolm to tell his own story in the witness-box, and called no evidence; in his speech, which Muir said was the finest effort of its kind he had ever heard, he dealt with the facts of the case in a quiet tone of confidence, in strong contrast to the eloquent flights more often heard in such circumstances. With the prosecution and the defence thus in agreement, what amounted to a verdict of justifiable homicide was certain. There was a scene of noisy enthusiasm in court, and when Malcolm left it, a free man, he was mobbed by people trying to shake him by the hand.

It was a case in which popular feeling was clearly right; but this instinct seems to have passed the border of sentimentality when, a few months later, David Greenwood was charged with the murder of Nellie Trew. A girl of only sixteen, she was found dead on Eltham Common on the night of February 12, 1918. She had been violently assaulted, and then strangled. Spilsbury's card of this case is one of those which make very painful reading. A great deal of sympathy, nevertheless, was worked up for Greenwood, because he had enlisted in the first days of the War when very young, had been buried alive by a bursting shell at Ypres, and was soon after invalided out of the Army suffering from shell-shock. This was rather beside the point, because the defence was not that Greenwood's mind was affected, but that he had not committed the crime, and, for medical reasons, could not have committed it. At the Old Bailey Mr Slesser, cross-examining Spilsbury, tried to extract an admission that a man discharged from the Service on account of shell-shock, neurasthenia, and a bad heart would not have had the strength to overpower a healthy girl of sixteen. On this point Spilsbury refused to express an opinion either way. Greenwood was convicted, but it took the jury three hours to make up their minds, and they added to their verdict a recommendation to mercy. When he was asked if he had anything to say Greenwood affirmed his innocence, but begged the judge to disregard this recommendation. Somewhat illogically, he then appealed, though in vain; but on the eve of his execution he was reprieved. Agitation on his behalf continued, and some years later a petition for his release was organized. He was freed after he had served fifteen years of his sentence.

The third of these cases which had the War as a background, though Spilsbury's part in it was a small one, is by far the most absorbing.

In January 1919 two elderly maiden ladies named Halse, one of whom was a talented sculptress, were living at No. 15 Clarendon Road, Holland Park. No. 13, next door, was the home of Sir Malcolm and Lady Seton. Late on the evening of January 13 the Misses Halse were startled to hear what sounded like several shots beyond the party wall between their drawing-room and their neighbours' dining-room. They knew the Setons quite well, and one of them, with considerable courage, went out into the dark and called at No. 13 to inquire if any help was needed. The front door was opened by a tall, swarthy man, a stranger to Miss Halse, who said he would ask Lady Seton. He returned with her thanks, and the message that she did not wish to see anyone. The caller went home, rather puzzled and ill at ease. If, as is very likely, she and her sister looked out of their front window they must soon have seen a succession of visitors arriving next door, including the police and the celebrated Dr Bernard Spilsbury. To the end of her days, at any rate, Miss Emmeline Halse could tell how that front door had been opened to her by a murderer.

The story behind the events of that evening went back over a dozen years, to the time when Sir Malcolm Seton's cousin, Miles Seton, was coached for a medical examination at Edinburgh by a young doctor named Norman Cecil Rutherford. The two became friends. Seton went to Australia, was commissioned in 1914 in the Australian Army Medical Corps, accompanied the Anzac Corps to the Mediterranean, and was later posted, with the rank of major, to the Australian Headquarters in London. Rutherford a lecturer at the London Hospital at the outbreak of war, had in the meantime become a lieutenant-colonel in the R.A.M.C., and a D.S.O. He was married, and had six children. The old friendship with Seton was renewed; the latter, the older of the pair, but a single man, was a constant visitor at the Rutherfords' homes at Mill Hill and Carshalton, and was godfather to their youngest child.

Those homes were not happy ones. There was a history of insanity in Rutherford's family, and he was given to violent fits of jealousy and vindictive rage. At such times he treated his wife abominably. At others he could be charming; and Seton must have found something likable in him, while at the same time feeling the greatest sympathy for Mrs Rutherford, who turned to him for advice. As the War neared its end her husband's abnormality became more noticeable and less bearable; like David Greenwood, he had been buried by a shell-burst, and his attacks of fury were dreaded by all who served with him. At home matters were not improved by the introduction of a young woman, his cousin, as companion help. He was seen going to her room one night. The facts of this episode were to be hotly disputed; but it is not surprising that the time came when Mrs Rutherford felt that she could put up with this sort of life no longer. No doubt she discussed the situation with Miles Seton, who seems to have acted throughout as a sincere friend of both parties. In the end she wrote to her husband, then in France, to tell him she would have to leave him, and to beg for a divorce.

Soon after this, in January 1919, Rutherford came home on leave. After a violent scene with his wife he locked her in her bedroom, raved at her through the door, and told a maid to pack his bag. The maid saw a revolver in his room. It was about nine o'clock on that night of the 13th when he left Carshalton; an hour later he was at Sir Malcolm Seton's house in Clarendon Road, asking for Miles Seton, who, as he had somehow learnt, was spending the evening there. The three Setons were upstairs, the two men in Sir Malcolm's smoking-room. Rutherford was shown into the dining-room, and his friend came down to him. Within a few minutes a regular fusillade was heard. To Lady Seton it sounded like some one rapping on the bannisters, but she came downstairs, followed by her husband. Miles Seton, in uniform, blood pouring from six wounds, was lying on the threshold of the dining-room, from which he had tried in vain to escape. Rutherford was by the window, a Webley revolver in his hand.

Under the stunning shock of the tragedy every one behaved in a strangely matter-of-fact and even well-bred manner. Rutherford, who appeared dazed, admitted shooting Seton, adding that he wished he had another bullet for himself. He agreed to stay in the house while Sir Malcolm went for a doctor, and as the latter hurried away was helping Lady Seton raise the body from the floor. A doctor could do nothing; Miles Seton was already dead. Lady Seton, in great distress, seated herself, supporting her cousin's head and shoulders against her knee. Hearing a click, and seeing Rutherford handling the revolver, she ordered him to put it down at once, and promise not to touch it again. Then, though he promised, she courageously told him to bring it to her. As he did so he begged her to do him a favour, and handed her a letter which he wished her to burn. She replied that he could go to the smoking-room and burn it himself; and it was as he returned from this errand that Miss Halse rang the front-door bell. The servants had gone to bed after Rutherford's arrival, and Lady Seton asked him to go to the door, and when he came back with Miss Halse's inquiry sent him again with her answer. This remarkable interlude, the more dramatic for its restraint, was ended by a second ring. The doctor had come; Sir Malcolm had gone on to find a policeman.

When in turn the latter arrived he seems to have been affected by the general atmosphere of good manners, for he allowed the confessed murderer to fetch his cap and gloves before taking him to the police-station. Rutherford maintained his unnatural calm, and after writing a note to his wife he crumpled it up, saying it would alarm her too much, and wrote again more briefly: "I am sorry; an awful thing has happened. Seton is dead."

What had really happened was now being reconstructed by Spilsbury. Rutherford and Seton had been together in the dining-room for about fifteen minutes. Spilsbury's opinion was that when the first shots were fired the two were facing each other across the dining-table, at the end farthest from the door. Seton backed towards this as Rutherford drew his revolver. The first two shots entered the major's chest; as he staggered back until his hand reached the door-knob two more bullets hit him in the chest, and while he slid to the floor Rutherford shot him twice more in the stomach and the arm, emptying his weapon. Rutherford had to step over the body as he went to meet Lady Seton.

The murderer gave the impression at the time of a man just roused from stupor, and not fully awake. The police surgeon thought that he did not realize what he had done. He was soon his old self, however, violent and difficult, insisting that his act was justified and that his lawyers should invoke what is called the Unwritten Law. Mr Rigby Swift and Travers Humphreys, who were briefed for the defence, and who soon discovered that their all-but-impossible client was insane, threatened to throw up their briefs if they were not allowed to conduct the case in their own way. They managed at length to convince Rutherford that if a plea of justification failed he would certainly be hanged. Insanity was not overtly suggested at the police-court proceedings; but by the time the trial came on a mass of evidence as to Rutherford's mental state had been collected. The jury was absent only a few minutes before returning a verdict of guilty but insane, and the accused was sent to the Criminal Lunatic Asylum at Broadmoor. Some years later he was released.

Another aspect of the case dragged on through the civil courts for three years. Mrs Rutherford petitioned for divorce, and the question of whether her husband had committed adultery with his cousin, the companion help, was argued in the lower court, which granted a decree nisi, before the Court of Appeal, which annulled the decree, and, finally, in 1922, before the House of Lords. The decision of Lord Birkenhead, the retiring Lord Chancellor, and his colleagues was that the decree nisi must be rescinded, and that a decree of judicial separation should take its place; but the president seized the opportunity to comment severely on the then archaic state of the divorce laws.

Chapter 6: THE EARLY NINETEEN-TWENTIES

IF the War made little difference to the nature of a busy pathologist's routine the peace made little difference either. On the morning of November 11, 1918, when the last shots were fired, Spilsbury was conducting a post-mortem on the body of a man who had died suddenly from heart failure following acute bronchopneumonia. The next morning, with the disillusioning 1920's already in sight, routine absorbed him once more.

In that era of melancholy 'blues' and general reaction and disappointment, people went on dying from the usual causes—old age, disease, accident. Suicides among the young were perhaps rather more frequent than before, lysol, of all things, becoming a popular means. A cause of a high proportion of tragedies was the unwanted child, and the abortionist was doing a brisk trade. At an inquest at Paddington in the spring of 1919 the sinister name of Dr Starkie is once more mentioned; and a year later Spilsbury was largely instrumental in bringing to book the abominable Nurse Hopton, of Gloucester, his cards instancing ten cases, two of them fatal, in which she was concerned within a period of a few months.

The termination of a Second World War has seen the repetition of a feature which marked the early 1920's—a series of murders carried out with great brutality. In the first four years after the Armistice Spilsbury was concerned in a number of such cases. In February 1919, while the Peace Conference was getting to work in Paris, he was again associated with Chief Inspector (soon to be Superintendent) Wensley in the case of Mrs Ridgley, of Hitchin, in Hertfordshire. Mrs Ridgley, who was fifty-four, kept a small general shop, and she was last seen alive when she closed this on the evening of Saturday, January 25. Soon after midnight she was heard moaning, but whoever heard her seems to have done nothing about it. The sequel was even more censurable. The poor woman was found dead on the Monday morning, and a diagram on Spilsbury's card shows lacerated wounds on the back of her head and on her face, and bruises on her back and arms. A 4-lb weight, bloodstained, was near her body, and her dog had been killed by a blow on the head. Yet, to quote Wensley, "the theory—unaccountable to me—had originally been formed that the woman had died as the result of an accidental fall." A man named John Healey was subsequently charged with the crime, but his trial at Hertford ended in an acquittal.

January was an ill-starred month at this time. A year afterwards Spilsbury was at Hastings, where Florence Nightingale Shore, an elderly nurse, lay dying from head injuries inflicted in a train from London. She was never able to make a coherent statement. A man was detained, but evidence of identification proved insufficient to justify a charge of murder.

Another twelve months, and in January 1921 Spilsbury was again in Hertfordshire on a case very similar to that of Mrs Ridgley. Mrs Seabrook, an infirm old-age pensioner of seventy-one, lived with two daughters at Redbourn, near St Albans. There had been a theft at her cottage, and when her daughters went out on the afternoon of the 27th they locked the front door. In the early dusk their mother was heard screaming. A neighbour found the cottage full of smoke, and Mrs Seabrook, though she was able to get to the window, so dreadfully injured that she died that evening. Once more there was bungling; before the local police took charge "the entire cottage," to quote a Press report, "was cleaned by kindly disposed neighbours—even a bent, blood-stained poker was washed." The inquest had been opened, and a doctor had described eleven wounds on the poor woman's head, before Spilsbury had an opportunity to examine the body, when he enumerated not eleven, but twenty-eight wounds, inflicted with great violence, some by a rod-like surface, others by a broader striking surface—"*e.g.*, knob of poker or head of hammer." Again the crime remained unpunished; no one was ever charged. It would be interesting to have heard Spilsbury's comments, and those of Inspector Crutchett of Scotland Yard—within a year they were to be together once more at Hay, in Brecknockshire—on the kindly disposed neighbours and the local handling of the case in general. The poker, and poor Mrs Seabrook's skull, were to be used by Spilsbury in a demonstration to the Medico-Legal Society.

A fourth January murder, at Paddington in 1922, was a replica in its sickening details of these previous New Year atrocities. Here, however, Scotland Yard was on its own ground, and able to act promptly; and within five weeks the murderer of Elizabeth Cooper was convicted.

A fifth homicide, that same January, was, for its singular features, of greater interest. After dark on the 14th Margaret Evans, aged twenty-eight, was pushed into the river Lea at Hackney. Unfortunately for E. H. Tunbridge, her companion at the time, there was a witness of the shadowy scuffle on the towing-path, and, what was worse, that witness was a police sergeant. The weakness of Tunbridge's first story, that he had not been with anyone, was soon made apparent to him, and he amended it when the body was dragged from the water. Margaret Evans, he said, had taken poison before jumping from the path. There was an element of truth in this version; analysis by Webster found the equivalent of 2.01 grains of prussic acid in certain of the dead woman's organs, equal to 4.84 grains of potassium cyanide, five grains of which can be fatal. But Tunbridge himself had been seen to throw a small object into the river, and a phial was dredged up which retained traces of KCN. Spilsbury's evidence at the trial was condensed on his case-card: "Impossible to say whether she was dead from KCN poisoning when thrown into water or whether she died from shock of immersion. Probably from poison." Tunbridge was found guilty.

In the intervals of this sequence of January crimes Spilsbury's daily round was varied by the unexplained mysteries of Fleetwood Willats and John Westcott; by the prosecution of two men named Warren and Morgan for the murder of Lucy Nightingale, who was tied up and gagged before she was strangled; by the case of George Grimshaw, another killing marked by great brutality; and by the murder of Henry Blackmore by Thomas Harold Thorn. Some of these cases present points of interest, and the first-mentioned remains not only unexplained, but almost inexplicable.

Fleetwood Willats was a man of seventy-two, a widower, who lived at Tottenham. On June 13, 1919, he had taken his usual glass of beer at the public house he frequented. On his way home he was stopped by two men who got into talk with him and offered him whisky. After drinking about two tablespoons of something that tasted like sweet wine and burnt his mouth Mr Willats sensibly refused more. But it was too late. Next day he was ill, and he died that evening in hospital. The cause of death was shown by Webster to be poisoning by hydrochloric acid. Willats was never able to describe the two strangers, and the object of this apparently motiveless act of devilry can only be conjectured.

Spilsbury's card dealing with John Westcott, thirty-five, is headed "Peeping Tom Case." Westcott's body was discovered in a Great Northern Railway tunnel near King's Cross, between the rails and the tunnel wall. On this were the marks of hands, the dying man having dragged himself along for some yards. His skull was fractured, and there were numerous other injuries, including a dislocated wrist. It was presumed that Westcott had got out on to the running-board of a carriage to look into another compartment, and had been knocked from his hold by the tunnel wall. The case was not so unusual as might be supposed.

In the case of Thomas Harold Thorn the moral is found in the sequel. In the spring of 1921, when Thorn was twenty-five, he was tried at the Central Criminal Court for the murder of Henry Blackmore, aged sixty-one, at Hampstead. Spilsbury filled three cards with the too familiar details of savage wounds on the head, twenty in all, some of them sketched. Thorn was found insane, and sent to Broadmoor. There he spent sixteen years, to be discharged in 1937 as a rational member of society. He set up as a tobacconist at Chester, and here, in the following year, he was in the dock once more at the Assizes, charged with wounding Alice Hannah Johnson with intent to murder her. In passing sentence of fifteen years penal servitude Mr Justice Singleton made the sound observation that there might be something in Thorn's mental condition that required attention. Alice Johnson must have wished that this supervision had not been allowed to lapse.

During these four years, 1919–22, Spilsbury handled some twenty other cases of murder. Of the whole series of over thirty it is probable that only four survive in popular memory—the first of the two murders on the Crumbles, the Armstrong case, the assassination of Sir Henry Wilson, and the trial of Frederick Bywaters and Edith Thompson. Spilsbury's connexion with the death of Irene Munro in August 1920 was limited to a visit to the Eastbourne mortuary, and the case may suitably be dealt with as a prologue to his second journey to the Crumbles in 1924, when the Officer's House was the scene of one of his most celebrated *tours de force*. The other three cases occurred in 1922, and with the exhumation at Hay, on the second day of the year, begins the most notable period in his public career.

2

Although Spilsbury was in every sense a born detective, taking pleasure in applying his powers of observation and deduction to a wider field than the pathological—a purpose for which they were often in demand—he was no reader of detective stories. It is believed, on the other hand, that at least one well-known character in this *genre* is in some part based on him. Apart from comparison of dates, inquiries show that this character is not Dr Thorndyke, as would seem in many ways fitting. The latter's creator, however, if he ever came across reports of the Cassendee case, must have read them with particular interest, for here is one of those rare problems of survivorship which always fascinated Thorndyke himself.

The case also comes as a welcome variation in the long tale of homicide which must form the backbone of any account of Spilsbury's public life. For once he was giving evidence not in a criminal court, but in the Chancery Division. The question at issue was which of two victims of an accident died first, and which of their wills was in consequence invalid.

On the night of October 3/4, 1920, Arthur Carroll Bazeley Cassendee and his wife, Beatrice, a couple in the fifties, were on board their yacht, moored in the outer harbour at Torquay. They were spending the night on board. A storm blew up, however, and became so violent that they must have decided to come ashore. At 6.30 on the morning of the 4th their bodies were discovered floating near some landing-steps 150 yards from the yacht. Close by was the upturned dinghy.

The time of the accident could be arrived at with some certainty, for Cassendee's watch had stopped at 3.40 A.M., and must have done so within half an hour of the immersion. It was calculated that it had been wound up approximately four hours before. Both victims were fully clothed, the man wearing a mackintosh, which helped to keep his body afloat; that of his wife was supported by a lifebelt, through which she had thrust her arm. Cassendee's body was limp, but Mrs Cassendee's was stiff throughout when brought ashore.

In the deliberate processes of law more than eighteen months went by before Spilsbury was called in to pronounce which of the two Cassendees survived the other. That he was expected to be able to do so, at that late date and on hearsay evidence, was a tribute to his reputation. In giving his opinion he began by presuming that when the dinghy capsized the pair were thrown into the water together. On the ascertained facts he held that the husband had died of drowning, this being, perhaps, accelerated by slight head injuries, for Cassendee was a strong swimmer. His lungs and stomach were full of froth and water. In the case of the wife there were none of the appearances of death from drowning. Her death was caused instantly by the shock of immersion, which would produce the immediate rigor that kept her arm through the lifebelt. "If they were thrown into the water at the same time," Spilsbury's notes conclude, "Mr Cassendee survived his wife by a few minutes at least."

Less than six weeks after Spilsbury delivered this opinion the detective-story motif was again in evidence in a sequel to a summons to Eaton Place, where Field-Marshal Sir Henry Wilson had been shot dead on the doorstep of his house. The late Chief of the Imperial General Staff was one of the many Irishmen who have attained high rank in the British Army. He entered politics as Member for North Down after the signing of the Irish Treaty. In May 1922 he was in Ulster, advising the Government of Northern Ireland on the policing of the new frontier. On the morning of June 22 he was returning home, in uniform, after unveiling a war memorial at Liverpool Street Station. He had paid his taxi, and was feeling for his keys, when two men came up behind him, pulled out revolvers, and shot him down as with an arm wounded by the first two bullets he half drew his sword. Nine bullets in all hit Wilson, and as the murderers ran up the street they emptied their weapons at passers-by who tried to stop them, wounding three, including a detective and a uniformed constable. After a vain attempt to seize a car they were captured half a mile away.

The body of the Field-Marshal had been laid on a couch in a darkened study, and Spilsbury's examination was carried out by electric light. Wilson, known throughout the Army as "Ugly," from his puckish, mobile face, was fifty-eight, and almost as tall as Spilsbury. He had been shot in the left forearm, twice in the right arm, twice in the left shoulder, in both armpits, and twice in the right leg. The armpit wounds were fatal, piercing the lungs.

When the examination was over Spilsbury's technician, Richardson, procured a taxi, and the pair set off for Bart's. As will be explained later, Spilsbury had now left St Mary's. They had not gone far when Spilsbury, who knew by now that the murderers had been caught, and that they were Irishmen, remarked conversationally, "Look behind. There is another cab following us. They must be the I.R.A."

Dr Thorndyke never encountered the I.R.A., but the ensuing chase was in the true Thorndyke tradition. After what had happened at Eaton Place Spilsbury can have had no illusions. He told his driver to avoid side-streets and to dodge among the traffic. The cab behind, however, was not to be shaken off. Pursued and pursuers covered the length of the Mall, crossed Trafalgar Square, and entered the Strand. Spilsbury's main concern was for the safety of Richardson and the taxi-driver, and next for his precious bag, in which were the bullets he had extracted, and he decided to jump out at the first opportunity and run into the nearest building, in the hope that the pursuers would follow or wait for him. Richardson was to go on to Bart's and lock up the evidence.

As the cab slowed down in the traffic of the Strand Spilsbury slipped out and ran for a hotel doorway. Apparently the ruse worked; by the time he had telephoned to Scotland Yard, walked through the hotel, picked up another taxi at the back entrance, and driven to Bart's, Richardson was already there. The black bag was under lock and key, and a detective had arrived to guard the laboratory.

Other police precautions were taken. Richardson was advised to vary his route home, a plain-clothes officer was detailed to follow Spilsbury, and a guard was put on the house in Marlborough Hill. The next morning Spilsbury received a letter threatening him with death if he gave evidence in the case. Unfortunately he seems to have torn it up. A similar letter, capped by a crude sketch of a skull, came to Mr Ingleby Oddie, the Coroner for Westminster and South-west London; but Oddie always suspected the writer to be his friend Danford Thomas, Coroner for the City, a notorious practical joker.

Identified as members of the so-called Irish Republican Army, the murderers were named Connolly and O'Brien. Connolly was a cripple. They were tried at the Old Bailey, before Mr Justice Shearman on July 2. Spilsbury, in giving evidence, was able in his precise way to describe where the murderers had been standing in relation to their victim, and even the order in which some of the wounds were inflicted. In his notes he wrote:

> Wilson was not shot after he had fallen. All nine wounds were inflicted when he was erect or slightly stooping, as he would be when tugging at his sword-hilt. The chest injuries were from shots fired at two different angles—one from right to left and the other from left to right. Either would have proved fatal and produced death inside ten minutes. The bullet through the right leg passed forwards and downwards, and therefore the shot came from directly behind. That in the top left shoulder had been fired from the left side and rather behind, and the downward direction proved that the arm was in a raised position as the bullet entered. The wounds in the forearms were inflicted from behind whilst the arms were still at the side of the body.

British courts of justice do not take the view that to shoot an unsuspecting man in the back because you do not like his political opinions is a crime in a different category from the battering to death of some old woman for her money. Both men were in due course executed.

To round off this review of the early post-War period, one other case should be touched on, because in a sense Spilsbury helped to engineer it, and had been waiting for it for a long time.

It has been said that he had been keeping a close watch on the career of his fellow practitioner Dr Richard Starkie. On his information the police had kept an eye on it too, with the added interest of old friends, for Dr Starkie had once been a police surgeon. He had prospered since those days. So far from his practice being adversely affected by his too frequent appearances as the doctor in attendance on women who died from abortion, in 1921 he was living in Brook Street, Mayfair, and his fees for certain operations, as Spilsbury noted on his cards, were sometimes as much as fifty guineas, as against the two or three pounds charged by Nurse Hopton and her like.

On July 17, however—it happened to be his birthday—Dr Starkie was taken into custody, charged with performing illegal operations on four unmarried women, and with administering a certain poison and noxious thing, with intent to procure abortion, to a married woman. He denied the charges, and he was in a different position from the unqualified persons so often convicted of similar offences. Some of them, then serving heavy sentences, may have felt that there was one law for the rich in their profession and another for the poor. The case illustrates the difficulties confronting the police when dealing with offenders of Dr Starkie's calibre, and explains why they were so long in bringing charges against him. His class of patient is more than usually reluctant to give evidence, and has means of avoiding doing so, while Starkie himself could afford to brief such a man as Marshall Hall for his defence. Whatever that brilliant advocate thought of his client, he threw all his vigour and virtuosity into the task of discrediting the prosecution's witnesses. In the teeth of Spilsbury's evidence the doctor was acquitted on the criminal charges, though sentenced to nine months' imprisonment for administering drugs. The result, due largely to Marshall Hall, must have been very displeasing to Spilsbury, after his patient accumulation of evidence, over several years, of Dr Starkie's misdoings; but he may have smiled a little later if he heard the story of the banquet given to the doctor, on the latter's release from Wormwood Scrubs Prison, by six hundred of his patients. Imagination, recalling the Light Brigade, suggests that the banquet could have been a very odd one. It was the final flourish, at any rate, of Dr Starkie's professional career.

3

A characteristic feature of Spilsbury's professional career is that there is no turning-point. There were not—until ill-health afflicted him at the very end—even any ups and downs. A graph of his progress during nearly forty years would show a steady climb to the highest level, and then onward an equally constant record of achievement and recognition, the cumulative effect of which was to give his public pronouncements an almost Papal infallibility. The feature is characteristic because the root of it was in the man himself; except for his good looks and charm of manner, against which had to be set a growing habit of reserve, few public figures of his eminence can have owed less to adventitious aids.

If, however, there are no accidents in his career of which it can be said, "This made him," or "Here he suffered a setback," certain periods have a significance of their own. The group of years now under consideration, 1919 to 1922, is one of them.

In August 1919 the Spilsburys' fourth child, Richard, was born. Of the three boys, only he has survived his father. In October of the following year the family had their first real holiday together since the visit to Cornwall in the eventful summer of 1914. Spilsbury was barely home and at work again when an unhappy event occurred which severed his long connexion with St Mary's.

No man could reach the position already attained by him without rousing jealousy, nor, unless he were inhuman, without sometimes being tempted himself into intolerance of opposing opinions which he believed to be wrong. That this phase in him was so fleeting, and that envy of his success was so rare and ineffective, is a testimony to the wide appreciation of his integrity and innate kindliness. Instances of overt antagonism will soon be recorded, and it is possible that the trouble at St Mary's arose from professional ill-feeling.

A member of the medical staff asked Spilsbury to preserve a specimen for him. Spilsbury considered it not worth preserving, and gave his reasons, it can hardly be doubted with his usual politeness. The other retorted that he must do as he was told. This was no way to speak to a colleague, and a distinguished one, still less to Bernard Spilsbury, with his strong sense of what was due to himself and to his position, and his conviction, on the trifling point at issue, that he was in the right. Even his equable temper was ruffled, and with his distaste for any sort of unseemly wrangle he must have been disgusted by the rather heated argument into which he was led. He demanded an apology. This being refused, the matter was referred to the Court of Governors, who convened a smaller court of inquiry. But Spilsbury felt too deeply affronted to await the decision of the court. On November 18, 1920, just over twenty years after his graduation and entry at St Mary's, he resigned his appointment there. In a few days' time the court of inquiry completely exonerated him. The other doctor was held to have behaved improperly, and was instructed to apologize. This he did, but it is said that he never again spoke to Spilsbury when they met, nor even to members of the court, except on professional topics.

Spilsbury's attitude throughout was typical. His decision to leave St Mary's must have been a wrench to him, but, having made it, he would not budge from it. He had no difficulty, of course, in obtaining new appointments immediately. Every hospital in the country would have welcomed him on its staff. Towards the end of the year, accordingly, the medical world at large, which knew nothing of the dispute, was surprised by the news that he was about to take up the post of Lecturer on Morbid Anatomy and Histology at St Bartholomew's.

The move to Bart's made little or no difference to Spilsbury's routine. In between lectures and demonstrations, coroners and the police kept him busy. The change resulted, however, in one interesting decision on his part. Many doctors are Freemasons, and members of the fraternity at St Mary's had often tried to persuade him to become one. The idea did not then appeal to him. In view of his traditionalist type of mind, and his interest in the past, it is an attractive conjecture that a change of view, following so soon upon a change of environment, was in part due to the influence of the oldest hospital in England, a parish in itself with its own parish church, the original of which, like so many of our Gothic churches, was perhaps built by Freemasons. Whatever the reason, Spilsbury was presently initiated a member of the Rahere Lodge, named after the founder of St Bartholomew's priory and hospital in 1123. Later he joined two other lodges, the Abernethy Mark M. and the Sancta Maria at St Mary's.

At a meeting in that summer of 1920 of the Medico-Legal Society he took part in a discussion which surviving hearers were to have cause to recall nearly a generation later. Dr Josiah Oldfield had given an address on "The Suicide Idea and Capital Punishment." After Earl Russell, who opened the subsequent debate, had spoken in favour of the abolition of the death penalty Spilsbury rose. Brushing aside the statistics upon which the earlier speakers had relied, he maintained that the only connexion between suicide and murder was to be found in the cases of greatly wronged persons who felt impelled to avenge the wrong, and then to destroy themselves. Except for such crimes of passion, murders were committed for gain of some sort, the murderers always believing that they stood a good chance of escaping the penalty. For that reason capital punishment was necessary to protect the community. Turning to suicide, Spilsbury said that the prevalence of hanging among the suicidal had nothing to do with the fact that this was the means of judicial execution in Britain. Shrinking from pain, and often unable to get poison, people chose the most painless method, available to all, of ending their existence. He repeated that he greatly doubted Dr Oldfield's suggestion that a person who took his own life would ever contemplate, except after a crime of passion, taking the life of another.

The alleged high proportion of suicides among medical practitioners, Spilsbury went on, was accountable only because they had a ready means of procuring death. Were poisons easily obtainable by the general public there was no doubt that an increase in suicidal attempts would result.

During these years he addressed the Medico-Legal Society on other occasions. At the annual dinner in December 1920 he declared his belief that in the teaching of medical jurisprudence Great Britain was lagging behind other countries, particularly the United States. Forensic medicine had made very little progress in Britain since Casper established the first principles. It was dependent on other sciences—not only medicine itself, but also physics and chemistry; but only in the last-named, in its application to toxicology, had adequate progress been maintained.

Next year he was taking part in a discussion by the Society of the medical evidence in the Staunton trial. In this famous case, in the 1870's, two brothers named Staunton, with the wife of one of them and her sister, Alice Rhodes, were charged with the murder by starvation of Louis Staunton's wife, Harriet. Harriet Staunton was a weak-minded woman possessed of considerable means. She was shut up in a room in appalling conditions of filth and discomfort, denied water to wash in, shoes to walk in, and, finally, food to eat. Though these facts were not in doubt, and all four accused were sentenced to death, they were reprieved, the three Stauntons being sent to penal servitude for life, and Alice Rhodes released with a free pardon. They had been in danger of their lives from a furious crowd, but afterwards it was rumoured that Harriet Staunton had died of tubercular meningitis, and not of starvation.

Spilsbury, who had read every word of the trial, pointed out that morbid anatomy was in its infancy in 1877. The doctors who conducted the post-mortem on Harriet Staunton knew less about the subject than present-day students, who often mistook for symptoms of tubercular meningitis those caused by other diseases. The complete absence of fat in Mrs Staunton's body was not a sign of a tubercular complaint. That bacon had been found in the stomach in an undigested state meant nothing; in cases of infants starved to death it was a common trick to give them food when they were beyond saving. In that of Mrs Staunton the absence of fat, and the translucency of the stomach and intestines, pointed to starvation. The findings of the post-mortem, in short, were "overwhelmingly in favour of that being the cause of death, as against tubercular meningitis."

Twice in 1922 he advocated in public a cause on which he felt strongly—the creation of a Medico-legal Institute. To the Medico-Legal Society, and again at Cambridge University, he stressed the point that a student's time was so fully occupied that a study of medical jurisprudence was possible only after graduation, and then the sole means of gaining practical experience was by post-mortem work at coroners' courts. For a young doctor this entailed pecuniary loss, such work bringing him only nominal fees. There had been no advance since Spilsbury's own student days, when his devotion to morbid anatomy led to late qualification and consequent loss of seniority. About this time, at the request of the authorities of London University, he gave a series of addresses there on forensic medicine, afterwards taking the students to his own laboratory at Bart's.

In 1921 there were rumours that he was going to retire, to devote himself to research and the compilation of a text-book on medical jurisprudence. If he had any such intention then, he would not admit it, and the rumours may have sprung from the fact that once more, and more seriously now, he was feeling the effect of unremitting work, and of travelling, at all times and in all weathers, in cold trains and draughty cars, from one end of England to the other. He suffered acute pains in the small of the back, which he called lumbago, and which made him stoop a little. His fellow-pathologists advised him to rest. They believed his trouble to be arthritis. They found it politic not to say so, however; Spilsbury would admit lumbago, but never arthritis. If he was deceived it must have been a case of self-deception. Fortunately the pains in the back, whatever their cause, subsided as the warmer weather came, and he soon seemed to be well again.

It was during these years, too, that he began to lose his sense of smell. He had always relied a great deal on this. Now he could work with his normal concentration, and with no sign of distress, in conditions which others found unbearable. Later it became his custom at a post-mortem to lay down his instruments from time to time and go out into the fresh air, running back to detect and differentiate the dreadful odours coming from the dead body.

The end of 1922, and of this post-War period, which found Spilsbury forty-five, was marked by a happy event. On December 21 he received a letter from the Prime Minister, Mr Bonar Law, informing him that in the New Year's Honours a knighthood would be conferred on him.

Chapter 7: THE ARMSTRONG CASE

When Bernard Spilsbury was entered at Manchester Grammar School as a tall, very good-looking boy of fourteen, with Oxford five years in the future, a young man who in appearance was his very antithesis had just come down from Cambridge to start a career that was to end, thirty-one years later, with the pair face to face, one in the witness-box and the other in the dock, in the Shire Hall at Hereford.

Herbert Rowse Armstrong began life with few advantages. Born in 1870 at Newton Abbot, in Devonshire, he must have been a puny child, for he grew up to be a diminutive man, not much over five feet tall and weighing only seven stone. His parents were in a very modest position; but relatives helped him to obtain a good education, and to go to Cambridge, where it is said he was spare cox for the University Eight. He studied law, and, having taken his degree, was admitted a solicitor in 1895, practising first in his native town, and later in Liverpool. He worked hard, and put money by. While at Liverpool, in 1906, he heard of an opening in the Welsh town of Hay, in Brecknock, where an ageing solicitor, one of the two in practice there, wanted a managing clerk. Armstrong put his capital into the business, and when the senior partner died the little man from Devonshire succeeded to the practice. These improved circumstances enabled him to marry, in the following year, an old acquaintance of his Newton Abbot days, Miss Katherine Mary Friend, of Teignmouth. He took a house in the little valley charmingly named Cusop Dingle, whose stream divides Wales from England, and where well-to-do people of Hay had villas. Three children were born to the Armstrongs in as many years, and then they moved into a larger house, Mayfield, also in the Dingle. This was in 1910, when young Dr Spilsbury was a newly married man living at Harrow, and another doctor, with an American degree, had recently lost his wife in Camden Town.

The scenes of famous murders have their atmosphere. That of the Ratcliffe horrors may owe much to De Quincey, but Hilldrop Crescent and Tollington Park call to mind Victorian suburban streets, dingy and declining, and the very name of the Crumbles suggests melancholy and decay. Few major crimes have for a setting that kind of countryside which Constable might have painted, and Gray or Wordsworth sung.

Hay stands in such surroundings, on the river Wye, on the very margin of Wales. It is so nearly in England that Spilsbury, misled perhaps by its railway station, which is in Herefordshire, seems to have thought that the town was in that county. Hills surround it, with the famous Brecon Beacons stretching westward almost to Llanelly, where another solicitor named Harold Greenwood was practising at this time. The town is small, with a population at the present day of barely 1500, but it is the business centre of a prosperous agricultural district.

The Armstrongs lived very comfortably, with a housekeeper and two maids. Mayfield, like Cusop village and Hay railway station, stands in England, a house of some size, with a considerable garden and a tennis-court. Armstrong, who liked tinkering about, was a keen gardener of the sort who must be always eradicating weeds. He kept a stock of weed-killer, and, knowing something of chemicals, he used to buy arsenic, the basis of most garden-pest exterminators, and brew his own concoctions. In contrast to his home, since business premises in Hay are not pretentious, the office in Broad Street which he took over from his late partner, Mr Cheese, was only part of a small converted shop, the remaining portion being occupied by a firm of estate agents. Across the street, almost opposite, was the office of the other solicitor practising in the town, Mr Griffiths.

Mr Griffiths was a Welshman, and well known in the district, as Mr Cheese had been; Armstrong was a stranger, and it seems that after his partner's death he had to battle with local conservatism, particularly strong in Wales. Time, however, might put this right, and if his own capital was tied up in the business Mrs Armstrong had the income of some £2000 of her own. Then, within a few years, came the outbreak of war. An old Volunteer and Territorial, Armstrong was called up with the rank of captain, and in time he was drawing the useful pay and allowances of a major. He went to France, but not for long, and from various depots in England he was able to supervise his business at Hay. In the meantime his rival, Mr Griffiths, was growing old and was in poor health. His son, who was to have joined him in the practice as soon as he was admitted a solicitor, was in the Forces abroad. Armstrong saw his opportunity, and offered his help, hinting at an amalgamation of the two firms. But Griffiths was already making other arrangements. Early in 1919 he took into his office on trial Mr Oswald Norman Martin, just demobilized with a head wound which afflicted him with a form of facial paralysis. Soon after Armstrong came out of the Army Martin became a partner. At the end of 1920 old Mr Griffiths died.

About this time all Wales, and all England as well, was following with absorption a trial for murder which the Armstrong case was to parallel in so many features that the sum of coincidence must be among the most remarkable in the annals of capital crime. Comparisons invite fascinating conjectures.[1] Both Herbert Armstrong and Harold Greenwood were solicitors practising in Wales; and though they lived fifty miles apart, in the dozen years after the former's arrival at Hay there must have been legal occasions in the Principality at which they could have met.

There can be no doubt at all—and here there is drama enough—that the Greenwood trial at Carmarthen was discussed by every one in Hay. What were Armstrong's thoughts as he talked it over with Dr Hincks when the latter called at the pleasant house in Cusop Dingle, or with the newcomer, Martin, with his stiff manner and twitching face, when they met on business? What were those thoughts when the subject came up, as it must have done, at his own dinner-table?

Armstrong shared with many small men, and others of various sizes, a characteristic attributed to all murderers. He was very vain of his ability and appearance, pushful in business, and a great talker in an egotistical style. Dapper in his dress, he was addicted to high collars and (like Spilsbury) to flowers in his buttonhole. He expected to be addressed by his military rank, as he was entitled to be, and at the time of his arrest he was still going about in his Army trench coat or British Warm, with fur collar. It was no doubt a comfort to him to be reminded of the days when he had been a personage of some importance wielding authority.

For life at Mayfield, at any rate, was very different from the freedom of base camps and messes. It was Mrs Armstrong who wielded authority there. She had many admirable qualities, and she was a devoted wife and mother, but she treated husband and children alike with a sternness which denied them many harmless pleasures. She was a crank, whose humourless austerity was perhaps a symptom of

[1] That, for instance, put forward by Sir William Willcox in his pamphlet *Toxicology with Reference to its Criminal Aspects*: "The Armstrong Case and the Black Case both illustrate the effect of imitation in the causation of criminal poisoning. It cannot be doubted that the sensational report of a noted case of arsenical poisoning (the Greenwood Case) led to the selection and use of this poison in these two cases."

the malady that later afflicted her. The stories of this curious *ménage* are well known: how little Armstrong was allowed to smoke in one room only, and never out of doors; how wine and spirits were forbidden him, except an occasional glass (in some one else's house) when he had a cold; how he was rebuked in public for keeping the servants waiting, or called away from some mild festivity because it was his bath night. In his behaviour under this well-meant tyranny one is reminded of Crippen, though the latter's provocation was, of course, far greater. Like Crippen, Armstrong was never seen to betray resentment, always keeping his temper and his manners—and his manners were excellent—and always treating his wife with consideration and affection. But also like Crippen, if for very different reasons, he must have found his domestic life inexpressibly galling. It is not surprising that he sought dubious enjoyments elsewhere, as one result of which he was under medical treatment at the date of his arrest. In Hay itself, though Mrs Armstrong was much respected, a good deal of sympathy was felt for the husband whom she dominated.

During the ten months between May 1920 and February 1921 a series of related events occurred, some of which were to assume startling significance later. Not all were known of at the time. In May 1920 Armstrong was in London, where he dined with a lady whom he had first met while he was stationed at Christchurch in the second year of the War. In July he drew up a will for his wife, or in her name, by which she left him everything she possessed, making no provision for their children. This completely reversed the conditions of an earlier will. It was apparently signed by Mrs Armstrong, but the signature was witnessed in a most irregular manner, as no one could have known better than Armstrong himself. Soon after he was making one of his periodical purchases of weed-killer, and by the middle of August his wife's state of health and mind was alarming Dr Hincks. She was suffering from delusions. Another doctor was called in, and the two practitioners having certified the poor woman as insane, she was taken to a private asylum at Gloucester. There she remained until January 1921, when she was so much improved that at her own desire, and in response to pressure from Armstrong, she was allowed to return home. Her husband fetched her in a car. Perhaps he talked to her about the garden, for though January is rather early in the year to worry about weeds, he had just bought another quarter of a pound of arsenic.

No doubt the reunited pair also talked about the trial of Harold Greenwood. This took place at the Carmarthen Assizes while Mrs

Armstrong was in the asylum, but Greenwood had been arrested in the summer, when she was at home in normal health. The trial, which lasted a week, resulted in a verdict of Not Guilty. The result must have been in Armstrong's thoughts when he made that last purchase of arsenic, on January 11, at the shop of his rival Martin's prospective father-in-law, Mr Davies, the chemist. It was an encouraging omen. For Greenwood, another gardener, was accused of poisoning his wife with arsenic obtained from weed-killer. Though he was acquitted, some one had given Mrs Greenwood arsenic. Now that history, up to a point, was about to repeat itself, Armstrong may well have felt that should suspicion arise in his own case the collapse of the proceedings against his fellow-lawyer might deter the authorities from taking action a second time in circumstances so similar, and so soon after. Probably he did not really fear suspicion. He had the murderer's conceit, and, unlike Greenwood, who was the subject of much local gossip, he had been careful to give no serious cause for scandal in his own town. The lady in the background lived far away from Hay. He was not far out, in fact, in his calculations: but for a later act of folly he would have escaped punishment.

Mrs Armstrong came home on January 22. On February 22 she died. Dr Hincks certified the cause of death as heart disease, the result of a long course of rheumatism, and itself bringing about nephritis. The patient had also suffered from acute gastritis. Three days afterwards the funeral took place in the churchyard at Cusop.

2

Ten months went by, and then—it was the afternoon of January 2, 1922—Spilsbury was in the train for Hay. The Home Office had decided on the exhumation of Mrs Armstrong's body. Hay did not yet know this, but it had enough to talk about. On New Year's Eve one of its two lawyers had been taken into custody, charged with the attempted murder of the other.

This was the climax of a remarkable tragi-comedy, though Mr Martin would not have used that term.

After Mrs Armstrong's death, life at Mayfield went on very much as before. Armstrong still had a housekeeper and a maid to look after him; his youngest child was at home, and he had the companionship of the other two during their school holidays. But there was one big difference: he was now master in his own house.

During this brief period of emancipation Armstrong must have seemed to be in an enviable position. He had a fair practice, he was clerk to the justices of Hay, Bredwardine, and Painscastle, and he had hopes of a similar post with the bench at Talgarth, where the incumbent was a man of eighty. If he had business worries only one was referred to at his trial. Martin was pressing him to complete the formalities, long overdue, arising out of a sale of property, in which connexion there was a matter of £500 paid to Armstrong as a deposit. Armstrong had nothing like the ready money to meet a claim for repayment. By his wife's second will, however, he became possessed at her death of £2300, and this capital was in the hands of the executor of her earlier will, who was also trustee of the marriage settlement, and a friend of both parties to it. The second will had been proved, and its validity was not questioned until after Armstrong's arrest. Yet up to that date he had made no attempt to realize any of the capital, except a small sum for costs. In short, the theory that he resorted to murder a second time within a year because he was short of money seems untenable on every ground, for Martin's death would not have helped him. The £500 would still have to be found. The mystery of the Armstrong case is not the husband's motive for poisoning his wife, but why he poisoned Martin—if he did.

For this, of course, was never proved, though Martin was undoubtedly poisoned, and by arsenic, and in circumstances which incriminated Armstrong, who then went on pertinaciously endeavouring to re-create them. Other cases of illness, and even the deaths of old Mr Cheese and his wife many years before, and that of an estate agent, were later attributed to Armstrong's machinations by public rumour. Such is the way of small country towns. It is said, however, that the Home Office was considering authorizing more exhumations.

From his own self-centred point of view Armstrong had strong reasons for resenting the very existence of Martin. To a certain type of egoist anyone who stands in his way, or who opposes him, has committed an offence. The motive of gain being absent, Martin must have been the victim of sheer vindictiveness. He had been warned, but he did not know it. About the time when he was beginning to press Armstrong to complete the sale of property a box of chocolates was delivered at his house. There was nothing to indicate the sender. Mrs Martin ate some, and then the box was put away, to be produced a few days later when there were visitors to dinner. One of the latter was afterwards taken ill. The remainder of the chocolates were preserved, and were later examined, when some were found to contain arsenic. This had been inserted through holes pierced in the base of the sweets, and the holes corresponded with the nozzle of a weed-eradicator used by Armstrong.

The relations between the two lawyers were amicable, but were confined to professional matters. Martin had not been to Mayfield for more than a year when, in October 1921, the leisurely business of the uncompleted contracts began to be speeded up. A brisk exchange of letters and telephone-calls went on across Broad Street. Armstrong always wanted more time. There were interviews in Martin's office, and at one of them, by his own account, Armstrong appeared much agitated. This was on October 20, and at the close of the meeting Armstrong invited Martin to Mayfield that same afternoon, to have tea. Martin proposed the 24th, but later postponed the visit. On the 26th, a Wednesday, he drove up Cusop Dingle in his car. After a walk round the garden with Armstrong he was taken to the drawing-room, where the tea-table was laid.

The maid brought in the tea, a cup was passed to Martin, and then Armstrong handed him a buttered scone, apologizing for using his fingers. Bread and butter followed, and the pair discussed various matters. The cancelled contracts and the £500 were not mentioned, though Martin could have raised the subject himself. He left Mayfield at half-past six to return to his own home in Cusop. That evening he was taken ill.

Dr Thomas Hincks, who was known to every one in and about Hay, where he had lived all his life, and where he had practised for twenty-five years, was called to the Martins' house early next morning. Martin was in bed, suffering from all the symptoms of a severe bilious attack, with one addition—a very rapid pulse. Dr Hincks continued to call daily, and the patient improved, but slowly, and his pulse-rate remained high. Somewhat puzzled, on the 31st the doctor forwarded a sample of urine to the Clinical Research Association for analysis. A week later, when Martin was at work again, the reply came back that 1/33rd of a grain of arsenic had been found.

From this report, in Dr Hincks's words, he "formed the opinion that Mr Martin's illness was caused by his taking a considerable dose of arsenic." The doctor, who made up his own medicines, had prescribed none that contained arsenic. He had, of course, questioned Martin about meals taken immediately before the illness developed. He knew that lunch and dinner on the 26th had been shared by Mrs Martin and the maid, who were perfectly well, and he knew of Martin's visit to Mayfield for tea that afternoon. Association of ideas recalled Mrs Armstrong's fatal illness to his mind. He had not encountered a case of arsenical poisoning for twenty years; but now that he had met one again he was struck by the similarity of the symptoms with some of Mrs Armstrong's. These must have been bad days for Dr Hincks; but he was an honest and a courageous man; he wrote to the Barnwood Asylum at Gloucester, and when the doctors who had attended Mrs Armstrong there agreed that they too might have been misled as to the cause of her physical ailments, he reported his suspicions to the Home Office.

In the meantime he held his tongue, except to Martin, who must be warned. During the latter's illness Armstrong had been sympathetic and helpful, calling at his rival's office for news, and conducting a sale for him. The pair were continually meeting again in Broad Street, Armstrong talkative and friendly, his blue eyes twinkling behind his pince-nez, Martin, no doubt, stiffer and more brusque than ever. Martin, indeed, was not out of the wood yet.

The Director of Public Prosecutions, with the recent Greenwood case in mind, took his time before acting on Dr Hincks's report. Eventually, after consultation with Superintendent Wensley, then senior superintendent of the C.I.D., it was decided to make inquiries on the spot, but with the utmost secrecy. Armstrong, if guilty, must not be put on his guard; if he was innocent there must be no talk about him. There had been enough trouble over Greenwood. Chief Detective-Inspector Crutchett, who had worked with Spilsbury in the case of Mrs Seabrook, was given charge of the investigation; strange policemen from London appeared in Hay after dark, and talked with the Martins, and Dr Hincks, and Mr Davies, the chemist. For all concerned it was a most harassing time. The doctor was actually attending Armstrong, for venereal disease; and as for Martin, he had barely accustomed himself to the idea that the little man across the street had tried to poison him when invitations to tea began to rain upon him.

As the two men handled between them most of the legal business for miles round, there was always some excuse for a meeting; and why not—now that the happy thought had occurred—why not at the tea-table? It was less easy to find excuses for declining, but Martin, inspired by recollections of buttered scones, somehow found them. Then Armstrong tried new tactics. He began having tea in his office; the telephone was busier than ever; surely Martin could find time to cross the street? But for Armstrong it was a case of jam (or buttered scones) to-morrow, but never jam to-day. Time was always at a premium with Martin; the best he could suggest was some morning, or at six o'clock. He was so hard-pressed, however, that he in turn sent to the local café for tea and buns in the afternoon. It was a tragi-comedy indeed, and if Martin, for some reason, seems scarcely a sympathetic figure, no man was ever more deserving of sympathy.

This extraordinary state of affairs dragged on for some weeks of that early winter of 1921. Martin, when in his office, was living in a state of siege, afraid to put his nose out of doors lest little Armstrong, smiling beneath his heavy waxed moustache, his glasses flashing, should come tripping across with another urgent invitation. And all the time official voices were ingeminating caution in Martin's ear. "Whatever you do, don't go. But whatever you do, don't let him think you suspect him." "But I can't stand this much longer," said poor Martin. "And I'm running out of excuses." To the police those three weeks might seem nothing; they were an eternity to Martin. After the first week of December, however, and rather suddenly, the persecution ceased. It may be significant that on the 6th, by letter, Martin once more raised the old affair of the rescinded contracts and the £500, which appears to have been in abeyance. He threatened to issue a writ unless the deposit was repaid by the 12th. This roused Armstrong to retaliate. No money came on the 12th, but a last invitation to tea, evaded as usual; on the next day Armstrong himself issued two writs, against Martin's clients. Subsequently, by his instructions, these writs were settled. He stated at the trial that he was in a position to complete the business early in December, but took no action because of the attitude of the other contracting parties.

Three days after Christmas, as if to show that there was no ill-feeling, Armstrong was in Martin's office with a renewal of his offers of hospitality. Would Mr and Mrs Martin come to dinner one evening that week? Martin, who knew that the end was near, talked vaguely of a later date.

3

In a pamphlet already quoted in a note to this chapter Sir William Willcox points out that the first law relating to the control of the sale of poisons in this country was the Arsenic Act of 1851. He gives the reason: "Arsenic produces symptoms so like those of natural disease that it has for all time been the most commonly chosen for criminal purposes."

Remarking elsewhere on the great advances made in toxicological chemistry in recent times—he was writing in 1938—Sir William goes on—"It may safely be said that to-day the criminal poisoner has little chance of escaping detection." Had he been dealing here with the particular case of arsenical poisoning, however, the writer would probably have qualified this assertion with some such words as "once the poisoner has given cause for suspicion." With a lethal substance producing symptoms similar to those of natural disease there will always be murders which escape detection. They remain unsuspected because the murderer has known when to hold his hand. Most convicted poisoners have given themselves away by their subsequent actions. Among major cases where arsenic was the means employed all those in which Spilsbury was concerned illustrate this point. Miss Barrow's body would not have been exhumed had Seddon put a check upon his greed and conciliated her relations; Armstrong was quite safe until he invited Martin to tea; it was the third death at Croydon which roused suspicion. The argument for undiscovered crimes in this *genre* is supported by the fact that even in Spilsbury's unexampled experience of homicides, and notwithstanding the popularity of arsenic among poisoners, these three cases stand isolated by long periods of time, and almost in a class by themselves.

Spilsbury knew what he had to look for when he left London for Hereford on that Monday, January 2, 1922. It was wintry weather; there were blizzards in the north, and snow lay in the streets of Hereford, where a police car met him. There were only three trains daily on the single line from Hereford to Hay. It was after six o'clock, and quite dark, when he arrived at the little churchyard of Cusop. With him were the Deputy Chief Constable of Hereford and other police officers, Dr Hincks, who had been picked up in Hay, and Dr Ainslie, of Hereford, who was to appear for the defence at the trial. Behind canvas screens the grave was opened, in the light of oil-lamps. The coffin was raised and trundled on a hand-bier to a small white house in a lane by the churchyard. Sacking was hung over a front-room window, and by the light of more oil-lamps Spilsbury made his preliminary examination. These were conditions against which he so often protested, and he left the real work of the post-mortem until next day.

Conditions were even more primitive in the tiny magistrates' court at Hay, where for years Armstrong had sat as clerk, and where he now stood under charge before his neighbours and colleagues. There were no lamps there at all, and the long-drawn proceedings, adjourned from week to week, closed when daylight failed. Armstrong's seat at the table below the bench was taken by Mr Cambridge Phillips, the clerk of Talgarth, aged eighty-one, to whom the prisoner politely offered his assistance. To every one there it must have seemed an extraordinary and unnatural business. Armstrong was one of them, a typical figure in a small country town, a professional man, Worshipful Master of the Hay Lodge of Freemasons, a churchwarden who read the lessons on Sunday, an active worker in everything that went on, from agricultural meetings and sport to whist-drives, dances, and concerts.

The alleged poisoning of Martin was as yet all that the Hay magistrates had to consider. The inquest on Mrs Armstrong had been opened, and adjourned for three weeks. The remains had been re-interred in the snow, and Spilsbury was back in London with specimens in jars for the analysts. He was to be busy between now and the trial at Hereford on two other capital cases—the murders of Margaret Evans and Elizabeth Cooper, already referred to, and with the case of Freda Kempton. Until Webster had completed his report on the specimens from Cusop the death of Mrs Armstrong was not on the agenda of the bench at Hay.

But on January 19 Armstrong was charged with the murder of his wife. At the adjourned inquest on the 24th the jury brought in a verdict of murder against him.

4

The severe weather of that winter—in January London was colder than Iceland—continued late into the spring of 1922. The Summer Assizes at Hereford opened early in April in a snowstorm. Armstrong was now in Gloucester Prison, and during his trial, which lasted ten days (as long as that of the Seddons), he was driven daily from Gloucester to Hereford and back again, covering in all more than six hundred miles in wintry weather. Against him the Attorney-General, Sir Ernest Pollock, led for the Crown; Sir Henry Curtis-Bennett was briefed for the defence. Armstrong had been anxious to secure Curtis-Bennett, because the latter was a Cambridge man. "Cambridge always wins," he said, and it may have seemed a good omen that on the day before his trial began Cambridge won the Boat Race, in shocking conditions, by 4½ lengths.

Mr Justice Darling was presiding over his last murder trial. He had now been a judge for nearly twenty-five years, and the outcry against his elevation to the Bench—the more venomous because it was political—had long been forgotten. Now seventy-three, a little, shrivelled man, scarcely bigger than Armstrong himself, Darling was the embodiment of common sense, and an example of the physical and mental toughness of lawyers. He lived until 1936, and was speaking in the House of Lords a month or two before his death at the age of eighty-six.

Darling afterwards said of the Armstrong case that it was perhaps the most interesting he ever tried. Spilsbury thought otherwise; in his own unique experience of capital crimes he put the Mahon case first, presumably because of the technical problems involved in piecing together the fragments of poor Emily Kaye. Interested though he was in human behaviour, science always took precedence. The fate of Armstrong, nevertheless, hung on the medical evidence, which takes up almost half the pages of printed testimony at the trial. As soon as Webster reported that the specimens from the grave at Cusop contained three and a half grains of arsenic, more than he had ever found before in a case of arsenical poisoning, only one defence, in the circumstances, was possible—that Mrs Armstrong, either inadvertently or by intention, had taken the poison herself. The Crown had to demonstrate, first, that she could not have done so, and, second, that no one but her husband had the opportunity to poison her, the motive, and the means.

On the first day of the trial, Monday, April 3, the Attorney-General's opening statement was interrupted, and the jury withdrew, while there was a legal argument about the admissibility of evidence bearing on the poisoning of Martin. On this charge a true bill had been found against Armstrong, but, Martin being still alive, the case had gone no further. In England murder is always charged alone. The prosecution wished to introduce the evidence to show, as Darling put it in summing up, "that the defendant had arsenic in his possession, and that he would use it to poison a human being"—in other words, to prove system, as in the case of George Joseph Smith, though this was not among those cited. The judge ruled that the evidence should be admitted. If he were wrong, he said, the Court of Criminal Appeal would put him right. The line which the defence would take was indicated when two witnesses, under cross-examination, agreed that Mrs Armstrong had asked whether a fall from the attic window of Mayfield would be fatal. Later a third witness, the executor and family friend, said that he had warned Armstrong against his wife's suicidal tendencies. The prosecution, however, regained ground with evidence that Mrs Armstrong had been incapable of leaving her bed for a week before her death, and for some days before it of even sitting up or lifting a cup to her lips; and with her words to her nurse on the last day of her life: "I am not going to die, am I? Because I have everything to live for—my children and my husband."

The lady from Hampshire was called to say that Armstrong had spoken to her of marriage only three months after his wife's death. Gardeners gave some rather contradictory evidence about the use of weed-killer at Mayfield, and then Martin told the story of his invitation to tea there, the incident of the buttered scone, and his subsequent illness.

Dr Hincks, the first in a procession of medical witnesses, said that in 1920 Mrs Armstrong began to show signs of delusions, with some incoherence of speech. She became physically ill, and her symptoms—mitral systolic murmur, stomach-pains, vomiting, and a rapid pulse—led him to diagnose organic disease of the heart and kidneys. Her delusions took the form of a belief that she was a wicked woman, unkind to her children, and in danger of arrest for defrauding tradespeople. Dr Hincks felt that she required the treatment and supervision which only a mental home could give, and she was taken to Barnwood House Hospital. There she was examined by Dr Townsend, the medical superintendent, Dr Hincks being present. Among other symptoms the doctors noted a marked cyanosed condition about the patient's lips, and a sallowness of the skin of her abdomen.

At that time, in August 1920, said Dr Hincks, no suspicion of poisoning, of any sort or kind, entered his mind. He did not see his patient again until her return home in January 1921. He found her condition then very much improved, but within a fortnight she was complaining of the return of a curious sensation from which she suffered at Barnwood—a feeling as of springs pressing her feet up from the ground. Dr Townsend, in a letter, had referred to this symptom as functional. Dr Hincks, when he had tried to make Mrs Armstrong walk naturally, and found her unable to do so, took a different view. The trouble, he thought, must be organic. Had it been functional—that is, caused by hysteria—she could have walked in a normal way had she made the effort.

There was a nurse at Mayfield, and she now put Mrs Armstrong to bed, where Dr Hincks examined her thoroughly. The reflexes of her nervous system were very weak; the knee-jerks were absent, and so poor was her control over her fingers that she had great difficulty in picking up a pen. The doctor had formed no definite opinion about her complaint when he left her that day, February 11. On the 16th he was summoned to Mayfield by telephone, to find a recurrence of the physical symptoms from which his patient had suffered before she went to Barnwood—abdominal pains, vomiting, rapid pulse, and dilation of the heart. Mrs Armstrong's lips were cyanosed, and there was a general coppery discoloration of the skin, which became more marked in the next few days. Her mind, however, was clear, and her great anxiety was to get better.

After that visit on the 16th he saw Mrs Armstrong daily until she died. She weakened very rapidly, and could keep nothing down. Morphia was injected to relieve pain. On the 21st the doctor told Armstrong that she was hardly likely to pull through. The next day, after he had seen her, he heard of her death.

Sir Ernest Pollock asked whether Mrs Armstrong was in a condition during the last days of her life to help herself to medicine. "Absolutely impossible," said Dr Hincks.

Martin's father-in-law, and his assistant in the chemist's shop, gave more evidence about Armstrong's purchases of weed-killer and pure arsenic, culminating in that made on January 11, just before Mrs Armstrong's return home. Armstrong then bought a quarter of a pound of pure arsenic. It was a rule that arsenic sold in this form should be coloured with charcoal, and whether this last purchase was so coloured was a disputed point of some interest. When Armstrong was arrested on New Year's Eve he was in his office. He was told to turn out the contents of his pockets, and these were roughly bundled in a piece of brown paper. It was asserted that he tried to tamper with this parcel; the contents, nevertheless, were not examined for some days, when a tiny packet of uncoloured white arsenic—three and three-quarter grains—was found caught in the flap of an envelope. Curtis-Bennett now sprang a surprise by producing another small packet of white arsenic, containing almost two ounces, which had been discovered stuck at the back of a drawer in Armstrong's desk, after his arrest, by his solicitor, Mr Matthews. As this discovery had been kept from the police, when Chief Inspector Crutchett was called he implied indirectly his doubts of this story by insisting that he had searched the drawer thoroughly, looking for arsenic. The defence relied a good deal on this second packet, but the surprise was to recoil on them, because the judge took a different view.

5

Police witnesses, and one or two others, having carried proceedings into the sixth morning, the prosecution then brought forward its heavy artillery, the medical experts, beginning with Spilsbury.

Photographs of the latter taken during the trial show him (when he is not hiding his face) looking very youthful for a man of his reputation in his forty-sixth year. Youthful he still was, in many ways; he had not yet succumbed to the tyranny of work, and his early addiction to the society of older men naturally became less marked as he grew older himself; there were even reactions when he sought and enjoyed the company of his juniors. There was a stereotyped side to much of his work as Home Office Pathologist at this time; as case followed case the legal element varied, but the medical witnesses for the prosecution, again and again, were Willcox, Webster, and himself. The three travelled together, stayed at the same hotels, compared their notes, and discussed the evidence they would have to give. Willcox was only five years older than Spilsbury, but twenty years' friendship had not quite eradicated the relation of master to pupil. There are one or two stories which illustrate Spilsbury's deferential attitude towards his old teacher, and the change in him when conferences were over for the day, and he was free until the next day's work began. During the long Armstrong trial, as usual, he and Webster and Willcox (by now Sir William) were in the same hotel in Hereford. There also were some of the lawyers. As an evening drew on Willcox, having, perhaps, been a little pontifical, would withdraw with his notes to the smoking-room; if he did not want Spilsbury the latter would go off to play billiards and have some whisky with junior members of the Bar. One of them says of him that he was like a schoolboy released, and this phrase has been used of similar occasions at this time.

Examined on the Saturday by the Attorney-General, Spilsbury described the exhumation at Cusop. After the post-mortem he took away sixteen jars containing organs and other parts of the body, sawdust and wood shavings from the coffin, and soil adhering to it. These specimens he handed to Webster for analysis. The body, after ten months' burial, was unusually well preserved, particularly such organs as the liver and kidneys, which arsenic in poisonous doses tends to preserve. He could find no evidence in these organs of any natural disease that would account for vomiting, diarrhoea, and death. There had been dilation of the heart, but no disease of the heart-valves. Speaking from experience, and in the light of subsequent analysis, he attributed the condition of the liver and kidneys to the action of arsenic in poisonous doses. In reply to a formal question from the judge, he said that he had considerable experience of poison cases, which were almost of weekly, certainly of monthly, occurrence.

After describing the condition of the kidneys, which did not suggest Bright's disease, but some form of poisoning, Spilsbury returned to the essential time factor. He was asked about a tonic mixture, containing one-twentieth of a grain of arsenic, prescribed for Mrs Armstrong at the asylum in October and November 1920, and he replied that it was quite impossible that this could have any bearing at all on the arsenic found in the body more than a year later. The Attorney-General then ended his examination-in-chief with a series of questions, the answers to which, in view of the witness's unique reputation, must have made a strong impression on all in the crowded assize court. For the answers summed up the case against Armstrong, and forestalled the still undeclared but easily conjectured line of defence. In Spilsbury's copy of the volume on this case in the "Notable Trials" series he has marked in the margin his reply to the first question.

"In your opinion, at what time must a dose or doses of arsenic have been taken in order to find what Mr Webster found in the organs which you gave to him?"

"From the amount of arsenic which was present in the small and large intestines it is clear that a large dose of arsenic must have been taken—I mean, a poisonous dose, possibly a fatal dose—certainly within twenty-four hours of death; and from the amount of arsenic which was found in the liver—over two grains—and from the disease which I found in the liver, it is clear that the poison must have been given in a number of large doses extending over a period, certainly of some days, probably not less than a week."

"Have you heard Dr Hincks's evidence as to the symptoms which Mrs Armstrong displayed about the time when she was taken to Barnwood Asylum in August 1920?"

"I have."

"What, in your opinion, was the cause of those symptoms?"

"She was, of course, suffering from mental disease, melancholia, but in addition the vomiting on the day of her admission, and the presence of albumen, are consistent with an acute or sub-acute attack of arsenical poisoning, and the rapid disappearance of albuminuria within a week after admission to the asylum, followed by the development of peripheral neuritis, point clearly to an acute toxæmia as the cause of these symptoms."

"Can you attribute these symptoms as likely to be caused by a particular poison?"

"They strengthen my view that the symptoms taken as a whole were due to poisoning by arsenic."

Finally, Spilsbury gave it as his opinion, from what he had heard in evidence, that the cause of Martin's illness was also acute arsenical poisoning. The amount of arsenic found in Martin's case could not be produced in any normal way.

Curtis-Bennett's examination, which took as long as the examination-in-chief and re-examination put together, could be summarized in a few words. It was an endeavour to get round Spilsbury's assertion that Mrs Armstrong had taken a fatal dose of arsenic less than twenty-four hours before death. Cases were quoted of persons who had lived for seven or eight days after taking large doses. If, however, a week or so had elapsed between Mrs Armstrong's last dose and her death the defence had to explain why there had been little or no remission of vomiting, which in all cases of poisoning naturally tends to become less severe after the first violent onset—unless more poison is taken. Curtis-Bennett put a hypothetical case of intermittent vomiting lasting a week. Spilsbury's answer, which he repeated, was quite definite. He would not expect such a state of things to occur through the action of arsenic alone—only if some other disease were present which of itself would cause vomiting. He had already said that he found nothing in the organs to suggest such a disease.

Curtis-Bennett then shifted his ground. He asked whether intermittent vomiting, with periods of remission up to twenty-four or thirty-six hours followed by renewed attacks, might not be the result of arsenic becoming encapsuled or encysted in the stomach. Spilsbury agreed that he knew of such cases. The action of the poison was then delayed. When it was freed from the cyst death ensued very rapidly. Then came the following questions and answers:

> "Then you would not like to exclude the case I have put of a patient taking a large poisonous dose of arsenic on Monday, suffering from vomiting, sickness, diarrhoea, and so on, on Tuesday, Wednesday, and Thursday, then a remission, I do not care whether for twelve or twenty-four hours, but slight remission, and then coming on again?"
>
> "I do not think I can agree to that—three days' sickness from a single dose, and then a remission due to this. I do not think it would occur."
>
> "Two days?"
>
> "I doubt that very much indeed."
>
> "I understand you to say that you did agree with the symptoms I put to you, but you would expect after death to find some other cause for them as well as the arsenic?"
>
> "Yes."
>
> "That you still say?"
>
> "Yes."
>
> "You are putting it now that the whole of the symptoms are due to arsenic?"
>
> "Yes, of course I am."

In the stiff and sometimes awkward wording of a transcript of evidence it is difficult to detect shades of expression, but this slight variation from monosyllabic assent may have been a reminder that the witness had been saying nothing else for some time, and was not in the least likely to be argued out of his considered opinion. Curtis-Bennett, however, continued to labour the point, that some other cause for the symptoms besides arsenic might have existed. He alluded to what he called the kidney disease from which Mrs Armstrong suffered before she went to the asylum. Spilsbury corrected him; he preferred the phrase "kidney damage." He would not agree that this meant very much the same thing, and the importance of the distinction is obvious. Curtis-Bennett had already touched upon the illness of 1920, and now it was gone into again at some length; but, as the judge had implied earlier, it was not what happened in 1920 that really mattered, but what killed Mrs Armstrong a year afterwards. The cross-examination need not be followed further. Like all great advocates, Curtis-Bennett, for the time being, identified himself with his client, whom, in fact, he rather liked, and whom he thought had a reasonable chance of acquittal. He had put a tremendous amount of work into the case, and he had made the most of the weak points in the evidence for the Crown. But he failed completely to shake Spilsbury's damaging pronouncements as to the cause of both illnesses. Webster and Willcox, who followed him in the witness-box, confirmed them.

6

In countering the case for the Crown the defence had three main difficulties to overcome. It was inevitable that such a defendant, an intelligent professional man, should give evidence on his own behalf. While in the witness-box, which he occupied for more than five hours, Armstrong had to render plausible his explanation of the arsenic found among the contents of his pockets, and in the drawer of his bureau. On the whole he was a cool and collected witness; but on these vital points, when he was taken in hand by the judge, he was very far from convincing. In a statement to the police, before his arrest, he said that he had no arsenic in his possession except in the diluted form of weed-killer. His story was that after he had been charged he discovered the little screw of paper containing white arsenic which had been in his pocket, and which he had forgotten. He said nothing about it, knowing that it must be found when the police went through his letters. Later he remembered the second package, in the bureau drawer. He said nothing about this either, except to his solicitor, Mr Matthews, whom he sent to look for it. It was produced only during the trial. It contained two ounces of white arsenic, probably representing half the last purchase from Mr Davies; and the defence argued that with its discovery all the pure arsenic in Armstrong's possession was accounted for, and that therefore the poison taken by Mrs Armstrong came from some other source—probably weed-killer, which was kept in the house, and which she could have obtained herself. Curtis-Bennett is said to have relied a good deal on this argument, but it postulated the truth of Armstrong's improbable explanation of the smaller, but still fatal, dose in his pocket—that this was the last of some twenty similar little packets used to eradicate individual dandelions on his lawn.

Secondly, the defence had to confute or minimize the evidence of system, as suggested by the poisoning of Martin and by Mrs Armstrong's illness in August 1920. Thirdly, and most difficult of all, they had to persuade the judge and jury, in the teeth of evidence to the contrary from the most experienced medical witnesses in the country, either that Mrs Armstrong had taken the fatal dose a week before she died or that she was capable of getting out of bed and going downstairs to fetch weed-killer on the day of her death.

The jury, listening to the cross-examination of Armstrong about the invitations to tea telephoned across Broad Street, may have thought to themselves that the fatal dose in his pocket would have come in very handy had Martin been induced to eat another buttered scone. Hard upon this, as the accused's long ordeal was drawing to an end, came penetrating questions about his strange forgetfulness at the time of his arrest, and his peculiar and elaborate method of disposing of dandelions. And then, as Armstrong was about to return to the dock, the judge intervened once more.

"Wait a minute, Major Armstrong."

More questions followed, going over the same ground, driving home to the jury the inadequacy of the replies. How did the witness account for having forgotten all about that arsenic, the only white arsenic he ever had? He had used some of it to make up twenty little packets, with nineteen of which he destroyed nineteen dandelions. That was very interesting, was it not? How, then, did he come to forget it? Did it not strike him, a solicitor, that it was very remarkable to forget it? As for the twenty little packets themselves, why go to the trouble of making up the arsenic in that way, instead of pouring it straight from the original paper into holes in the ground?

"I really do not know," said Armstrong. "At the time it seemed the most convenient way of doing it."

The quiet, dry voice from the bench went on. Why, when he did remember this interesting experiment, did he not tell the police? Why, when he remembered the two ounces in his bureau, did he not tell them about that? He was a man accustomed to criminal procedure. If he thought the police were certain to find the arsenic, as he said, would it not have been better to have made a clean breast of it, and take the credit of telling them himself?

All accounts of the trial agree as to the effect of this intervention by the judge. When Armstrong returned to the dock the jury had perhaps made up their minds, if they had not done so before. They heard more evidence for the defence, the most important being that of two doctors who held that Mrs Armstrong's first illness, and that of Martin, might well have been due to natural causes, and that if Mrs Armstrong eventually died of arsenical poisoning it was several days after she had taken the last and fatal dose. This, in short, was to assert that Spilsbury and Webster and Willcox did not know what they were talking about. But the jury knew all about these eminent witnesses; it was well aware of their reputations; and before them it had heard Dr Hincks, who was known, or known of, all over that part of the Welsh border. Dr Hincks was an honest man who made a mistake and admitted it, and with his new knowledge he was the first to use the phrase, of the propositions now being put forward, "absolutely impossible." Again and again, by Spilsbury and Willcox, that phrase had been repeated. Could Mrs Armstrong have lived for a week after taking the last large dose of arsenic? Absolutely impossible. Could she have got out of bed, or lifted a glass to her lips, during the last day or two of her life? Absolutely impossible. Those emphatic words must have been in the minds of the jurymen all the time they listened to Dr Toogood and Dr Ainslie striving to demonstrate the opposite.

The tenth day came, the final speeches had been made, and the judge began his summing-up. Darling made short work of the arguments about the arsenic in the bureau proving anything except possession. The greater part of his charge to the jury related to the medical evidence about Mrs Armstrong's last weeks. In the words he had used earlier, what concerned the jury was what and who killed her. When he had finished he can have left small doubt as to his own views.

All judges had a high opinion of Spilsbury, not merely as the leading authority on forensic medicine, but because of his striking qualities as a witness. Darling seems to have had a particularly high regard for him in this respect. Such qualities made a special appeal to the judge's own neatness and lucidity of mind and strong common sense. In this summing-up Darling made appreciative reference to the abilities and standing of Webster and Willcox, but he went out of his way to emphasize once more the impression made on him by the man he had once called "that incomparable witness." He said to the jury:

"Let us consider who these doctors are. It is for you—you have been told you are the judges of this case, not I. Do you remember Dr Spilsbury? Do you remember how he stood and the way in which he gave evidence? Do you remember how if there were any qualification to be made which told in favour of the defence he always gave it without being asked for it? Did you ever see a witness who more thoroughly satisfied you that he was absolutely impartial, absolutely fair, absolutely indifferent as to whether his evidence told for the one side or the other, when he was giving evidence-in-chief or when he was being cross-examined? You should recollect and consider the demeanour of every witness in every case that you try; and when you consider Dr Spilsbury, when you have to say whether you trust the opinions that he gave, you are entitled then to remember his demeanour, and to form your own opinion as to what it was, and to act accordingly."

Towards the end of the summing-up Darling linked Spilsbury and Willcox in the following remarks:

"Now you see there is the evidence of those doctors who were called for the defence, who, however the arsenic was taken, are confident that it was taken on the 16th or early on the 17th of February; that it was one large dose, and that she never had any other. . . . There is the evidence of Dr Spilsbury, who actually made the post-mortem examination; and he tells you what he found, and he says he is certain from what he saw himself that that arsenic was taken within twenty-four hours of death. He is not merely theorizing; that is from what he saw. There is Sir William Willcox, who is admitted to be as great an authority as any on the subject, and he says he is satisfied that there must have been this dose within twenty-four hours of death; and he used the remarkable expression that what was found put the theory of suicide out of court. . . ."

In the minds of the jury, no doubt, it had long been put out of court, and after reading this summing-up it is surprising to hear that an acquittal was very generally expected. In Hereford they were betting five to one on it. What seems even more surprising—for apparently it was a sincere expression of belief—Curtis-Bennett himself said to a newspaper-man, "I have been in forty-eight murder trials, for and against, and I have never known the verdict so open." Perhaps great advocates sometimes convince themselves by their own advocacy, and memories of the Greenwood case may have prompted popular misconceptions, which were encouraged, even in the Shire Hall, by the absence of the jury for fifty minutes. Armstrong, always buoyant, must have felt increasingly confident as time went by.

Yet, in fact—or so the story goes—almost as soon as the jury had retired it was all over. It is possible that the eloquence of Curtis-Bennett and the Attorney-General was rather wasted on the eight farmers, the fruit-grower, and the three "gentlemen," who made up the jury, but for ten days they had been doing what Darling recommended them to do: they had been studying the demeanour of the witnesses, including the accused. At any rate, eleven of them, it is said, were for a verdict of guilty outright; the twelfth man wrote on his slip of paper, "Not proven." But he hastened to explain this to the foreman. "Well, Tom, you know what 'not proven' means. I think he did it." This twelfth man bore a grudge against Darling, before whom he had once lost a civil case, and he seized the opportunity to be obstructive. On such things may justice sometimes turn; but in this case the obstructionist, having made his gesture, fell into line with the rest. "After which," to quote Filson Young, "the foreman, finding they were all agreed, was alleged to have said, 'We've heard enough of the case, and we needn't discuss it any more. Let's have a quiet smoke before we go back into court.' "

Darling had reminded the jury that if he was wrong in admitting as evidence the story of Martin's poisoning that would be enough to upset the whole proceedings. The Court of Criminal Appeal could quash them on the ground of misdirection. That court, however, upheld his action, and on May 16 Armstrong's appeal was dismissed. During the last fortnight of his life the English climate performed one of its celebrated transformations: a bitter winter and spring were succeeded by a heat-wave. At the end of the month Spilsbury, less busy than usual, was engaged on the case of George Grimshaw, murdered by the Yeldhams, who were arrested on the 29th. The P. and O. mail steamer *Morea* had returned to Plymouth from the Mediterranean, and a young steward or writer named Frederick Bywaters was spending in London the last leave he was ever to complete. On the 31st Armstrong was hanged.

Chapter 8: UNPLEASANT THINGS ON THE CRUMBLES

WHEN Spilsbury was giving evidence against Patrick Herbert Mahon in the County Hall at Lewes his thoughts must have gone back to another trial for murder held there four years earlier. The same judge presided; counsel now leading for the prosecution and the defence had been in that trial too, and similarly opposed; he himself had played a part in the case, though for once only a small preliminary one, in the background. Nor did coincidence end there. The scene of both crimes was the same strip of the Sussex shore called the Crumbles, and since he must have followed the earlier trial at the time, he may now have recalled the unwittingly prophetic words of Marshall Hall, who had defended one of the accused. Hall asked a witness whether the Crumbles was not a place where unpleasant things happened. "I am not suggesting," he was careful to add, "that murders go on there."

Murders, however, were among the unpleasant things that were to go on there.

The Crumbles is the aptly descriptive name of a melancholy stretch of shingle, more than two miles long with a greatest depth of nearly a mile, which extends from Eastbourne to Wallsend, on Pevensey Bay. The road from one place to the other forms its western boundary. In the early 1920's its dreariness was diversified by a fringe of tough undergrowth beside the road, a few sheds, a seaplane base at the Eastbourne end, and a railway-track, a branch of the London, Brighton, and South Coast Railway, used to collect shingle for ballast. Along the Wallsend Road were dotted cottages and bungalows, among them being a group of buildings, to become notorious, which had been a coastguard station.

On August 20, 1920, the body of a girl was found roughly buried in the shingle near the terminus of the railway-track, a few hundred yards from high-water mark. She was identified as Irene Munro, a seventeen-year-old London typist on holiday in Eastbourne. Her head had been terribly injured by a blow or blows from an ironstone brick and from some implement like a stick.

Two post-mortems were performed, the first by the local police surgeon, the second, at the request of the Home Office, by a London pathologist. In the meantime two young men named Field and Gray were detained by the Eastbourne police, only to be released two days later. It was at this point that the Home Office called upon Spilsbury to give his opinion on the injuries; on his case-card he wrote as follows:

> Injuries to the left face consistent with a single blow by the blood-stained stone if the head was resting on the shingle on the right side, accounting for right injuries. From amount of blood extravasated, slow rate of bleeding and shock. Probably survived for short time—might have been ½ hour, but would be deeply unconscious all the time. Death might have been accelerated by weight of shingle on body compressing chest. Thus death may have been due to combined effects of shock and loss of blood and asphyxia. *May have* been blood on assailant.

It was only in this advisory capacity that Spilsbury came into the case. He did not give evidence against Field and Gray, who had been taken into custody a second time and charged with the murder. Tried before Avory at the Sussex Autumn Assizes, both were convicted and executed. This fleeting association with the Crumbles was not, however, to be the end of Spilsbury's connexion with that sinister tract.

A man and a woman who were to know it only too well were no doubt among the millions who read and discussed the tragic story of Irene Munro. At that time they had not met. Like Miss Munro, Emily Beilby Kaye began to earn her living early in life, at seventeen, the age at which the other girl was to die. She came of a substantial middle-class family, and was a practical, intelligent woman, who no doubt thought, as she read of the pathetic victim of Field and Gray, that here was a case far outside the possible experience of such as herself. She was not in the habit of forming promiscuous acquaintanceships with dubious young men.

In 1920 she was no longer young; she was thirty-four, but still unattached. In 1923, when she went to live at the Green Cross Club in Guilford Street, Bloomsbury, she was employed as shorthand-typist by a firm of chartered accountants with offices in Copthall Avenue. One of the partners, Mr Hobbins, for whom she worked, had been appointed, as the result of a debenture holder's action, receiver and manager of a concern called the Consols Automatic Aerators, Ltd, of Sunbury-on-Thames. In turn Mr Hobbins had appointed, as sales manager under him, a salesman with the firm named

Patrick Herbert Mahon. Mahon often visited the offices in Copthall Avenue, and so became friendly with Emily Kaye.

If Mahon had tried to scrape up acquaintance with her in the street, as he did with Ethel Duncan and, no doubt, many others, she would probably have put him firmly in his place. She was accustomed to look after herself, and she was not like Irene Munro. But this friendship, in every respect but one, was quite in order; Mahon, four years younger than herself (though to him she gave her age as twenty-nine), was a man in an excellent position, earning an excellent salary, and the trusted deputy of her Mr Hobbins. He was good-looking, dressed well, and had an easy charm that made him popular not only in her office, but in Richmond, where he lived, and where his social gifts made him in demand. He was honorary secretary of a bowls club there, and in a book in which members appended facetious descriptions of themselves he wrote beside his name, "A Broth of a Bhoy, who deserved to have been born at sea." He had been christened plain Herbert, but Patrick seemed more in keeping with his surname and with the character he sedulously cultivated. He was very vain, and must always, even in the most daunting circumstances, make a good impression. He had other interesting qualities: he quoted the Latin classics and spoke French fluently, and, like St Francis, whom he resembled in no other way, he had a remarkable influence over animals. Those who like to think that animals know good people from bad will be distressed to learn that Mahon had only to whistle and birds came to him, and that dogs and cats deserted their masters and mistresses to follow him home.

With Emily Kaye his blandishments succeeded only too well. She was at a dangerous age, and she fell passionately in love with him. It was a slight drawback that he was married, a fact he could not conceal at her office had he wished to, since Mrs Mahon was also employed by the firm in Sunbury, and was often on the telephone. She had, indeed, found her husband his post there, after a curious episode of which Miss Kaye, at any rate at first, knew nothing. Mahon doubtless spun to her the tale he told Miss Duncan, probably his regular gambit—that his married life was a tragedy. The courage and ready smile with which he bore his sorrows may further have endeared him to Mr Hobbins's secretary, who seems to have made no attempt to discover the truth about his home life, as, in the circumstances, she could easily have done. Mahon, in fact, owed everything to his wife, of whom nothing but good is known; and hers was the tragedy.

In view of events, and of Mahon's character as a persistent

philanderer, his version of the relationship between him and Emily Kaye may very well be true—that she was a determined and possessive woman, who would not let him go. Moreover, after they began to go about together the inevitable happened, and early in 1924 she probably knew that she was going to have a child. Edgar Wallace tells a story, which, if authentic, explains why Mahon could not escape from the entanglement. It will be referred to later.

In the meantime Miss Kaye's employment in Copthall Avenue had been terminated. With her experience and excellent references she should have found other work easily, but, except for a month, when she took a temporary post, she seems to have done nothing after October 1923. Having money put by, she was in no immediate need of work; and, besides, she had a different future in view.

At the Green Cross Club, where Mahon sometimes called for her, he was known as Derek Patterson, or "Pat" for short. This apparently was her own suggestion; a girl at the club had friends who knew him, and it would be a nuisance if rumours reached his wife. It was all one to Mahon, who would call himself anything. Wife or no wife, he was now Emily Kaye's fiancé, and in March 1924 she was showing her friends a diamond and sapphire engagement ring, and writing to her sister about going to South Africa with "Pat," who had a good post waiting for him there. She was realizing her invested capital of rather over £600, and nearly half this sum, in three £100 notes, passed into Mahon's hands. His story of transactions in francs was not convincing, still less his explanation of the different false name and address he gave when changing each note; but, as the judge observed during the trial, this financial episode was of secondary importance. Miss Kaye undoubtedly gave the notes to Mahon. On April 7 she herself was buying 7400 francs with most of the balance of her capital. She had already arranged to give up her room at the club; and that same day she finally left Guilford Street.

Ten days later, on the 17th, her friend Miss Warren received a letter from her. Though dated the 14th, and written on the notepaper of an Eastbourne hotel, it had been posted only the previous evening, that of the 16th, and in London, in S.W.1. In it was the news that "Pat" and Emily Kaye were together, and were going to Paris for Easter, which fell on the following week-end. They would be in London for a short time before setting out on their "final journey." It is improbable that this really meant a voyage to South Africa; Mahon's story is worth nothing, and he certainly had no intention of leaving England; and it has been seen that Emily Kaye, having burnt her boats, had no scruples about small deceptions. Whatever plan was in her mind, by the time her letter reached Miss Warren she had already gone on her final journey.

2

At the Pevensey end of the Crumbles, on the Wallsend Road, stood what had been Langney Coastguard Station—a terrace of small white-washed, single-storied quarters and a larger detached residence, with half a dozen rooms, still known as the Officer's House. The whole group of buildings was enclosed by a brick and concrete wall, from which the shingle sloped to the sea. Inland stretched a flat and desolate country, and the next nearest habitation, in 1924, was some distance away. Close at hand was the spot where Irene Munro's body had been found. It was not, it might be thought, an ideal scene for a romantic and illicit love affair.

People lived there, however, and the Officer's House, which for letting purposes was styled a bungalow, was the property of a Mrs Hutchinson. At the end of March that year she asked her friend Mr Muir, who lived in the Victoria neighbourhood, to advertise that the bungalow was to let. The advertisement appeared in the *Daily Telegraph* of April 4, and that day a Mr Waller telephoned about it. There was an interview, Mr Waller saw the bungalow, and agreed to take it from April 11 at a rent of 3½ guineas a week. On the following day, as it happened, Muir again met Mr Waller, who was carrying a bag, in Victoria Street. He was to have cause to remember the date and place of that meeting.

Easter came and went—Good Friday was the 18th—and in a boarding-house in Pagoda Avenue, Richmond, Mrs Mahon was beginning to worry about her husband's erratic movements. For two week-ends he had been away, sending her telegrams from Eastbourne, Bexhill, and Vauxhall Bridge Road, and giving explanations more plausible than convincing. An acquaintance had seen him at Plumpton Races on Easter Monday, which suggested that he was up to old tricks that had cost her dear before—though not so dear as some of his other ones. As one more week-end came round, the last in the month, and he was absent again, she searched the pockets of his numerous suits for a clue. She found a cloakroom ticket from Waterloo. A friend who had been in the railway police agreed to investigate. At Waterloo he withdrew a locked Gladstone bag, and by forcing open the ends discovered enough to send him straight to Scotland Yard.

This was on May Day, a Thursday. Chief Inspector Savage

examined the bag that evening, and left an officer to watch the cloak-room. For a few hours more Mrs Mahon was left in ignorance of the fact that the contents of the bag were beyond her worst imaginings. She was told only that they had nothing to do with betting or book-makers, as she had feared. The ticket was back in her husband's coat pocket, and her mind must have been more or less at ease, for he was with her that night, and she held her tongue.

The next evening, that of Friday, May 2, a very good-looking young man, whom Mr Muir was to recognize as Waller, called at Waterloo for his Gladstone bag, and was stopped by Detective-Constable Thompson. Taken to Kennington Road Police Station, he was asked to explain how this piece of luggage came to contain a number of bloodstained articles, including a cook's knife, and a racquet-case marked E.B.K., all sprinkled with disinfectant. A story about dog's meat failed to account for the blood, for it was human; and presently, after long intervals of silence—they must have been terrible æons to Patrick Mahon—he told a very different tale.

It was not the truth either; that was to be laboriously established, largely by Spilsbury, in what, technically speaking, was one of the masterpieces of his long and immensely varied professional career.

3

Spilsbury was once asked at a banquet which of the famous cases in which he was concerned he considered the most difficult. He said he thought the Crumbles case the most interesting he had had. After sifting all the evidence available it was obvious that the police could not make out a very good case against the accused, yet nothing was to be gained by waiting, and it was agreed to take the case to court with but a poor hope of success. As it proceeded, the case against the accused gradually revealed itself, until by the end there was no shadow of doubt about his guilt. "It gradually took shape as in building up a jigsaw puzzle," said Spilsbury.

These are very instructive observations, if only because they read rather surprisingly to-day, when the case against Mahon appears to have been as complete from the beginning as such a case could be. No one now believes his story, nor did the police believe a word of it then; the difficulty lay in disproving it beyond that 'shadow of doubt' which haunts every jury in a trial for murder. Spilsbury's remarks are instructive, again, because they are typical; there is not a word to suggest that his own enormous labours, and the weight of his reputation, put the coping-stone on the no less thorough constructive work of the C.I.D.

Mahon's story, told at Kennington on May 2, brought the local police to the Officer's House the next day; and on the morning of Saturday, the 4th, Chief Inspector Savage and other officers travelled to Eastbourne. With them were Spilsbury and his new assistant, Mrs Bainbridge. The widow of a former professor at Bart's who had been Spilsbury's friend, she had applied for work at the hospital after her husband's death. Sent to the pathological department to help in the museum, she developed an interest in post-mortem work, and was allowed (an unusual privilege) to watch Spilsbury in his laboratory. A highly intelligent woman, she became before long his assistant, and wrote up his findings at his dictation as he went along. She held this post until her early death a few years later. Spilsbury soon appreciated the convenience of having a secretary, and as Mrs Bainbridge's nerves proved equal to the most grisly tasks she was presently accompanying him on cases that took him far from the hospital, and even out of London. The crime at the Crumbles was the first major investigation in which she shared.

It was to prove the most shocking. After that long day's work at the Officer's House, much of it in the spring sunshine in a small high-walled courtyard which was part of the shingly garden, Spilsbury himself, inured to horrors, said the human remains discovered there were the most gruesome he had ever seen.

The front door of the house opened into what was now called the lounge, comfortably furnished in a commonplace style, with a wall-paper of shrubs in pots, a cretonne-covered settee and chair, a good carpet, and two oil-lamps on a corner cupboard. An incongruous addition—the police had brought it from the scullery—was a two-gallon saucepan on the brick hearth. In the more utilitarian dining-room another big saucepan stood in the fireplace, beside a saucer and a flimsy coal-scuttle in the form of a cauldron with hollow tripod legs, one of them bent. There was solid, old-fashioned stuff in the bed-rooms, and in one of them, as well, a capacious fibre trunk with the initials E.B.K. painted on it, a leather kitbag, and a square hat-box. A galvanized iron bath and an enamelled basin had converted a large scullery into a bathroom.

When Spilsbury and his companions, watched by a growing crowd of spectators, entered the bungalow on that May morning, the sauce-pans had been uncovered, and the contents of the trunk and the hat-box, which now stood in the scullery, lay exposed. Spilsbury put on his long white apron and rubber gloves and went from room to room, picking up objects, examining them, turning them over, and collecting them in the scullery. He looked at the appalling luggage, peered into the saucepans and the bath and the basin. Then he had the kitchen table taken into the little courtyard, beyond which the police were digging among the pebbles and coarse grass of the garden. For three hours he worked there, Savage and other officers standing by, and Mrs Bainbridge making notes. Altogether Spilsbury spent eight hours in the bungalow that day. When he left, after dusk, hundreds of people still stood staring on the Crumbles, and among the cars drawn up on the road.

There had been found, in the order in which Spilsbury described them at the trial:

On a rusty tenon saw, grease and a piece of flesh. Articles of female clothing, greasy and bloodstained, some with soot or coal-dust on them. On the cauldron-shaped coal scuttle, two minute specks of blood. In the saucer near it, solidified fat. The two-gallon saucepan in the same fireplace was half full of a reddish fluid, with a thick layer of grease on the surface; this contained a piece of boiled human flesh, the skin adhering to it. The metal fender was splashed with grease. There was more grease deposited in the second saucepan, and smeared in the bath and basin. In the hat-box, among soiled articles of clothing, were thirty-seven pieces of flesh, cut or sawn. All were human, and all had apparently been boiled. The big fibre trunk held four large pieces of human body, sawn apart, but not boiled. On one of these pieces, a left chest and shoulder, there was a bruise over the shoulder-blade, the result of a blow inflicted before death; if only a few minutes before, it had been, in Spilsbury's opinion, a heavy blow. There was also in the trunk a biscuit-tin containing various organs.

This was not all. The police had already found a large stain of human blood on a carpet, the blood having soaked through to a felt drugget beneath, and then to the floor-boards. In the leather kitbag were a woman's brush and comb, a gold wrist-watch, and jewellery. There were six hats, and other articles from a woman's wardrobe, in the bedrooms. There was an axe, its haft broken. Among the cutlery, an inventory of which was in Mahon's pocket, was a carving-knife; the distinction between this and the cook's knife found in the Gladstone bag at Waterloo, emphasized by Spilsbury in his evidence at the trial, had an important bearing on Mahon's own story. So had the construction and condition of the coal-cauldron. Finally, in fireplaces and in a dustpan was a quantity of coal and other ash; and this Spilsbury sifted with his customary infinite care, recovering from it nearly a thousand fragments of calcined bone, much merely dust, but many of the splinters still identifiable as human. Some he was able even then to fit together.

In short, these horrible *disjecta membra* comprised most of a female human body. The skull and upper part of the neck, and the lower portion of one leg, were missing. Flesh and bone went back with Spilsbury to Bart's; and that night, after the staff had left, he began his final task in the preparation room, next to the post-mortem room. He worked till 6.30 the next morning, carried out his usual duties during the day, and resumed work on the remains in the evening. By the second morning, that of May 6, he had discovered all that it was possible to discover, medically speaking, about the fate of Emily Kaye.

If this was not much it was as a feat of reconstruction probably one which no other man could have accomplished. Remnants by the hundred, such as Spilsbury himself never before or after handled, boiled and burnt, sawn, hewn, and pulverized, all fragmentary and many minute, were pieced together during those two nights' single-handed labour. Trunk and organs were reassembled; from a mound of brittle incinerated bone-dust portions of the legs, the tibia, the right femur, and left radius were sorted and united. There were particles of both hands. When Spilsbury employed the hackneyed comparison of the jigsaw puzzle to describe the case as a whole he must have been thinking of its grimmer application to his own masterpiece.

His conclusions are set out in sufficient detail in his evidence at the trial, when he said:

> "All the material which I have examined, portions of the trunk, the organs, pieces of boiled flesh, and those fragments of bone which I have been able to identify, are all of them human, and correspond with parts of a single body: there are no duplicates at all. The four pieces of chest and abdominal wall fit accurately to form one trunk, and the organs in the tin box, together with the fragments of organs attached to the four pieces of trunk, form a complete set of human organs, with the exception of certain missing portions, of which the uterus and one ovary are the most important. The body was that of an adult female of big build and fair hair. She was pregnant, in my opinion, at the time of her death, and at an early period, probably between one and three months. There was no indication of any previous pregnancy or of pregnancy which had run its full term. The organs were those of a healthy person, and the adhesions round the right lung were the only indications of previous disease. No disease was found to account for natural death, and no condition which would account for unnatural death."

4

As these last words reveal, in one sense all this patient and intricate work went for nothing. Before Spilsbury left London for the Officer's House he knew that the remains were those of a woman named Emily Kaye. What the police wanted to be told was how she had died; and that not even he could tell them.

He could, however, say how she had *not* died, and so undermined the whole structure of Mahon's defence.

If Mahon's detention at Waterloo had not taken him completely by surprise, or if he had given thought beforehand to the story he might some day have to tell, it is just possible that he would have escaped the gallows. But among the lies he told three were fatal; one was easily disproved by routine police inquiries, and the other two by Spilsbury.

Mahon had not been detained for many hours before the police discovered that they knew a good deal about him. Of Liverpool-Irish stock, with a certain quick intelligence as well as plausible manners and good looks, his youth had been outwardly exemplary. Like Thorne and other murderers, he was regular in attendance at Sunday school, and later at church, and active in various social affairs. He was good at games. He married, in 1910, when he was only twenty, a girl two years younger. A year later he was taking another girl to the Isle of Man with money obtained by forged cheques. Bound over for this offence, he was soon sentenced to twelve months for embezzlement. This was in Wiltshire; some time after his release he appeared at Sunningdale, in Surrey. He could not keep away from women, and apparently the notoriety of his love affairs cost him his job there. He picked up others where he could, chiefly on race-courses, and then, in 1916, he broke into a bank and stunned a maidservant with a hammer. It was in character that he lingered until his victim had recovered her senses, when he tried his blandishments on her, kissing and fondling her, and explaining that he had not really meant to hurt her. He was tried at the Guildford Assizes before Darling, who proved insusceptible to charm of manner; and when Mahon went to prison again it was for five years.

It was this episode, according to Edgar Wallace, which gave Emily Kaye a hold over him. She was lining a drawer with a clean sheet of newspaper, and as she pulled out the old sheet she saw on it a report of the trial at Guildford.

Young Mrs Mahon had stood by her husband throughout. There

were two children of the marriage, but the younger one, a boy, died while his father was in prison. Mrs Mahon, in the meantime, had come to London and found work with the Consols Automatic Aerators Company at Sunbury. When Mahon had served his sentence her recommendation secured him a position with the firm as salesman. She herself, by her own endeavours and ability, in time became secretary. Mahon, it will be noted, always came back to her; and it is a tragic aspect of this case that with her help he might now have made something of his life. When the company was put in the hands of a receiver he too was promoted, at a salary of £750 a year. Not a soul in Kew or Richmond, except his wife, knew that he was an ex-convict, and still under observation by the police.

Murderers who have to account for a dead body adopt one or other of certain well-worn explanations. Some, like Voisin, talk of a plot; some, like Thorne, put their trust in suicide. The variant used by Mahon was the quarrel, the struggle, and the accidental death. But his story, concocted during that nerve-racking evening at Kennington Road police-station, was full of improbabilities and more serious defects, and later versions did not improve it.

Miss Kaye travelled to Eastbourne on April 7. Mahon joined her on the 11th, a Friday, to take over the Officer's House, returning to London for the night. He had already given false names, addresses, and references all over the place—when changing the first two £100 notes and to Mr Muir. Meeting Muir the next morning, that of Saturday, the 12th, in Victoria Street, he told another and apparently unnecessary lie, either from force of habit or as part of a plan already formed, but never carried out. He was then on his way to the bungalow, and after the meeting he made some purchases, among them a cook's knife and a tenon saw, also called a cook's saw. In his first statement to the police Mahon said he bought these implements on the 17th, when Emily Kaye was dead; only at the police-court hearing at Hailsham, when a duplicate invoice from the ironmonger's shop was produced, did he admit that, as he put it, he had made a mistake about the date. It was a vital and fatal 'mistake.' The reasons he proceeded to give for making such purchases while Miss Kaye was alive carried no weight at all when produced at so late a stage.

Since, however, this afterthought was his only counter to the charge of premeditation, Mahon attempted to bolster it up by denying that he used the cook's knife on the body. Emily Kaye had handled it, and for sentimental reasons he preferred to cut her up with the carving-knife belonging to the bungalow. At the trial Spilsbury was recalled to dispose of this nauseating piece of hypocrisy. The carving-knife could not have done the work. "It would be no good to cut through skin." A much sharper knife had been used. Nor was there the faintest trace on the carver of the blood which must have spurted over it and into the junction of blade and handle; on the contrary, grease and emery-powder showed that it had last been used for normal domestic purposes. On the cook's knife, designed to slice raw flesh, Webster's tests had found suggestions of blood.

The next most disastrous mistake in Mahon's story was his account of how his victim died. In a struggle with him Emily Kaye fell backward, carrying him with her, and striking her head on the cauldron-shaped coal-scuttle. These scuttles were sold for a few shillings by the thousand—insubstantial things of which the legs tended to buckle and the bottoms to wear through quickly. When Spilsbury was in the witness-box Curtis-Bennett, who led for the Crown, questioned him on this point, as did the judge.

Curtis-Bennett first asked, "In your opinion could Miss Kaye have received rapidly fatal injuries from falling upon that coal-cauldron?"

"No, in my opinion she could not," replied Spilsbury.

Mr Justice Avory then intervened: "Just put it in another way. Do I understand in your opinion a fall upon that coal-cauldron would not cause her rapid death?"

"That is so."

In answer to J. D. Cassels, for the defence, Spilsbury amplified these concise replies: "No fall on the coal-cauldron such as you have described would be capable of inflicting such injuries to the head as to cause rapidly fatal results. If that particular cauldron, filled with coal, were the one referred to, a sufficiently severe blow to produce such injury would have crumpled up the cauldron."

Setting aside all Mahon's other shifts, prevarications, and downright lies, probably nothing did him more harm with the jury than the true story of Ethel Duncan. Late on the evening of April 10, the day before he and Emily Kaye took over the Officer's House, he met Miss Duncan in Richmond. Out of work and unhappy, she was walking home in the rain; Mahon, heedless of his entanglement with Miss Kaye, to say nothing of his devoted wife waiting for him a few streets away, or of plans of murder which probably were then taking shape in his thoughts, succumbed at once to the impulse to philander with a nice-looking young woman. A few days later, on Wednesday the 16th, Miss Duncan was having dinner with him at Victoria. Emily

Kaye had been dead barely twenty-four hours. While her body lay locked in a spare bedroom, Ethel Duncan spent the next week-end, that of Easter, with Mahon at the bungalow. His explanation of this episode, so tragic for Miss Duncan, and so extraordinary at first sight, was that for some days after the murder he could not bear to be alone in that house; and this no doubt was the truth. But it did not go down well with those who heard and saw him.

For he made a poor impression in the witness-box. He did his best; he bought a new suit for the occasion, and contrived somehow to darken his face to give the effect of tan. (An innocent reporter wrote of him in the dock: "The bronzed hue of his fine features was a tribute to the extent to which prisoners are now allowed open-air exercise.") He is said to have been confident, almost until the end, that his looks and charm would spellbind the jury, and even Mr Justice Avory. But his manner was either too jaunty or too dramatic. Avory, in his most chilling way, kept recalling him to the point with such interjections as "All this is so vague," or "You were asked what you did, not all this imagination." Under Curtis-Bennett's cross-examination Mahon must have begun to feel hope slipping away; and, before that, a startling coincidence shattered his self-assurance. At Brixton Prison he had told Cassels how he built up a great fire in the bungalow, and in it placed Emily Kaye's severed head. The day was stormy, and as the long fair hair flamed up the dead eyes opened, and, at the same instant, thunder crashed overhead and lightning blazed. Terrified, Mahon ran out into the rain. Now, on the third day of the trial, Cassels was again questioning him about those fearful hours when he was cutting and sawing and boiling the remains of the woman who had loved him. The July weather was dark and sultry, and as Cassels began to ask about the head, and Mahon replied, again a thunderclap reverberated through the court-room, and the lightning flashed. Mahon shrank back, gripping the edge of the witness-box. He was white and shaken as he answered the further questions with which the day's hearing closed.

He was not acting then; but there remains an element of mystery about his disposal of the head. The most ghastly item in this catalogue of horrors is his account of how he broke it up with a poker. Spilsbury's meticulous sifting of ash and bone, which produced so much else, found no trace of it. It was considered doubtful whether it could have been wholly destroyed by an ordinary coal-fire, though to settle an argument Spilsbury put a sheep's head on such a fire and reduced it to unrecognizable ashes in four hours. Yet speculation is still unresolved. Did Mahon get rid of the head, half burnt and pounded to powder, by throwing it into the sea, or (as he got rid of certain other remains) from a railway carriage? It is believed that he killed Emily Kaye by a blow with the axe on her head or neck so violent that it splintered the haft. In such a case he must cause the head to disappear completely, so that should suspicion fall on him he could put forward his story of the quarrel and the accident. Prolonged efforts were made, in vain, to find the head. Dogs were employed, and acres of shingle were raked and riddled. There was rejoicing over the discovery, in a brickfield near Pevensey, of bone fragments and a dental plate; but the bones were not human, and the plate was not Miss Kaye's. Nor was a human leg found on Wimbledon Common the limb missing from the Crumbles remains.

5

Mahon having been convicted, his appeal failed, as it was bound to fail, and he was hanged on September 9. According to the biographers of Curtis-Bennett,

> he was "doubly hanged." It seemed that he had a certain amount of knowledge of the procedure of the executioner. He knew that his feet must stand within two chalk-marks as the rope was adjusted round his neck. He knew that immediately after the fixing of the hood the executioner would move swiftly to a lever and cause the platform on which he stood to swing away from under him. As he sensed that Pierrepoint moved to the lever, Mahon jerked his bound feet forward in a wild attempt to place them on the stationary part of the platform. At that moment the lever was pulled and his body swung back, the base of the spine striking with terrific force against the sharp edge of the platform. That blow killed him, and half a second later the spine was again broken at the neck by the jerk of the rope.[1]

Spilsbury's case-card notes that the spine was dislocated between the fourth and fifth cervical vertebræ, and that between the sixth and seventh vertebræ there was much displacement backward of the upper part. There is no mention, however, of any bruise resulting from the blow against the edge of the platform, which seems to dispose of the story.

At this point it may be asked how Spilsbury's filing cabinets come to contain a card for the murderer, as well as one for his victim; and the answer is of considerable interest.

[1] Roland Wild and Derek Curtis-Bennett, *"Curtis"; the Life of Sir Henry Curtis-Bennett, K.C.* (Cassell, 1937).

A reporter who knew Spilsbury was surprised to meet him at Wandsworth Prison on the morning of the execution. He was carrying the inevitable black bag. Asked why he was there, he replied that he was performing the post-mortem on Mahon's body. He was doing the routine work of the prison, and doing it in his usual painstaking way. The normal practice in such post-mortems is to open the neck to confirm the obvious cause of death. Spilsbury, however, opened the body right down, and then spent another hour examining the brain, a portion of which he took away with him. To the coroner, who suggested that he was being unnecessarily thorough, he said, "I must do this in my own way."

It was his first autopsy of this kind, but by no means his last. It had occurred to him that here was a form of sudden death, not uncommon, which no one before had thought of investigating with the thoroughness applied as a matter of course to other fatalities. It must also have struck him that a series of such investigations would have a comparative value of their own. In every case the time of death would be known to a second, and the post-mortem could be carried out at the statutory hour, or at any other precise interval, after hanging. From 1924 onward the heading "Judicial Hanging" is found once or twice a year among his cards, and latterly much more often. Altogether he must have performed at least fifty of these prison post-mortems. Whether or no his researches advanced medical science, they produced one curious and interesting by-product. He went into the whole matter with his friend Bentley Purchase, the coroner, who has had his own wide experience of judicial executions; and at their recommendation the drop, which is varied according to a formula involving simple calculations of weight, and which, for obvious reasons, must not be too long, was increased on humanitarian grounds by three inches.

Spilsbury's remarkable work in the Mahon case was generally recognized. The Director of Public Prosecutions, Sir Archibald Bodkin, wrote to him in these terms:

My dear Spilsbury,

I feel quite sure that you will not have expected to receive a letter from me, but at the same time I think I ought to write and acknowledge the extreme value of the services to the public which you have once more afforded in the case of Mahon. Your visits to Pevensey and your investigations there, and the subsequent minute examination of those gruesome exhibits in London, must have entailed upon you very considerable labour, but at the same time I know you will not have grudged that when you appreciate as fully as I that you were throwing light upon what is generally described as one of the foulest crimes which has been committed, certainly in recent years, and I am sure that the learned Judge and jury, Counsel, and last but not least myself, have deeply appreciated the care and skill which you have brought to bear upon the matter.

Chapter 9: THE THORNE CASE—SPILSBURY AND BRONTË

THE crimes of Patrick Mahon and Norman Thorne are linked by time, place, and circumstance, and perhaps by the sincerest form of flattery. Both were committed in Sussex, and in the same year. Both murderers had the same lower-middle-class background; Thorne's Sunday school was Wesleyan, and he was a member of the Band of Hope and an organizer of boys' clubs. Like Mahon, he was caught up in an amorous entanglement from which he wished to free himself, and throughout the former's association with Emily Kaye, the second victim, Elsie Cameron, was visiting the squalid poultry farm at Blackness, near Crowborough, only twenty miles from the Crumbles. She was murdered three months almost to a day after Mahon's execution, and the two crimes are marked by very similar features. This may not have been accidental; Thorne followed the earlier case closely, collecting newspaper cuttings about it, and it has been remarked that he profited by his studies, avoiding many of Mahon's mistakes. Like Mahon, he was finally trapped by one of those chances against which method and foresight cannot guard. He too was tried at Lewes, and once more, for the third time in little over four years, familiar figures appeared in the County Hall—Curtis-Bennett and J. D. Cassels, Inspector McBride, of New Scotland Yard, with his photographs, and Spilsbury. Now, however, the judge was not Avory, and there was a picturesque newcomer, with a flavour of the Battle of the Nile and *Wuthering Heights* about his name, in the person of Dr Robert Matthew Brontë.

The two cases, moreover, are linked in Spilsbury's career. The second followed close upon the first; its problems were similar; and, if they did not afford him opportunities for so remarkable a feat as the piecing together of the Crumbles remains, upon that technical triumph ensued one of personality and prestige. The trial of Thorne was to bring him, for the first time for many years, into conflict with an array of prominent men in his profession. The outcome was a public display of the professional jealousy of his outstanding position which, in some quarters, had long been coming to a head.

Its medico-legal aspect apart, the case of Norman Thorne is of real interest only to psychologists. Thorne had none of the *panache* which Mahon possessed in abundance; he was a rather dull, though not unintelligent, young man, who must have had very strong nerves, and who was to prove himself a good actor and a most plausible liar. Something coldblooded about him altogether alienates sympathy, and his smaller vices were sordid. Up to his twenty-fourth year he had led an outwardly respectable, but seldom prosperous, life, and in December 1924 he had been struggling for two years to make a success of his poultry-farm near Crowborough. But he was in difficulties again, and largely to save money he was then living in squalid conditions in a small hut built as a brooding-house, set in a waste of mud and wire netting, and with only the depressing company of hens.

Elsie Cameron is an equally unattractive figure—neurotic, not even clever, unable to keep a post because of ill-health or inefficiency, her little mind filled almost exclusively with thoughts of sex and marriage. It may be to Thorne's credit that for two years he seems to have made no serious attempt to break the ill-starred engagement into which the pair had drifted. On the other hand, he was never during that period in a position to marry, so that he may have felt that there was no need to bother, and Elsie Cameron was only too ready to offer him what he seems to have valued above looks or brains. Elsie Cameron herself, however, held different views. By the summer of 1924 she was continually talking of marriage, money or no money; a fortune-teller had told her that the wedding would be in December. She had often stayed in the neighbourhood of the poultry-farm, and sometimes spent the night in Thorne's hut, and next she was telling him that she was pregnant—which was not true, though she may for a time have believed it—and urging him to hasten things. But by now Thorne had got to know a more attractive local girl, Elizabeth Coldicott, and by the end of November that year he was writing to his fiancée to say that he was between two fires. After the angry reply which he may have hoped to provoke he went further, not hesitating to blacken the character of his new friend. This brought Elsie Cameron down to Groombridge station and the brooding-house on the afternoon of December 5, full of the violent determination of the weak. She was not going to leave Thorne again.

Nor did she. Five days later her father was telegraphing for news of her, and Thorne was telegraphing back that he did not understand, writing the same day to say that he had been expecting her on the morning of the 6th, but that she had not arrived. The police began inquiries, and found him anxious to be helpful. He readily allowed them to search his farm and his hut; he called at Crowborough Police Station with queries and suggestions. He talked freely to everybody, including Pressmen, who photographed him feeding his fowls and holding them in his arms. To one of them Thorne said he wanted his portrait taken at a particular spot. What impulse of cynicism or bravado moved him can only be conjectured; it was the spot where Elsie Cameron's body was soon afterwards found.

Two men, one of whom knew the girl by sight, had seen her in the dusk of the late afternoon of December 5 walking towards the poultry-farm, carrying her small dressing-case. Their stories do not seem to have interested the Crowborough police. Another neighbour, a woman, also saw her, actually turning into the gate of the farm. Somehow this witness did not hear of the local mystery until more than a month later. It was only then, on the strength of her report to the police on January 10 or 11, that Scotland Yard was called in. On the 14th Thorne made a long statement which was merely an amplification of earlier ones. But while it was being taken down at Crowborough digging had begun at the poultry-farm; and the next day Elsie Cameron's dressing-case was found. Thorne, who had been detained, was told that he would probably be charged with causing her death. The game was up; and he made yet another statement, his last.

It is not surprising if such ultimate versions, elicited by necessity, and contradicting everything said before, are viewed with some cynicism by the police. They have heard so often the opening formula, "I want to tell the truth about what happened," and they have so seldom found it to be anywhere near the truth. Thorne's new story was that of Mahon over again, with one exception; he was perhaps too intelligent to copy slavishly, and Elsie Cameron's neurotic temperament would suggest the idea of suicide. He had, indeed, once told her sister that she had threatened to throw herself out of the train. The story was, in short, that the girl had come to his hut unexpectedly on that afternoon of December 5; that she announced her intention of staying until he married her; and that, having gone out later to keep an appointment with Miss Coldicott and her mother, he returned towards midnight to find Elsie Cameron hanging from the cross-beam of the hut.

Of the many murderers who have concocted fictions in this *genre*, very few have had the nerve to behave at the time as they would have done were their stories true. Thorne's immediate actions conformed to type. He made no pretence of behaving like an innocent man, by seeking help or advice. He proceeded to saw the body into four portions. The head he forced into a tin box, so tightly that it was extracted with difficulty. The trunk and the severed legs were wrapped in sacking. This horrid work must have taken much of the night. In the late winter dawn roosting Leghorns were disturbed by frenzied digging in their run. Elsie Cameron's few simple belongings were interred with her dressing-case in a potato-plot. That same afternoon Thorne was going to the cinema with the other girl.

Considering this behaviour, and the aplomb with which he carried on his deceptions, including well-simulated anxiety and distress, for six weeks afterwards, it is difficult to take seriously those who suggest that he may have been speaking the truth after all. It is possible that the basis of this theory lies outside the facts of the case altogether, being part and parcel of a legend, created at the time of the trial, and fostered since, about the medical evidence.

2

The remains of Elsie Cameron were dug up on the day after Thorne had made his final statement. Two days later, on January 17, Spilsbury was examining them at the Crowborough mortuary on Beacon Hill. On the 26th the assembled relics were decently interred at Willesden. But they were not allowed to rest; after another four weeks had passed they were exhumed. Spilsbury was again present, to watch a second post-mortem performed by another pathologist whom he was to come to know very well.

Dr Robert Brontë was an Irishman, of the same County Down family of Brunty as the Brontës of Haworth. He had been Crown Analyst to the Government of Ireland, but on the establishment of the Irish Free State in 1922 he came to England to start a fresh career. A common acquaintance introduced him to H. R. Oswald, then Coroner for the Western District of London, for whom he was soon busy on post-mortem work. He was presently appointed pathologist to Harrow Hospital.

Brontë was the typical Irishman, as that abstraction is understood by the English—clever and quick-witted, voluble, combative, sociable, possessed of the gift of making friends and partisans. An infirmity which compelled him to have a specially constructed car had not soured his mercurial temperament. But he was also pushing, self-opinionated, with little sense of dignity, and rather boastful. At the Thorne trial, the first big case in which he was concerned, there is a significant contrast between the casual references made by Spilsbury and other medical men to their qualifications and the long list reeled off by Brontë, who mentioned every post he had ever held. Curtis-Bennett, in cross-examination, did not miss the opportunity thus offered. "You have been asked by Mr Cassels," he said, "as to all the different positions you have held over a number of years. I did not ask Sir Bernard Spilsbury all those questions. . . ." In later years, when Brontë was sometimes called in as witness for the Crown, he took to describing himself, in general terms, as Home Office Pathologist. There was then, in fact, only one Home Office Pathologist, Spilsbury, for whom the honorary appointment had been created.

A graver complaint against Brontë was that he was slapdash in his work. A fellow-analyst of great experience in an official capacity, one of the kindest of men, who knew him well, describes him as "rather careless." Criticism by many others associated with him professionally, both doctors and lawyers, is less restrained. One of the most distinguished judges of the past half-century has said of him:

> At the time when people were saying that Spilsbury was 'laying down the medical law,' a so-called pathologist, Brontë, was frequently called on to contradict him in criminal cases. The only time I heard Spilsbury let himself go was on an occasion when an opinion of Brontë's was in question. "I cannot believe," he said, "that any man with a knowledge of anatomy ever said that." We got a celebrated surgeon to say ditto next day in the witness-box.

Such was the man whom those conducting Norman Thorne's defence called in to redress the balance of Spilsbury's great reputation. They called in other doctors, too; but the tussle was to be between Spilsbury and Brontë. Circumstances, or design, were to make it only the first of many. In nature, method, and point of view the two men were fundamentally different. If the Irishman had the characteristics of his race, many of those held to be peculiarly English were carried to extremes in Spilsbury—reserve, cautiousness, thoroughness, the habit of understatement and of using the minimum of words. It is probable that he had never before met anyone quite like Brontë: having met him, he did not like him; and he never saw cause to change his views. Being Spilsbury, when the pair did meet he was always courteous. Brontë, for his part, seldom failed in public to speak with respect of his eminent antagonist. But disparaging insinuations would often follow; Spilsbury reserved his adverse comments for private circulation. In his lighter moods he would remark drily that when Brontë did a post-mortem there were never any stomach contents. But after some instance (and there were many) of what he considered to be carelessness or guesswork, in his eyes unforgivable sins, he would refer scornfully to "that person," or "that man." This contempt and antipathy is noteworthy, because no other man seems to have aroused a similar feeling in him.

By the time of the second post-mortem on Elsie Cameron's body, nearly three months after death, it had undergone great changes, especially by the action of water. Brontë, nevertheless, was able to form conclusions opposed to those arrived at by Spilsbury a month earlier, when decomposition was much less advanced. In these views Brontë was supported by another medical man who was present at his examination. No fewer than six other doctors gave evidence for the defence at the trial, which opened at Lewes, before Mr Justice Finlay, on March 4, 1926. The value of this massed testimony, as against Spilsbury's single voice, will be considered later, in connexion with the legend built up upon it.

In few trials of modern times, not even in that of Mahon, has the medical evidence played so predominant a part. All that the police had to prove was that the beam in Thorne's hut, from which he said he found Elsie Cameron hanging, showed no trace of cord or rope. The beam was produced in court, the hut having been dismantled for the purpose. Thorne was in the witness-box for the best part of a day; the equivalent of two more saw it occupied by doctors. Spilsbury was there for a whole afternoon, and on the fifth and last day he was recalled.

A good deal of time was consumed over arguments about bruises. They amounted to little more than an attempt by the defence to confuse the issue—an attempt that was, perhaps, a mistake. The subject was a particularly dangerous one on which to controvert Spilsbury, who throughout his life made a special study of bruises, as his cards and notebooks testify. He had no doubt, he said, that those on Elsie Cameron's body were caused before death—two on the head last of all. One of these, on the temple, was the result of a crushing blow which pulped the tissues. Brontë, hampered by the advanced decomposition of the body when he examined it, argued that such a blow would break skin and cheek-bone, which had not happened. He said further that some of the bruises were caused before death, some during death, and some afterwards. This confused the issue too thoroughly, for Thorne denied that there had been even a scene before he left the girl alone in the hut, and the jury must have wondered how she could bruise herself so severely before hanging, and still more while hanging. All this, in fact, was irrelevant; there was only one essential question before them, and it had nothing to do with bruises. Had she, or had she not, been hanged?

On this question Thorne's case stood or fell. Spilsbury's conclusions are summed up in his replies during re-examination on the second day of the trial.

> "I made a thorough search of the neck on the 17th of January because of the suggestion that the woman had died by hanging—not only externally, but of the tissues under the skin. After I had turned the skin back I cut across the creases and in between fifteen and twenty such cuts I found no single area which suggested hæmorrhage or which suggested crushing of the tissues, and no thickening or reddening of the skin itself resulting from pressure by a rope. There was no sign of any sort or kind of damage resulting from attempted hanging or actual hanging. It was therefore not necessary at that time to make any microscopic examination or to make slides. When the post-mortem was conducted by Dr Brontë on the 24th of February the condition of the tissues was then such that no examination, microscopic or otherwise, would help. When the marks which I say were normal marks found on most women's necks were seen on the 24th of February by Dr Brontë he made the remark which I took down at the time that they were 'the normal creases on the skin.' I have not the slightest doubt that they were. I have had for over twenty years continuous experience in microscopic work and the making of slides, applied more especially to medical-legal problems. I took samples of the same parts of the skin of the right cheek and right side of the neck that Dr Brontë had, and I made slides from those examples. The inevitable action of water by soaking into the tissues had destroyed all the elements of the blood, so that it was impossible to find extravasation. It was quite impossible for me to identify the slides or the matter which was in the slides. I formed an opinion on the 17th of January that there was no sign at all of congestion of the brain."

Spilsbury then went on to deal with the theory of the defence, already developed in his cross-examination by Cassels, and put in the fewest possible words by the judge in a question to the latter. "Is it this: attempted hanging, cutting down before death, and death from shock immediately, or almost immediately, after cutting down?" Cassels agreed that that was the hypothesis. Spilsbury said of it:

> "I found nothing in my examination externally or internally to justify the proposition that there had been attempted hanging, cutting down before death, and death occurring immediately after. I found signs to rebut such a suggestion, which were injuries on the head, face, elbow, legs, and feet, which together were amply sufficient to account for death from shock, and death which must have occurred very shortly after those injuries were inflicted."

Of these injuries, and their consequences, he had already said as much and more definitely. "Death was caused by shock due to bruises on the face, head, legs, and feet—to the combined effect of all the bruises. *I found nothing else at all to account for death.*" He now emphasized this conclusion by pointing out that attempted and successful hanging would leave very similar signs. A laundry rope had been produced; he said that suspension by it "would immediately make a mark on the neck . . . and that would in this case have certainly been found when I examined the body on the first occasion. *There was no such mark.*"

Here was the crux of the argument. There were indeed marks on the neck; Spilsbury said they were natural creases, to be found on most women's necks. His reasons for this opinion have been cited. At his own post-mortem he made sections of these marks, and of the bruises, but did not examine them microscopically. Decomposition was not then so far advanced as to make this necessary. The most careful of men, he made a note at the second post-mortem that Brontë agreed with him. At the trial Brontë denied this. He had used the word 'creases,' but had not described them as natural or normal. The marks were those of a thin rope or cord, and later he substituted 'grooves' for 'creases'; the words, he said, meant the same thing. A dictionary would have told Dr Brontë that they do not, and when the point at issue is whether a mark is a natural fold or the impression of a rope the difference in connotation is wide. He further disagreed with Spilsbury on the question of extravasation, or the breaking of blood-vessels by violence or pressure; he found evidence of this in the sections of the neck prepared for him. Spilsbury had already said that he found no such evidence in the specimens, and that, in view of their advanced decomposition, it would be impossible to find it.

There was much discussion about these slides from Brontë's post-mortem. He had given sections of the creases and bruised areas to Spilsbury, who, as always, prepared his own slides, numbering them in accordance with Brontë's similar specimens, and describing them. Brontë was less thorough. His slides were prepared, not all in his presence, by a pathologist who was the brother of another medical man called for the defence. Like all exhibits produced in court, these specimens had to be proved, and Brontë's casual methods made it difficult to trace their history. They were so decomposed that no one could determine by inspection what they were, and when Spilsbury was asked in cross-examination whether he recognized them as the slides in question he made the rather crushing reply: "These might have been made anywhere, at any time. I cannot tell at all." A conference of counsel and others engaged in the prosecution, which he attended, was largely devoted to a discussion of these slides, and how Brontë obtained some of them.

Brontë's examination-in-chief by Cassels was a long one, and would have been longer if the witness had had his way. Having said that in his opinion the cause of death was shock following an unsuccessful or interrupted attempt at self-strangulation, he added that his experience of people intending to die by one means and dying by another was considerable; he had brought records of between four and five hundred cases, if the judge would care to hear them. "There are limits," said the judge. Later, when Brontë had somehow got on to the subject of chickens, which run about after decapitation, Curtis-Bennett intervened. "I am very anxious not to interrupt, but I do not know how we are to stop at this sort of thing." "I feel the difficulty," the judge observed. "Could not Dr Brontë state things in his experience?" In Brontë's persistence, volubility, and irrelevancies there is a faint echo of another Irishman, Dr Kenealy, in the Tichborne trial.

Thorne himself was a remarkably collected witness, but he had too much to explain away. He had told so many lies, and juries, since they read the papers, are no doubt, like the police, sceptical of eleventh-hour explanations of carved-up bodies. A very telling point was made by Curtis-Bennett in a question to a friendly witness who had just described Thorne as a model of excellence. "Could you have imagined, from your knowledge of the defendant, that he would be able to dismember a body?" "Certainly not," said the witness. Bennett had opened his cross-examination of Thorne with a few simple questions equally damaging.

"On the morning of the 5th December were you still in love with Elsie Cameron?"

This seemed easy, and Thorne answered confidently that he was. The next query opened vistas of trouble.

"On the morning of the 5th December were you in love with Miss Coldicott?"

Thorne hesitated, and said, "Yes."

"On that morning which of those two girls that you were in love with did you desire to marry?"

What was he to say? After some quick thinking he replied that he was not particularly anxious to marry anyone at that time.

Later, when he was being asked about Elsie Cameron's last visit to his hut, came another of those deadly questions to which there was no rational answer.

"If your story is correct, when you went out at half-past nine she still believed from you that you were going to marry her if she was pregnant?"

"Yes."

"Then why should she commit suicide?"

Thorne could only reply that as she left no message he could not suggest a definite reason.

Not knowing what his chief medical witness was going to say, he was in difficulties again over the bruises. He said he saw none. Two other points brought out while he was in the witness-box, one evidential, the second an unfortunate invention, must have told heavily against him. Some of Elsie Cameron's clothes were found, wet and muddy, buried in the potato-plot, but some Thorne admitted he had burnt, and these included a woollen frock and other outer garments which, if there had been an attack and a struggle, might have shown signs of it. Then he had said that on his return to the hut, to find the girl hanging, her eyes were open, but screwed up. He stuck to this story under cross-examination, and it was to confute it that Spilsbury was recalled on the last morning of the trial, when he said, "Assuming unconsciousness had intervened, if not death, the eyes would have been in the condition of paralysis. That is to say, the eyes would not have been completely closed, or completely open; a half-open condition, with flexive lids; certainly no puckering."

The judge having taken this opportunity to question Spilsbury on other points, one of the medical witnesses for the defence, Dr Hugh Galt, a pathologist, was recalled for his opinion on them. He and Spilsbury, as he put it, agreed to differ. In cross-examination Curtis-Bennett asked him about the slides. Spilsbury's, said Dr Galt, were exceptionally well prepared and well stained. To the next inquiry, whether they compared well with those produced by Brontë, the witness replied, "Very; they were, I should say, better than the others." The defence could not let this pass unchallenged, and in answer to Cassels Dr Galt said, "There was nothing about the preparation of the slides of Dr Brontë which would interfere with the formation of an opinion by me. They were perfectly good."

When the judge, in his charge to the jury, had traced the known history of the case and had come to the medical evidence he remarked of this bone of contention, the slides, that the position was rather curious. "I am far from saying, gentlemen of the jury, that the slides are not of importance in the case; that they are of decisive importance you may well think." He had already spoken of Spilsbury in terms which were later called in question as being tendentious. "Sir Bernard Spilsbury would be the first to disclaim infallibility in matters of this sort, but his opinion is undoubtedly the very best opinion that can be obtained. . . ." The argument about extravasation was reduced to rational proportions. Spilsbury had found no evidence of it, either on his slides or on Brontë's. "That is one view," said the judge. "Another view is that there was some slight extravasation at the girl's neck. I suppose it was very slight and very local. . . . I suppose that would be an indication that the injury to the neck causing extravasation was slight." This could hardly be the result of hanging; and so the jury thought. They were less than half an hour in bringing in a verdict of guilty.

An unusual application was made when the case was taken to the Court of Criminal Appeal—namely, that the medical evidence should be referred to the arbitration of a medical commissioner appointed by the Court, which under a section of the Criminal Appeal Act had power to take this step. In delivering the judgment of the Court the Lord Chief Justice said that there was nothing in the case which made it desirable to have recourse to this special and exceptional power. With regard to criticisms of the judge's summing-up, there was no foundation for them. The appeal was dismissed; and a last-minute attempt to influence the Home Secretary failed likewise. Thorne was executed just a month after his trial.

3

It is often said, especially of capital cases, that the Crown always has the big battalions. Thorne, for one, could not have complained on this score. In few trials of this nature have the big battalions been so predominantly on the side of the accused. The decisive factor was the medical evidence, and eight doctors were called for the defence, against two (one of them a police surgeon, who would have been called in any event) for the prosecution. Nor was this all. When the case went to the Court of Criminal Appeal another K.C., Mr William Jowitt, later to be Lord Chancellor, was brought in to lead Cassels and his juniors, who had done all that able and devoted advocates could do at the Assizes. This throw failed too; but in the meantime other influences had been at work, and now the Press took a hand. Whatever the influences were, the motive of the agitation was scarcely concealed. The fate of Thorne was made a vehicle for an attack on Spilsbury.

Letters appeared in the newspapers, mostly on similar lines to the following, written by a "medico-legal expert" who preferred to remain anonymous:

> For some reason or other, Sir Bernard Spilsbury has now arrived at a position where his utterances in the witness-box commonly receive unquestioning acceptance from judge, counsel and jury. He can do no wrong. But a reputation for infallibility such as that which appears of late to have been thrust on Sir Bernard (I am sure he never claimed it for himself) is quite out of place in medical and surgical matters. The unquestioning acceptance by the jury of Sir Bernard Spilsbury's evidence in the face of conflicting testimony, due, as it may have been, to the singling out of this particular medical witness for eulogy by the judge, seems a legitimate point for comment in putting the case for Thorne.

Among others, Conan Doyle entered the lists, with the honours of Oscar Slater upon him. He was not quite easy about the case; there seemed to him a faint doubt existing. Doyle was always on the side of the underdog; he had no axe to grind, and no prejudice against Spilsbury. It was different with *The Law Journal*, which, after pontifically rebuking the Lord Chief Justice, went on to say: "The verdict of a jury on a question of pathology is valueless. Thorne is entitled to feel that he has been condemned by a tribunal which was not capable of forming a first-hand judgment, but followed the man with the biggest name." This was the whole point of the article, which was published immediately after the dismissal of Thorne's appeal, and, in asserting that the Court of Criminal Appeal should have used its powers to appoint a commissioner to review the medical evidence, *The Law Journal* added its weight to the campaign to persuade the Home Secretary to reopen the case.

The Home Secretary was unamenable to pressure, and Thorne was hanged; but the implication that he was a victim of injustice, because the jury "followed the man with the biggest name," was not allowed to die. Four years after his trial the first fairly full account of it was published, in the "Famous Trials" series. This series must not be confused with Hodge's "Notable British Trials," being certainly inferior in this respect, that evidence is not printed in full, but is selectively condensed at the discretion of the editor. The volume on Thorne, published in 1929, is edited by Miss Helena Normanton, a barrister. Her long introduction is a very clever piece of special pleading, designed to perpetuate the legend that Thorne, whether guilty or innocent, did not receive a fair trial.

Miss Normanton's main line of argument may be summarized as follows. Rather oddly, for a lawyer with a trained mind, she succumbs to the fallacy of the big battalions. She relies on the counting of heads; because eight medical men disagreed with Spilsbury, the odds are eight to one against his opinion being correct. She enumerates the qualifications of some of these witnesses for the defence. From only one of them, however, did she seek help or advice. Acknowledgments in her preface to Dr Brontë are scarcely needed, for internal evidence suggests that he was indeed of much assistance.

Now, more than twenty years later, the Thorne legend is still alive. The following might have been written by Miss Normanton:

> Spilsbury was the Crown's sole expert witness. The defence had four or five, at least three of whom could boast qualifications on a par with Spilsbury's own. They agreed between themselves, and disagreed with him, so that the defence enjoyed an easy lead on a mere counting of heads.

This is Edgar Lustgarten, another lawyer, in his account of the trial of Thorne in *Verdict in Dispute*, published in 1949. He goes on:

> How then did Spilsbury's evidence acquire such vast importance? . . . The answer is simple. Juries are formed from members of the public, and the British public believed Spilsbury infallible. . . . Spilsbury had indeed done what few can hope to do; he had become a legend in his own lifetime. To the man in the street he stood for pathology as Hobbs stood for cricket or Dempsey for boxing or Capablanca for chess. His pronouncements were invested with the force of dogma, and it was blasphemy to hint that he might conceivably be wrong.

Admitting that Spilsbury's qualities were genuinely outstanding, Lustgarten says: "Even so, it was a situation fraught with danger." He quotes from Cassels' final speech for Thorne:

> "We can all admire attainment, take off our hats to ability, acknowledge the high position that a man has won in his sphere. But it is a long way to go if you have to say that, when that man says something, there can be no room for error."

Cassels' words are special pleading with every justification. He was fighting for a man's life. But commentators writing long after the event, and aiming at a judicial presentation, should be more objective. Arguments from the general to the particular are out of place. The question is not whether an eminent man, in this case Spilsbury, was invariably right, but whether he was right in the single instance under review, which is the trial of Norman Thorne. Those who say that he may have been wrong adduce various reasons, but their chief criterion is Miss Normanton's and Edgar Lustgarten's mathematical "counting of heads"; and by that they must be judged.

What was the value of the evidence of these eight medical men called for the defence? Eminent though some of them were, their professional qualifications seem to have carried little weight with the judge and jury; and the reason is plain. Of all the ten doctors in the case, only four saw Elsie Cameron's dead body—Spilsbury and the police surgeon first, and then, in greatly changed conditions a month later, Brontë and his assistant, Dr Gibson. Dr Gibson made no claim to be a pathologist. He was in general practice in Acton. Of the remaining six medical witnesses for the defence, three were pathologists, but the testimony of all six was based solely on what they had heard in court. It has been shown again and again that evidence of this kind makes little impression on juries. They prefer, and it would seem reasonably, the man who has seen what he is talking about. In the Thorne case, for practical purposes, this meant two doctors out of ten—Brontë, of whose methods something has been said, and Spilsbury. The jury chose to believe Spilsbury.

For this they were told by *The Law Journal* that their opinions were valueless. Miss Normanton and others have said very much the same thing. To ignore the human element may perhaps be a weakness of legal training. As compared with their armchair critics, juries have the advantage which Spilsbury and Brontë possessed over the rest of their colleagues in the Thorne trial: they have the evidence of their own eyes and ears. They see and hear the accused and the witnesses. Sometimes they go astray, of their own accord, as in the Wallace case, or because of misdirection, as in that of Edith Thompson; but on the whole justice is well served by the rule of common sense laid down by Darling in the Armstrong trial: "You should recollect and consider the demeanour of every witness." Having recollected and considered the demeanour of Thorne and Spilsbury and Brontë, the jury at Lewes made their choice—in twenty-five minutes.

Spilsbury possessed a copy of Miss Normanton's book. He has scarcely marked it at all—in fact, in only two places. One pencilling is against a significant passage in the police evidence, to the effect that while the upper beams in Thorne's hut were thick with dust, there was no dust on the lower beams, from one of which Elsie Cameron was said to have hanged herself. The other pencil-mark is no less significant. It appears beside a characteristic assertion by Brontë: "I have occupied for the Crown of Ireland a corresponding position, I suppose, to the position occupied in this country by Sir Bernard Spilsbury. It was exactly similar." Further comment, as, no doubt, Spilsbury felt, is unnecessary.

Part Three

SPILSBURY AS OTHERS SAW HIM

Chapter 1: BENCH AND BAR

Few men so well known to the public that they have become, in words already quoted, a legend in their lifetime can offer to biographers, at first sight, less material on the personal side than Bernard Spilsbury. If a questionnaire were addressed to the thousands who knew him, in one degree or another, it is safe to say that every answer would begin, "I really can't tell you much about him." The minority in constant contact with him would add, "He never talked of himself. He seemed to have few friends. His only interest was his work." This absorption in work, coupled with methods patient and thorough almost to excess, isolated him in later life even from his family, who would catch only brief glimpses of him at a hasty lunch, or during a week-end, in between endless, increasing, over-riding labours for the police, in coroners' courts, or in the laboratory.

Out of all these negatives, nevertheless, the proverbial affirmative takes shape. Those who saw most of Spilsbury in his professional capacity, when they search their memories, inevitably turn out to know a good deal about him, and to have formed definite views as to his attainments and character; and, if he had few close friends, what friendships he did make were lasting.

As the shadowy figure becomes substantial, a most striking feature is the unanimity of the opinions that build it up. The same words and phrases are used again and again. This applies to every aspect of Spilsbury's career—as a medical man, as a researcher, as a scientific witness, and as a private individual. To take the last first, during discussions about this book, which is the work of a team, it has often been said that to make a living figure of Spilsbury somebody must be found who cordially disliked him. It appears that this is an impossibility. From time to time many of his colleagues differed from him; instances of professional jealousy have been mentioned, and more will be said of antagonisms based on the grounds that he became too dogmatic and that his mere name carried too much weight; but no one has been found who will say, "I didn't like the man." On the contrary, there is an overwhelming mass of testimony, not only to his outstanding professional qualities, but to a humanity and likability amounting to charm which sprang from goodness of heart and thoughtfulness for others. In a more general sense, Spilsbury made friends everywhere—among judges and counsel, fellow doctors and students, police officers of every grade, constables in the ranks and coroners' officers, the waiters who served him at the restaurants he used day after day, strangers whom he helped as a matter of course without thought of the trouble involved. To employ a cant phrase, it was all done by kindness. There was never any conscious attempt to please; he was too preoccupied for that; and increasing power and prestige made no difference at all. He was always the same to everybody.

Nothing could reveal more clearly the universal liking felt for him than the willingness, and, indeed, eagerness, shown alike by associates and mere acquaintances to pay tribute to his memory. The usual gambit, "I really know very little about Sir Bernard," will be followed, almost as invariably, by a story of some act of kindness, or a reference to the unaffected courtesy which is among the predominant recollections of all who met him. Instances which throw light on this side of his character will presently be cited, but the same feeling of respect and regard colours even formal estimates of his professional accomplishments.

It is a happy consequence of the longevity of lawyers that there are those still living whose active careers overlap Spilsbury's own. Sir Travers Humphreys' memories of the past have already been drawn upon. He became acquainted with Spilsbury during the preliminaries of the Crippen case. The pair met constantly after that, in the courts as counsel and witness, and then as judge and witness, and in later years as members of "Our Society," the Crimes Club founded by H. B. Irving and others. Now, forty years after the trial of Crippen, the opinions then formed by Sir Travers of his younger colleague remain unchanged, or, rather, have been confirmed and enhanced by long experience:

> Spilsbury in the witness-box was to my mind the ideal scientific witness. He was unemotional, simple in speech because he was clear in mind, absolutely fair, quite indifferent to the result of a case, paying little or no attention to those parts of the evidence which did not affect the medical or scientific aspects of the matter. He spared no pains in seeking out anything, fact, theory, or latest discovery, which could properly affect his judgment. He learned from Willcox early in his career the art of helping a muddled or halting cross-examiner to put his questions in such a way as to enable the witness to agree with his proposition. A frequent

answer of his in the witness-box would be: "Put in that way, I am afraid I cannot agree; but if you ask whether the evidence is consistent with such and such a theory, you are quite right." At one time medical and legal critics thought that Spilsbury was becoming too didactic, but I think it must have come to his notice, for he quickly reverted to his old formula, "I have no doubt," or "That is my definite opinion," followed by some such phrase as "others may take a different view," or, where he knew that his knowledge was a little ahead of that of many of his colleagues, "That is the most modern view." His own knowledge of his subject was, of course, immense. His medical colleagues will no doubt testify to that, and to his pre-eminence as a lecturer.

Sir Travers ends on a familiar note: "As a man I knew very little of Spilsbury. I doubt if he had many close friends. He seemed to me to be too much immersed in his work to be very interested in other matters or people."

A memory which goes even further back is that of Sir Archibald Bodkin. As he says, as Treasury Counsel he examined Spilsbury many times. Afterwards, when Sir Archibald was Director of Public Prosecutions, the two came in even closer contact. Again, in his words, appears the perfect witness, the reserved man, and the insatiable inquirer after knowledge:

> Spilsbury will be a very difficult subject for a biographer. He never talked about himself, or except on strictly relevant lines about his cases or his methods.
>
> I have examined him as a witness many times, and was always struck by his absolute fairness and moderation as an expert, and both Judges and Juries accordingly accepted his evidence implicitly. He had a gift of making abundantly clear to a layman the difficult questions which arose in connexion with his cases, and always in the simplest and least technical phraseology.

In referring to Spilsbury's habit of examining the soil in exhumations where poisoning was suspected, Sir Archibald goes on to give a further illustration of this thoroughness in a case in which arsenic had been used:

> I forget the details, but Spilsbury for some reason wanted to see the place whence the body had been removed—a wood not far out of London. He and I one Sunday set off and inspected the place. What his reason was I never found out, but that he had a good reason is certain.

In discussing the trial of George Joseph Smith, Sir Archibald mentions the experiment made with one of the baths, in which a nurse took part, and raises a curious point which probably would occur only to a lawyer:

> To their astonishment and distress Spilsbury[1] and Willcox found that sudden immersion in such a bath by lifting the legs so as to immerse the head might well cause death, not by drowning or any heart disease, but by the resulting shock. The nurse in question very nearly died—so the story ran—but the experiment enabled the experts to found a theory of the cause of death which I think the jury accepted. It would have been a very interesting question whether, if the nurse had died, any offence had been committed.

Like all who had professional dealings with Spilsbury, Sir Archibald emphasizes his lack of interest in money.

"When I was Director of Public Prosecutions after Sir Charles Mathews," he writes, "I used to engage Spilsbury whenever required, and was always struck by the extreme moderation of the fees he claimed for his services."

Beside these judgments by distinguished lawyers, who knew Spilsbury well, can be set that of another lawyer, equally eminent, but in another country, who, except for the two occasions referred to, can have known him only by repute. The occasions are of particular interest, because they are among the few criminal proceedings in which Spilsbury appeared for the defence. This, since until the end of his life he was employed for the Crown, he could seldom do in England; but there was no bar to his services being called upon by the Pannel, as the defence is styled in Scotland. Lord Alness, who as Lord Justice-Clerk presided over both the trials in question, has very kindly written an appreciation of Spilsbury's part in them, which he calls "A Scottish Chapter":

> Sir Bernard Spilsbury's evidence was usually and naturally given in England, but it is interesting to note that on occasion he also gave evidence in Scotland. In point of fact, he appeared as witness—not for the prosecution but for the defence—in two Scottish murder cases. They were both tried before me—with, of course, a jury in each case—and I had a full opportunity of assessing the worth of Sir Bernard's testimony. I have read and re-read the official record of his evidence in both cases, and I have this to say about it. No one could fail to be impressed by the cogency and thrust of his testimony, and also by its measured and moderate character. Its fairness made the impact none the less deadly.
>
> The first of the two cases to which I have referred was officially designated "H.M. Advocate *v.* Peter Queen." The accused was tried in

[1] But see Part Two, Chapter 3: "The Brides in the Baths."

Glasgow in the year 1932. The case lasted for five days, and attracted widespread public attention. It concerned the alleged murder by the accused, a young man, of his paramour, who was also young. She was found dead, with a ligature round her neck, which admittedly caused her death. The Crown case was that the accused placed the ligature in position, and so murdered her. The defence was that the young woman committed suicide. In supporting the latter theory, Sir Bernard adduced five reasons. The jury, however, refused to be convinced by this and other evidence led for the defence, and found the accused "Guilty as Libelled." I sentenced him to death. I understand, however, that he was subsequently reprieved.[1]

The second case referred to by Lord Alness was the trial at Edinburgh, in 1927, of John Donald Merrett for the murder of his mother, and also for uttering forged cheques. By a peculiarity of Scottish law the two charges were combined. This famous trial will be considered in a later chapter. "The jury," says Lord Alness,

> found the accused guilty on the second charge, but on the first charge, to which Sir Bernard's evidence was confined, they returned what I respectfully regard as the unsatisfactory Scottish verdict of "Not Proven." In the course of his speech for the defence to the jury, Mr Craigie Aitchison, in dealing with the murder charge, paid a unique, and, if I may say so, a deserved tribute to Sir Bernard Spilsbury, which I take the liberty of quoting in full:
>
> > "I need not remind you that in this case we have had the great and learned assistance of Sir Bernard Spilsbury. I do not dispute that Professor Littlejohn and Professor Glaister are men of eminence, but I do not hesitate to say that there is no name in Britain, there is no name in Europe, on medico-legal questions on the same plane as the name of Sir Bernard Spilsbury; and I am certain that you cannot have failed to be impressed by the moderation and restraint and fairness, and by the complete absence of partisanship displayed by him in the evidence which he gave in the witness-box yesterday. Standing the evidence as it does, I claim that on this, the medical aspect of the case, it is emphatically in my favour."

"I venture to think," Lord Alness concludes, "that no truer or finer estimate of Sir Bernard's eminence in his profession could be penned, and I, for one, do not propose to essay the task."

[1] Queen made an unsuccessful appeal, but his sentence was commuted to penal servitude for life.

2

There is scarcely a book on criminal or medico-legal matters published in this country in the past thirty-five years which does not contain some reference to Spilsbury. All such references of a personal nature agree upon his qualities, as a witness, of precision, lucidity, and moderation. Of the impact of these qualities upon a jury, when coupled with Spilsbury's enormous prestige, Lord Alness is not alone in using the word "deadly." It is natural for judges to be grateful for gifts which clarify to the layman obscure scientific issues, and no less naturally Treasury Counsel and others concerned with prosecutions tend to imply, when writing their memoirs, that their star medical witness can do nothing wrong. But there is another side to all prosecutions. Among the most recent books on the subject are two by Sir Patrick Hastings, who belongs to a rather later generation than the other distinguished lawyers just quoted. As an advocate Sir Patrick has frequently acted for the defence, and in a number of murder trials he was on the opposite side to Spilsbury. This lends a special quality to his observations about the latter as a witness.

Of the trial of the Polish officer known as Captain "X" Sir Patrick writes, in his autobiography:

> To anyone who knew Sir Bernard as I did, the deadly nature of this evidence was immediately apparent. I had cross-examined him too often to be under any possible illusion. As a witness he was always strictly impartial and scrupulously fair, but his knowledge was immense, and once he had formed a definite opinion it was always extremely difficult to shake him in his views. Spilsbury's evidence was the cause of my main anxiety throughout the case. . . . I was very glad to see him leave the witness-box.

In *Cases in Court* Sir Patrick carries the matter further. He is dealing with the trial of Mrs Elvira Barney for the murder of Thomas Scott Stephen. The defence was that Stephen's death was accidental, and everything had to be done, in Sir Patrick's words, "to bring the evidence into line with this theory, and above all to meet in advance the evidence of Sir Bernard Spilsbury . . . of all the witnesses to be called against me the one I feared most."

"By this time," he goes on,

> Sir Bernard had become recognized as an almost inevitable witness in a prosecution for murder, and I had cross-examined him on many previous occasions. He was an absolutely fair witness, and a most knowledgeable and skilful medical man, but unfortunately there had grown up a practice among some prosecuting counsel to treat him almost as an expert on

murder. He was invariably permitted to sit in Court throughout the trial, and a question of this sort was not infrequently put to him by the prosecution: "Sir Bernard, you have been in Court and you have heard the suggested defence put forward on behalf of the prisoner. In your opinion, is that defence consistent with the results of your examination?" To which Sir Bernard could only reply, "No." In my opinion this was a most unfortunate question. If Sir Bernard was not cross-examined, his opinion remained unchallenged; if he was, he was entitled, and indeed bound, to give the reasons for that opinion, and those reasons given with all the weight of his skill and experience must be most deadly for the defence. I spent much anxious thought in deciding upon the best method of avoiding this particular danger in the case of Mrs Barney.

It is a striking tribute to the apprehensions felt by defending counsel when Spilsbury was to appear against them that Sir Patrick's meditations resulted in his taking an unprecedented step. The jury having been sworn, he rose to make an application:

> I asked that Sir Bernard should not be allowed to remain in Court during the opening of the case and the calling of the evidence. As far as I am aware, such an application had never been made before—purely medical witnesses are almost invariably permitted to remain in Court, but the judge ruled that I was within my rights in making the application, and Sir Bernard left the Court.

Having summarized the earlier evidence, Sir Patrick describes how his astute move was utilized:

> And then came Sir Bernard Spilsbury. His evidence was purely medical and given with absolute accuracy and firmness, and that evidence was in no way inconsistent with the defence, but, inasmuch as he had so far been out of Court, he had not heard of any theory of suicide, or any other suggested defence, and therefore no question could possibly be asked of him as to his opinion on such a theory; that, no doubt, would come when he was rigorously and severely cross-examined. Possibly to the disappointment of some people, he was not cross-examined at all; no single question was asked of him,[1] and when he left the witness-box the last opportunity for the prosecution to offer any expert opinion as to the plausibility of the defence was gone. I never remember to have felt greater pleasure at seeing a witness leave the box. One of our greatest dangers had disappeared.

No lawyer can have appreciated more fully than Spilsbury himself the cleverness of this manœuvre. It has been well said of him—by Edgar Lustgarten—that he had become "a professional cross-

[1] Sir Patrick was trusting to memory. He put three questions to Spilsbury, but three only. See Part Four, Chapter 8.

examinee . . . as used as any counsel to the atmosphere of the courts; as trained in the rules, as familiar with the tricks." As he left the box he must well have understood how the defence had scored by their masterly inactivity. So the event proved: Mrs Barney was acquitted.

Sir Patrick, with first-hand knowledge, confirms an observation made by others, that to cross-examine so experienced a witness required a special technique. "A long experience," he writes,

> had taught me the only hopeful line of cross-examination; ask as little as possible for fear of making the case worse than it already was, and trust to the not wholly unreasonable comment: "doctors are not infallible, and are so often wrong."

Few juries took this view of Spilsbury; it may or may not be significant that probably the only one that did, in a capital case, was the Scottish jury at the trial of Peter Queen. Grumblings about infallibility cut little ice in England, waspish though they sometimes were, as when it was said, "Sir Bernard is no more qualified than would be a medicine man or a witch-doctor." Sarcasm fared no better. "Sir Bernard," said one learned counsel,

> comes here with a great reputation and a great name, and, as so many do when they reach the top of the tree, becomes a little dictatorial. One does not like to criticize a man in his position, but the witnesses for the defence are entitled to have their opinions respected as much as the great Sir Bernard Spilsbury. Are the jury going to convict on the assumption that Sir Bernard cannot be wrong?

The jury were, and did.

These complaints seem in the main to belong to one period, the years immediately after the Thorne case, when the lively appearance on the scene of Dr Brontë gave the Adullamites a rallying-point. An observation of Sir Travers Humphreys, cited earlier, suggests that there may have been some slight justification—that there was a time when Spilsbury allowed himself to show intolerance of opposition. Some one then dropped him a hint, and he never offended in this way again. He reverted to his old formula, in Sir Travers' words. The latter, in conversation, has put this in a rather different way—namely, that Spilsbury was always ready to acknowledge points made against him, but would always have an explanation to meet them. "In general, So-and-so was quite right," he would say, "but he had not considered the problem in relation to this particular case."

"During cross-examination," writes another old friend,

> if some suggestion that countered his evidence were put to him he had a pleasing, almost an engaging way of accepting it; he might even put it

into simpler words, so that all could understand it. Then he destroyed it, and made it clear to all that it had no foundation in the facts that he had described. Under that pleasing manner, and with the sole desire of ascertaining and maintaining truth, there remained a remarkably alert mind that never got perturbed by theories that might be speciously or earnestly propounded to it.

Stories are told of how, in this "pleasing, almost engaging way," Spilsbury would lead on the most distinguished counsel for the defence until they thought they had at last got him in a corner. "Yes," he would say to their questions. "Yes." "Yes." "I agree with you." Then, as they made their penultimate point, and were ready to spring, a few quiet words would demolish the whole structure they had been building up. "That is a very ridiculous question, Mr So-and-so." With Spilsbury, in fact, the business of giving evidence, especially under cross-examination, because an art, the practice of which, in such circumstances as these, appealed to his sense of humour.

The old friend quoted above goes on to say:

> Sometimes Spilsbury's experience in the particular matter that was the subject of a criminal trial was challenged. The writer can recall an occasion on which Spilsbury was being cross-examined at the Old Bailey in a trial for criminal abortion, and was asked how long it was since he had attended a woman in childbirth. After due reflection to assess the period exactly, he replied, "Thirty-seven years." He added that the process, however, had not, he thought, changed during that length of time, and he maintained entire control of the situation. Soon afterwards, the period was reduced to zero, owing to the sudden demand for a doctor at Spilsbury's club, where, after dinner, he found himself dealing with one of the female staff as an emergency measure.

The trial referred to was that of a man well known in his time in the East End as "The Threepenny Doctor," and it was he who put the question to Spilsbury.

Spilsbury, in short, always had an answer; and one critic has deduced from this that he regarded his conclusions as indisputable. A very senior official at New Scotland Yard, who knew him for more than twenty years, and greatly admired him, agrees that he did not always take kindly to contradiction in professional matters. Sir Patrick Hastings has been quoted on the difficulty of shaking him in his views, and plenty of other evidence could be adduced of this attitude of absolute certainty. Conveyed with studied brevity and moderation, it was one of the secrets of his enormous influence with juries. On the other hand, he never gave an opinion unless he *was* certain; and not only was his experience unrivalled, but no man ever took so much trouble to ensure certainty. A medical colleague at the Home Office, of experience almost as long, has said that no pathologist before Spilsbury's day was so thorough, and none has been so thorough since. The whole argument about infallibility would seem to be answered by another who knew him well, a one-time Chief Inspector of the City of London Police. "A less cautious man enjoying that reputation might well have exposed himself to some damaging rebuffs in the courts, but I never saw him do it, and I doubt if anyone did." Sir Travers Humphreys may be quoted again on this point, for he once put it in another way. Spilsbury's friend Dr Eric Gardner describes the incident:

> Travers Humphreys once defended Spilsbury when Norman Birkett played a forensic trick on him by warning the jury not to accept certain opinions just because they came from a man whose reputation was so great that he had come to be regarded as infallible. The judge pointed out that for twenty-eight years—ever since the Crippen case—Spilsbury had undergone in the witness-box the most severe cross-examinations a man could be subjected to, yet, as counsel had just admitted, he was dangerous precisely because after all these years and all these ordeals people still took his word at its face value.

In short, as a witness in the criminal courts for nearly forty years in all, Spilsbury never experienced a serious rebuff, though a host of able counsel and medical witnesses tried their hardest. They would perhaps have been surprised to hear Spilsbury himself on the subject. The same acquaintance quoted above once heard him say that an expert was a man who went on learning more and more about less and less, until at last he knew everything about nothing. His critics might have been equally surprised had they known how relatively often he admitted being at a loss. Among his thousands of cases there are quite a number in which, with all his assurance and vast experience, he could not find a cause of death. He always said so, without any qualification; if the evidence was not there he refused to guess.

Enough has been said about him as a witness, but no small part of his authority derived from his remarkable good looks, his stature, and the care he bestowed upon his dress—his only form of vanity. In his younger days he was a far more elegant figure than is customarily seen in the witness-box. When morning coats were still the thing he wore a morning coat, carried a top hat, and had a flower in his buttonhole, usually a carnation. While he was at Bart's a newspaper published a photograph of him with the caption "The Handsomest Man in London." It is hardly necessary to say that, to his embarrassment, for he was not vain about his looks, the students pinned this up in the Common Room. Some time later he was described (probably by a Conservative) as "looking in court like Lord Curzon in the present House of Commons." In after-life the lean, athletic figure and the clean-cut features filled out, until with his plump, pink face, his glasses, and his silver hair he might have been a benevolent general practitioner or a prosperous farmer.

Even his authority as a public figure was but a very partial indication of the extent to which his influence was felt and his knowledge sought behind the scenes, from the most unlikely quarters, and about the oddest happenings. His views were asked on certain aspects of a divorce case that took place before he was born, and about the cause of death of James Hepburn, Earl of Bothwell, the third husband of Mary Queen of Scots, whose embalmed body was exhumed in Sweden nearly four hundred years after his imprisonment as a pirate in the castle of Malmö. In doubtful cases Spilsbury was constantly consulted beforehand by the Director of Public Prosecutions, and many innocent persons, and not a few guilty ones, escaped being charged because he considered the medical evidence inadequate. The strength or weakness of a case in other respects was no concern of his. A colleague at a post-mortem once exclaimed, half in irritation, "You're a rotten pathologist, Spilsbury—you won't go beyond your facts"; and the following queer story is worth telling because it also illustrates this scrupulous attitude to guess-work. The incident occurred during the last years of Spilsbury's life.

The body of a newly born infant, in a state of mummification, its mouth crammed with cotton-wool, was found among some luggage in a basement near Victoria. The child had been so long dead that the police surgeon would not say that it had been born alive. The woman to whom the luggage belonged had disappeared. A year afterwards she was discovered in Bloomsbury. While she was being questioned at the police station her room was searched. The body of another newly born infant came to light, its mouth also full of cotton-wool. It had not been dead many weeks, and the police now felt confident that they had a certain case against the assumed mother. They were the more confident, perhaps, because the inquest would be held by Bentley Purchase at St Pancras, where Spilsbury would perform the post-mortem. He did, but to their considerable annoyance he would not say what they wanted and fully expected him to say. The police officer concerned admits that a good deal of pressure was applied.

There was nothing, unless it were abortion, about which Spilsbury felt more strongly than offences against children and infants, but though he was now a sick man, and prematurely aged, his professional conscience was as rigid as ever. It was no good talking to him about cotton-wool: he refused to assert, on the medical evidence, that the child had had a separate existence. The woman in the case escaped with the light penalty for concealment of birth. It is of interest to recall that many years before, when the bodies of no fewer than four newly born infants were found at Romford, Spilsbury gave the same negative opinion. He had not changed.

This attempt to show him as he appeared to those who knew him chiefly as an official witness will fittingly be concluded by drawing once more upon the recollections of the old friend with whose estimate this chapter began. Speaking of Spilsbury's habitual reserve, which amounted to reticence, Sir Travers Humphreys suggests that it sprang partly from knowledge of his own limitations. Having so few interests outside medicine, he did not feel himself sufficiently well-informed on many general topics of the day to be drawn into discussing them. His son observes that he was hampered all his life, and probably was conscious of it, by the defects of his early education. Owing to his own father's restless ways, Spilsbury went to three schools in different parts of England in scarcely more than as many years; only when he was at Magdalen was there any sort of continuity and by then he had decided on his life's work, and what a contemporary has described as "one long grind, mostly in the laboratory and the museum," left little time for other interests. The "long grind" was to preoccupy him for the rest of his life.

In this connexion Sir Travers has compared him to Sir William Willcox, a man of great versatility, who successfully took on many tasks outside his daily round as Home Office Analyst. There ought, Sir Travers has said, to be a book about Willcox. So, no doubt, there should be; but for every one who would read it a hundred want a book about Spilsbury. The most cogent reasons for this mus ıbe sought beyond the obvious: they are to be found in the character of the ınan himself. Diffidence allied to supreme confidence, curious limitations of outlook, manifest sincerity, scrupulous fairness, reticence and elusiveness combined with good looks and prestige, formed together, in the public eye, a figure of mystery. It was, of course, the very last attribute Spilsbury would have claimed for himself. He knew very well that he was nothing if not normal. What he was as a boy he remained to the end. But the public would not have it so.

The reference to Willcox is a reminder that for many years he and Spilsbury were the Castor and Pollux of the criminal courts. They were constantly appearing together. Sir Travers Humphreys still tells a pleasant story which he first told a long time ago in *Criminal Days*. In his last case as Treasury Counsel, when he was prosecuting a clerical reprobate named Bacon, the great twin brethren were as usual due to give evidence. While the trial was in progress, Mr Travers Humphreys was raised to the Bench, and took the oath before the Lord Chancellor, Lord Cave. He asked that the public announcement of his elevation might be postponed for twenty-four hours, so that, although now a judge, he could once more, for the last time, examine his old friends Willcox and Spilsbury.

Chapter 2: DOCTORS AND STUDENTS

In the early 1920's a young doctor practising in Wales gave evidence at a coroner's inquiry into the cause of the death of a woman who had undergone an illegal operation. Largely as a result of his testimony, a charge was preferred, and the case went to the Assizes. In the meantime, the young doctor met with a certain amount of criticism from professional colleagues who disagreed with his opinion. He was seriously worried—so much so that he took the unusual step of writing for advice to a man he had never met, or corresponded with, but whom he considered the highest authority on the subject. "By return," his account of this episode runs,

> I had a long *hand-written* reply, setting down in minutest detail what would and could have happened in the circumstances. I went to the Assizes armed with this knowledge, was cross-examined carefully, and was complimented by the Court at the end of the case.

"Now Sir Bernard knew quite well," the doctor goes on,

> that I was a general practitioner working in an out-of-the-way district, with nothing whatever to recommend me and with no hope of my ever being able to repay his kindness or to do him honour in any way. Neither had I been a student under him or had anything in common with him; I had only heard of him by repute, and had carefully followed his evidence in celebrated cases.
>
> I consider that this was one of the greatest kindnesses I have ever had bestowed on me, given at great length, with complete authority, cheerfully, and without hope of any kind of reward.

Twenty-three years later, in 1946, an old lady living in Derbyshire had recently lost her husband. One of his closest friends, and best man at his wedding, had been Lady Spilsbury's brother, Dr Horton. The old lady had known the Spilsburys slightly as a young married couple at Harrow; she had not seen them since that time, and had so completely lost touch with the family that she was not sure that they were still alive. After her husband's death she made inquiries on this point, because she wanted news of Dr Horton, and then wrote to Spilsbury, whom she had last met thirty-six years before. In reply she received two long letters, from which, as she says, she learnt for the first time "that he had been through great suffering and loss."

When the unknown young doctor in Wales was worrying about the evidence he would have to give at the Assizes Spilsbury had just been knighted, and was rapidly becoming the busiest man in England, and, in his own line, the most sought-after. Twenty-three years later he had only a year to live, and there were times when he was so crippled that he could hardly write at all. From the long interval between, many identical acts of kindness could be quoted—lengthy, detailed letters to mere acquaintances, students, strangers, people who wanted favours. Such acts, small, perhaps, in themselves, throw a clear light on character when they are found repeated, again and again, over a lifetime. The recipients of these careful answers to sometimes trivial inquiries would have been surprised to hear, from anyone who knew Spilsbury well, that he was far from a good letter-writer. His ordinary correspondence, in fact, was hasty and scrappy in the extreme. He had no time for letter-writing—except when somebody needed help, or when he himself had a kindness to repay. In his last years, when, after his first stroke, he was for a time compelled to use two walking-sticks, the Department of Public Prosecutions always sent a car when it required his services. He never failed to write a note of thanks. This was not a formality. He was genuinely touched, and a little surprised, by goodwill shown towards him.

Doctors and laymen all over the country, old students of St Mary's and Bart's, those from other hospitals who met him only when they came trembling before him for examination have retained long-lasting impressions of his courtesy and thoughtfulness. In examiners these qualities may make all the difference to a nervous examinee, of either sex; and in the medical profession there was for a long time a prejudice against women candidates. If Spilsbury, with his old-fashioned outlook on some things, ever shared it he never allowed it to appear in his manner. One woman doctor, who was examined by him more than thirty years ago, records that he treated her with a sympathetic understanding and kindliness she had never met in any other examiner. With his good looks, his morning coat, and his top hat, he still recalls to her "all the charm and dignity of the Edwardian era—the age of 'carriages at eleven.'" Not many examiners, in any subject, leave this sort of memory. Dr Doris Bell Ball, known as Josephine Bell to a non-clinical clientele which probably did not include Spilsbury himself, no reader of detective stories, remembers him as

> the one and only outstandingly kind examiner I came across in my laborious passage through my finals in medicine. His kindness and consideration undoubtedly carried me through a difficult and important moment in my career, and I shall always be grateful to his memory.

Thus set at her ease, like many more, she was, in fact, carried through her next ordeal at the hands of an examiner of another type, "curt and bullying," and she passed. Like the first lady, Miss Bell was struck by Spilsbury's fine presence and handsome appearance—"a most unusual thing, this, in examiners."

Such phrases as these—"I can give an example of Sir Bernard's great kindness of heart"; "an act of kindness I shall never forget"; "I was much impressed with the trouble which such a busy and distinguished man could take over an entirely undistinguished student who was one of a class of about seventy"—constantly occur in letters of appreciation written after Spilsbury's death. One begins, "To the memory of one of the noblest and most ill-requited of men," and several more, from doctors and lawyers whose acquaintance with Spilsbury was mainly in the law-courts or at coroners' inquests, refer in strong language to the inadequacy of the material rewards he earned. "I should imagine," one letter runs, "that Sir Bernard had no idea of the value of his services to the country, and that the Home Office took advantage of this, paying him the most paltry fees for his work. Of course, I do not know the circumstances regarding the payment of Home Office Pathologists," the writer adds; but, on this, and on Spilsbury's attitude to these things, Dr Keith Simpson's views are similar. "The fees assigned to this work," he says, "were at that time absurdly small, however skilled the service and however time-consuming, but Spilsbury took no interest in such matters, desiring only to satisfy the court and his own conscience." Dr Mervyn Gordon, who when Spilsbury was at Bart's was Lecturer on Bacteriology there, after saying that the latter's "outstanding services to the state in medico-legal cases were grossly underpaid," goes on to give the following instructive comparison:

> What shocked me was Spilsbury's answer to a question I put to him after he had done a long and trying examination in one of the criminal cases in which he was called in. . . . His reply was, "Ten guineas."

The case in question was one of those which entailed a long journey; and Dr Gordon goes on:

> In a case where I happened to be called in for the purpose of identifying an infection, and where the services of a consulting physician were also

required, a considerable distance had to be covered, and I charged the same rate as the physician—two-thirds of a guinea a mile, which amounted approximately to 60 guineas. Now you will see why I consider that Spilsbury was grossly underpaid.

In criminal cases Spilsbury, of course, received his travelling expenses, but neither these nor his fees were at the rate of two-thirds of a guinea a mile. The fees seem to have varied greatly. For the Armstrong case, which lasted ten days, the payment was not inadequate; on other occasions it was. Spilsbury's Home Office appointment being honorary, he received for this work only his fees for individual cases and £100 a year towards the upkeep of a laboratory. Underpaid, in the long run, he undoubtedly was. A private case has been cited for which his fee was commensurate with his great reputation, but he did very little private work. His income, which at its highest seems to have been about £3000 a year, was derived partly from Home Office fees and partly from his teaching posts, but chiefly, and increasingly, from his work for coroners. The normal payment for a post-mortem examination before the First World War was two guineas; it was afterwards raised to three guineas. In Spilsbury's busiest years, at the end of the 1930's, he was performing between 750 and 1000 post-mortems annually. If he sometimes received the higher fees which can be demanded by specialists of his standing it was not often at his own request.

Something has been said of his generosity, of the simplicity of his habits, and of his very few personal extravagancies. For a long time he smoked cigarettes everywhere (except in mortuaries) at the rate of fifty a day. Eventually he came to believe that the practice was affecting his heart, and he cut it out altogether. He enjoyed good food and wine, but would not put himself out to obtain them. When he had rooms in Verulam Buildings, and later, during the last War, was living in Hampstead and doing his laboratory work at University College, in Gower Street, he lunched either at the Holborn or at the station restaurant at Euston—usually alone, with a book or a journal, unless some member of his family was with him. He was probably scarcely aware that in the most straitened period of rationing his unsought popularity with the staffs brought him special dishes.

Though a fondness for buttonholes was a symptom of a genuine love of flowers, Spilsbury was never a gardener, and after his tennis days were over his only regular recreation was listening to music. He did not play any instrument himself. As a medical student he began to attend Henry Wood's promenade concerts, and in later life he was often seen in a concert hall, especially if Beethoven or Mozart was on the programme. He went two or three times to Glyndebourne. On the stage classical music seems to have appealed to him less than light opera. His taste in literature, which latterly he found little time to indulge, suggests that, like so many essentially simple men, he was at heart a romantic. Tennyson, Wordsworth, and Kipling were among his favourite writers. A set of Molière may have been a wedding present. Archæology was another early hobby for which necessarily he had less and less leisure as time went on. Here, as his son points out, the detective instinct came into play; as in pathology, he was faced with such questions as, "What situation in the past caused the observable evidence existing now?"

He once took his son Richard on one of the Hellenic cruises popular in happier days, and it was characteristic of him that even this sort of holiday must be turned to account, and the ground prepared beforehand. A notebook, apparently compiled during the homeward voyage, contains rough essays on the attitude of Sparta towards Athens, the Peloponnesian War, and the foreign policy of Pericles. From his days on the classical side at Manchester Grammar School Spilsbury remembered his Latin and Greek, and he quotes Aelian, Diodorus, Thucydides, Plato, and Socrates in the original, as well as modern authorities whom he must have studied for this purpose. He was little interested in modern history and language, but he learnt enough German to read text-books in that tongue.

As might be expected, he was not in the ordinary sense a clubbable man, though for many years he was a member of the Junior Carlton, and latterly of the United Universities, where he usually hid himself in the library. But his reputation for unsociability is belied by his enjoyment of company and talk in clubs of another sort. In addition to the Medico-Legal Society, he belonged to a number of others which met for the discussion of medical and forensic topics, and of science in general, such as a small dining club founded at Bart's by Dr C. Lovatt Evans, the Sydenham Medical Club, which was in existence before 1775, the small, informal, and select Organon Club, nearly a hundred years old, and, as before mentioned, "Our Society." This body of criminologists heard him discuss, among other curious affairs, the two tying-up cases in which he himself figured, and the mystery of the death by shooting of Mrs Luard, his observations on which must have been of great interest.

What he had to say on these occasions was backed by so much knowledge that most of his contemporaries would no doubt have agreed with Dr Lovatt Evans, who says of the discussions at his dining club, which for years Spilsbury attended regularly, "we usually learnt more from him than he did from us." As a speaker, he was more concerned with matter than with manner, and did not perhaps always realize beforehand how his detailed disquisitions on extremely gruesome subjects might affect less hardened audiences. In great demand by medical societies all over the country, he found time now and then to address such bodies in towns near London; and in the early 1920's he twice spoke to the newly formed Cambridge University Medical Society. On the second occasion he so wrought upon his hearers that one screamed, threw an epileptic fit, and bit the chairman's thumb, and two or three more fainted.

Such a scene was far from funny at the time, but Spilsbury may have seen its comical aspects afterwards. He had a rather schoolboyish sense of humour—a type not unknown, by the way, in other medical men. There is a story that in his younger days, when, however, he was married and on the road to fame, he carried home part of a human leg and left it in the kitchen under a dish-cover, to test the cook's reactions—which were violent. His family still possesses another relic of the post-mortem room, a thigh-bone once tied with ribbon and given as a Christmas present to the dog. With a bent for this sort of joke, Spilsbury was not likely to overlook opportunities suggested by his famous bag, which with its contents, whatever they might be at the moment, often went with him from the mortuary to a friend's house. Miss F. Tennyson Jesse, after remarking that, though to the general public he seemed rather a grim figure, he was very far from that, and, indeed, to a criminologist a delightful, because informative, conversationalist, tells how she met him one evening at a dinner-party given for Mr Harry Hodge, the publisher of the "Notable British Trials" series, and his wife. Spilsbury, almost always punctuality itself when on business, arrived three-quarters of an hour late, but "quite calm," says Miss Jesse. One of the courses at the delayed meal was partridge on toast, and as she always had difficulties in carving this bird she asked him to cut it up for her, adding, "You ought to be good at this, Sir Bernard." "It is a curious thing," said Spilsbury, "but I am no good except with my own instruments—which, by the way, I happen to have with me." Miss Jesse replied that it was a still more curious thing, but if he were to cut up her partridge with his instruments she would be unable to eat it.

None of Spilsbury's professional colleagues came to know him so well as Dr Eric Gardner, whose painstaking methods and flair for criminal investigation were almost on a par with his own. They first met on the occasion of a murder in Surrey, where Dr Gardner was County Pathologist. The latter had already performed a post-mortem on the body of the victim when Spilsbury was called in. He examined the body and the specimens taken from it with his usual care and in his usual silence. He listened to Dr Gardner's report. Then he put on his coat and prepared to go. The police officer in charge of the case said to him, "I suppose you will be sending your report, Sir Bernard." "You don't need a report from me," said Spilsbury. "Dr Gardner's is all that is necessary."

As a result of this meeting mutual liking and esteem, and a community of outlook and interests, grew into a close friendship—how close will eventually appear. Professionally, the two men were often associated in criminal cases, but Dr Gardner's opinion of Spilsbury can fittingly be included here.

"It was his honesty and integrity, and the fact that he could be relied on," Dr Gardner writes,

> that put him in the position he attained. My own opinion is that he was a great man. He made no attempt to pass as such, for he was—except in the witness-box—rather shy and unassuming. Any attempt at display would have been quite foreign to his nature. His greatness was due to his honesty and to the fact that his investigation of any material submitted to him was so thorough that even though his conclusions might not be accepted (though they generally were), they were received even by his opponents with the greatest consideration.

Dr Gardner tells a story which illustrates how wrong an impression of Spilsbury was sometimes formed by those who had not met him, and how rapidly a meeting altered their views:

> A man at my club pointed to Spilsbury and said to me, "Do you know that new member? All my life I have loathed that bombastic fellow Spilsbury, laying down the law in the witness-box as if he alone knew anything. I have spent several delightful evenings with him here, and have been more than charmed to find out what an unassuming, courteous gentleman he is. I use that much-abused word in its fullest meaning. I have only just found out that he is my pet aversion, and I can hardly understand it. I have seldom met a more delightful man to talk to—so different from what I had thought." The two became good friends.

2

Spilsbury's professional appointments included, at one time or another, those of Lecturer in Pathology at St Mary's and curator of the museum there, which he virtually founded; Lecturer in Morbid Anatomy at St Bartholomew's, and in Forensic Medicine and Toxicology at the London School of Medicine for Women; Examiner in Pathology at the University of London, and in Forensic Medicine at six universities. In 1924 he was Lettsonian Lecturer to the Medical Society of London. At the Centenary Meeting of the British Medical Association he was vice-president of the section of Forensic Medicine. He was for many years secretary to the Medico-Legal Society, contributing many papers to its proceedings.

If he did not hold more official positions of this kind it was for two reasons. Practical work and the calls of the Home Office, the police, and coroners encroached more and more deeply into his time; and while he enjoyed discussion on professional matters, and reading written papers to learned bodies, and was an admirable examiner, he did not love teaching or lecturing. Perhaps they were not his forte, and he realized it. All who sat under him agree about his complete lack of hesitation and the fund of example and analogy he could draw from his immense experience; but, as one old student puts it, this mass of information, of the most detailed and accurate character, was poured out in a rather mechanical manner. Others have said frankly that as a lecturer he was dull. A monotonous method of delivery, the mere fact that he was never at a loss for a word, tended to cause attention to wander, and he was less successful than others in getting his students through the theoretical side of their examinations.

When it came to practical work it was a different story. Those who were bored by the lecturer crowded to watch him demonstrating in the post-mortem room. Some stayed on after the demonstration was over, knowing that Spilsbury was always willing to stay on himself to clear up doubtful points, and even to go through the whole lesson again for their benefit. "I made it a habit, whenever possible," says the student already quoted,

> to stay behind after the other chiefs and students had left, when Sir Bernard would go meticulously over all the subjects and demonstrate to me the true cause of death, which had often been missed by the most eminent physicians and surgeons. Through his kindness and help I acquired more knowledge of pathology from him than from any other source. His clear expositions, on every word of which one knew one could rely, but which often were touched with his own characteristic quiet humour, were fascinating to listen to, and were of inestimable value to me later on in my examinations and after I had qualified.

The interesting point here is the transformation of the "rather mechanical" lecturer into the executant whose expositions became "fascinating" as soon as he could talk about something he was actually doing. Of this practical side another old student employs the same word: "To watch Sir Bernard, as I used to do at Bart's with fascination and awe, demonstrating on a brain, or a kidney, was—I should imagine—like watching Turner paint. What a master demonstrator!" The same writer refers to Spilsbury's "funny little box, and old instruments—there were no frills at all. He could have used a penknife.".

Some time later this same student, now qualified, was among the many who had cause to be grateful to his old teacher for a kindly and tactful thought. He had the misfortune to lose a patient under an anæsthetic. At the inquest Spilsbury's evidence completely exonerated him. As the pair drove away together Spilsbury said, "You mustn't let this affect you, Copeland. Every anæsthetist has a case like this. I knew a man who did *not* have one, and after twenty-five years his nerve went, as he thought each case he took would be that one, and he had to give up." Whether the anecdote was true, or whether it was made up on the spur of the moment, as Dr Copeland seems to suspect, it was just the right thing to say at the time.

Spilsbury's old instruments were well known. Some are said to have been of a type quite strange to his colleagues. They served his purpose, which was all he cared about; he was not interested in the latest thing, because it was the latest, but when any instrument could be improved upon he saw that it was done. Probing forceps, of his own invention, have become a standard for pathologists. The original pair is preserved at Bart's, together with the suit of white rubber overalls which gained for him the name of the Great White Chief. He was the inventor also, and apparently remains the sole user among pathologists, of detachable shirt-sleeves and of a special set of overalls described as being rather like a diver's suit.

His classes averaged between sixty and seventy. At the beginning of each course in pathology he would go round the class, examining the students' microscopes. On one occasion a new student, being, as he says, hard up, was found to be using an antique affair which had belonged to his father and grandfather. Spilsbury, remembering, perhaps, the new microscope, his own father's present, which influenced his choice of a career, sent to the laboratory for two modern types, and told the student to select the one which suited him best. During these courses at Bart's he gave three lectures a week on special pathology, and a series on forensic medicine, and for every course he prepared his own specimens and slides, sometimes as many as two hundred. This work alone took up much of his time for weeks beforehand. In the end he had to ask for a second assistant to take over this work of preparation. It was the custom for examiners who went to universities with well-equipped laboratories to use slides prepared for them there, but here, again, Spilsbury preferred to be equipped with his own. These visits to universities he heartily enjoyed; when he went to the provinces he might be away for a week, meeting old friends in fresh surroundings not associated, as were so many of his travels, with crime and horror. At least once, however, at Oxford, he combined lecturing with criminal investigations.

A born organizer, when he went from St Mary's to Bart's, from a fairly modern building to a congeries of older ones, he found a good deal that called for improvement, especially in his own department. Certain sections of the Medical School were being run on rather haphazard lines, and the classrooms were badly planned. He rearranged his own, so that every student could see what was being demonstrated. The post-mortem room, on the top floor, was not at all to his liking; he had the position of the tables changed, and the concrete floor replaced by one of mosaic, which was more easily and thoroughly washed down. His private laboratory was a small room on the first floor, its window looking out upon Smithfield Market. Here, as later at University College Hospital, his microscope was to help to solve many murders.

Something will be said later, in connexion with his work for coroners and the police, of his methods when performing a post-mortem. When demonstrating to students they were just the same—swift and certain in technique, and extremely thorough. Nothing was left to conjecture. Such demonstrations took two hours, followed by an hour for question and answer. No smoking was allowed, partly because the act of putting a pipe or cigarette to the mouth in close proximity to a dead body might convey disease, but quite as much in Spilsbury's case because tobacco fumes confused his poor sense of smell. Defective though this was, he relied a great deal on it. Students and others, who had to endure almost unbearable conditions in which he was perfectly happy, often wished it was keener.

It was while he was at Bart's, where he was soon working twelve hours a day, that constant calls by the police at all times decided him to take quarters more centrally situated than the house in St John's Wood, so that when necessary he could spend the night there. He found what he wanted in a set of chambers in Verulam Buildings, in

Grays Inn. Here he established another laboratory, and here, instead of an occasional night, he was before long spending the entire week, returning to his home only at week-ends. There were rare occasions when members of his family saw him at the hospital, and one of these is perpetuated by what is perhaps the only photograph showing him in an undignified position. In July 1923—the year in which he was admitted a Freeman of the City of London, under the style of "Sir Bernard Henry Spilsbury, Knt, Citizen and Fruiterer"—a fair was held in West Smithfield, outside the gates of the hospital, to celebrate the eight hundredth anniversary of its foundation, and to raise funds for its work. Lady Spilsbury and the children, hunting in the crowd among the swings and roundabouts for the eminent head of the family, found him sitting on the ground, in his usual dark suit, spats, and light grey Homburg, surrounded by students who had waylaid him, his legs clamped in a pair of stocks.

At Bart's, as everywhere, he was greatly liked and respected, and the hospital was proud of his gifts and reputation, yet his move there from St Mary's, the result of what in a man more given to impulse might have been called a fit of pique, turned out to be not wholly successful. At St Mary's, where he had, so to speak, grown up, he was one, and the most distinguished, of the brilliant band which had made its Medical School famous. Because in every branch of practical pathology, and as a demonstrator, he stood supreme, allowances, were any needed, were made for shortcomings as a lecturer and teacher in theory. At the older, and perhaps more old-fashioned, hospital there may from the first have been a scarcely conscious tendency to criticize. The failure of some of Spilsbury's students at Bart's to pass in morbid anatomy and histology was the subject of comment. On his side, well aware as he was of his pre-eminence in other respects, and particularly in post-mortem work, he was disappointed because he thought the staff kept too much of this in their own hands, giving him less than he expected and considered his due.

Chapter 3: THE POLICE

When Spilsbury was asked what he would do when he retired he replied, prophetically, "I shall go on to the end, and die in harness." The phrase in his case is singularly apt; and not only in the Biblical sense of the warrior. There never was a more willing horse, as the police with whom he worked in the happiest association for forty years are the first to testify. If they drove him very hard it was at his own wish.

To the C.I.D., indeed, he was the perfect collaborator. He knew as well as they did the importance of time in a criminal case. What are called clues may be destroyed through delay, and changes in the body after death, and its removal from the place where it was found, can confuse the medical evidence. Spilsbury never wasted a minute. At the height of his fame he was on call, like a general practitioner or the newest detective-constable, at any hour of the twenty-four, on every day in the year. Sundays or holidays made no difference; once at least he was fetched from home on Christmas Day.

It was not only for strictly medical reasons that the police valued his prompt appearance on the scene of an unnatural or unexplained death. He often helped them to reconstruct a crime of violence on the spot, which he almost invariably visited, even though the body had been removed. A Scottish judge once said that when a medical man sees a dead body he should notice everything, and no one believed more thoroughly in this maxim than Spilsbury. His remarkable eye for detail, and his acute gift of reasoning from observed facts, made his views valuable on questions normally outside the province of a pathologist. But he had to be asked for those views: he never volunteered them. Even when reporting on purely medical evidence he would confine himself to the facts, until asked what he deduced from them. There is no doubt, however, that he became keenly interested in every aspect of criminal investigation. He had thought much about criminals—especially about murderers. He had a theory that something always compelled them to refer obliquely to their crime, and that a study of their recorded words after the event might disclose incriminating phrases. Instances to support this theory, which seems psychologically probable, can at once be called to mind. Louis Wagner, the murderer of Smutty Nose, said, as he pointed to a boot thrown on the floor of a cobbler's shop, "I have seen a woman lying as still as that boot." George Joseph Smith warned Miss Pegler against the danger of baths.

Spilsbury, as has been said before, was the first medical detective, giving that word its narrow, accepted usage. From instinct and training his methods in every respect resembled those of his friends the police, as the latter fully appreciated. On the scene of a crime he could be trusted (unlike some others who should know better) to touch nothing, except the body, and to miss nothing. When he had finished his medical examination he would keep his hands in his pockets—a favourite trick at all times, which, perhaps, sprang from a habit of restraint. The police knew that material evidence was as safe in his keeping as in theirs; when a case came to court there would be no difficulty in proving Spilsbury's exhibits, because they had been handled by no one but himself and the analyst. The latter, in the witness-box, would begin his evidence, "On such and such a date I was handed so many jars by Sir Bernard Spilsbury"; and this was a statement of fact. Some pathologists leave to the police or mortuary attendants the packing of specimens and their dispatch for analysis, but this was not Spilsbury's way. In his bag, which was necessarily a large one, he carried not only his instruments, overall, and rubber gloves, but also his own jars and supply of formalin. From the moment he began his examination no one was permitted to touch this bag, not even to carry it for him to a car. He himself placed the organs he required in the jars, sealed them, wrote on them, and then took them in person to the hospital where he would find the analyst, whoever it might be—Webster or Willcox, Roche Lynch or Ryffel. Similarly, he made his slides himself; he did not let others make them, still less, like Brontë, allow them out of his sight.

2

Those who remember Spilsbury in his prime draw amusing comparisons between his unobtrusive arrival on the scene of an investigation, alone, polite but preoccupied, carrying his large bag, and the bustle and ceremony which sometimes attend the pathologist to-day, behind whom may trail a retinue of assistants, secretary, and other doctors, the subsequent examination of the body being accompanied by a running commentary and (if the scene is a mortuary) the rattle of a typewriter. For the last twenty years of Spilsbury's life, after the death of Mrs Bainbridge, he had no assistant for outside work. Watched respectfully by those present, he conducted his examination or autopsy almost in silence, unless asked a question; and while his faculties were at their keenest he made no notes at the time—often not until several days later. When he did make them he had forgotten nothing. Latterly, when he was ageing, but was still overwhelmed with work, there were times when the police wished he would not do quite so much himself. Reports which they needed promptly were unduly delayed.

Spilsbury's thoroughness has become proverbial. He scrutinized every inch of a body, front and back, before opening it, which he would do from the lower neck downward, not from the chin, as is more customary. He took the organs out one by one. A colleague, contrasting Spilsbury's method of hastening slowly and taking nothing for granted with the procedure sometimes in use to-day, tells a story which Spilsbury himself would have appreciated. A woman had been stabbed to death. The wounds, front and back, had been photographed. At the post-mortem the pathologist, presumably thinking that this was enough, began to open the body without turning it over, and drew out the organs in a bunch. The officer in charge of the case being present, he suggested that it would be as well to look at the back before going further, as he wanted to know whether the wounds there were separate ones, or the points of exit of stabs delivered in front. It was now necessary to take the body off the table and hold it upright, while the organs were with difficulty replaced and held in position. The narrator, paraphrasing Sergeant Brewster, remarked of this rather grim business that it would not have done for Sir Bernard.

The latter's trained eyesight and profound knowledge enabled him to detect symptoms invisible to the keenest vision of others. Many colleagues and old students record instances of this. When Dr John Cahill was with Spilsbury at St Mary's there was a case of a young woman who died of blood poisoning following a miscarriage. "Sir Bernard," says Dr Cahill, "called our attention to a minute punctured wound (the mark of a toothed instrument) in an internal organ. Not one of us could see it. But, with a lens, it became just visible." Dr Mervyn Gordon tells of a later case at Bart's where tuberculosis of the spine had been diagnosed. The patient died, and Spilsbury conducted a post-mortem. Dr Gordon found him still at work very late, and asked what was delaying him. "The notes," Spilsbury replied, "say that the lesion is tuberculosis of the spine, but I am convinced that it is not." Dr Gordon now recognized the body as that of one of his own patients from whom, while alive, he had taken a sample of pus containing actinomyces—the ray fungus. "Few pathologists, I venture to think," he says, "would have perceived with the naked eye the trace of chronic inflammation and suppuration which proved that another factor than tubercle was present."

This ability to dispense on occasions with the microscope was sometimes challenged in criminal cases, particularly in the Thorne trial, as a result of which so many latent causes of complaint against Spilsbury's authoritative position were given an airing. There is not, however, one recorded instance of a considered opinion by him, based on what he could see with the naked eye alone, being reversed by microscopical examination to the satisfaction of a judge and jury. He never formulated such an opinion, still less uttered it from the witness-box, unless he was absolutely sure. If he had the faintest shadow of doubt he applied his microscope. His supreme confidence in deciding when he could or could not do without this instrument is shown in his reply to a question by Dr Gordon as to the proportion of cases in which his first diagnosis was unchanged after microscopical examination. Spilsbury said that it was approximately 60 per cent.

There are many stories, some perhaps *ben trovato*, about the virtuosity to which he had raised even his defective sense of smell. One was told at the time of the Croydon poisonings. Spilsbury arrived at the grave-side dressed in his usual immaculate manner—according to the story, in a top hat. When the coffin was raised he ran his nose along it, straightened himself, and remarked, "Arsenic, gentlemen." In *Light and Shade at Scotland Yard* H. M. Howgrave-Graham, who was Secretary of the Metropolitan Police for nearly twenty years, relates how he asked a senior C.I.D. officer who had attended a good many post-mortems whether he found them unpleasant at the start. "Yes, sir, I did indeed," the officer said.

> I well remember my first case with Sir Bernard. It was a particularly unpleasant corpse, an exhumation case. I walked into the room, and there it was all laid out ready for examination. I was terribly afraid I should made a fool of myself, which would never do for a C.I.D. officer, so I put on a cigarette and tried to think of something else. After a while Sir Bernard came in. He sniffed twice, looked round the room, and said, "You mustn't smoke, please, Johnson. I can't smell the smells I want to smell." He then bent down over the corpse and sniffed away as if it was a rose-garden.

There was a very clear distinction in Spilsbury's mind, not always recognized by some who thought his methods old-fashioned, between what could not be improved upon and what needed improvement. If he used old instruments he invented new ones, and in the endless battle of science against crime, with which his name is chiefly associated, he was responsible for progress as radical as any he brought about in the less spectacular routine of the coroner's court. A familiar figure at the Metropolitan Police Laboratory (only recently removed from Hendon to join the photographic and finger-print departments at New Scotland Yard), he kept himself abreast of physical as well as of medical science, and tested any and every theory which might help him in his work. The by-products of chemical discoveries as applied to police investigation are interesting and curious, and no one studied them more closely than Spilsbury. Because he was able to prove that the fluorescence from a medical dressing worn by a man accused of murder differed from that given out by a similar piece of dressing found on the scene of the crime the man was discharged.

Among the C.I.D. specialists, Chief Superintendent Cherrill, by reason of his seniority, and because, next to the photographers, the finger-print experts are most often in demand where crime is suspected, probably saw more of Spilsbury than any other. Their work, too, lay on common ground, and their co-operation sometimes produced remarkable results, as will be instanced in a later chapter. It was not confined to crime. A patient from a skin hospital, suffering from a very rare complaint—complete absence of sweat glands—was once sent to Spilsbury. Even he was baffled, and recommended that the patient should see Mr Cherrill, whose lifelong study of finger-prints has resulted in his becoming an authority on skin diseases.

Spilsbury was by no means preoccupied with the purely scientific side of criminal investigation. At his suggestion many improvements and innovations were introduced into the practical outdoor methods of the police. One is of particular interest. When he was called in on the Mahon case in 1924 he was horrified on his arrival at the Officer's House on the Crumbles to find Superintendent Savage handling the dreadful remains of Emily Kaye with bare hands. Practically no special equipment for use on the scene of a crime was then issued to the police. They had no rubber gloves, no tapes or compass, no portable finger-print apparatus. With the help of Dr Scott Gillett, Spilsbury evolved what is now so well known as the "murder bag."

In writing of the happy relations which existed between Spilsbury and the police, who for so many years saw so much of him, the word 'friends' has been used, and deliberately. There were two main reasons for this bond of friendship. One is to be found in Spilsbury's unique position *vis-à-vis* the Force itself. Officially he was Honorary Pathologist to the Home Office, which meant the Department of Public Prosecutions; but he was also, to all intents and purposes, an honorary member of the C.I.D. The extent to which his advice and co-operation were sought cannot be defined; it must be enough to say that in all important investigations in which he was concerned his part was far from finished when he had performed a post-mortem and made his report. No outside consultant had ever occupied such a position before.

Implicit in this highly confidential status was the character of the man himself. Nowhere was he held in greater liking and respect than among the police of every grade. In conversation with them these sentiments are at once apparent; they are revealed by expression and manner with the first words used about him. "Every inch a gentleman," an expression employed by a very senior officer, sums up the opinion of them all. Chief Constable Wensley put it another way. "It is an education for any young officer to work with Sir Bernard," he once said.

Among many stories which help towards an understanding of this attitude there is one worth telling for itself. Some human remains were found in a zinc bath on the bank of the river Wreake, in Leicestershire. Two doctors, having examined them by torchlight, thought the matter sufficiently suspicious to warrant further investigation, and Scotland Yard was called in. Though by the time C.I.D. officers arrived the local police were satisfied that the remains, which included the mummified bodies of several infants, were anatomical specimens, Spilsbury also went down to Leicester, where he confirmed this opinion. The remains, in fact, were the property of a doctor, described as "a curious man who has since left the district." This affair, of which the Chief Constable of Leicester observed that it was "a wild-goose chase with a certain element of comic opera," gave Spilsbury an opportunity for one of those actions that gained him so many staunch friends among the police.

The remains had been taken to an infirmary. When Spilsbury came to inspect them, accompanied by two Scotland Yard officers and others of the Leicester City force, the superintendent of the institution was inclined to be obstructive. Looking at the police officers, he said, "You won't want these men with you, I suppose?"

Spilsbury turned to his companions. In the words of one of them, he looked right through them.

"I don't see any 'men,'" he said. "These officers will of course accompany me."

It is notable, too, how policemen, like judges, counsel, and professional colleagues, employ the same phrases in describing him and his methods. His kindliness and courtesy, combined with aloofness (this word is constantly used), his excellence as a witness, his fixed ideas and almost excessive thoroughness—these impressions, when reiterated again and again, give the effect of a stereotype. They are the unmistakable stamp of a personality which had no hidden side.

Chapter 4: CORONERS' COURTS

To those who know a pathologist only as an expert witness in criminal cases his career resembles an iceberg, nine-tenths of which are hidden. The actual disproportion between his cases which make news and those which are his real life's work is, of course, far greater. Of Spilsbury's 25,000 post-mortems, perhaps 250, or 1 per cent., had to do with murder. The remaining 24,750 represented day-to-day routine in hospitals and coroners' courts. The work he did for coroners enormously exceeded in bulk all the rest put together.

There are some two hundred and eighty coroners in England and Wales, holders of a judicial office so old that its origin, in the words of a standard work on the subject, "is lost in obscurity." *Jervis on Coroners*, the first edition of which was published in 1829, is a mere infant compared with some of the authorities it cites, such as the Articles of Eyre of 1194. "To put it shortly," says the Introduction to the seventh edition of *Jervis*, "the evidence points to the office of coroner having been first instituted in England as a Crown office by the Normans." In the Preface to this edition, issued a hundred years after the first, the editor's acknowledgments of help include one to Spilsbury.

Among the original functions of the coroner, as *custos placitorum coronæ*, or keeper of the King's pleas, was the collection of certain chance revenues due to the Crown, such as "chattels of felons, deodands, wrecks, royal fish and treasure trove." The last-named duty survives to-day, and the coroner can still act upon occasion in place of the sheriff. Another function as old, which keeps him more busy than ever before, and which provided Spilsbury with his main source of income and experience, is that of investigating sudden—*i.e.*, unexpected—deaths and the holding of inquests on the bodies of those killed by violence or accident, or dying in prison.

With these ancient powers, and as a direct officer of the Crown, chosen for life or during good behaviour, the coroner is a very important person—next to the sheriff, said Lord Campbell, the most important official in the county. The supreme coroner over all England is the Lord Chief Justice, and justices of the High Court are also sovereign coroners and can hold inquests in any part of the country, though they never do. In the days when all landowners had to have a smattering of law, the coroner seems usually to have been a knight; and until 1926 a property qualification was a condition of office.

Coeval with the office itself is the coroner's jury, summoned by warrant, and now numbering not fewer than seven or more than eleven "good and lawful men." The coroner can accept a majority verdict if the minority is not more than two. In certain circumstances he can sit without a jury. In general, he is allowed by custom a very wide latitude in his conduct of an inquiry, and one of his best-known duties is that of issuing a warrant for arrest after a verdict of murder or manslaughter.

Though in theory, until very recently, almost any person with some means could be a coroner, it has long been the general practice to appoint lawyers to the office. "Crowner's Law" has sometimes had a dubious connotation, but common sense has always been the basis of most of it, as is illustrated in the discussion by the two Clowns of the case of Ophelia. This also shows that even at inquests rank then had its privileges.

How rarely, until recent days, coroners had medical knowledge appears from *The Lay of St Gengulphus*:

> Here's a corpse in the case with a sad swell'd face,
> And a Medical Crowner's a queer sort of thing!

Only by the Coroners (Amendment) Act of 1926 was it laid down that coroners must be barristers, solicitors, or legally qualified medical men, of not less than five years standing. In the 1930's it became the practice in the huge area controlled by the London County Council to appoint coroners who were both lawyers and doctors, but this combination is nowhere obligatory, and is still rare in country districts.

The wide discretion allowed to coroners may occasionally be abused—among Spilsbury's cases, the inquest on the body of Willie Starchfield will be recalled in his connexion—and tenure of office for life sometimes results in incumbents continuing to hold it long after they should have made way for younger men. The valuable and helpful work accomplished daily in coroners' courts throughout the country far outweighs any such shortcomings, and to attend one of these courts, and watch an experienced coroner dispose of case after case with thoroughness and sympathy, without hurrying, and yet with dispatch, is to come away impressed by the workings of a system which, like so much else in English life, has developed in course of time from custom and tradition. Mr F. J. Waldo, himself a distinguished coroner, closes his Introduction to Sir John Jervis's standard work as follows: "The gradual growth of the coroner's office has beyond a doubt contributed throughout many centuries in no small degree to the protection of the lives of our countrymen."

This was Spilsbury's view, and no one, not even a coroner, knew more about the system than he. He was familiar with it twenty years before the present senior London coroner took office. He gave evidence at inquests from end to end of the country—some of them held in long-established courts, with the Royal Arms emblazoned behind the coroner's dais, some in village halls and inn parlours. If, as has been said, his knowledge of the ways and means of procedure in criminal courts was greater than that of any judge or counsel, in coroners' courts, where he spent so large a part of his professional life, he was even more at home.

As far back as 1914 the *St Mary's Hospital Gazette* contained an article on the subject attributed to him. There had recently been a good deal of criticism of coroners, and he came out strongly in defence of the system. "Prominent among the various opinions and criticisms," he wrote,

> is that of the modern reformer who favours complete abolition of the coroner's court on the ground that it is an anachronism, that a great part of its work is of no value to the state, and that the remainder could be better performed by a court of law.

"It must be emphasized," he went on, perhaps with recent cases in mind,

> that a coroner's inquisition has not as its objective the arraignment of a person suspected of the death of another. Its primary duty is to inquire into the cause of death, on view of the body, in all cases where death may have been caused or accelerated by the wilful act or negligent conduct of another person, in all cases recent or remote where an accident my have been the cause of accelerating death, and in all cases of sudden death where the cause is unknown. These, together with deaths in asylums and judicial executions, comprise the work as it affects the medical profession.
>
> If the result should bring a guilty person to justice it is, though important, entirely subsidiary to the above. For this reason hearsay evidence is allowed in a coroner's court and not in a court of law.

Spilsbury goes on to discuss the results of the Workmen's Compensation Act with regard to coroners' inquiries. There was a great tendency on the part of relatives to attribute death to the nature of the employment or to an accident connected with this. A large proportion of cases ended in findings against the claimants. Much time and expense in lawyers' fees was saved by dependents accepting the verdict of a coroner's court. Even if a case did go to the civil courts the findings and medical evidence at the inquest were of the greatest assistance.

Inquests, moreover, he added, cleared up to the satisfaction of all concerned many fatalities where some person rested under unjust suspicion. This applied, for example, to deaths under anæsthetics, because of the possibility of negligent administration.

"All deaths from remote injury," he concluded, "described by a person just before death, or remembered by friends, should be reported by medical men to the coroner."

His own records were to illustrate all the points he made, in those early days, on behalf of that ancient institution the coroner's inquiry. In particular, he was concerned in many cases "where some person rested under unjust suspicion," where his own evidence was the decisive factor in clearing that person's good name, and where, but for the inquest, it might never have been cleared. Some of these stories have been told, or will be told. Among others, there was that of Harold Glendinning, whose body was exhumed at Huddersfield because of rumours that he had died of antimony poisoning. Spilsbury showed that the cause of death was uræmia due to polycystic kidneys. Through no fault of his own he was too late in clearing the name of Samuel White, of Hordle, in Hampshire, whom village gossip accused of murdering his wife. White committed suicide before the adjourned hearing of the inquest at which Spilsbury's evidence proved that Mrs White had died from narcotic drugs taken to relieve insomnia. And in a third and more remarkable case he confounded a fellow pathologist and disposed of another charge of murder. A man was found dead of head injuries in a wood; the pathologist pronounced that three hairs found on a branch lying beside him came from his head, and the local police, following this lead, began to look for his murderer. Fortunately, being at a standstill, they called in Scotland Yard. The officer given charge of the case had his doubts, and said, "We must have Sir Bernard in on this." Spilsbury made short work of the hairs, which were those of a deer, a rabbit, and a dog. The dead man, who had been a sailor, had fallen from the tree, or, possibly, Spilsbury thought, had dived from it.

2

Many of the coroners' courts with which Spilsbury became acquainted at the start of his career are still standing, in part unchanged, but elsewhere greatly altered. Forty-five years ago the mortuaries attached to these courts were bare, whitewashed rooms, bitter in winter. There were no effective means of preserving bodies. Post-mortems had to be performed promptly, which is among the reasons why there were far fewer than there are to-day. Mortuaries are now tiled and warmed, and large refrigerators can keep a dozen corpses in cold storage. They have on occasion been employed for other purposes; soon after one of the massive affairs was installed a rush of business necessitated the use of all twelve compartments, when the twelfth was found to contain the mortuary-keeper's case of beer.

The normal coroner's court resembles in miniature other courts of law. There is, of course, no dock. The coroner sits raised above the floor of the court, with the witness-stand on his left. In some courts the jury-box is behind this, but more often it is on the coroner's right. Below him is a table for counsel, solicitors, and others watching a case on behalf of interested parties. Facing him and filling the rest of the court, are benches for witnesses, the public, and the Press. On the wall behind him—occasionally, as at Westminster, in transparency on a window—are the crimson and gold of the Royal Arms, the symbol of his office as King's Coroner. As a mark of respect for this office, every one rises as he enters and leaves a court.

The coroner has a deputy and a staff of officers, who are policemen attached to the court. One of these on duty opens the proceedings with a preamble beginning, "Oyez, Oyez, Oyez," and then calls witnesses by name and administers the oath—"I swear by Almighty God that I will speak the truth, the whole truth, and nothing but the truth." The coroner then examines the witnesses, and he can allow them to be further examined by counsel. He has power to conduct an inquest in secrecy, "for the sake of decency or for respect due to the feelings of the family of the deceased," and he can summon a pathologist to make a post-mortem without holding an inquest at all if the medical report justifies his belief that the death is natural and that further inquiry is unnecessary.

Such were the surroundings and routine amid which Spilsbury spent the greater part of his working life, day after day for forty years, either in the mortuary or in court. Of his pre-eminence as a witness it might seem that enough has been said; but coroners, especially when, as in London, they are doctors as well as lawyers, can appreciate better even than judges and counsel the qualities that raised him to this position. "As a witness," says the one who knew him best of all,

> he was incomparable. He used terms that all could understand. He called a bruise a bruise. . . . He never trifled with the facts as he saw them. He buttressed his position in every case by considering them carefully before he expressed an opinion; he did not confuse his facts with his conclusions. It was this clarity of decision that labelled him comparatively early in his professional career as one upon whom reliance could be placed, and he repaid this opportunity by setting a high standard in the giving of scientific evidence; in short, he put forensic science into the witness-box on its own separate importance, and not as being ancillary to anything else. His example has been far-reaching. . . . He was not one whose opinion changed, once it was well-founded, or whose evidence seemed to bear more than one facet as the case proceeded. What he said in the first instance he stuck to, and he was able to do this because he knew that he was right. . . . If the facts did not, in his view, merit a firm opinion he never flinched from admitting it. It can be all too easy for a pathologist or morbid anatomist to lean towards the adoption of some plausible condition as a cause of death when the possibility of its being adequate is not entirely certain. It takes a good pathologist to admit that what looks as if it were a simple, natural death has, temporarily at least, defeated him. Spilsbury had no qualms about this; he did not do his work against time and produce the answer in any given period. He was entirely unaffected by the possibility that he 'might have missed something'; he missed nothing. His scope of experience was almost limitless at his prime, and his memory was such that he could bring it to bear upon any matter at very short notice.

The writer, Bentley Purchase, may have had in mind an inquest at St Pancras, one of the few cases in which Spilsbury did admit himself defeated, only to have it proved, a little later, that his provisional diagnosis was correct. Such was his reputation that his admission made headlines in the Press. An elderly man had been found dead in bed. His relatives professed to know of no complaint that might have hastened his end, and Spilsbury said that he could find no cause of death. Under some pressure he added that it might be one of several things, the most probable being an obscure form of epilepsy. The relatives, recalled to the witness-box, admitted that for family and insurance reasons they had concealed the fact that the deceased had, in fact, suffered from occasional epileptic fits.

The same old friend speaks of the card index of which so much use has been made in this book. "In each case the autopsy appears to have been complete. The fact that the deceased was run over by a tram did not deter Spilsbury from seeing whether or not his heart shewed brown atrophy, or whether his spleen was soft." Another coroner, Ingleby Oddie, who employed Spilsbury a great deal, suggested that he was doing more detail in post-mortem examination than the facts of some of the cases required.

> Spilsbury would have none of it. He preferred to go to the same degree of detail in each case. He saw nothing unnecessary in his opening each body himself; he was not satisfied till he had examined every organ; though he did not produce museum specimens, he would cheerfully sit up into the small hours looking at frozen sections, prepared by himself, of organs the condition of which was not really material, except as a scientific exercise.

This quality of thoroughness, which made Spilsbury what he was, had one defect, apparent as he grew older. Satisfied only with the best, he found that life was not long enough for the amount of work he imposed upon himself. His health suffered, and, to some extent, the work itself suffered too, as he toiled ever harder to get ahead of time. "It must be admitted," Bentley Purchase says, "that, with the passing of years, his delivery deteriorated. . . . He overworked himself. Being an individualist and one who refused assistance to himself (though he gave it freely to others), he was likely to do so." This was an old story; many years before Sir William Willcox had said to his son, "Spilsbury is a fool: he'll kill himself with work done for nothing."

In Spilsbury's view it was not done for nothing, but in one sense the verdict is true, as towards the end of his life he realized. One of the saddest features of his case is that his most cherished aim, the object of so much of this overwork, not only was not attained, but was not even begun. "His fellow pathologists," one of them writes, "while recognizing his great merits, can but reflect ruefully on his disinclination to record, collate, or in some permanent way comment on his vast experience in forensic matters." There was no disinclination; on the contrary, for years he was collecting material for the book he was going to write on the application of post-mortem work to forensic medicine. For this purpose he summarized 6000 cases on his cards, and almost to the day of his death he was still summarizing, and still talking of his book. But increasing age, infirmities, the necessity of earning a living, and, perhaps not least, inability to call a halt to note-taking until, in his opinion, his material was complete—an unattainable state of things—these obstacles combined to postpone for ever the task on which his heart was set. Not a line of the book was written.

These remarks are appropriate here because "the very problems that Spilsbury learnt to solve so successfully," to quote the colleague mentioned above, were solved in the mortuaries of coroners' courts. At the mortuary tables was acquired the unrivalled knowledge that was to have been the basis of the unwritten book.

3

Before and after Spilsbury had given evidence at an inquest he would sit in court writing his notes or filling in forms. Form-filling was one of the things that took up too much of his time. Secretaries and typewriters were not for him. "He preferred to write out his reports himself in longhand; if two were required, he wrote out two. He thus gave himself extra work which others, but not himself, thought unnecessary." These reports were sometimes very long, and he insisted on reading them in full. At a criminal trial a judge once commented rather pettishly on this habit, but the impatience of others never hurried Spilsbury.

Ninety per cent. of his post-mortem work was done in London, and if there was some waiting for him in the mortuary he went there as soon as the court proceedings closed.

His recommendations and advice led to many of the modern improvements in mortuaries. The refrigerating system was one which he wished to see extended. At the Medico-Legal Society, after listening to a paper by Dr Blench on "Crime Investigation in Paris," he spoke on his favourite theme of the backward state of forensic medicine in England, due to inadequate facilities for medico-legal studies, and he instanced the lack of anything like the Paris Morgue, where bodies could be preserved for reference for any length of time. In a case of murder it would often be useful, in his opinion, if the corpse of the victim was available at the time of the trial.

One improvement failed to meet with his requirements. In later life he suffered greatly from the cold, and no heating system, short of a hypocaust, will warm cement floors constantly washed down. At one mortuary the attendants devised a species of duckboard walk round the tables specially for Spilsbury, but as his hands became chilled he dropped instruments through the slats. It was at this court, during a severe winter, that the heating of the court-room failed. The coroner, a man who did not know the meaning of cold, went happily on with the windows open while the witnesses froze. Among them was Spilsbury, muffled to the ears, his nose turning blue, trying to write his notes with icy fingers. This spectacle at last caught the coroner's attention, and the windows were shut.

Like every one else who saw much of Spilsbury, mortuary attendants and coroners' officers speak of him with genuine affection. He was always the same—preoccupied but courteous, strict but appreciative of the rather grim little jests current in mortuaries, which appealed to the schoolboyish sense of humour he never lost. One true incident made a story which it always amused him to tell. A medical witness collapsed in a faint while being rather sternly handled by the coroner, and had to be carried out. Soon after this Spilsbury arrived in court. Other witnesses having been heard, the coroner asked if Dr So-and-so was now in a condition to resume his evidence, and was surprised to hear that the doctor not only had recovered, but had gone. When he was removed insensible from the court, there being no couch available, he was laid on a long office table, of much the shape and hardness of a mortuary table. There he regained consciousness, and had barely done so when he saw Spilsbury's face bent over him. This was enough, and he fled.

At his busiest Spilsbury sometimes performed a thousand post-mortems a year. He used to say that a pathologist might do eleven hundred or twelve hundred, but certainly no more if a proper standard of thoroughness was to be kept up. Medical men asked to be present when he was at work, and he allowed students to attend some of his autopsies in police cases. To these witnesses he would talk, if questioned; otherwise he worked in silence, unless he wished to draw attention to some unusual feature, or, as he took out the organs, one by one, weighed them accurately by hand.

His cards, the material for the unwritten book, deal with mortality from almost every conceivable cause, but the great number of instances he preserved of certain diseases and means of death suggest that these held a particular interest for him. Such are pulmonary embolism, fibrosis, especially of the heart muscles, abortion, and asphyxia. He had made a prolonged study of asphyxia, and thought that doctors too frequently failed to distinguish between the two types—internal asphyxia, and that caused by some external process, such as strangulation. During a conversation at his club with Dr Eric Gardner the latter made a remark to the same effect. Spilsbury sat up in his chair. "What made you think of that?" he asked. "We must have been working along the same lines. I shall have a lot to say about asphyxia in my book."

He would have had a lot to say, too, about the thymus, the condition of which he seldom omitted to mention, as whether it was large or small, and what it weighed. A red-covered notebook headed "Thymus Cases" contains the records of ninety post-mortems, whose only consistent feature is a note of the size of the thymus gland.

As a student Spilsbury had experimented upon himself with carbon monoxide. The records he preserved of cases of coal-gas poisoning, the means by which he was to take his own life, are very numerous.

Part Four

THE FULLEST YEARS

Chapter 1: MURDER IN VARIETY

THAT part of Spilsbury's career which made his name a household word falls conveniently into three periods. In the first fifteen years, from his debut at the Crippen trial in 1910 to the end of 1925, he appeared in between twenty and thirty capital cases. Among them were the classics of the past half-century—the Crippen case itself and those of the Seddons, G. J. Smith, Thompson and Bywaters, Armstrong, Mahon, and Thorne. It has been possible to treat most of these at some length. The outbreak and collapse of the campaign against Spilsbury which followed the Thorne trial, and which left him firmly established for life at the head of his profession, brings this first period to an appropriate end. Moreover, after a comparatively uneventful twelve months in 1926, the police began to make enormously greater demands upon his services in connexion with this class of crime. During the next fourteen years, to the end of 1939, a date that put a period in every sense to all that had gone before, he was concerned in about 130 murder investigations. In view of the limitations of a book, it is as well that few of these cases are likely to become classics in the old style. There is a slump in great murders during this second period. For every reason, therefore, the mass of material has to be dealt with by a method differing from that applied to the first fifteen years. Selected cases are grouped under various headings. There will be a few overlappings, backward into the past—for example, the Bywaters-Thompson trial in 1922, and that of Alexander Mason a year later, are included in chapters on stabbing and shooting cases—and forward into the third and final period, that of the Second World War and Spilsbury's last years.

To begin with, some half-dozen cases spread over the middle period, difficult to classify or presenting unusual features, are considered together here.

2

The year of the Charing Cross Trunk Murder, 1927, found Spilsbury at work on the victims of other murders at Southwark, Grimsby,

Kingston, Sheffield, and Tonbridge. The Tonbridge case was in every sense a tragedy: an elderly woman, dying of cancer—Spilsbury gave her only two months to live—was poisoned by her daughter, who took arsenic from a doctor's surgery to put her mother out of her misery. The daughter was found unfit to plead. The Kingston autopsy, a month earlier, was the sequel to the discovery of the body of a young woman in Richmond Park, and it is possible that in this case the murderer was also on the borderline of insanity. Constance Oliver, who was twenty-one, had been missing from her home for two days before her body was found on October 2. She had been strangled with strips of material from her dress, after being stunned by blows on the head which drove the teeth of a comb into her scalp. Other injuries, and the trampled bracken round her, pointed clearly to a struggle. As well as these familiar details, Spilsbury noted a curious feature: part of her clothing and the top of a stocking had been burnt, and the skin of her thigh was scorched and blistered. If this was evidence of an attempt to burn the body, as was suggested, it indicates strongly the workings of an irrational mind.

A few days before her death Constance Oliver had introduced to her family a new acquaintance, described as "a delightful young man." It was a sad misfortune that he did not return the compliment by taking her to his own home, where she might have inferred that he was not as delightful as he seemed. He had a record of abnormal habits, some of them vicious, and his mother went in fear of him. His name was Sidney Bernard Goulter, and he was twenty-four. In December he stood his trial for the murder at the Guildford Assizes, before Mr Justice Horridge. Insanity was not pleaded. The proceedings lasted only a day, and the jury found the accused guilty after an absence of less than ten minutes. He was executed early in the New Year. Spilsbury performed the post-mortem after the hanging.

Though the rather artificial hubbub arising out of the Thorne case had died, it had set a fashion. When Spilsbury's evidence left counsel for the defence with little to work on there was always the forlorn hope of a declamatory appeal to the jury not to be overawed by a great reputation. A fortnight before the trial of Goulter, Spilsbury carried out a post-mortem on the body of the young wife of a retired naval officer. His findings led to a charge of manslaughter against a medical electrician with a Mayfair address. The defence was that the woman had died of shock while undergoing electrical treatment; Spilsbury agreed that the cause of death was shock, but said that it was due to an illegal operation. At the trial at the Old Bailey in January 1928 he gave reasons for this opinion which were incontrovertible. No amount of electrical treatment would produce the effects of an injection giving the chemical reactions for soap. Norman Birkett, for the accused, relied in his final speech less upon argument than upon the forlorn hope. "It will be an evil day," he said in this rhetorical appeal, "when, in the criminal courts, merely because of attainments, distinctions, and experience, the words of any expert are accepted as final and conclusive. Sir Bernard Spilsbury is not infallible yet, and his word is not the final word in this case." Once more, however, it was, and the accused was sentenced to seven years penal servitude.

Like "Man Bites Dog," "Murder at the Zoo" is news, and when the motive for the murder is said to be a white elephant the realm of pure fantasy seems to be reached. The story behind the domestic crime which shocked the Fellows of the Zoological Society in the autumn of 1928 had its pathetic side. San Dwe was a young Burmese who had come to the Zoo in the previous year in charge of a white elephant. The London climate did not suit the animal, and it was returned to Burma. San Dwe remained, but fretted over the loss of his large companion. He longed to rejoin it in its native forests and swamps. In his simple way he may have echoed Alice's plaint to Jumbo:

> If you really love me, as you say you do,
> You wouldn't go to Yankeeland and leave me in the Zoo.

He had, moreover, a less sentimental cause for dissatisfaction. The chief elephant-keeper at the Zoo was Sayed Ali, a Mohammedan from Calcutta. Like the white elephant, Sayed could not stand the English winter, and, being a very fine trainer, and therefore a valuable man, he was allowed to return to India after each summer season. During his absence in the winter of 1927–28 San Dwe deputised for him. A profitable part of the work was the charge of two elephants used for carrying children about the grounds.

When Sayed Ali came back as usual in June of the latter year he again took over this job, which was worth 30*s.* a week in tips. San Dwe was relegated to such tasks as looking after the elephant cart. Nevertheless the two men, who shared rooms over the Tapir House, were said to be on friendly terms.

The Tapir House is close to the Outer Circle of Regent's Park, from which it is separated by an iron railing and a privet hedge. On the night of August 24 two police officers heard groans coming from behind the hedge. One of them climbed the railing and found San Dwe lying at the back of the Tapir House. He had a wounded foot and was hysterical. His story—he could speak a sort of English—was that four men had broken into the building and killed Sayed Ali with a pickaxe. They had tried to kill him too, while he hid under his bed, but he escaped.

Sayed Ali was indeed dead, shockingly battered about the head and body. Spilsbury made drawings of four of the lacerated wounds on his case cards. The Mohammedan's room was in great disorder. A wooden box had been broken open, and on top of it were two bags full of coppers. A wallet in the bed contained £36, and a Post Office Savings Bank Book showed deposits amounting to £60. A blood-stained pickaxe and sledge-hammer were found on the premises.

San Dwe was taken from hospital to a police station, where he was kept for a day and a half before being charged with the murder. At his trial in November Mr Justice Swift commented severely on this detention. Curtis-Bennett, for the defence, called no evidence, submitting that the prosecution had not proved their case. No one, however, believed in the four intruders, and the Burmese was found guilty. The sentence was commuted to one of penal servitude for life. In 1932 it came up for revision by a special board, and San Dwe was released and sent back to Burma, where, it is to be hoped, he found his large white (or greyish) friend.

His crime was that of a child, as was no doubt felt at the time. It emerged from several rambling statements how passionately he desired to return to his own country. Having killed Sayed Ali, panic or conscience drove him away before he could finish his search for money. It was all quite senseless, for not only had he £40 of his own, but if he had told the authorities at the Zoo of his wishes they would have let him go and paid his passage.

3

At 6.45 on the evening of January 10, 1929, a telegram from Mr McCormac, Chief Constable of Southampton, was received at Scotland Yard:

> A case of murder has occurred here. A man has been found shot in a room the door of which was padlocked. The body was found to-day and has probably been in the room some eight or nine weeks. Will you please send an officer down to investigate the matter.

More than a year later, on March 4, 1930, at the Winchester Assizes, Spilsbury went into the witness-box to give evidence against the man accused of this crime. He began by saying, "In my opinion death was caused by fractures to the skull and injuries to the brain, consequent on blows on the head with some heavy blunt object. The head of this hammer might have caused all the injuries."

Vivian Messiter, who was not shot, but hammered to death, had been reported missing from his lodgings in Southampton as far back as November 1, 1928. He was living with an ex-policeman, or his disappearance might not have been notified as promptly as it was. The subsequent lack of interest in his whereabouts was one of the striking features of the case. A West Countryman, educated at one of the smaller public schools, Messiter had studied medicine before becoming an engineer. He had been abroad most of his life. During the 1914–18 War he came home to enlist, and as a captain in the Northumberland Fusiliers received a wound which left him slightly lame. In 1928 he was fifty-seven, a reserved, solitary man, divorced from his wife, and he had returned to England only that year from another long absence in the United States and Mexico. Yet he had relatives in this country, and he had a job, and the fact that he was lost to sight and knowledge for more than two months without any serious efforts being made to discover what had become of him throws a curious light on the casual attitude of his acquaintances and of the firm which not only employed him, but had recently made him a director.

Messiter's job was that of local agent for the Wolf's Head Oil Company. He used a garage in Grove Street as a store. After his disappearance from his rooms was reported the Southampton police did indeed get in touch with his firm, and a sergeant went to Grove Street, where he found the garage padlocked on the outside, and came away again. Nothing more was done, though it seems to have been known that the landlord of a public house near at hand had a spare key. It was assumed that Messiter had suddenly decided to go on his travels once more, but taking nothing, not even a change of clothes, and without informing anyone. His firm was so little interested in pushing business in Southampton that ten weeks went by before a Mr Passmore came to take over the agency. The publican who had the spare key being out, Passmore and a friend forced the padlock. In the garage, which was stacked with drums and cases of oil, stood the firm's car; still unperturbed, the pair spent some time trying to get it to start. Only when they found the tank was empty did they trouble to explore the premises. Behind a high tier of wooden cases they found the body, and the police were summoned.

What followed illustrates a point which is perhaps rather often overlooked—that very few police officers in the lower ranks of the uniformed branch ever meet a case of murder. Members of the C.I.D. are accustomed to the difficulties caused because some constable first on the scene of a murder does not recognize it as such, or misreads what he sees, or forgets all the precautions he was instructed to take when he was under training. At least three policemen saw Messiter's body lying in the garage. The head had been terribly battered, the skull, in Spilsbury's words, "being fractured everywhere except on top." Blood was splashed on the boxes round to a height of several feet, an almost sure indication of blows by a weapon used as a club. There was no money in his pockets, and the building was padlocked on the outside. Making allowance for the damage wrought by time and rats, it is still surprising to read that for some hours he was thought to have died of a hæmorrhage. Then it was supposed that he had been shot. A doctor examined the body that morning, but the shooting theory was still held when the Chief Constable sent his telegram in the evening. The real cause of death seems to have been recognized before Chief Inspector Prothero and Detective-Sergeant Young arrived at Southampton from Scotland Yard late that night. The weapon used, the hammer, was found three days later, between some cases and the garage wall. It was a punctured wound over Messiter's left eye, made with the point of the hammer, which was at first mistaken for a bullet-hole.

Spilsbury went to Southampton on the 15th, five days after the discovery of the crime. He describes on his cards the results of his examination of the body in the presence of the doctor who performed the first post-mortem, and he adds his conclusions:

> At least three blows on the head, any one producing immediate unconsciousness. The head of a large hammer, used with great violence, would account for injuries. Those across base and on right side produced when the head was on a hard surface. Position of injuries at back suggest that deceased was bending forwards. Punctured wounds on top of head—? striking edge of tin box in fall.

By this date Chief Inspector Prothero was already beginning to be interested in the movements of a man who was, in fact, the murderer, and who was then known as William F. Thomas. His real name was William Henry Podmore. More than a year was to pass, as has been seen, before he was brought to trial for the crime, and it was after this that Spilsbury, filling in his cards from his notes, appended the following brief history of the case:

> Oct. 28 Podmore came as assistant to deceased. He was a motor engineer, aet. 29. "The Man with the Scar," passing as Thomas. He

was to sell oil for deceased. Deceased last seen alive Oct. 30, 1928. Body found Jan. 10, '29, lying on floor in garage. Blood on floor and splashed on cases some feet from body. No money or valuables on body. Gold watch missing, but swivel ring of watch on floor. Heavy hammer found with human bloodstains upon it and a hair corresponding with eyebrow hair of deceased. Hammer had been borrowed from Morris works at Southampton. Evidence from books of two false transactions for which Podmore was charging deceased. Fictitious names were those of persons living near Podmore's home in Potteries. Messiter had written out invoices to be sent to these people at fictitious addresses in Southampton. Prisoner said that an agent—Maxton—was with deceased when he last saw him, and that they were in dispute. No such person traced. Prisoner talked to two fellow prisoners while on remand in Wandsworth Prison, charged with robbery for which he was serving a sentence when charged with the murder. Convicted of murder. Winchester. Lord Hewart. March 8, 1930.

All that need be added to this adequate summary, written on both sides of a card measuring five inches by three, are the details of the speedy tracking down of Podmore, which is an excellent example of combined police routine work. The first clue, which by itself might have led nowhere, was Messiter's order-book. Some of the front sheets were torn out, and carbon transfer sheets gave names and addresses of customers in and about Southampton that proved to be non-existent. In a memorandum book, also lacking its front pages, was a receipt signed "H. F. Galton." This was genuine, but concealed, like a palimpsest, another clue of great importance. In Messiter's rooms was found a reply to an advertisement for local agents, dated October 23 and signed "William F. Thomas." At the address given it was learned that Thomas and his wife, having stayed a fortnight, had left on November 3, three days after Messiter was last seen alive. Thomas left an address in Chiswick which turned out to be fictitious. The search of the Grove Street premises next brought to light a crumpled note from Messiter to Thomas, undated, saying that he would be at the garage at 10 A.M., but not at 12.30. In the meantime the police had published a description of a youngish man seen with Messiter at the end of October. A building contractor in Downton, a small Wiltshire town, came forward to say that a mechanic named W. F. Thomas, answering to the description, had been in his employ from November 3 to the third week in December. A large sum of money in pay packets having disappeared, on December 22, the Wiltshire police questioned Thomas, who, with Mrs Thomas, vanished next day. He had given the police an address compounded of the imaginary firm in Chiswick and one of the equally imaginary streets in Southampton found in Messiter's order-book.

All this being known to Mr Prothero by January 15, the day when Spilsbury examined Messiter's body, it will be understood why the Chief Inspector felt a good deal of interest in W. F. Thomas. He was soon to feel more. Thomas had made a bad slip, perhaps a fatal one, when he fled from Downton. He did not wait to pack his belongings, or tidy up his room. On scraps of paper there were found the words "Podmore" and "Manchester," and the printed heading of a firm in that city. It was such a piece of luck as sometimes rewards the drudgery of a police investigation. Podmore, a motor mechanic, had left the employ of the Manchester firm on October 17, three days before Mr and Mrs Thomas took rooms in Southampton, and his description tallied with that of Mr Thomas.

Nor was this all. The Criminal Record Office at Scotland Yard knew nothing of W. F. Thomas. But while a fuller description of him was being circulated—it mentioned a scar on his temple, actually very slight, but seized on by the newspapers to make a headline—the C.R.O. was searching its files for William Henry Podmore. And there he was, if not an habitual criminal in the technical sense, a man who had been several times in the hands of the police, and who at that very moment was wanted in Manchester for fraud. To round off a neat case, Podmore was a Staffordshire man, and the fictitious names and addresses in the order-book and given by him were those of persons and streets familiar to him in his native county.

Podmore was soon found, on the information of the woman who had passed as his wife. He was not trying to hide, but was in London under his own name, on his way to Southampton, or so he said, to tell what he knew. He had been described as an unusually clever criminal, and, having by now realized his position and decided on a course of action, he thought out his story, with its half-truths and lies and admissions, and never varied from it.

The gist of it was that, being on the run from trouble in Manchester, he went to Southampton, accompanied by the person whom the Rev. Cornelius Whur might have called a faithful female friend, in the hope of getting abroad. He had good reasons for using an assumed name. Though his employment by Messiter began only on October 28, by the 30th he had decided to take the better job at Downton. The contractor there, however, was not ready to take him on, and that evening, and again on the 31st, he called at the Grove Street premises, but found them locked. The morning of the 30th was the last time he saw Messiter. During their short acquaintance the latter was twice in the company of another agent called Maxton or Baxton.

Messiter had given him a list of customers. Some of them he failed to find, among these being a firm listed as Cromer and Bartlett, of 25 Bold Street. This was one of the fictitious addresses in the order-book; but though there is no Bold Street in Southampton, there is one in Hanley, in the Potteries, and others in Midland and northern towns known to Podmore. Podmore, of course, had never heard of them, and he had his usual ready answer when asked why he gave the Wiltshire police the name of another imaginary firm in this non-existent street. Having stolen the pay-packets at Downton (as he now admitted doing), he naturally gave a false address, borrowing the street from Messiter's list.

He was detained on January 17, and at the end of the month was charged at Manchester under the warrants out against him and sentenced to six months' imprisonment. In the Messiter case, in the meantime, another hopeful clue had come to nothing. An engineer at the Morris works at Southampton, which were near Grove Street, identified the hammer found in the garage as one he had rather confidingly lent to a stranger in the last days of October. But at an identification parade neither this witness nor his foreman recognized Podmore as the borrower.

However convinced Chief Inspector Prothero might be that he had found the murderer, more evidence was needed to make a case that would satisfy the Director of Public Prosecutions. The result of the adjourned inquest did not forward matters. A most important piece of evidence had, in fact, by now come to light; but in spite of this the coroner's jury returned an open verdict.

If ever officers of the C.I.D. in charge of a case feel like kicking themselves it must be on those rare occasions when, after weeks of patient and tedious work, it is found that some vital point has been overlooked. From the day when Mr Prothero arrived at Southampton he had in his possession the evidence which probably hanged Podmore; and for nearly two months he had not known it. It was the receipt for *2s. 6d.* commission on the sale of oil signed "H. F. Galton." As it was a genuine receipt—Galton worked for Messiter in his spare time—the sheet of the memorandum book on which it was entered, though handled scores of times, received no special attention. Only on March 7, when scrutinizing it once more, did the Chief Inspector perceive indentions beneath the writing. They had been made by a pencil on the page above, which was one of those torn out. When photographed at a suitable angle under a powerful light the indentations were clearly readable as another receipt.

October 28th, 1928

Received from Wolf's Head Oil Company commission on Cromer & Bartlett, 5 galls at 6d. 2/6d. W.F.T.

Here at last was proof of what had long been assumed—that Podmore, during his few days with Messiter, who did not know Southampton well, had been drawing commission on imaginary sales, borrowing names and addresses from his native Staffordshire and elsewhere. After the murder, presumably, he had torn the incriminating pages from the order-book and the memorandum-book.

Though this discovery was made in March, Podmore was not charged with the murder until December that year (1929). He was in safe keeping; no sooner had he finished his sentence for the Manchester fraud than he was rearrested, charged with the theft of money at Downton, and given another six months. It would seem that the authorities felt that the murder case against him still needed strengthening, and hoped that something more would turn up. This rather Micawberish attitude may have been influenced by the verdict of the coroner's jury. How the authorities would have acted had Podmore not been in custody is, however, an interesting conjecture.

In due course something more did turn up: two of Podmore's fellow-prisoners at Wandsworth, one of them a man of colour, reported statements by him, of which one amounted to a confession. On December 17 he was at last charged with the murder, and he was tried at the Winchester Assizes in March 1930, fifteen months after the crime, before the Lord Chief Justice, Lord Hewart. He was convicted, and his appeal against the conviction was dismissed. An attempt to carry the case to the House of Lords having failed, pressure was applied to the Home Secretary. When he declined to alter the course of the law the Independent Labour Party had the effrontery to censure him, as a Socialist, for not doing so, and received a well-merited rebuke. Podmore was hanged on April 22.

Those behind this agitation who were sincere were influenced by the delay in bringing Podmore to trial, and by the calling as witnesses of two convicted criminals, but chiefly by the common misunderstanding of the value of circumstantial evidence. In the volume on the case in the "Famous Trials" series the authors, one of them a lawyer, point out that the case against Podmore rested not only on what was found, but on what was not found.

Had the books been unmutilated, had the missing invoice and the missing receipt been there, they would indeed have established a case of swindling against the prisoner, but it is more than doubtful whether any jury would have held that they established more—it is a very long step from false pretences to wilful murder. But they were not there, and there could have been but one hand that removed them—the hand of the man who had fabricated the orders and signed the receipt. And that removal must have taken place after Messiter's death, for before it would have been useless. That was what really convicted Podmore.

What happened, no doubt, was that Messiter discovered the swindle, and taxed Podmore with it, threatening him with the police. This meant more than a short sentence for misappropriating a few shillings; there were the warrants out in Manchester. Podmore, who had never before used violence, lost his wits or his temper. The hammer was there—lying about, perhaps borrowed by Messiter himself, or in Podmore's own pocket; as Messiter turned away he was struck down. The most shocking feature of the attack, which no doubt the jury bore in mind, was that while the unconscious man lay with his head on the cement floor his assailant rained more blows on him. Podmore's callous insensitiveness once he had recovered his nerve—leaving his victim locked in the garage, he took his faithful friend to Downton "for some fresh air" in Messiter's car—must have created almost as bad an impression.

Spilsbury's share in this case was limited to showing that the hammer was the weapon used. Out of this grew one of those newspaper legends, the inaccuracy of which did much to strengthen his almost morbid aversion to publicity. "Two Hairs hanged this Man!" may be a good headline, but it bears no relation to the truth. "The revealing lens," says the author of this caption, "had focused two tiny hairs on the weapon. Sir Bernard made up his mind very quickly. Hair . . . human . . . male . . . eyebrow. . . . Those two hairs pointed the killer out to the police." There was one hair, not two, on the hammer, and since it was Messiter's, not Podmore's, and the hammer was never traced to Podmore, a whole scalp would not have pointed the killer to the police. "The most vital clue of all" was not even a clue. "Messiter," the reader is told later on, "discovers that he had been systematically swindled for months," the actual period being two days; and a remarkable metaphor describes Spilsbury's evidence at the trial. "Crisp, forceful, direct, he prodded Podmore's feeble alibi with a hammer. . . ." As the late Professor Moriarty said to Mr Holmes, "Dear me!" When nonsense of this sort was brought to Spilsbury's notice— his normal periodical reading went little farther than medical journals and *The Times*—he must have prayed to be delivered from his friends.

4

Fifteen months after Podmore's trial a case occurred in which Spilsbury's evidence probably did turn the scale, and which deserves mention for another reason. Though the *mise en scène* and the actors were squalid in the extreme, an age-old problem, that of the disposal of the body, was tackled in a novel way by the use of local facilities so rarely available that in this country only writers of detective stories have been able to employ the method since.

On June 2, 1931, a blackened human hand was seen protruding from a smouldering rubbish-dump at Scratchwood Sidings, on the Midland Railway between Mill Hill and Elstree. The rest of the horrid remains having been dug out, Spilsbury examined them at Hendon mortuary that afternoon. They were those of a man of middle age, his whole body terribly charred by the intense heat generated in the mass of rubbish. The right arm was burnt away to the shoulder, and the legs were half destroyed. The skin of the face peeled off with the sacking in which the head had been wrapped. It was the Rouse case with a difference—the roasting effects of slow combustion as against the swift searing of a petrol flame. From the degree of putrefaction of unburnt parts protected by the man's clothes Spilsbury put the time of death at from two to three days before the discovery. It had been caused by a violent blow on the left temple, and he made a sketch of the curious rectangular fracture of the skull.

The fragmentary clothes were those of a labourer. The left forearm, the hand of which, beckoning from the dump, had betrayed the crime, was tattooed with a red heart transfixed by a sword. This ornament, and what was left of a moustache, identified the victim as a member of a constantly shifting colony of casual workers, unemployed and unemployables, who lived like gypsies in some shacks near the railway sidings. Most of these were rough characters, far from popular in the local public houses, who preferred to be known only by nicknames. The dead man was "Pigsticker." A witness came forward who had seen him attacked on the night of May 30, by two other denizens of the encampment, "Tiggy" and "Moosh." These picturesque appellations would hardly do in a police court; and, the pair having been separately apprehended, they were charged with the murder in their real names of Oliver Newman and William Shelley. "Pigsticker" was Herbert Ayres, aged forty-five.

Under the floor of Newman's hut was found a bloodstained axe. Spilsbury fitted the rectangular back of the blade into the fracture on Ayres' skull. In spite of this the accused, who could not deny that there had been a fight, said that Ayres had the weapon, while they used only their fists; and at the trial at the Old Bailey counsel for the defence made much of certain bruises on the dead man's left hand. Spilsbury's opinion was that the bruises were caused as Ayres tried to protect his head from the blows of the axe. Shelley's counsel writes, in an account of the case, "We lost, of course, because, as every barrister knows, once Sir Bernard had made up his mind, nothing could shake him." There is more in this admission than perhaps appears.

An interesting point in the trial was a protest uttered by Rigby Swift, the judge, in his most energetic vein, against the use made of Spilsbury's earlier evidence at the police-court proceedings. In a transcript of this, questions put to Spilsbury were made to look as if they were his answers. The judge's comments were:

> "In the witness-box counsel listens to him, and if he finds an 'i' not dotted, or a 't' uncrossed, he says, 'This man is saying something different to what he said below.' It happens day after day, and it is painful to see what the art of defending criminals has descended to. I will not tolerate it, and it is a perfect outrage to put that to Sir Bernard Spilsbury and suggest that that is his evidence. It is an outrage. It is shocking!"

The two accused having been sentenced to death, Shelley made the curious remark that it ought to have happened twenty years before.

5

If there are degrees of wickedness in murder, only a shade less atrocious than the killing of children is the deliberate battering to death of elderly women living alone. These crimes are almost always committed for gain. In the majority of cases the murderer picks out some one known to him—a woman keeping a small shop, or with a reputation for hoarding money—but the evidence shows that there is also a type of monster who sets to work, by a system of trial and error, to find a suitable victim. Though murder may not always be intended, whether it results or not seems to be a matter of indifference to this class of criminal. From his point of view the victim is usually better dead; and only too often, the hammer or poker having silenced her, the bloody task is completed.

Such brutes are always with us, as the newspapers show, and their crimes recur with terrible frequency in Spilsbury's records. Some of these cases have been mentioned. Among those occurring in this middle period of his career two stand out—the murders of Miss Wren at Ramsgate and of Mrs Kempson at Oxford.

The Wren case, which in its shocking details differs little from a score of others, is remarkable for the character and behaviour of Miss Wren herself. She was eighty-two, and she had a small sweet-shop in Ramsgate. She possessed some house property, and had money in the bank. Like so many people of her age and class, she kept cash in tin boxes and other receptacles stowed away in various hiding-places. This dangerous habit got known, as it usually does, and her hoards, no doubt, were much exaggerated, the more so because she lived like the traditional miser, in squalor and discomfort.

About six o'clock on September 20, 1930, a girl of twelve who lived opposite the shop was sent across the street to buy a blancmange powder. The shop door was locked; peering through the window, the girl saw Miss Wren sitting in her back room. When eventually the old woman came to the door blood was streaming down her face, and she could only whisper; but though, in fact, she was suffering from injuries that might have killed her on the spot, she went behind the counter and fetched a number of packets for the child to choose from. The girl ran back to her parents, and to their horrified inquiries Miss Wren gave the unlikely explanation that she had fallen over the fire-tongs.

She was taken to hospital, where she lingered for five days. She had been savagely attacked, and on the third day Scotland Yard was called in. As her mind wandered she made rambling and contradictory statements, from which glimpses of the truth emerged, to the nurses and the police, and to the magistrate who, later, waited beside her bed. It was an accident; a man had attacked her with the fire-tongs; he had a white bag; it was another man with a red face; it was two men; then, again, it was an accident with the tongs. Once she admitted that she knew her assailant, but she would not name him. "I don't wish him to suffer. He must bear his sins. . . ." Just before the end she said, "He tried to borrow ten pounds." More than this they could not get from her, and to Superintendent Hambrook, who was in charge of the case, she was the most determined, inflexible woman he ever met. On the afternoon of the 25th she died, still keeping her secret.

Performing the post-mortem on the following day, Spilsbury enumerated eight wounds and bruises on the face, and seven more, lacerated or punctured, on the top of the head. In addition, there had been an attempt at strangulation. The injuries were undoubtedly inflicted with the tongs which figured in the poor woman's stories, and on which hairs were found.

The circumstances of this murder suggest that it may not have been premeditated, as it so often seems to be in similar cases. Miss Wren was seen alive and well at 5.30, and she usually kept her shop open after six. At that hour, in September, with Summer Time in force, it was not dark. There were people going up and down the street, and children playing. If violence was intended it was an extremely rash project. On the other hand, there can be no doubt that the murderer came for money, and, like all his type, was prepared to go to great lengths to get it. It was probably he who locked the shop door. Perhaps disturbed by another caller—for no money seems to have been taken—he escaped by the backyard. Apart from the evidence of Miss Wren's admissions, it is clear that he knew of her habits, and was familiar with the premises.

At the inquest certain persons were referred to by letters of the alphabet. Superintendent Hambrook says that there were six suspects, of whom *A*, *B*, and *C* were able to clear themselves. One of the remaining three *D*, *E*, or *F*, was the murderer. Miss Wren knew which, and the police may know too. But it has never been possible to pin the crime on him.

Eleven months later came the murder of Mrs Annie Louisa Kempson at Oxford. There was no lack of premeditation here, and from the circumstances and the murderer's record it may be inferred that he was working on the empirical method earlier alluded to—"If at first you don't succeed, try, try again"—and that if poor Mrs Kempson had been less trusting, or more lucky, he would have sought another victim elsewhere.

On the evening of August Bank Holiday, 1931, Chief Inspector Horwell, being then first on the Chief Inspectors' rota for duty, was called up from Scotland Yard and told to take the midnight train to Oxford, where a murder had been committed. Early next morning he telephoned to Spilsbury, who arrived "in an incredibly short time." In the mortuary Spilsbury examined the body of Mrs Kempson, Horwell standing by, for she had been dead for at least a day, and time was precious. Except for one feature, Spilsbury's notes are almost a replica of many others made in similar cases. There were half a dozen lacerated wounds on the head, inflicted by some such implement as a hammer. The first blow had been delivered from behind, and she had not attempted to defend herself. Other blows followed as she lay stunned. In Spilsbury's opinion she was then moved from the entrance-hall, where the attack took place, to the dining-room, and there, as she was still alive, the murderer used another weapon, a sharp cutting instrument, which he drove through the neck, severing the carotid artery. She would have died almost immediately. It was a shockingly cold-blooded business.

Mrs Kempson was the widow of an Oxford tradesman. She was fifty-eight, and lived in a small semi-detached house called The Boundary in St Clement's Street, which is that part of the London Road joining the Iffley Road and the High Street at Magdalen Bridge. Like Miss Wren, she owned house property, and, though better educated and in better circumstances, had the same foolish habit of keeping considerable sums of money in her home. She had a lodger, a Miss Williams, but the latter was away for the Bank Holiday weekend. Mrs Kempson herself was to have gone to London the same Saturday afternoon, and it was her failure to arrive at her destination that led to inquiries being made of her brother, a servant at Jesus College. On the Bank Holiday itself, Monday, August 3, at a second visit to The Boundary, the brother and his son broke in, to find Mrs Kempson's body, covered with a mat and three cushions, on the dining-room floor. The house had been ransacked.

In establishing the time of death, an essential factor in the investigation, Spilsbury's evidence was to be decisive. It is interesting, however, in this connexion, to find him changing an early opinion—a very rare occurrence. He was extremely busy that autumn; from the Oxford mortuary he went straight back to London to perform more post-mortems at St Pancras in the afternoon; and his notes on the Kempson case seem to have been made at different times. From the condition of the body he would only say that death had occurred not less than twenty-four hours before his examination. Of the stomach contents he says first, "Chiefly starchy and fat. No articles of food identified." But on the last case-card—there are four—he gives the result of what can only have been a later re-examination and analysis: "Food in stomach. Light meal, bread, butter and egg." And in the witness-box at the Oxford Assizes in October he added tomatoes.

The importance of this was that it confirmed other evidence which put the time of the murder as far back as the morning of Saturday, two days before the Bank Holiday. The previous evening Mrs Kempson had eaten tomatoes for supper. When last seen by Miss Williams the next morning she was dressed in the black frock in which she was found two days later, but she had not breakfasted. The police found a used cup and saucer, bread, butter, and the remains of some egg custard laid out on the kitchen table, and in the scullery, still unwashed, were a cup and saucepan used by Miss Williams on the Friday night, with her breakfast things. Upstairs Mrs Kempson's bed had not been made. As she was methodical and house-proud, all this pointed to an interruption of her daily routine soon after her breakfast on Saturday. It came out later that on that morning, for the first time for ten years, she failed to renew the flowers on her husband's grave.

This case might be cited as another model of police-work. Scotland Yard and Spilsbury were called in at once, and within a fortnight, starting from nothing at all, house-to-house inquiries by the Oxford Constabulary, the help of the Criminal Record Office and the police of Buckinghamshire and Brighton, some scientific detection after Spilsbury's own heart, and a further contribution by his microscope, had combined to bring about the murderer's arrest. It is well to recall what Chief Constable Horwell (as he became) says of the toil involved in such a case. "We all worked day and night throughout that period, seldom getting more than an hour or two for sleep, and missing our meals, which we snatched at odd times. . . . As far as my own staff was concerned, one of them nearly died."

The murderer was Henry Daniel Seymour. A photograph shows him as a well-dressed, rather mild and attractive-looking young man. St John was right; for Seymour, who was about forty, had eleven previous convictions for serious crimes, including housebreaking, counterfeiting, theft, and unlawful wounding. This last was significant; the charge had been reduced from one of attempted murder, and the victim was a woman living alone. Seymour had a wife in Oxford, and he had been employed there for a time selling vacuum cleaners. He had sold one to Mrs Kempson. At the end of July 1931 he was staying at a hotel in Aylesbury. On Friday, the 31st, he left without paying his bill, and that afternoon he was in Oxford, where he called on another customer, Mrs Andrews, with a story of having lost his money. With 4*s*. 6*d*. lent him by Mrs Andrews he went straight from her house to an ironmonger's, where he bought a hammer and chisel. Fortunately, perhaps, for his helper, her husband was at home when Seymour returned to ask if he could put up for the night. He had missed his last bus to Thame. He was given a bed, and after leaving next morning, with his hammer and chisel, spent his last 6*d*. on a shave. Three hours later, however, he was in a public house having drinks. He may have needed them, for in between he had murdered Mrs Kempson.

His crime had brought him only a few pounds, for in his frenzied ransacking of The Boundary he had overlooked a box full of pound notes and some gold. He was back at the hotel in Aylesbury in the afternoon. Found in the room he had occupied, where his suitcase remained, he gave the excuse that he wanted his shaving things. As he had not enough to pay his bill, he was not allowed to take the case. In it, when the police traced him there, was the hammer. The maker's label had been removed, and the whole implement washed and scraped. When Horwell held the suitcase upside down, and shook it, among the fluff and scraps that fell out were tiny particles of rolled-up paper. Treated with drops of water, like a Japanese puzzle, they unfolded, and when fitted together made up most of the label from the hammer.

The results of Spilsbury's first examination of the hammer were disappointing. The head, in his view, was too small to have caused the wounds which struck Mrs Kempson down. It was suggested that a piece of material might have been wrapped round the hammer, and Spilsbury made experiments on these lines with wrappings of different thickness, until he produced indentations on a board of the same dimensions as the injuries. With the microscope he found a minute thread caught between the head and handle of the hammer, and this proved to consist of cotton and linen fibres.

A blotting-pad from the commercial room at the Aylesbury hotel, when held to a mirror, showed an address at Brighton. There was nothing to indicate that it was Seymour's, but the Brighton police were asked to inquire there, as a matter of routine. And there they found him, under the name of Harvey, in the house of a woman who, like Mrs Kempson, was a widow. Seymour had stayed there with her before; this time he had arrived on the day after the crime at Oxford. He was given a room above his landlady's bedroom, where, as he may have known, she kept her ready money at night. When he had paid her £2 *6s.* he was almost penniless, and he gave her the second instalment of this sum after she found two eyeholes bored through the floor of his room with some tool like a new chisel. Together they gave a good view of the bedroom below.

If Seymour murdered Mrs Kempson he must have committed the crime between 9.30 and 11 on the Saturday morning. During his trial, at the Oxford Assizes before Mr Justice Swift, witnesses swore to seeing Mrs Kempson out shopping later in the day. One said she was posting a letter. But no one came forward who had received the letter. No one admitted being the man seen at her front door just before ten o'clock. Neither Swift nor the jury had any doubts about who he was, and Seymour was convicted and hanged.

As a rider to these examples of murderous attacks on lonely women, it may be of interest to make a very brief comparison, in the manner of Plutarch, between Spilsbury's career and that of one of his contemporaries. The two were almost of an age, Harold Dorian Trevor being the younger by a couple of years. Both were educated men, with solid, comfortable backgrounds; both had a good appearance, and possessed great charm of manner, in the one exercised almost unconsciously, by the other deliberately exploited. Each, throughout life, pursued a single aim, and each, in a sense, may be said to have died of it. Their careers, for long parallel, converged together for the first and last time when both were in the sixties.

Trevor's aim was to live in comfort without working, by means of the spell cast upon credulous women by his charm, his eyeglass, and his tales of money always coming, but never there. As, however, he spent forty of his sixty-two years in prison, and ended on the scaffold, the sport seems scarcely to have been worth the candle. Though his principles were those of George Joseph Smith, even the police, who came to know him so well, thought him a likable fellow; and one of them gave him a kindly warning. As he grew old his attractions would fade; he would become desperate, and resort to more serious crime. Perhaps to murder. . . . Trevor was amused. He was not such a fool.

In 1941 Spilsbury was called to a house in Bayswater, where Mrs Greenhill, a woman of sixty-three, had been murdered. Early one morning in March of the following year he was at Wandsworth Prison; and presently another card was added to his files:

> Trevor, H. D. 62. Judicial Hanging. Dislocated Spine and Injuries to Brain and Spinal Cord.
>
> *Exterior*. Well nourished. Ht. 5 ft. 11½ in. Wt. 168 lbs. Drop 5 ft. 11 in. . . .

As in Plutarch's parallels, there should be a moral here somewhere.

Chapter 2: MORE POISONING CASES

WHEN, during the trial of Armstrong, Spilsbury said that he dealt with cases of poisoning almost monthly it was a typically conservative estimate. The ten poisoning cases preserved among his cards for 1922, for instance, could no doubt be doubled. After 1927 he began to accumulate more material, in the form of cards, for the book he hoped to write; totals of over 270 cards for 1928, and again for the following year, include respectively twenty-seven and twenty-six cases of poisoning.

From the trial of the Seddons in 1912 to those of Greenwood, Armstrong, and Black nine or ten years later there were no outstanding cases of this kind, but the rest of the 1920's saw a series which attracted much popular interest. It will be convenient to deal together here with the three in which Spilsbury was concerned. In one only, the first, was a definite conclusion reached, when Jean-Pierre Vaquier was convicted of the murder of Alfred Poynter Jones.

It was a stupid and not very interesting crime, and its attraction for the public was due to the strange love affair involved, the scene of the murder—a large public house in a suburban upper middle-class district near London—and the nationality of the accused, a Frenchman, who, like Voisin, spoke hardly any English, but who, unlike Voisin, was a man of some education and considerable intelligence, though this deserted him when he set out to poison his mistress's husband.

In August 1923 Alfred Jones, with money said to be his wife's, purchased the business and became the licensee of the Blue Anchor Hotel at Byfleet in Surrey. He was then thirty-seven; he had married in 1906, and there were two children. Mrs Jones had carried on various businesses, not all of them successfully, and in November 1923 she was threatened with bankruptcy. In the carefree manner of bankrupts she went off to Biarritz for what she described as a rest, and there, at the Hotel Victoria, by no means one of the cheapest, she met Jean-Pierre Vaquier. Vaquier, an excellent and inventive mechanic, was employed by the hotel to work his wireless-set in the drawing-room. He was forty-five, a native of Niort, not the town near La Rochelle, but a small village in the Department of Aude. In the first of his numerous statements he said he was living apart from his wife; in his evidence in the witness-box the separation had become a divorce. A typical Mediterranean product, he was small, volatile, and excitable, very vain of his appearance and wearing a spade-shaped beard and bushy moustaches combed outward and carefully tended. During his trial (like Patrick Mahon, whose own trial, in the next county, was to begin a fortnight later) Vaquier paid particular attention to his looks and dress, scenting himself and pomading his hair. He posed for the Press photographers, and almost to the end appeared to regard the proceedings as a tiresome formality, but in which at any rate he was the central and most interesting figure.

At Biarritz he had fallen passionately in love with Mrs Jones, who returned his affection to the extent of going to live with him at a less expensive hotel. It was a remarkable affair, for she could speak no French, and he no English, and they exchanged endearments by means of a dictionary—a labour of love indeed. A telegram from Mr Jones put an end to the idyll, but Mrs Jones did not hurry home, spending a night with Vaquier in Bordeaux, and several in Paris. For he too was on his way to England, where he hoped to sell the patent rights of a sausage machine he had invented. Mrs Jones left Paris for Byfleet on February 8, 1924, and the little Frenchman followed to London next day.

During the ensuing week Mr Jones, who also had his financial troubles, and also felt in need of a rest, went off to Margate for a few days. In his absence his wife saw Vaquier at his hotel in London, and spent a night with him there. A chambermaid found them together, and the peculiar difficulties of such a liaison are illustrated by Mrs Jones's account of the episode. Asked at the trial what she had said to Vaquier, she replied,

> "I told him he had put me in a nice plight or position—something like that."
>
> Mr Justice Avory: "Did you say that in English?"
>
> "Yes."
>
> "By that time was he understanding?"
>
> "No; he simply got the dictionary."

Returning to Byfleet that morning, the 14th, Mrs Jones was followed by Vaquier, who arrived at the Blue Anchor in the evening with his dictionary, but without money or luggage. The Blue Anchor had a considerable staff, and bedrooms for guests, and there the Frenchman stayed for more than six weeks, paying his bill in London, and so retrieving his luggage and sausage-mincer, with money borrowed from Mrs Jones. Before he left, to spend his last fortnight of freedom at another hotel, in Woking, Alfred Jones was dead.

Jones had returned from Margate suffering from influenza, which induced congestion of the lungs. He was in bed, or convalescing, for nearly three weeks. By the second week of March he was quite well again. On the 28th of that month there was what was described as a party at the Blue Anchor, and a good deal of drinking, carried on till midnight, when two of the guests had to be put to bed in the hotel. Vaquier, who had retired early, came down next morning at seven o'clock, and took his coffee in the bar parlour, wearing his overcoat, though he usually sat in the warmer coffee-room. He refused to move when the room was being swept and dusted. Jones was downstairs before nine, and, having gone up again to dress, and then having played with his dogs, came into the parlour for some bromo salts, a bottle of which always stood on the mantelpiece. He was a heavy drinker, and was in the habit of taking a dose of these salts after an evening's carouse, as Vaquier, invariably an early riser, very well knew. Watched by the little Frenchman from an armchair, Jones swallowed a dose, and almost immediately became violently ill. His doctor was summoned, to find the unhappy man on his bed, fully dressed, in fearful convulsions and great terror. He died of asphyxia in less than half an hour.

Dr Carle at once formed the opinion that the cause of death was poison, and poison with an action similar to that of strychnine, and that this had been taken very shortly before. Jones had eaten nothing that morning, and the doctor accordingly pocketed the bottle of salts. He also scraped some crystals from the floor of the bar parlour. Two days later he performed a post-mortem, and the stomach and small intestine, the bottle, and the crystals were sent to Webster for analysis. In all these specimens Webster found traces of strychnine.

Three weeks went by before the police investigations, directed by Superintendent Boshier of Woking, led to the arrest of Vaquier. In the meantime Mrs Jones had been taken to the Director of Public Prosecutions for a severe interrogation, and Vaquier had volunteered four statements. His love of posing for photographers hastened his undoing, for on April 16 his photograph in a newspaper caught the eye of Mr Bland, partner in a firm of chemists in Southampton Row, a few hundred yards from the London hotel where Vaquier had stayed. Bland went to the police, and on the 19th Vaquier was charged with the murder. He then made yet another statement.

He was tried before Mr Justice Avory at the Surrey Summer Assizes at Guildford. Marshall Hall appeared in what was the uncommon rôle for him of counsel for the Crown, led by the Attorney-General, Sir Patrick Hastings; Curtis-Bennett led for the defence, and found his client very difficult to deal with. The trial, which opened on July 2, and was prolonged over four days because everything had to be translated to the prisoner, was held in conditions against which judge after judge had protested. The court-room at Guildford was a hall used for dances and similar festivities. It was next door to a theatre, with which it had a common corridor for holders of stall tickets. Old pieces of bunting hung from the roof, the witness-box was borrowed from elsewhere, and the dock was carpentered for the occasion. Avory expressed himself forcibly about this state of things, and not long after Guildford lost its assizes, which were moved to Kingston-on-Thames.

The evidence, as reported, throws little or no light on the most interesting feature of the case—what went on, during Vaquier's six weeks at the Blue Anchor, between the three principal actors in the very curious triangle there. Alfred Jones scarcely emerges at all, except as a man who, unlike his wife, spoke French, and who drank too much. It is impossible to tell whether he knew or suspected the relations between his guest and his wife, both of whom denied impropriety at the Blue Anchor itself. Mrs Jones was in the witness-box for as long as all the other witnesses put together, but Curtis-Bennett devoted much of his cross-examination to attacking her character. He had written instructions from Vaquier that the line taken by the defence must not involve her in the charge of murder. The Frenchman insisted throughout that she had no hand in her husband's death, but in earlier statements he alleged that she had other lovers, and that his own presence in what he called a house of pleasure, "where things happened that are unknown in brothels," was embarrassing alike to patrons and staff. He accused in particular a potman named George, prophesying darkly, "I think that the second act of the drama will be the disappearance of the wife of George, as mysteriously and also as tragically as Mr Jones." By the time of the trial he had thought of a new murderer, and the Jones's solicitor had to be fetched at the last moment to deny that he had asked Vaquier, whom he scarcely knew, to buy strychnine for him. The judge, in summing up, dealt faithfully with this improbable story, in which there was no mention of the perchloride of mercury, another deadly poison purchased by Vaquier at the same time as the strychnine; and the jury was advised to disregard Mrs Jones's evidence, since her credit had been attacked, and to concentrate on that of other witnesses from the hotel who had no cause to tell anything but the truth.

Vaquier's wild accusations and emotional behaviour ensured that there were few dull moments in the trial, which was conducted with great patience and fairness, the Attorney-General even waiving his right to make the last speech to the jury, because the accused was a foreigner. Personalities and outbursts from the dock, however, tended to obscure the real basis of the prosecution's case—the medical evidence. This was brief, and took only an hour or two on the third day, but it was preceded, the evening before, by the damning story of Mr Bland, the chemist of Southampton Row.

Between Vaquier's arrival in London in February and the first week of March he paid several visits to Bland's shop, buying toilet articles and a few harmless chemicals which he said he needed for his wireless experiments. Bland could speak French, and the two became on friendly terms. Vaquier gave his name as Vanker, which, when it came to an entry in the poison book, he spelt Wanker. This happened on March 1, when he brought to the shop a list of chemicals he required, among them 20 grammes of perchloride of mercury, or corrosive sublimate, and ·12 of a gramme of strychnine hydrochloride. These two being poisons on the scheduled list, and of a particularly deadly nature, Bland, who had never heard of their use in connexion with wireless, hesitated to supply them. Vacquier, always plausible, and making out that he was a well-known inventor in his own country, where he could buy these poisons by the pound, eventually persuaded him.

Bland was followed by Dr Carle, and Dr Carle by Spilsbury. After Dr Carle had performed his post-mortem on Alfred Jones, the results of which confirmed his immediate opinion about the cause of death, the landlord of the Blue Anchor was buried in Byfleet Cemetery. But the authorities were taking no chances, and a week after Vaquier's arrest the coffin was dug up. Spilsbury made a second examination of the remains, and took away more organs for analysis.

He began his evidence with a statement which makes puzzling reading, possibly due to the omission of an explanatory sentence in transcription. Having said that for some years past he had been pathologist to the Home Office, he added, "I have now practically retired, and only come in for special cases when I am asked." He was, in fact, now acting for the Home Office in an honorary capacity, and was giving up hospital appointments in order to have more freedom for research. A relative dearth of "special cases" about this time may have encouraged a hope—it cannot have been a very flourishing growth—that Home Office calls on him would abate. If this were so, events, and his own intense absorption in the practical side of his life's work, soon proved altogether too compelling. From 1927 onward official demands were to keep him busier than ever before.

His examination by the Attorney-General—it was quite short—was limited to questions about the effects of strychnine, the peculiarities of saline preparations like bromo salts, and the condition of the body. Spilsbury said that, having heard Dr Carle's evidence, he agreed that the symptoms observed were those of strychnine poisoning. Half a grain of strychnine had proved fatal on several occasions. From the amount found in the organs analysed more than one grain, and not much less than two grains, must have been taken. There was nothing in the condition of the body when he himself examined it indicative of death by natural disease, and no natural disease would cause the symptoms described. His examination otherwise tended to confirm Dr Carle's opinion.

Curtis-Bennett's very brief cross-examination was mainly directed to underlining Spilsbury's estimate of the amount of poison taken. Webster followed to give the exact figures of his analysis. In the organs delivered to him by Dr Carle and by Spilsbury he found altogether rather more than seventeen-thirtieths of a grain of strychnine, or round about the minimum fatal dose of half a grain.

Vaquier had purchased from Bland ·12 of a gramme of strychnine, and the medical evidence had now shown that Jones died of at least as big a dose as this. The poisoner, of course—as the judge pointed out in summing up—could have obtained more elsewhere. There was, in fact, more strychnine—much more—on the premises of the Blue Anchor; but this fact did not come out until after the trial.

An official of the Marconi Company having stated that he knew of no uses for strychnine in the chemistry of wireless telegraphy, the defence was opened by Vaquier leaving the dock for the witness-box. Vain and confident, he was probably among the few—Seddon had been another—who in his situation did not dread this moment. At last he was to be in the centre of the stage. He told some very tall stories, as that he had lent Jones £150. (When arrested he possessed only a few shillings.) He contradicted Bland, the chemist; he had ordered 25 grammes of strychnine—an enormous amount—but no perchloride of mercury. It was now that he introduced the tallest story of all, that the strychnine, enough to kill a regiment, was for the Jones's lawyer, who wanted to destroy a dog. He did not think it peculiar that a stranger in a foreign country, whose name he did not even know, should make such a request.

No other evidence was called for the defence. The Attorney-General and Curtis-Bennett made unusually brief speeches. Nor did the summing-up take long: Avory was never prolix. A little man, like Darling, but entirely without Darling's saving grace of humour, at any rate in court, it was said of him that he was spare of flesh and sparing of compliments, but never spared criminals. As Treasury Counsel he had prosecuted Adolf Beck, and his objection to a certain line of cross-examination—an objection upheld, it is true, by the judge—was partly responsible for a miscarriage of justice. It was characteristic, perhaps, that Avory always maintained that he had correctly interpreted the law. When a judge himself he won a reputation for severity second only to that of Hawkins, but very few of the convictions in the many capital cases that came before him were seriously challenged on appeal. He was at his best in his charge to the jury which convicted Vaquier, and it has been said that in the hands of a judge less strong there might even have been an acquittal.

That charge, as it happened, was delivered in ignorance of certain facts later revealed. Their revelation did not help Vaquier, but had Avory known of them his references to Spilsbury's evidence would have been differently phrased.

Speaking of Vaquier's purchase of strychnine, he said:

"·12 of a gramme is something slightly less than two grains; two grains are equal to ·13—that is to say, thirteen-hundredths—of a gramme. What he [Vaquier] had was twelve-hundredth parts, and therefore you can appreciate that it was only something very slightly less than two grains. Now, assuming that he never had any more than that, learned counsel invites you to say, on the evidence of Sir Bernard Spilsbury, that there must have been more than two grains used by the person who committed this crime. That is based upon the statement of Sir Bernard Spilsbury that, assuming seventeen-thirtieths of a grain is found in the organs after death, and assuming that the deceased had spat out some of the poison, and assuming that he had vomited twice and brought up some of the poison, then he estimates that probably two grains must have been taken, and possibly more."

Avory then went on:

"That, you will observe, is a mere estimate based upon a number of hypotheses. . . . You cannot be sure, therefore, that the man ever spat out any of this poison, and how much he would have brought up in vomiting is all again a matter of conjecture. You must say whether you think that argument really justifies you in coming to the conclusion that the accused could not have been the person who put this poison in, because he never had more than two grains, and never had, according to the case for the prosecution, quite so much as two grains of strychnine, bearing in mind what Sir Bernard Spilsbury has said, that, even if there were only half a grain in the dose, that of itself would be enough to cause death."

Referring to the entries in Bland's poison book, Avory then quoted the chemist's words in evidence: "I am sure that the list did not specify twenty-five grammes of strychnine." Further, said the judge, Bland had stated that at that time he did not possess anything like twenty-five grammes of the poison, nor had the accused suggested that he had taken away that amount.

It would be interesting to know Avory's afterthoughts on these observations. For, as to the strychnine, there was more to come, in every sense. The jury, having been absent for nearly two hours, brought in a verdict of guilty; Vaquier, all his airy illusions dissipated by one word, was sentenced and removed, shouting abuse. Within a few hours, however, he was seeing the governor of Wandsworth Prison with a new story. After the death of Alfred Jones he had seen a woman, either Mrs Jones or the manageress of the hotel, go to a tool-shed in the garden. Later he had gone there himself, and had found, behind a brick, the bottle of strychnine which he had bought for the solicitor. The police now went to the tool-shed, and there was the bottle. There were two bottles, in fact—one containing twenty-three grains of strychnine, the other some of the poison in solution.

Here, roughly, was the amount of strychnine that Vaquier said he had ordered from Bland. The latter's poison book showed that only ·12 of a gramme had been sold, and the chemist had sworn that all the chemicals bought by Vaquier were wrapped in paper. Where the Frenchman obtained this enormous amount of the poison—for it cannot be doubted that he had hidden the bottle—was never discovered. Had he disclosed its existence to his counsel before or even during the trial the fact might or might not have assisted the defence; coming when it did, the revelation merely showed that he knew where to lay his hands on enough strychnine, in the words of Sir Patrick Hastings, to poison 740 people. At the Court of Criminal Appeal the Lord Chief Justice disposed caustically of the new theory that vital evidence could be suppressed during a trial, and brought forward only if the verdict went against the accused. "If this sort of thing is to be allowed," he said, "the oath to be taken by prisoners will have to be altered to 'I swear to tell the truth, five-eighths of the truth, and nothing but the truth. I will keep the remaining three-eighths for the Court of Criminal Appeal.' "

Leave to appeal was dimissed, and Vaquier, shouting again and clinging to the dock, vanished from public view for the last time.

2

In the year of the murder at Byfleet another man of French descent, Hilary Rougier by name, a native of Guernsey, came to live in Surrey, and within six miles of the Blue Anchor. He was a retired farmer, and much older than Vaquier. Four years later he was to play the opposite rôle in the familiar drama of murder and victim. The means was again poison.

On March 16, 1928, Spilsbury was once more at Woking, by appointment with his old acquaintance Superintendent Boshier. The circumstances were very similar to those of their last meeting, even to the French background. The scene was now the churchyard of St John's, in Woking itself. Again a grave was opened and a coffin raised. When, however, Spilsbury began his post-mortem in the town mortuary he did not know what he was looking for, or even whether there was anything illicit to find. Hilary Rougier had been dead for nearly two years, and the manner of his death had at the time roused no suspicion of foul play outside a very small circle. Why this exhumation was eventually decided on is indicated on Spilsbury's case-cards. He needed three, and they summarize the whole case in unusual detail.

"Before his death," he wrote, "most of deceased's money had passed into the hands of the Lerwills. ? Forged cheques."

William Knight Lerwill and his wife were a young couple who came to know Rougier in his solitary old age. He lived with them for some years as a paying guest—a highly paying guest, as was to appear—at several places in Southern England. Finally the Lerwills moved to Lower Knaphill, which is about as far to the west of Woking as Byfleet is to the east. Here they took a house called Nuthurst, at 4½ guineas a week. A Dr Hope had lived and died there, and his daughter, on letting the house, locked a cupboard containing some of her father's medicaments and drugs. She retained the key. Among the drugs was a bottle of laudanum, otherwise tincture of opium, of which an alkaloid is morphine.

In 1926 Rougier was seventy-seven. Until a short time before his death he was active for his age, doing a good deal of gardening. What happened in the summer of that year is thus described by Spilsbury:

Dr Brewer first called in July 23, 1926. Told that his [Rougier's] voice was weak lately and that he had a cough. Appeared healthy for his age. Found nothing wrong but slight bronchial trouble. Very subdued; never spoke for himself. Mrs Lerwill did all the talking. Gave cough mixture. Saw him again July 28. Much as before. Mental condition normal. Mrs L said medicine had eased cough. Next saw him August 6. Condition as before. On August 14 urgent call about 8 A.M. Found unconscious in bed. In dying condition and beyond aid. Livid. Breathing quiet. Pulse very feeble. Was told he was all right previous night. Diagnosed severe cerebral hæmorrhage. Later in morning informed of his death. Certified—Senile decay, cerebral hæmorrhage.

Money is the root of most exhumations. Rougier's solicitor, who had prepared the old man's will in 1919, knew that the estate should be worth between five and six thousand pounds. It had dwindled in seven years to less than £80. No cheque-book could be found, but entries in Rougier's bank pass-book showed payments of large amounts to the Lerwills. Cheques for sums ranging from £950 to £40 were made out to William Lerwill, and a bearer cheque for no less than £1850 had found its way into Mrs Lerwill's account. From Rougier's bank in Guernsey everything had been withdrawn.

Rougier's family—he had a married sister and a married niece—not unnaturally put a sinister interpretation on this state of affairs. Suspicion was strengthened by other curious features. Dr Brewer never saw his patient alone: Mrs Lerwill was always there, and, as has been seen, did all the talking. When funeral arrangements were being discussed she wished the body to be cremated. There would seem, in fact, to have been a strong case for exhumation from the start; but for reasons unknown the Home Office would not then move. The Lerwills had another lodger, a trained nurse, who had helped to look after Rougier, and who found him unconscious on the morning of his death, and it is possible that her evidence tended to confuse the issue. Equally obscure are the reasons that caused the authorities to change their minds nearly two years later. Superintendent Boshier, no doubt, always had his eye on the Lerwills, who remained at Nuthurst, and in view of what was to happen afterwards it may be suggested that some action by William Lerwill finally tipped the scale.

Spilsbury, in his thorough way, describes on his cards how the grave was opened in his presence, what soil lay at different depths, and the wood and fittings of the coffin. During the post-mortem Dr Brewer stood by—yet another busy general practitioner placed in the unenviable position of watching a faulty diagnosis exposed. It was a situation which Spilsbury disliked intensely, unless, perhaps, when he suspected negligence; he never failed to show sympathy with a colleague found out in an excusable error. His own conclusions now, made on the spot, were definite: "Death not due to cerebral hæmorrhage, and no other disease of the brain. Some senile changes, *e.g.*, in arteries and kidneys. No disease to account for death or symptoms preceding it."

The organs were dispatched for analysis, and the cards go on:

> *Analysis—Roche Lynch.* Morphine present in all organs as oxydimorphine. Definite reaction in most organs. Suspicions in others. Amount too small for estimation. But traces 18 months after death means considerable amount shortly before death.

Morphine tends to disappear as putrefaction proceeds. During life, or after death, it may undergo a change, becoming oxydi-morphine or pseudomorphine.

All this, and much more, came out at the inquest, which was not held until May. Spilsbury and Roche Lynch gave evidence. Dr Brewer admitted his mistake. Miss Hope said that the contents of the locked medicine cupboard at Nuthurst did not appear to have been tampered with. It was shown, however, that the cupboard had a defective hinge, and could be opened without a key. The bottle of laudanum, which was graduated in sixteen divisions, was more than half empty. Roche Lynch explained that the average fatal dose of the drug in this strength would be four or five divisions, but the equivalent of two divisions had been known to cause death.

The Lerwills were the chief centre of interest at these proceedings. William Lerwill agreed that the body of the cheque for £1850 was made out by him; only the signature was Rougier's. This and other payments made to him and his wife were free gifts. The total was between five and six thousand pounds. Mrs Lerwill professed to know nothing about money matters, and both she and her husband denied knowledge of the laudanum bottle. Lerwill said he once bought laudanum for Rougier, who wanted it for his dog's claws. This purchase was never traced.

Though the position of this pair was, to say the least, a very awkward one, the jury would seem to have decided, even before retiring, that only one thing had been proved—Hilary Rougier died of a dose of morphine, not self-administered. A verdict to this effect was returned within half an hour.

From this curious and unsatisfactory case certain inferences may be drawn, but are better left unspecified. Events were to prove, however, that William Lerwill was a thorough wastrel. With the bulk of £5000 obtained from two newspapers which he sued for libel, he went to Canada, abandoning his wife and child. He was back in England in 1933, and a year later, almost penniless, with a trail of worthless cheques behind him, he was stopped by a police constable in Combe Martin, Devonshire. A postscript scribbled on Spilsbury's last card tells the sequel: "Wm Knight Lerwill. Poisoned himself March 1934 with HCN (Prussic Acid) when about to be charged by Police with fraud."

3

A reliable guide to the incidence of capital crime in the London area, using that term in its widest sense, could be compiled from Spilsbury's cards. Applied to a map, it would show that in that area far more murders are committed north of the Thames than south of it, and that on the north bank they tend to cluster along the rather squalid arc which leaves the river at Fulham and sweeps round by Hammersmith, Shepherd's Bush, Notting Dale, Paddington, and Islington to merge in the East End. One of the busiest years of Spilsbury's busy, single-centred life was 1931. In that year murderers were busy too; and the man who a short time before professed to have all but retired from departmental work lent his services to the Home Office in twenty cases of homicide, not including the usual annual tragedies of the unwanted newly born. Ten of these major crimes were committed in London, eight of them north of the Thames, and five of these in the Paddington-St Pancras district. Two, on the other hand, startled the more decorous and recently rural neighbourhood of Hendon.

There are obvious reasons for the relatively light calendar of violent crime on the South Side. It follows that when such crimes occur there they are as likely as not to happen among the salaried and higher income groups of modern jargon, 'respectable' people, in semi-detached villas or large houses with grounds, who attach great importance to appearances. In the late 1920's a series of poisoning mysteries in one family (all to this day, so far as the general public is aware, mysteries still) were the talk for months of the most sedate residential district of Croydon.

The Sydneys and the Duffs were typical of the South Side. Mrs Violet Sydney, of Birdhurst Rise, was the well-to-do widow of a barrister. An unmarried daughter, Vera, lived at home with her. Near at hand, in South Hill Park Road, was her son, Thomas, with his wife and children. A second daughter, Grace, had married Edmund Creighton Duff, a Commissioner of Northern Nigeria. Two children of this marriage had died young, and it was afterwards remembered that there had been a third death in the household—that of an old lady who lived with Mrs Duff while the latter's husband was in Africa. When Edmund Duff retired he joined his wife and the two surviving children in a house near Thomas Sydney's in South Hill Park Road.

This was the situation in 1928—these three related groups congregated close together in a neighbourhood whose very street names suggest comfortable means, pleasant homes, well-tended gardens and well-dressed children, servants, cars, golf, and, perhaps, a certain smugness. In the year Mrs Sydney was a healthy woman of sixty-eight. Her children were in middle age, and Edmund Duff was fifty-nine.

On the evening of April 26 the latter returned from a fishing holiday in Hampshire. It was afterwards thought that he had eaten something poisonous on the train, but he seemd to be in excellent health when he arrived home. The Duffs' back garden ran down to the railway-line, and, passing the end of it on his way from the station, he threw a heavy suitcase over the wall before walking round to the front door. Mrs Duff had finished her supper, and had left out for him a plate of cold chicken, some potatoes, and two bottles of beer. Some time after eating this meal he complained of feeling unwell, and, as he went upstairs to bed, of cramp in the calves of his legs. Next morning he was suffering from abdominal pains, and the family physician, Dr Binning, was summoned. Duff was a man who made the most of little ailments, and at first the doctor did not take the case seriously. He diagnosed a mild attack of colic. Within a few hours, however, there was a violent change; and that evening Edmund Duff was dead.

Dr Binning was puzzled by the later symptoms of vomiting and shivering, and no doubt by the cramp. Irritant poisons, among them arsenic, produce this symptom. He had called in his partner, Dr Elwell, and, both suspecting food poisoning, an inquest was held. Portions of certain organs were removed by Brontë for analysis, but no trace of poison was found, and death from natural if perplexing causes was assumed.

Nearly a year went by, and then in February 1929 there was illness in the house in Birdhurst Rise. Vera Sydney, in her own words, had been feeling seedy; on the 14th, after lunch with her mother and an aunt, she became really ill, and was vomiting all night. Her aunt and the cook were ill too, and so was the cat. All appeared to recover, and the next day Miss Sydney took a hot bath and went out in her car in bitterly cold weather. She was a hardy and athletic woman of forty, who did not believe in cosseting herself. Later that day she was violently sick, and all night and next day was ill and in pain. Dr Binning called in a specialist, who agreed with him that it was a case of severe gastric influenza. Vera Sydney died that night.

March came, and on the morning of the 5th Mrs Sydney, who had been terribly distressed by her bereavement, was taking a dose of a well-known tonic, prescribed by Dr Binning. She said to a servant that it tasted nasty. After lunch she was sick, and once more Dr Binning, and then his partner, hurried to the house. Mrs Sydney, now in bed, insisted that her medicine had poisoned her. The doctors found sediment clinging to the sides of the bottle, which Dr Binning pocketed. The case followed the course now so familiar, with vomiting, cramp, and pain, and in a few hours Mrs Sydney died, as her daughter and son-in-law had died. Dr Binning, nevertheless, apparently reassured by the statement of the chemist who supplied the tonic that it was the normal commercial product, again fell back on the well-worn theory of food poisoning; and a third victim was laid beside the other two in Croydon Cemetery.

Sir Archibald Bodkin, while Director of Public Prosecutions, is quoted by Mr H. L. Adam in *Murder by Persons Unknown* as saying of doctors, "They never think of poison." It is said of Dr Binning that he did think of poison, in the criminal sense, but dismissed the idea because he knew the family so well. Thomas Sydney, after his mother's death, exclaimed, "This must be seen into," and it was so far seen into that another doctor made a bacteriological examination of certain organs. He found nothing abnormal, but nothing, on the other hand, to account for death, which is something of an abnormality in itself. This appears to have satisfied the family; to people like the Sydneys and the Duffs inquests and publicity are abhorrent—and their medical men know it. Somebody, however, whether Mr Jackson, the coroner for the district, an anonymous informer, or the police themselves, now drew the attention of the Home Office to these last two deaths, occurring in the same house within three weeks. The Home Office acted promptly. On March 22 the bodies of Mrs Sydney and her daughter Vera were exhumed.

Spilsbury performed the post-mortems. In each case the usual organs—stomach, intestines, kidneys, and liver, with specimens of muscle and tissue—went to Dr Ryffel, one of the Home Office analysts, who was also given Mrs Sydney's bottle of tonic. At the inquests, held separately and repeatedly adjourned, so that proceedings dragged on for months, Spilsbury said that in his opinion both deaths were caused by arsenical poisoning. The symptoms during illness were characteristic, as were the results of his own examination, notably the condition of the stomachs, the inflammation of the intestines, the fatty state of the organs as a whole, and, in the case of Vera Sydney, the well-preserved state of the body after six weeks' burial. Dr Ryffel's analysis extracted 1·48 grains of arsenic from Miss Sydney's organs. In view of the rapidity with which arsenic disappears from a body, this was the residue of a much larger dose. The minimum fatal dose of arsenious oxide, the form apparently employed, is two grains. In the case of Mrs Sydney, more recently buried, 2·38 grains were actually recovered, and as much as another grain was traceable. From arsenic in her hair and nails the older woman must have been taking it, in small doses, for about a week before her death. No medicine containing arsenic had been prescribed for her. In the tonic bottle, which contained a single dose, Dr Ryffel found liquid of the normal deep-red colour, and a sediment. Mingled with the ingredients of the harmless tonic was a strong solution of arsenic, and the penultimate dose, presumably the last taken by Mrs Sydney, must have produced obvious symptoms of poisoning.

At this point Dr Brontë reappeared on the scene, and on the witness-stand; it is not clear why, for his evidence merely confirmed the obvious—namely, that Dr Ryffel's findings proved poisoning by arsenic. His reappearance, however, was timely, if not perhaps in a sense he would have wished; for by now the authorities were extending their inquiries over the whole sequence of fatalities associated with this ill-starred family, back in time to the deaths of the Duff children in 1919 and 1924. In the end these cases, and that of the old lady who died in the Duffs' house, were allowed to rest. But there was still Edmund Duff, in whose remains the analyst had failed to find any trace of poison. This opinion notwithstanding, Mr Duff's body was exhumed on May 18, and again Spilsbury carried out the post-mortem in Brontë's presence. The latter was found to have left the major part of the intestines unexamined and intact, and it appeared more than probable that organs from another body examined by Brontë on the same day had become mingled with those of Duff. At any rate, what with Brontë's jealousy of Spilsbury, and Spilsbury's low opinion of Brontë, by then equally well-known, though no doubt

SIR BERNARD HENRY SPILSBURY

Photo Elliott and Fry

SPILSBURY AT THE AGE OF EIGHT

SPILSBURY AT THE AGE OF FOURTEEN

SPILSBURY
IN THE EARLY DAYS
OF HIS CAREER
Photo Topical Press

SPILSBURY
IN THE STOCKS
AT WEST SMITHFIELD
IN 1923
[*See p.* 201.]

CRIPPEN LANDING, UNDER ARREST, AT LIVERPOOL

Photo Mirorpic

THE REMAINS IN THE CELLAR OF NO. 39 HILLDROP CRESCENT, INVESTIGATED BY SPILSBURY

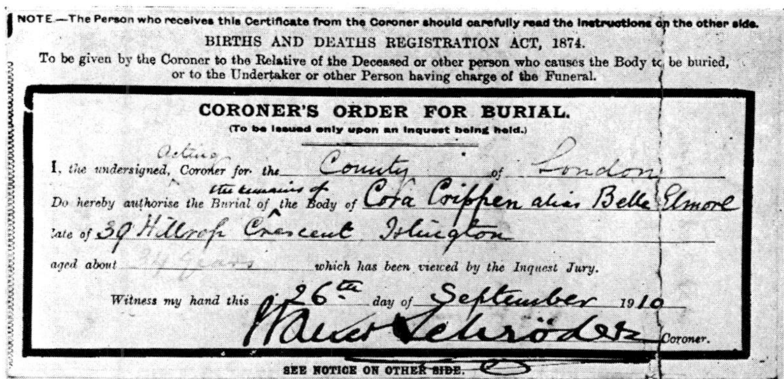
NOTE.—The Person who receives this Certificate from the Coroner should carefully read the Instructions on the other side.

BIRTHS AND DEATHS REGISTRATION ACT, 1874.

To be given by the Coroner to the Relative of the Deceased or other person who causes the Body to be buried, or to the Undertaker or other Person having charge of the Funeral.

CORONER'S ORDER FOR BURIAL.

(To be issued only upon an Inquest being held.)

I, *the undersigned,* Acting *Coroner for the* County *of* London

Do hereby authorise the Burial of the remains of *the Body of* Cora Crippen alias Belle Elmore

late of 39 Hilldrop Crescent Islington

aged about 34 Years *which has been viewed by the Inquest Jury.*

Witness my hand this 26th *day of* September 1910

Walter Schröder Coroner.

SEE NOTICE ON OTHER SIDE.

THE CORONER'S ORDER FOR THE BURIAL OF THE REMAINS OF CORA CRIPPEN

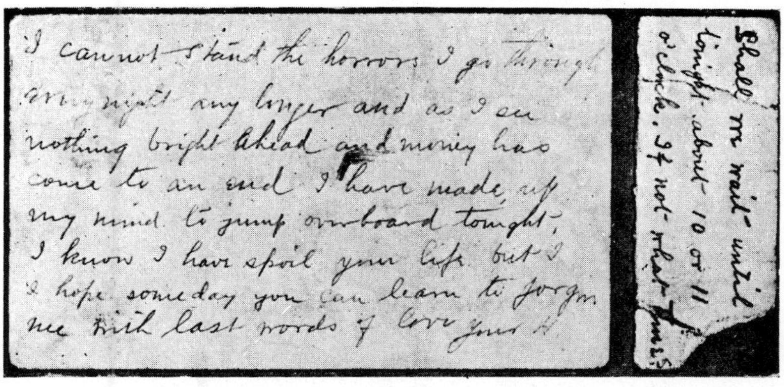
I cannot stand the horrors I go through every night any longer and as I see nothing bright ahead and money has come to an end I have made up my mind to jump overboard tonight, I know I have spoil your life but I I hope someday you can learn to forgive me with last words of love your H

Shall we wait until tonight about 10 or 11 o'clock. If not what time?

PART OF A LETTER WRITTEN BY CRIPPEN ABOARD THE S.S. "MONTROSE"

SEDDON ARRIVING AT THE INQUEST ON ELIZA MARY BARROW

Photo Mirorpic

GEORGE JOSEPH SMITH IN THE DOCK

Photo Mirorpic

[*See pp.* 70–92.]

THE CHARLOTTE STREET MURDER: VOISIN'S KITCHEN

THE CHARLOTTE STREET MURDER: VOISIN'S CELLAR, SHOWING THE CASK IN WHICH SOME OF THE REMAINS WERE FOUND

[*See pp.* 98–106.]

A FAMILY GROUP AT THE TIME OF THE FIRST WORLD WAR

Sir Bernard is on the left; the others are his parents and his brother, Leonard.

A SELECTION FROM SPILSBURY'S CASE-CARDS

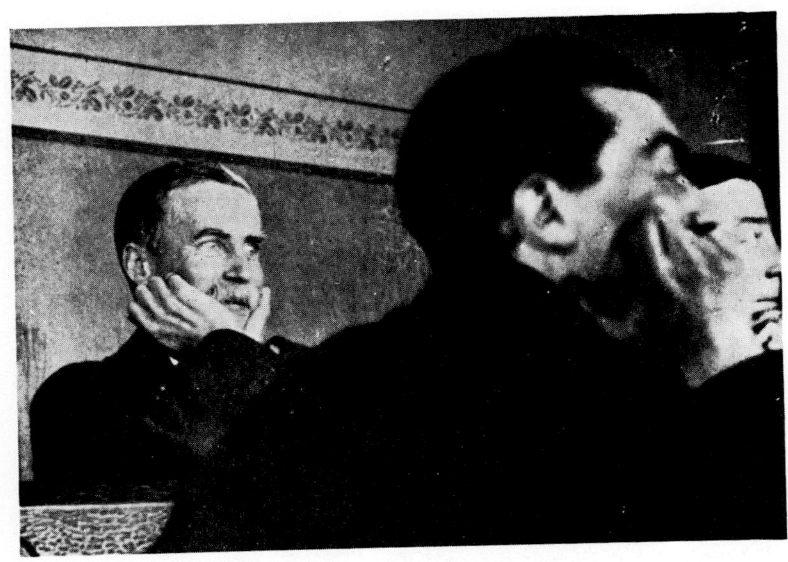

ARMSTRONG IN THE DOCK AT THE MAGISTRATES' COURT AT HAY

Photo Mirorpic

ARMSTRONG'S OFFICE AT HAY

Photo Topical Press

FEBRUARY 2nd Month 1921	1921 28 Days FEBRUARY
20 Sun—2nd in Lent. Sun sets 5.21 Nurse Lloyd here for night Confirmation – Bishop of Hfd	24 Th Wrote Arthur Arthur Came Mrs Seymour Came
21 Mon K. worse. Bevan [illegible] 1 Tin Petrol	25 Fri K's funeral 3 pm Cusop Mr [illegible] Came
22 Tues—○ Full Moon 9.32 a.m. K died	26 Sat Mrs Seymour left Arthur left
23 Wed 3 p.m. [illegible]	Memo

A PAGE FROM ARMSTRONG'S DIARY

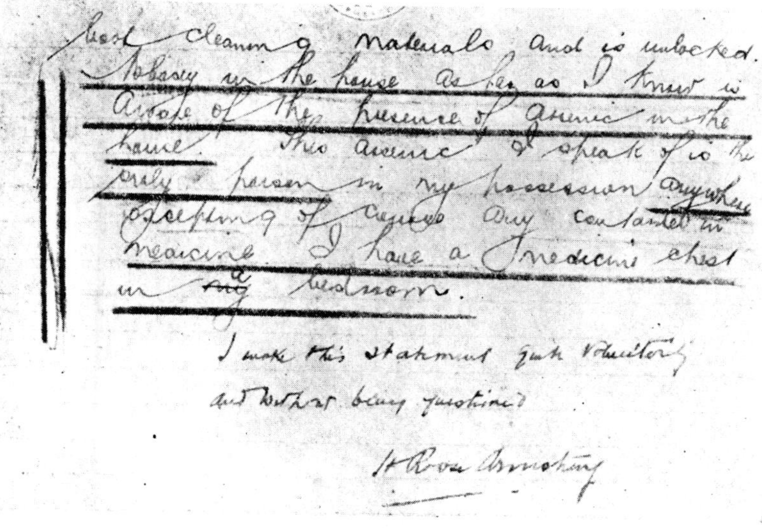
[illegible] cleaning materials and is unlocked. Nobody in the house as far as I know is aware of the presence of arsenic in the house. The arsenic I speak of is the only poison in my possession anywhere excepting of course any contained in medicine. I have a medicine chest in a bedroom.

I make this statement quite voluntarily and without being questioned

H Rowse Armstrong

ARMSTRONG'S FINAL STATEMENT

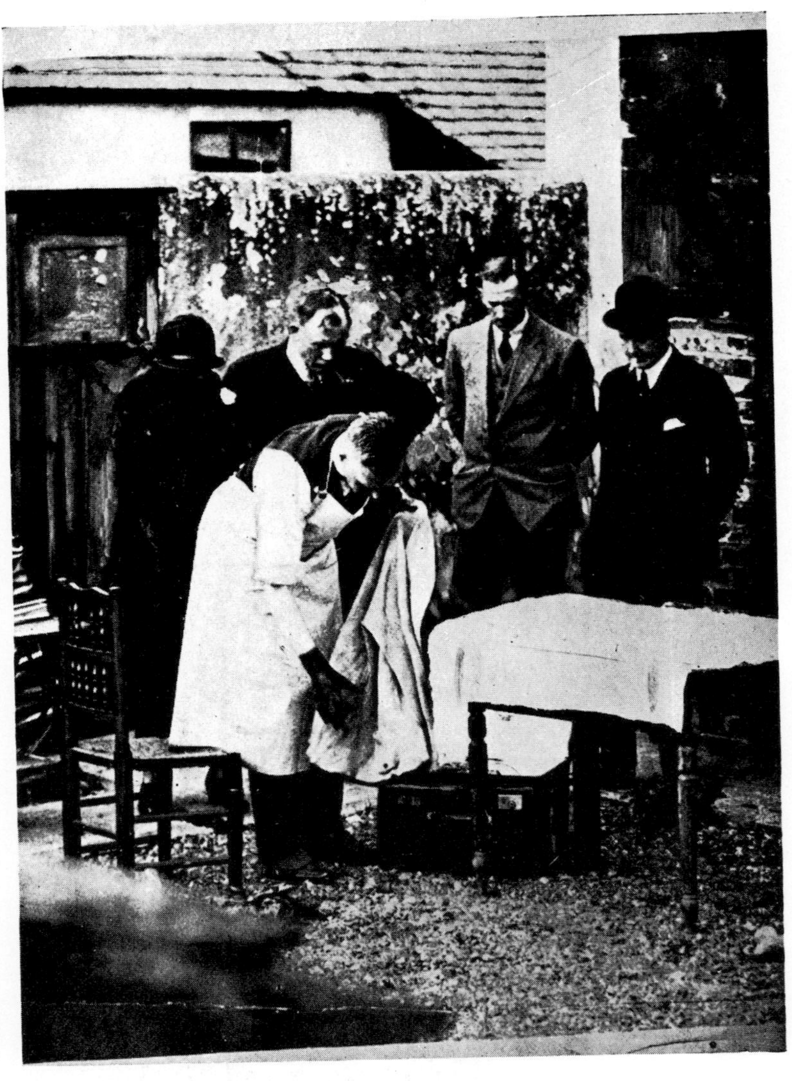

THE MAHON CASE: SPILSBURY EXAMINING THE REMAINS IN THE GARDEN OF THE BUNGALOW

Photo L.N.A.

THE MAHON CASE:
THE SITTING-ROOM

THE MAHON CASE:
THE BEDROOM

NORMAN THORNE AT WORK ON HIS FARM

THE CROWBOROUGH CASE: INTERIOR OF THORNE'S HUT

GEORGE BELCHER'S CARTOON OF SPILSBURY

The following lines appeared beneath the cartoon:

When arsenic has closed your eyes,
  This certain hope your corpse may rest in:—
Sir B. will kindly analyse
  The contents of your large intestine.

By kind permission of the Proprietors of "Punch"

SPILSBURY'S LABORATORY AT UNIVERSITY COLLEGE, LONDON
The cabinet contains the famous case-cards.
Graphic Photo Union

MICROSCOPE SLIDES IN SPILSBURY'S LABORATORY
Graphic Photo Union

SPILSBURY AT THE
WEDDING OF HIS DAUGHTER EVELYN
IN 1934
Photo Topical Press

SPILSBURY WITH HIS SON RICHARD

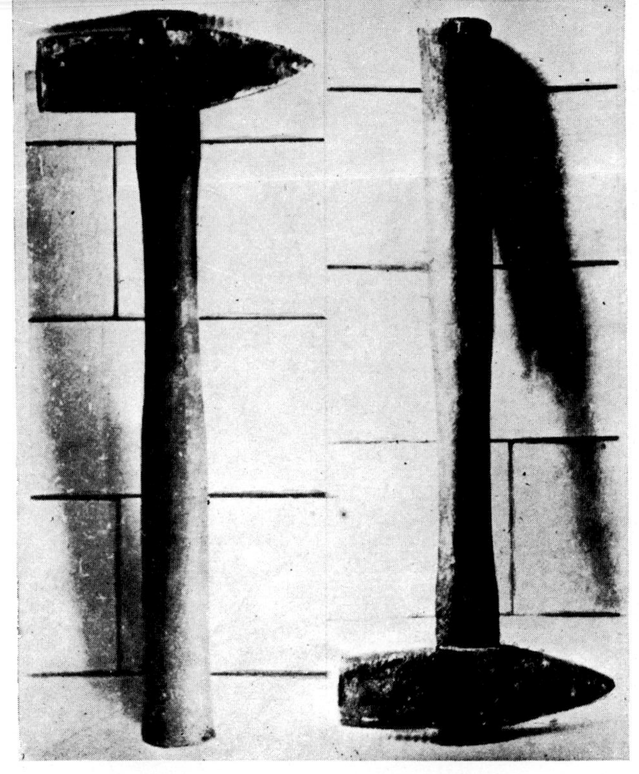

THE HAMMER WITH WHICH VIVIAN MESSITER WAS MURDERED

Photo Topical Press

MISS WREN'S SHOP AT RAMSGATE

Photo Topical Press

[*See pp.* 232–233.]

RUBBISH-DUMP MURDER: SHACK IN WHICH NEWMAN AND SHELLEY LIVED

RUBBISH-DUMP MURDER: SIDINGS AND DUMP IN WHICH THE BODY OF AYRES WAS FOUND

[*See pp.* 230–231.]

MR JUSTICE AVORY LEAVING THE COURT AT GUILDFORD DURING THE VAQUIER TRIAL
Photo Central Press

VAQUIER LEAVING THE COURT
Photo Central Press
[*See pp.* 238–246.]

BYWATERS UNDER ARREST AT ILFORD POLICE STATION

Photo Topical Press

EDITH THOMPSON AND BYWATERS IN THE DOCK

Photo Mirorpic

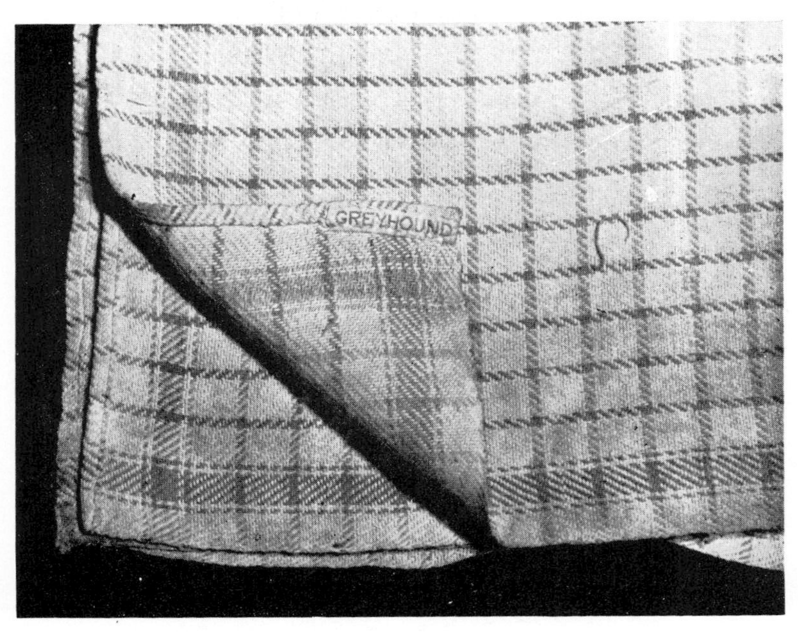

THE DUSTER FOUND IN THE TRUNK IN THE CHARING CROSS TRUNK CASE

RECONSTRUCTION OF THE ROOMS IN THE HOTEL METROPOLE, MARGATE

[*See pp.* 336–343.]

THE FIRST BRIGHTON TRUNK CASE:
THE WRITING ON THE BROWN PAPER IN
WHICH THE BODY WAS FOUND

Photo L.N.A.

[*See pp.* 277–280.]

THE CHARING CROSS TRUNK CASE: THE TRUNK IN WHICH
THE REMAINS OF MRS BONATI WERE FOUND

Photo Mirorpic

THE SECOND BRIGHTON TRUNK CASE:
THE TRUNK

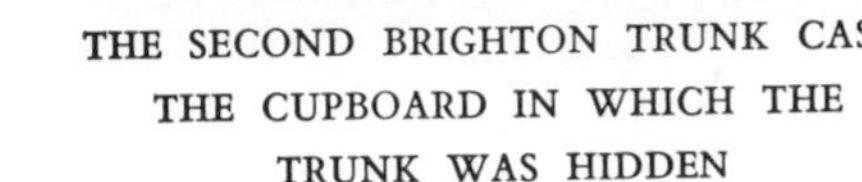

THE SECOND BRIGHTON TRUNK CASE:
THE CUPBOARD IN WHICH THE
TRUNK WAS HIDDEN

[*See pp.* 280–284.]

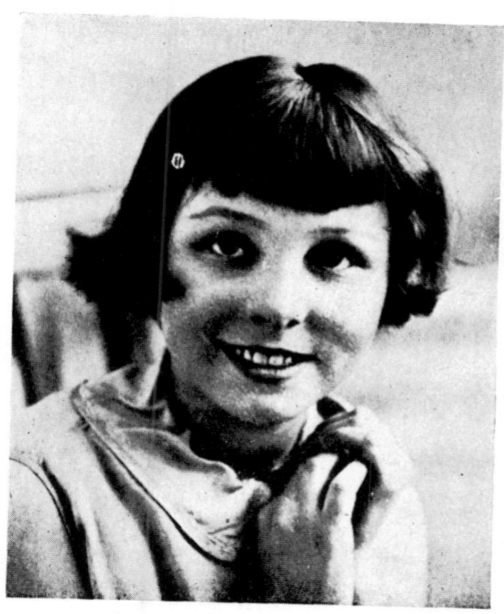

VERA PAGE
Photo Topical Press

DETECTIVES AT THE SCENE OF THE VERA PAGE MURDER IN KENSINGTON
Photo Planet News
[*See pp*. 308–312.]

THE TELEPHONE IN MRS BARNEY'S FLAT

Note the police number above the telephone.

[*See pp.* 355–360.]

SPILSBURY ON HIS WAY TO ATTEND AN INQUEST

Photo Central Press

THE BODY IN THE CELLAR OF THE EQUESTRIAN PUBLIC HOUSE, BLACKFRIARS ROAD, SOUTHWARK

SPILSBURY LEAVING SOUTHWARK MORTUARY AFTER CONDUCTING THE POST-MORTEM ON THE BODY FOUND IN THE EQUESTRIAN PUBLIC HOUSE

Photo Planet News

[*See pp.* 370–371.]

THE MAX KASSEL CASE: SUZANNE BERTRON'S SITTING-ROOM, WHERE KASSEL WAS SHOT

(*Left*) LACROIX AFTER BEING ARRESTED BY THE FRENCH POLICE; (*Right*) THE REVOLVER USED IN THE CASE
Photo Central Press

A PAGE FROM THE DIARY KEPT BY SIR MICHAEL O'DWYER'S MURDERER

[*See p.* 387.]

SPILSBURY LEAVING THE HOUSE WHERE THE BODY OF MAPLE CHURCH WAS FOUND

Photo Keystone

[*See p.* 391.]

THE CASSERLEY CASE: THE SILVER LAID OUT TO SUGGEST AN ATTEMPTED ROBBERY
[*See pp.* 362–364.]

SPILSBURY ON HIS WAY TO THE OLD BAILEY TO GIVE EVIDENCE IN THE ANTIQUIS MURDER TRIAL IN 1947
Photo Planet News
[*See pp.* 406–408.]

concealed by an impassive mask of courtesy and concentration, witnesses of that meeting at the Croydon mortuary may have found the atmosphere a little strained.

A third inquest was opened. Spilsbury's examination had revealed the familiar signs of arsenic. The analyst this time was Roche Lynch. Edmund Duff having been dead a year, traces of the poison had almost vanished from the organs, but it was discovered in every tissue tested, the total amount being nearly a grain. The fatal dose had been taken within twenty-four hours of death.

There was little doubt as to the vehicle employed in each of the three deaths in this family, two of which were certainly murders. The remains of the chicken eaten by Edmund Duff were consumed next day by his wife without ill-effects. Of the two bottles of beer he had drunk, one was afterwards missing. At the lunch after which Vera Sydney, her aunt, and the cook were taken ill Mrs Sydney shared every course except the soup. As the maid was bringing this in the telephone rang, and she set the soup-bowl down while she answered the call. The caller muttered unintelligibly, and rang off. Some of the soup had been made, and safely consumed, the day before. Beer and soup were therefore almost certainly the means by which arsenic was administered to Duff and his sister-in-law; in Mrs Sydney's case it was the tonic. Spilsbury, in his evidence at the inquests, pointed out that liquid arsenic has very little taste, and would be disguised by beer or soup. White arsenic, in crystals, would not have made the beer flat.

The family, to all appearance, was a united one. Thomas Sydney, a concert entertainer, was constantly in his mother's house after his marriage. He was there on the day before Mrs Sydney's last illness, discussing Vera Sydney's will. Miss Sydney had between £4000 and £5000 of her own, and by her will, of which her brother and sister were co-trustees and executors, her mother received a life interest on £2000. On Mrs Sydney's death this capital sum was to be divided equally between Thomas Sydney and Mrs Duff.

The latter was also at the house in Birdhurst Rise almost daily. On February 14, hearing that her sister was unwell, she called to see her before the lunch that was to have so fatal a sequel. The attack which followed did not at first alarm Mrs Duff, who, like the doctors, attributed it to gastric influenza, then prevalent; but she was at the invalid's bedside much of the next day, the last of Vera Sydney's life.

Weed-killer, which so often figures in poisoning cases, came into the picture, for Thomas Sydney used it in his garden, and the police collected a tin from him. Both houses concerned had back doors, never locked in the daytime and near to larders or pantries, and the theory that some person unknown had thus entered and tampered with the food and drink at least found some support in the improbability of such a massacre being committed by a member of the family. It does not appear that any of them was in need of money, and no other motive for the crimes was openly suggested. The theory of the homicidal maniac was, of course, put forward; this, like all others involving an outsider, presents some difficult problems. Whatever the truth, certain points are clear. There was much method in this madness, there was only one poisoner, and he or she was well acquainted with the habits of the Duff and Sydney households.

Finally, were there three murders or two? Death by arsenical poisoning is a dreadfully painful one, and it is difficult to imagine Mrs Sydney, who was normally well-balanced, pilfering weed-killer from her son's garden, or somehow obtaining arsenic elsewhere, in order to kill herself by such means. Her words to the servant, when she tasted her last dose of medicine, could be twisted into an expression of surprise because the poison, when combined with other chemicals, had a nasty taste; but this implies a knowledge of the properties of arsenic scarcely to be expected. On the other hand, Mrs Sydney had been in a distraught state since her daughter's death, and the verdict of the coroner's jury in her case was that there was insufficient evidence to show whether she had killed herself or had been murdered.

Verdicts of murder against some person or persons unknown were returned at the inquests on her daughter and son-in-law. The proceedings in the three cases, repeatedly adjourned, had dragged on until August 1929. An immense amount of work was involved for all concerned, and the coroner, Mr Jackson, being on the verge of a breakdown, received medical attention from Spilsbury. The police may have, as they are said to have, definite opinions about all three deaths, but there the matter rests to this day.

Chapter 3: THE USE OF THE KNIFE

KNIVES are not commonly carried in this country, except by seamen, and this no doubt is the basis of a prejudice that has none in logic. The knife is at least a cleaner weapon than the poker or piece of lead piping favoured by young men who set out to murder old women. The young men, not having been brought up to the use of it, feel that it is less sure—and perhaps less manly.

Spilsbury's filing cabinets, an index to death in all its forms, show whole years which do not include a single death caused by the knife, suicides excepted. Other years bear out the popular belief that such crimes are as often as not committed by foreigners. The year 1931, for instance, made use of elsewhere as a criterion, shows the high number of five killings by this means. One of the accused was adjudged insane, and a second acquitted; of the other three, two were named Anastasiou and Martinucci. Nine years before this Spilsbury had given evidence in the most famous of all cases in England in this category, to be touched on later. His first public appearance as pathologist for the Crown, in 1911, was in connexion with the murder of Alice Linfold, the weapon being a razor.

It was a tragedy marked by peculiarly shocking circumstances. Most murders are committed in secret, but this was a premeditated crime of jealousy or frustrated passion carried out in the most open manner. Alice Linfold lived with her parents at Finchley. A good-looking girl of twenty-two, of blameless character, she was being pestered by the attentions of a young man named Pateman. On the last day of her life, April 29, as she was going out in the evening, Pateman met her at her garden gate. When she rejected some demand he made upon her he drew a razor from his pocket. On Spilsbury's case-card is a scale drawing of the frightful wound inflicted on the girl's throat. He goes on to give a characteristic reconstruction of the attack. Apparently Miss Linfold had turned away, probably to go back into the house; Pateman grasped her from behind, bruising her arm and slashing her coat and even her hat-brim as she struggled to free herself. His furious grip broke the handle of the razor. The poor girl was able to stagger nearly fifty yards along the garden path to the kitchen, where she died.

A case of suicide in the next month, May, in the neighbouring borough of Hornsey, must be included because it illustrates Spilsbury's thoroughness, not only in reconstructing events, but in interpreting them to show the workings of a man's mind. Always interested in the human brain and its thought-processes, what he saw at the mortuary took him to the scene of the tragedy, of which he made a close examination. A man named Surgey, employed by an insurance company, had cut his throat in the street, dying soon after of air-embolism caused by the wound. The weapon was a new pocket-knife; he had closed it, and replaced it in his right jacket pocket. He was gripping a bloodstained handkerchief in his right hand. Beside him lay a copy of a weekly paper. Another scaled outline on Spilsbury's card shows the suicide's determination. The exterior jugular vein was completely severed. Yet, having realized with horror an instant after what he had done, the dying man walked nearly a hundred yards before he collapsed. Spilsbury paced them, and his quite masterly deductions from this and other features of the case, which he outlined later that year in an address on air-embolism to the St Mary's Medical Society, were summarized as follows in the *Hospital Gazette*:

> Dr Spilsbury showed two cases of cut throat, and clearly demonstrated by his intricate arguments that the mantle of Sherlock Holmes has fallen on his shoulders. In one case he had a few stains of blood along a foot-path, a post-mortem examination, and a dilated pupil, by which he developed in detail every movement and every thought of the victim from the time of his self-inflicted wound to his death. How his temporary insanity was turned into logical reasoning was shown (1) by a gap in the drops of blood where the suicide had attempted to arrest hæmorrhage by the use of a handkerchief, and (2) by the direction of his steps towards the house of his medical adviser and not towards his home. Dr Spilsbury thrilled his audience by describing how, after turning a corner, the man removed his handkerchief, unconscious of the knowledge that by so doing he was letting air into his veins and thereby determining his death. The pressure on the neck must have paralysed the sympathetic nerves—hence the dilated pupil.

Some years later a stabbing case at Stockton-on-Tees shows him helping the police to a conviction by demonstrating how, and therefore by whom, the wound was inflicted. Patrick Swift, an ironworker, was found killed by a knife-thrust in the kitchen of his house. His wife maintained that after a drunken quarrel he had stabbed himself.

No one else had been present, and though the police doubted her story, they could not disprove it until Spilsbury was called in. A fierce downward stroke had pierced Swift's chest near the heart; he was a right-handed man, and Spilsbury showed that he could not with that hand have stabbed himself at such an angle, nor with his left hand have used sufficient force. The knife had been brought down from over the shoulder of some one facing him.

Though in the least complicated cases of death by stabbing, or by shooting, Spilsbury made his usual exhaustive examination of the organs, crimes of violence in this class seldom give the pathologist that scope for virtuosity provided where there is an element of doubt, as in death by poison, or where a body has been dismembered and its fragments, perhaps (the Mahon case is the classic), made to undergo a change. One murder by the knife, however, otherwise celebrated, is possibly unique, because Spilsbury's post-mortem was directed to seeking evidence of previous attempts to kill by other means.

2

This was not the only remarkable issue arising out of the murder of Percy Thompson at Ilford in 1922. It is no novelty to find little interest felt in the victim himself; a long procession of these unfortunates—the Pritchard family, John Parsons Cook, Camille Holland, Miss Barrow, Mrs Armstrong, Jones, of the Blue Anchor—have long ago passed as unremembered shades, while the looks and words and postures of their murderers are still recorded and discussed. This is markedly the case when the accused is a woman, to instance only Madeleine Smith, Mrs Maybrick, and Adelaide Bartlett. The striking feature of the trial of Frederick Bywaters and Edith Thompson is that the limelight was stolen by that one of the pair who, in the technical sense, was certainly not a murderess. And it was stolen, not because she was a woman, but because of the sort of woman she was.

Percy Thompson was a shipping clerk. That is really all that can be said about him, except that perhaps in this very featurelessness lay the seeds of disaster. If his wife is to be believed, at his best he was a pernickety and trying husband, and, at his worst, sometimes a brutal one. We have not got his version of their life together. He was only thirty-two at the time of his death, when Edith Thompson, who had been Edith Jessie Graydon, was twenty-eight. They had been married for seven years. Before the marriage, and after it until her trial, Mrs Thompson was employed by a firm of wholesale milliners in Aldersgate Street. She rose to be bookkeeper and manageress, and was described by her employer as a very capable and businesslike woman.

It is plain that the Percy Thompsons were a most ill-suited pair. They lived in a world of orderly conventions, where every one, outwardly, behaved alike. All the men, and some of the women, left home after breakfast and returned before supper. The intervening hours were spent in what to most was merely a dull way of earning a living. Only when they came home were they free, and then only within limits. Into this world Percy Thompson probably fitted perfectly, a neat little round peg in its appropriate neat little round hole. But his wife was made of different stuff. If appearances and conventions also meant much to her, it was as matters of habit and environment, not of character.

There are plenty of good business-women, and not a few who are romantic escapists. The two types cannot often be found in one personality, still less often in such as Edith Thompson. Her success in business implies that she enjoyed her work, which in time gave her more responsibility and scope than her husband ever knew, and a salary at least as big as his. It brought her in constant touch with a wider and more variegated life than that of Ilford. But another and very powerful element in her nature demanded a different life altogether. She found this in her own dreams, and in novels; and the more Ilford, and all it stood for, irked her, the deeper she withdrew into this life of fancy. The case is common enough, but Mrs Thompson was a most uncommon woman, as few who have read her letters can doubt. She was the escapist *par excellence*. It has often been remarked that the published photographs of her might be the portraits of as many different women. The very features appear unlike. She had that chameleon quality of the oversensitive and imaginative mind which so takes on the colour of whatever at the moment possesses it, whether reality or make-believe, that it seems to remould the face. Unhappily, in her, the mind was wholly untrained and uncontrolled. It was the mind of a child, absorbing rubbish, and worse than rubbish, as readily and credulously as the stuff of value it was quite capable of appreciating. Because, indeed, it was a very lively and intelligent mind, this inability to discriminate brought disaster. In the famous letters lies and self-deceptions are so mingled with the truth that judge and jury, taking the easiest course, appear to have assumed the lies to be truth, and much of the truth to be lies.

Beside the extraordinarily vivid impression, for good or bad, which is all that remains of Edith Thompson the picture of Frederick

Bywaters, like that of his victim, is sketchy in the extreme. Probably there was not much in him except virility and a sort of good looks. The rest was supplied by Edith Thompson's imagination. Though old in some ways for his years, he was, in fact, eight years her junior, and, being a writer, or steward, on the P. and O. liner *Morea*, he was out of England for many weeks at a time. These circumstances, menacing her with fears that he might tire of her or become estranged during their long partings, were always in her mind. There are signs towards the end that he had moments of doubt about this passionate entanglement, and it is then that she begins the obscure campaign of incitement which was to be the ruin of both of them. It is not in his favour that he kept her dangerous letters, while she faithfully destroyed his, and Filson Young, who describes him as "a virile degenerate," is not alone in thinking him capable of blackmail. When poor Mrs Graydon asked her daughter how she could write such letters Edith Thompson replied, "Nobody knows what kind of letters he was writing to me." The views of a kindly and impartial witness of these protagonists in the tragedy may perhaps be inferred from one of those marginal pencillings which are so often a clue to Spilsbury's thoughts. In his own copy of the relevant volume in the "Notable Trials" series he has marked this passage. He marked others, and, as will be seen, on the whole these annotations confirm the impression that his opinion of Edith Thompson was not that of the judge and jury. It is interesting to note that for him, as for everybody else, she held the centre of the stage. There are no pencil-marks for Frederick Bywaters.

The latter had known Edith Graydon when he was at school with her brothers. His own home was with his widowed mother at Norwood, but in 1921, when he had been in the merchant service for three years, he took a room in the house which Percy Thompson and his wife now occupied in Kensington Gardens, Ilford. It was too big for their needs, for they had no children. Just before this Bywaters had been away with them for a holiday in the Isle of Wight, and a photograph taken there of Edith Thompson and her husband (probably by Bywaters himself) shows this baffling and fascinating woman—for fascinating she will always be, whether from pity or aversion—in one of her chameleon moods, looking her happiest, but quite unlike herself in any other portrait. Percy Thompson, in a yachting cap, looks, it must be admitted, merely dour and uninteresting.

If his wife looked her happiest during that holiday at Shanklin it was because she was then for the first time, and passionately, in love.

Two months later some sort of quarrel between Bywaters and Thompson led to the former leaving the house at Ilford; and from that date whenever his ship was in dock at Tilbury he and Edith Thompson met constantly and furtively elsewhere—that is to say, though others knew of these meetings, Percy Thompson was not supposed to be one. Before long, however, or so his wife asserted in her letters, he began to suspect what was going on. All this time the letters, in a stream, followed the *Morea* to Marseilles, to Port Said, to Bombay. Most of Bywaters' replies came to the office in Aldersgate Street. On September 23, 1922, the *Morea* docked once more from the Mediterranean. During the next ten days he and Edith Thompson met frequently. If in the long partings his ardour cooled, as soon as they were together her fascination, and the intensity of her passion, again swept him off his feet.

Their last meeting of this relatively carefree kind was on the afternoon of October 3, at a café in Aldersgate Street. That evening the Percy Thompsons went to the Criterion Theatre. About midnight, in Ilford, in a street near Kensington Gardens, a woman's voice was heard crying out, "Oh, don't! Oh, don't!" in what was described as a most piteous manner. Some people on their way home met Edith Thompson running for help for her husband, who was lying bleeding on the pavement. A doctor was fetched, and when he told the distracted woman that Percy Thompson was dead she exclaimed, "Why didn't you come sooner, and save him?"

She said nothing at this time about the presence of any third person. To a police sergeant she said, "They will blame me for this." She seemed then to be hoping that her husband was still alive. He had, in fact, been stabbed three times in the neck, one thrust piercing the carotid artery, and there were other minor slashes on his body and clothes. No knife had been found.

Superintendent Wensley was given charge of the case, but before he arrived at Ilford Police Station the following afternoon the local police had got on the track of Bywaters. He was brought in for questioning that evening, and detained. Edith Thompson was at the police station later, and was also detained. Neither of the pair knew that the other was in the building until next day, when it so happened, or was so contrived by Wensley, that Mrs Thompson was taken along a passage from which she could see, through an open door, Wensley himself interrogating Bywaters. Under the shock she cried out, in what seem to be the spontaneous accents of truth, "Oh, God, what can I do? Why did he do it? I did not want him to do it!"

It was after this that she admitted seeing Bywaters running down the dark street from the scene of her husband's death. She still denied, and denied to the end, any foreknowledge of his plans or movements that night. She appeared then to be in no serious danger herself; but Bywaters' room in his mother's house was now being searched, and his cabin on the *Morea*, and the damning letters were being avidly read. He was charged with murder that day, and in due course both he and Edith Thompson were committed for trial at the Central Criminal Court on a whole series of charges—as to Bywaters himself, murder and conspiracy to murder, and as to his alleged accomplice, murder conspiracy, soliciting murder, administering poison with intent to murder, administering a destructive thing with the same intent. Those who drew up the indictment had done their best to leave no loophole.

3

Macaulay remarks somewhere that the British people are prone to rather ridiculous fits of self-righteousness. It was Edith Thompson's fate to run head-on against a representative section of the public, a judge and jury, in its most priggish mood. For Bywaters, of course, there was never any hope; nor did Mr Justice Shearman, in his charge to the jury at the Old Bailey, waste many words on him. The judicial sarcasms and moralizings were reserved for the woman in the case. Shearman did not, and could not, remind the jury, as judges are so fond of doing, that a court of law is not a court of morals, because to adjudicate on morals was precisely what he did, and no doubt intended to do from the first. In his summing up he said that he was anxious not to take a side; but he had already taken it. He had intervened in Curtis-Bennett's final speech for the defence to warn the jury, almost in so many words, not to listen to advocacy which might distract their minds from the only thing that mattered—that they were trying a vulgar and common crime. It was in allusion to this speech that he said later that he did not like invocations to the Deity, and that the jury must not be frightened by them. Since the word 'adultery' was always on the judge's lips, he would have done well to remember that the jury was there to try a breach of the sixth Commandment, not the seventh. The following, with its tendentious parenthesis, is a typical observation:

"This charge really is—I am not saying whether it is proved—a common or ordinary charge of a wife and an adulterer murdering the husband."

A few more *obiter dicta* should be quoted:

Of the letters in general—"Gush." "This insensate, silly affection."

"You are told this is a case of great love. Take one of the letters as a test. 'He has the right by law to all that you have a right to by nature and by love.' If that means anything, it means that the love of a husband for his wife is something improper because marriage is acknowledged by law, and that the love of a woman for her lover, illicit and clandestine, is something great and noble. I am certain that you, like any other right-minded persons, will be filled with disgust at such a notion."

Of such authors as Robert Hichens and W. B. Maxwell—"They write chiefly about so-called heroes and heroines, probably wicked people, which no doubt accounts for a great many of these tragedies."

(Mr Hichens, Mr Maxwell, *et al.*, must rightly have resented this preposterous inference.)

Of the witness who declared on oath that he heard Edith Thompson cry out, "Oh, don't! Oh, don't!"—"You know he was some way off. I am not saying it is true."

Lawyers—or some lawyers—profess to see nothing wrong in this summing-up, because there was nothing wrong with its law. It was soon generally recognized, however, that as regards Edith Thompson it was thoroughly bad; and it certainly seems that even in law, or in what is supposed to be synonymous, equity, it fell sadly below the high standards of the English Bench. There were serious and inexcusable omissions. The judge failed to remind the jury that Edith Thompson's capacity for make-believe, or plain lying, was extended to trifles. She invented domestic scenes and squabbles. And not a word was said about Spilsbury's evidence. Because, it can only be supposed, it was as much in favour of the defence as of the prosecution it was completely ignored.

It was the letters that brought Spilsbury into the case. He was not needed to explain how Percy Thompson met his death, and the latter had been buried for some time before the study of his wife's letters to Bywaters opened new and entrancing vistas to the prosecution. They had got her now; Spilsbury would find traces of the poisons and the powdered glass which, if words mean anything, as Mr Justice Shearman would have said, she had persistently mingled with her husband's food.

A month almost to the day after the murder the body was exhumed. Spilsbury performed the post-mortem, and he found nothing—nothing, that is, of any use to the prosecution. Not a trace of poison, or of the passage of powdered electric-light bulbs. Webster's analysis confirmed these findings. Spilsbury's case-card mentions one symptom which might be construed as indicating that poison had been administered: there was fatty degeneration of certain organs, and no sign of disease to account for it. Rather oddly, when the Solicitor-General, Sir Thomas Inskip, had Spilsbury in the witness-box, he did not raise this point. He was content with extracting the admission that after a lapse of months poison or powdered glass might leave no trace.

Perhaps Inskip would have liked to dispense with so unsatisfactory a witness altogether. But that was impossible: once Spilsbury was called in all the world knew it. The less, therefore, heard about his negative findings the better. In one of the latest studies of this famous trial Edgar Lustgarten says of the episode: "The Crown produced this tremendous piece of evidence in a shabby, grudging, discreditable way." Nothing was shabbier than the judge's omission to mention it in his summing-up. This must have been deliberate: judges did not forget, or underrate, Spilsbury, to say nothing of Webster. But if this pair were right—and how often were they wrong?—words might mean nothing, after all. It was a terrible thought for lawyers.

The proceedings at the Central Criminal Court, which lasted five days, were dominated by the reading of extracts from Edith Thompson's letters, and by her ordeal in the witness-box. She insisted on giving evidence; Curtis-Bennett, faced with the familiar dilemma, would have preferred not to call her. He said afterwards, to a friend,

> I know—I am convinced—that Mrs Thompson would be alive to-day if she had taken my advice. She spoiled her chances by her evidence and demeanour. I had a perfect answer to everything, which I am sure would have won an acquittal if she had not been a witness. She was a vain woman and an obstinate one. She had an idea that she could carry the jury. Also she realized the enormous public interest, and decided to play up to it by entering the witness-box. Her imagination was highly developed, but it failed to show her the mistake she was making. I could have saved her.

Probably Edith Thompson soon realized her mistake. Standing alone, the eyes of a hostile judge and of a puzzled jury, waiting for his lead, unwaveringly upon her, nerves and hope deserted her. She made a bad, implausible witness. After she left the box the end soon came. Bywaters, to his credit, had done his best to dissociate her from the crime; when, after the verdict, in his case inevitable, he said that he was not guilty of intentional murder he added that she was not guilty either—meaning of incitement. The acoustics of the Central

Criminal Court are poor, but every one heard her own anguished cry: "I am not guilty! Oh, God, I am not guilty!"

Correct in law, Mr Justice Shearman's summing-up, and the verdicts, were upheld in the Court of Criminal Appeal. The Lord Chief Justice, in delivering the two judgments, might have omitted moralizings very similar to those too often heard at the trial. The case was "squalid and rather indecent"; it was "essentially a commonplace and unedifying case." A less commonplace case has never been tried, and, by moralists, the upshot should have been thought highly edifying.

The general public thought it so, being then in a moral mood. It is often said that Edith Thompson was not reprieved because a weak Home Secretary had been frightened by the popular reaction to the reprieve of Ronald True. Curtis-Bennett, who should have known, always held that if anything influenced the Home Secretary it was popular feeling, expressed in the newspapers, of another sort—indignation against a wicked woman who had led astray a youth of good character, much younger and more innocent than herself.

Time and opinions have changed. Much has been written about this case, and the famous letters have been studied in their entirety. This was not possible at the time. Upward of sixty of these letters, from Edith Thompson to Bywaters, were found in his possession. Only some thirty were produced in court, and from these only extracts helpful to the case for the Crown were read. Why the others were not produced, or at least quoted by the defence, which had copies, remains unexplained.

What was in these letters? They were long and rambling: to use the writer's own word to express what this correspondence with her lover meant to her, she did not write, she "talked"; and, shorn of Mr Justice Shearman's "gush," the common stuff of love letters, quite remarkable talk it sometimes is—spontaneous, naïve, almost witty, and often moving. There is a great deal about novels of the romantic type, *The Guarded Flame*, *John Chilcote, M.P.*, *The Common Law*, *The Fruitful Vine*, and *Bella Donna*, and characters are discussed as though they lived, as, indeed, they did to Edith Thompson.

"We ourselves," she writes,

> die and live in the books we read while we are reading them and then when we have finished, the books die and we live—or exist—just drag on through years and years, until what? Who knows?—I'm beginning to think no one does—no, not even you and I, we are not the shapers of our destinies.

Were they not? All this, at least, is Edith Thompson to the life. She wrote again: "The endings are not the story. . . . Do as I do. Forget the end, lose yourself in the characters and the story, and in your own mind make your own end." She lost herself; she made her own endings, and her own end. Many of these novels she sent to Bywaters, among them *Bella Donna*, in which a wife poisons her husband. She sent other things, more incriminating—Press cuttings about poisoning cases, and questions about the action of poisons. Two of the cases were Spilsbury's—the deaths from cocaine of Freda Kempton and Lilian May Davis. She did more: she "talked" with incredible recklessness of what seemed, "if words mean anything," to be attempts on her husband's life.

At the start of the trial Curtis-Bennett argued that the letters were inadmissible as evidence. The judge ruled against him, and the hand-picked extracts were read by Travers Humphreys, who was with the Solicitor-General, but whose far superior talents were otherwise wasted. There were such examples as these:

> Now I think whatever else I try it in again will still taste bitter—he will recognize it and be more suspicious still and if the quantity is not successful it will injure any chance I may have of trying again when you come home.
>
> You said it was enough for an elephant. Perhaps it was. But you don't allow for the taste making only a small quantity to be taken. It sounded like a reproach—was it meant to be?
>
> Now your letter tells me about the bitter taste again. Oh darlint I do feel so down and unhappy. Wouldn't the stuff make small pills coated together with soap and dipped in liquorice powder—like Beechams—try while you are away.
>
> 'It must be remembered that digitalin is a cumulative poison, and that the same dose, harmless if taken once, yet frequently repeated becomes deadly.' Darlingest boy, the above passage I've just come across is in a book I'm reading, *Bella Donna*, by Robert Hichens. Is it any use?
>
> I had the wrong Porridge to-day, but I don't suppose it will matter, I don't seem to care much either way.
>
> I'm going to try the glass again occasionally—when it's safe—I've got an electric light globe this time.
>
> I was buoyed up with the hope of the 'light bulb' and I used a lot—big pieces too.
>
> I used the 'light bulb' three times but the third time he found a piece—so I've given it up—until you come home.

Such extracts could be multiplied. What did they mean? Were they literal statements? If they were, what was Percy Thompson doing about it? Apparently nothing at all. When he was not picking pieces of glass out of his porridge, or complaining because his tea tasted bitter, he was leading his normal domestic life, eating meals prepared by the wife who was trying to kill him, taking her to the theatre. . . . The letters, in fact, do not make sense, unless they are accepted as nonsense.

Of Bywaters it was said, even at the time,

> it is extremely probable that he entered into this grim and shocking game of correspondence about poisoning meaning it as little as she did; and it is probable that they both found an erotic stimulus in giving full play on paper to their jealousy. And when the letters ceased, and they met again, they had worked themselves too far; and to avoid anti-climax this jealous lad was forced to the climax of the knife.

The writer of this was present throughout the trial. His theory is now widely accepted. In support of it, and in fairness to Edith Thompson, one or two other extracts from her letters not produced at the Old Bailey should be cited.

It is rather terrible now to read the following, written, with its characteristic misspellings and lack of punctuation, only four months before the end, and long after incitement to murder was alleged to have begun:

> Darlint, your own pal is getting quite a sport. On Saturday I was first in the Egg & Spoon race & first in the 100 yard Flat race & 3rd in the 50 yards last race.
>
> Everybody tells me Im like a racehorse—can get up speed only on a long distance & my reply was 'that if a thoroughbred did these things then I felt flattered.'
>
> Then I was M.C. for the Lancers we stood up 10 Sets had some boys in from an adjoining cricket field. I sat on the top of the piano & made a megaphone of my hands & just yelled. . . .
>
> It was rather fun on Thursday at the Garden Party—They had swings & roundabouts & Flip Flaps cocoa-nut shies Aunt Sallies Hoop La & all that sort of things. I went in for them all & on them all & shocked a lot of people I think. I didnt care tho' & going home Mr Birnage said he'd like some fried fish & potatoes—Id rather a posh frock on—wht. georgette & trd. with rows & rows of jade ribbon velvet & my white fur & a large wht. hat, but all that didnt deter me from going into a fried fish shop in Snaresbrook & buying the fish & chips. Getting it home was the worst part—it smelt the bus out. I didn't mind—it was rather fun. . . .

"It was rather fun." Two months later, two months before the end, she could still find contentment in little things. "I have been amusing myself making jam, chutney & mincemeat with the apples from the garden. . . ." These scarcely sound like the moods of a calculating murderess.

It is a fair inference that among those who did not believe her to be one was a witness at the trial whose knowledge of human behaviour was even then exceptional. In Spilsbury's copy of *The Trial of Frederick Bywaters and Edith Thompson* these passages are marked by him.

From Filson Young's Introduction:

> She wished him [Bywaters] to believe that there was nothing she would stop at; though, in fact, she had no intention whatever of running the risks that such attempts would have involved.
>
> By keeping these letters Bywaters brought ruin to the writer. She kept none of his; she was too loyal for that.
>
> I think the defence made another mistake in not having the whole of the letters put in as evidence instead of that portion of them selected by the prosecution.
>
> In my opinion, the real explanation of the passages relating to definite attempts on the husband's life by means of poison, glass, etc., is that these two people were playing in their letters a very dangerous kind of game, in which Mrs Thompson's too fertile imagination cast her for the role of that heroine with whose existence in fiction she was very familiar.

From the cross-examination of Bywaters:

> "As far as you could tell, reading these letters, did you ever believe in your own mind that she herself had ever given any poison to her husband?"—"No, it never entered my mind at all. She had been reading books."

From the cross-examination of Mrs Thompson:

> "Now, Mrs Thompson, is it not the fact that you knew that Bywaters was going to do something on this evening?" "That is not so."

From the Letters:

> Yes, I like you deciding things for me. I've done it so long for myself. . . .
>
> I want you so badly to lean on and to take care of me to be kind and gentle and love me as only you can.

Other passages marked, the implications of which are favourable to Edith Thompson, are her words to her mother about Bywaters' letters to her, her outcry in the dark street at midnight when her husband was struck down, and a reference to her passion for the outward conventions of respectability. Also pencilled is Bywaters' statement that a "compact" mentioned in the letters referred to a suggestion (by her) of suicide. Did Spilsbury believe this? She was as capable of 'talking" glibly about suicide as about murder, without meaning what she said in either case.

On the contra side there are marks against one or two of the "poison and powdered glass" extracts, and a pen has been used to indicate what no doubt was agreement with the general sense of the judge's condemnation of the intrigue between these two young people. No one will suppose that Spilsbury, with his rigid views on certain moral lapses, felt anything but disapproval of such behaviour. But it did not make Edith Thompson a murderess; and though the judge, the jury, the Court of Criminal Appeal, and the Home Secretary chose to send her to the gallows, the rather cryptic marginalia of their leading medical witness would alone suggest that he knew better where the truth lay. In a letter to the *Daily Telegraph* (1951), Miss Tennyson Jesse has revealed that Spilsbury "considered Mrs Thompson guiltless of any attempt to poison her husband or in any other way to try to get rid of him."

Chapter 4: TRUNKS AND TORSOS

On May 11, 1927, Spilsbury was at the mortuary of the Westminster Coroner's Court in Horseferry Road, examining some exceedingly grisly luggage deposited five days before at the main-line cloakroom of Charing Cross Station.

The fashion in trunk murders in this country seems to have been launched by Crossman, who cemented the remains of a Mrs Sampson in a tin case in 1902, when Spilsbury was a young student demonstrator at St Mary's. Three years later Crossman's method was copied by Arthur Devereux, a chemist's assistant, who sent the bodies of his wife and twin children, packed in a similar air-tight container, to a furniture repository. The idea may have been in Devereux's mind for some time, for he had once bought a trunk at Herne Bay, where George Joseph Smith was later to buy a bath. The lady who was then passing as Mrs Devereux became for some reason suspicious, and left him in haste.

The owner of the piece of luggage collected by the police at Charing Cross was a less careful criminal than Devereux. His trunk was a large, round-topped, wicker-work affair of a familiar type, covered with black American cloth and fastened with a broad strap. It was very far from air-tight, which accounted for the cloakroom attendants beginning to wonder about its contents so soon after it had been left with them on May 6. A police constable was fetched from his beat, and the trunk was opened. In it, under some brown paper, was the body of a woman divided into five parts by amputation at each shoulder and hip-joint. The constable, however, a man who took his instructions literally, would not allow these horrid remains to be removed to the mortuary until a police surgeon had certified that the woman was dead.

Putrefaction was advanced, but Spilsbury was able to enumerate a number of bruises on the temple, abdomen, back, and limbs. These bruises were all recent, all caused before death, and made almost at the same time, one on the temple and another on the right hip being of earlier origin than the rest. After examination of the lungs, air passages, and tongue Spilsbury gave the cause of death as set out on his case-card: "Asphyxia from pressure over mouth and nostrils whilst unconscious from head injury and other injuries." Death had taken place about a week before the discovery of the body. The woman had been short and rather stout, and between thirty and forty years of age.

In describing the amputations Spilsbury used words reminiscent of the murder of Mme Gerard in Charlotte Street ten years earlier: "Clean dismemberment of parts suggests experienced slaughterman." In this later case the murderer's luck or judgment led Spilsbury into one of his rare errors of deduction. He admitted it readily afterwards. The way in which the left hip was severed and two tentative cuts, one opening the peritoneum and the second at the back of the right knee, should, he said, have told him that the operator was unskilled.

The story behind this crime proved to be of a very common type, and the case is chiefly remarkable for the thorough but rapid work which enabled the police to identify first the victim, and then the murderer, and because of the circumstances of the murder itself. It must be almost the only one committed opposite a police station. This fact, when discovered, and the added impertinence of the murderer in hailing a taxi just paid off at the very door of that station, and having the trunk and its contents put on it in full view of any police officers who happened to be looking out, must have lent a peculiar zest to the pursuit.

There was no direct evidence in the trunk of the victim's identity. It contained, besides the naked torso and limbs, wrapped in paper, articles of women's clothing, a pair of shoes, a duster, and an empty handbag. On one piece of clothing was a linen tab with the name "P. Holt" in block letters, and on another garment were two laundry-marks—581 and 447. On the trunk itself the letters "I.F.A." were painted in white, and on a tie-on label was written "F. Austin to St Lenards." F. Austin had nothing to do with the case; but the misspelling of St Leonards, and the laundry-marks, played their part in the investigation.

The attendants at Charing Cross cloakroom had no recollection of the trunk's depositor, which was not surprising, for they handled some two thousand pieces of luggage that day. The porter was found who fetched the trunk from a taxi, but again it was the luggage he remembered, not its owner. By an odd chance the cloakroom ticket for the trunk now turned up; a shoeblack had found it in the station yard. According to one story, he saw it thrown from the window of a departing taxi. A snapper-up of unconsidered trifles, he put it in his pocket; five days later there was a hullabaloo about a trunk, and he produced his find. He was to have his sixty seconds of fame when he was the first witness to be called at the subsequent trial.

As in the Voisin case, the laundry-marks brought information about the dead woman within twenty-four hours. The marked garment came from a household in Chelsea, where, some time before, a Mrs Rolls had been employed for a week as a cook. Her employer recognized the remains from the trunk. The next day Mr Rolls was found; the dead woman, who had lived with him for a while, was Minnie Bonati, the wife of an Italian waiter. In another few days Bonati was run to earth, and removed all doubts by positively identifying certain peculiarities in the body, including a crooked finger his wife had had from birth. By now a good deal was known about Minnie Bonati and her way of life: she was thirty-six, and of promiscuous habits, and the last person found who had seen her alive was the Chelsea relieving officer, whom she visited on the afternoon of May 4.

The provenance of the trunk had also been traced. A dealer in second-hand luggage in the Brixton Road came forward to say that he had recently sold it—he thought on or soon after the 4th. Unobservant as well as rather unbusinesslike, he remembered little or nothing about the purchaser.

When nearly a week had gone by since the discovery of Mrs Bonati's remains the evidence of a taxi-driver gave a definite and final turn to the inquiry. To the police of Rochester Row it was a startling development. Shortly after 1 P.M. on May 6 the cabman drove two passengers from the Royal Automobile Club to that police station. He was then hailed by a man standing in the doorway of a block of offices across the street. He helped the man lift a very heavy trunk on to the cab, and drove him to Charing Cross Station. The significance of this journey, out of all those made by taxi-cabs with trunks to Charing Cross that day, was apparent as soon as times were checked. The police had found the person who received the cloakroom ticket preceding that issued for the only trunk they were interested in, and the latter, it was thus established, was deposited at about 1.50. The summonses at Rochester Row for that day were turned up, and the taxi-driver's passengers from the R.A.C., two men charged with a motoring offence, were shown to have arrived at the police station at 1.35. The times fitted; the taxi-driver identified the trunk; and every officer at Rochester Row now looked with a new and devouring (and rather scandalized) interest at the familiar façade of No. 86 across the street.

An immediate investigation of the premises was undertaken by Chief Inspector (later Superintendent) Cornish, who was in charge of the case. The principal tenants were a firm of solicitors, and one of their staff had seen a trunk in the lower hall soon after 1 P.M. on the 6th. Among others with offices in the building, one was missing—Mr John Robinson, who carried on the business of an estate agent in a single, poorly furnished room. Mr Robinson had written to the landlord on the 9th to say frankly that he was leaving because he was broke.

The first search of his room produced nothing to connect him with the crime, but he had to be traced. It was a matter of routine to find his lodgings, but he was gone from there too. A returned telegram (the addressee being unknown) now took the police to the Greyhound Hotel, Hammersmith; and there they found not Robinson, but his wife, to whom he had sent the telegram. The mistake of a new maid, who did not know that Mrs Robinson worked there, had saved Chief Inspector Cornish and his men a good deal of trouble. Robinson was a most unsatisfactory husband, but he kept in touch with his wife, and she was meeting him that evening—it was now May 19—at the Elephant and Castle.

Between six o'clock and seven Robinson was at Scotland Yard. He had no objection to being put up for identification, but the trunk-dealer, the taxi-driver, and the station porter failed to recognize him. He had, of course, never bought a black trunk, and knew nothing of the crime beyond what he had read in the papers. Cornish had to let him go.

He remained, however, the most likely among the tenants of No. 86 to be the man the Chief Inspector wanted, and two days later Cornish carried out a fresh search of the empty office. In the waste-paper basket he found something that had been overlooked—a bloodstained match. In the meantime the clothing and other articles from the trunk were examined anew. The duster, which was very dirty, was washed, and soap and water brought up the word "Greyhound," printed on a tab on one corner. Robinson was brought back to Scotland Yard. Thinking, as so many have done before his time and since, that the police knew far more than they did, instead of holding his tongue, he made yet another of those fatal statements which begin, "I'll tell you all about it. . . ."

If Devereux set a fashion in trunks the Mahon case has had a fascination for later dismemberers. Robinson's story was Mahon's, with suitable variations. On the afternoon of May 4 he was accosted by Minnie Bonati, and took her to his office. When she asked for money, and he said he had none, she became abusive and violent. She tried to strike him, and he struck back, and she fell. Believing her to be only shaken and dazed, he then left the office, expecting her to get up and go when she recovered. Returning the next morning, he found her still lying there, dead.

Behind all these stories of murder and dismemberment is one common feature which can only be guessed at—the murderers' thoughts and emotions when they face the dreadful task of disposing of their victims. The feelings they describe when they make their hackneyed statements smell of the blue lamp, and words, in any case, can but faintly convey what they must have gone through at the time. The sense of guilt and horror, however, will vary greatly according to whether the crime is or is not premeditated. Mahon, a hardened criminal already, knew beforehand what he would have to do. There is nothing to suggest that Robinson was a ruthless egoist of this type. A shiftless rolling-stone who had been almost everything by turns, but nothing long, he was far from scrupulous, but it is most unlikely that he ever contemplated committing murder. It is probable that up to a point his story was true. His denial that he had known Minnie Bonati before the afternoon of May 4 was not disproved, and by killing her he had everything to lose and nothing to gain. For some reason there was a quarrel and a fight; and since by all accounts she was a virago, it may have been the very presence of the police station across the street that drove him, in the heat of temper, to silence her before she could run out screaming vindictively for help.

Then he was faced with the consequences. A man of his kind would be an avid reader of sensational news, and his thoughts would now turn to the behaviour of others in his predicament. It was only three years since Mahon and his methods had filled the papers. Robinson himself now required a carving-knife; and it cannot have been coincidence that took him next day, the 5th, to the shop in Victoria Street where Mahon had bought his own cook's knife and saw. There must have been cutlery shops in the neighbourhood of Kennington Oval, where he was lodging. To all who, like Spilsbury, are interested in the workings of a murderer's mind this episode will perhaps seem the most bizarre and curious feature of an essentially commonplace crime. For some time afterwards, incidentally, anyone asking for a kitchen knife at that Victoria Street shop must have received one or two queer looks. It may be crediting Robinson with too subtle a mind to suggest that when later he buried his weapon under a may-tree on Clapham Common it was because it was the month of May.

On the morning of the 6th he was purchasing the trunk in Brixton and conveying it by omnibus to Rochester Row. Though light when empty, it was an awkward and conspicuous piece of luggage, and it is not fanciful to picture him, as he carried it into No. 86, looking nervously over his shoulder at the building with the blue lamp across the way.

His trial at the Old Bailey before Mr Justice Swift opened on July 11. It lasted only two days. His counsel were faced with the difficulties inherent in all defences in murder trials which have the appearance of being afterthoughts, and which are contradicted by expert medical evidence. Some one must be found to rebut that evidence, and when it was Spilsbury's that was not easy. Having weathered the storm, such as it was—and it was a storm in a tea-cup—which arose out of the Thorne case, Spilsbury was now in a more impregnable position than ever. Few of his fellow pathologists would care to go into the witness-box to say that he was wrong on no better grounds than such a story as Robinson's. There was one, however, always ready to rush into the lists; and once more Brontë took up the gage. Though no doubt he believed sincerely that the theory he put forward was as likely to be correct as Spilsbury's (and so experienced an observer as Ingleby Oddie believed it had a chance), the wish was father to the thought. With the combative Irishman, in whose make-up there was a touch of Jack the Giant-killer as well as of the showman, the personal element entered. Sooner or later he must, and would, shake that serene, infuriating confidence which, for nearly a generation, had hypnotized jury after jury. He never did; and it was an attitude of mind that Spilsbury himself could scarcely understand.

From the tactical point of view this repeated calling in of Brontë to grapple with the giant, though perhaps sometimes unavoidable because no one else would take on the task, was probably a mistake. The only type of medical witness who might have persuaded an English jury to doubt Spilsbury's pronouncements was one as English as himself, as lucid and restrained, as detached, and as palpably convinced that he was right. Celtic verbosity and cocksureness, the slipshod phrases and worse indiscretions that so often called down rebukes from the Bench, hampered rather than helped the defence, and did an injustice to Brontë's own genuine gifts.

Nearly thirty witnesses at the trial testified to the thorough spadework of the police, but they were scarcely needed, for Robinson elected to go into the box and admit almost everything except intention to murder. The methods used by the police in obtaining his statements were challenged, but this matter was not pressed, and prosecution and defence then got down to the crux of the case, the medical evidence.

The divisional police surgeon, in the presence of a pathologist, had performed a post-mortem on the body the day before Spilsbury saw it. This examination disproved Robinson's story of the struggle which no doubt took place. The bruises could not have been caused by a fall, as he said, but were the result of direct blows and pressure, probably by the knee. Death had occurred very soon after, from asphyxiation. The two doctors agreed that this could scarcely have been caused by the folds of the threadbare office rug produced in court; a cushion, also exhibited, was a more likely instrument. A slight leak of gas in the office could have had nothing to do with so rapid a death, nor was there any evidence to support the theory of an epileptic fit, that red herring so often dragged into capital cases since the days of George Joseph Smith.

Spilsbury, in the box, drove home these points. As to Robinson's final statement, he was asked:

> "From the bruises you saw do you accept that as a true explanation of the way she came by her injuries?"
>
> "No."
>
> "How, in your opinion, were those bruises caused?"
>
> "Most of them were caused by direct violence."

Having explained what he meant by direct violence, Spilsbury said that his own examination of the organs showed symptoms of congestion at the back of the lungs, an indication that for some time after death the body was lying on its back. If Mrs Bonati had met her death face downward, from suffocation by the carpet, the front of the lungs would have been congested. This countered Robinson's assertion that when he returned to the office on the morning after the struggle he found her lying on her face. Spilsbury went on to say that there were no indications of coal-gas poisoning, heart disease, or epilepsy; in short, he could not attribute death to normal causes.

"To what abnormal cause?" he was asked.

"In my opinion, asphyxia or suffocation brought about by covering the nose or nostrils, and after the woman had been violently assaulted."

By this time there were certain moves in the game always played, if opportunity offered, when Spilsbury was in the witness-box. An attack on his reliance on observation by the naked eye was one of them; and now in cross-examination it was suggested, as usual "with great respect," that without a microscope it was impossible to tell how long before death bruises were caused. Spilsbury, who must have been getting tired of this particular question (which was purely rhetorical, for counsel who put it knew what reply they would get), retorted quite brusquely for him:

"In the case of recent bruises a microscopical examination will not help in the least. With the naked eye, after they have been cut into, one can tell quite distinctly."

A little later, when agreeing that women bruise more easily than men, he made an interesting comment which suggests that the former are getting tougher:

"Some women bruise very easily, but I think there are fewer than there used to be."

His evidence closed the case for the Crown. The defence opened with Robinson himself in the witness-box, where he spent an uncomfortable and unconvincing hour and a half. He was followed by Brontë, who immediately got into trouble. Asked if he thought that Mrs Bonati could have been suffocated by lying unconscious for some time with her nose and mouth buried in the carpet, he made the curious reply: "Speaking as a layman, yes." He was sharply reminded by the judge that he was not there to speak as a layman, but as a scientific witness. The rest of his evidence was a series of ingenious assumptions adapted to Robinson's story that he found the dead woman lying on her face—as that if she was not suffocated by the carpet she might have been stifled through getting her mouth and nose into her bent elbow. A leak of gas while she was unconscious "could not do other than diminish her chances of recovery." As at the Thorne trial, Brontë gave it as his view that only microscopical examination could determine how long bruises had been caused before death.

The judge, in his charge to the jury, made it clear enough where his own opinion lay, particularly in respect of the medical evidence. He made a pronouncement on the onus of proof which seems to have attracted little attention at the time, but which, when he repeated it some years later, became famous as the Woolmington Misdirection. The jury was out for more than an hour, but no one, it has been said, least of all the prisoner, seemed surprised at their verdict of "Guilty."

2

There is an old music-hall song which runs:

> To Brighton, to Brighton,
> Where they do such things
> And they say such things,
> In Brighton, in Brighton;
> I'll never go there any more.

Brighton is proud of the fact that every one has heard of it, but at one time it found itself acquiring the sort of notoriety that no seaside resort relishes. When, not very long before, the decorum of its select neighbour, Eastbourne, had been shattered by the shooting of a constable in the streets, followed by two atrocious murders on the Crumbles, Brighton had perhaps felt a little smug. In spite of its racecourse and other attractions for the populace, they did not do such things there. Presently, however, and within less than a year, Brighton had a similar series of undesirable sensations of its own, and nervous people were saying, in the words of the old song, "I'll never go there any more."

The series began at Portslade, which is not Brighton, but is almost as near to Brighton as the Crumbles is to Eastbourne, and, to the ignorant, seems, with Hove, to be just part of the same huge, sprawling town. Here, in November 1933, there was a brutal murder in a shop. Spilsbury was called in, and two men named Parker and Probert were convicted of the crime. A few months went by, and the summer crowds were swarming on the front at Brighton. On Derby Day, 1934, some inconspicuous person left a plywood trunk at the cloakroom at Brighton Station. On June 17, eleven days later, the seven-year-old story of the Charing Cross cloakroom was repeated. An offensive smell was traced to the plywood trunk, and when this was taken to the police station there was found in it the torso of a woman. The missing head and limbs had been sawn off.

Some quick work followed. Immediate instructions were issued by telephone to cloakroom attendants throughout the country, and the next day a suitcase was opened at King's Cross. It contained a pair of legs, severed at the knees.

Spilsbury was at Brighton on the 19th. The following day he examined the legs at St Pancras mortuary. The coroner had them packed up and sent to his colleague at Brighton, and the sawn thigh-bones were found to fit accurately to the torso discovered there. Spilsbury's conclusions were that the remains were those of a woman at least twenty-one years of age, probably twenty-five or over, well-proportioned and about 5 feet 3 inches in height. There was no evidence of serious disease or cause of death; she had led an active life, and was in a healthy condition, but was between four and five months pregnant. A few loose light-brown hairs found on the body were acutely bent and twisted from the action of heat, from which Spilsbury deduced a not very recent permanent wave. Sunbathing had bleached the hair on the legs. The dead woman had taken care of her appearance; her armpits were shaved, her hands and feet well kept, and she had worn well-fitting shoes. Death had occurred two or three days before the torso and legs were deposited at the two cloakrooms. Dismemberment had been performed after death, and showed no anatomical skill.

These details of personal appearance are of great interest in view of what followed—or, rather, of what did not follow. Here, plainly, was a woman who dressed well and mixed with the world, if only the half-world. She must have been known to many people, who would now be wondering what had become of her. In spite of the fact that her head was missing, it was confidently expected that a few hours or days would clear up the mystery of her identity.

In the meantime there were the trunk and the suitcase to work on. The trunk, the tray of which was missing, was a cheap thing of plywood covered with brown canvas and strengthened by cane bands, and was quite new. The torso when found in it was wrapped in brown paper tied with six yards of venetian-blind cord. Congealed blood which had soaked through a piece of paper half obliterated a word written in blue pencil, only the terminal letters 'ford' being decipherable, preceded by what might be a 'd' or an 'l.' There was also in the trunk a face flannel and some cheap cotton-wool.

The limbs in the suitcase from King's Cross had been done up in brown paper and newspaper saturated with pure olive oil. From one piece a wine-glass of oil was extracted. The pure article is sometimes used by surgeons to stop profuse bleeding. It was not considered likely that restaurants or cookshops would stock it in such quantities.

From these beginnings began routine inquiries about which a considerable pamphlet might be written. For sheer dogged, patient work by the police, going on for months and covering the whole British Isles and extending to the Continent, this case must stand in a class by itself. As, however, Spilsbury's part in it was to begin and end with his examination of the original remains, it cannot be dealt with at length. The following facts and figures will give some idea of what it entailed.

Of over 700 missing women under thirty all except seven were traced. Inquiries were made at every clinic and hospital to which women came for pre-natal advice, and out of five thousand recent cases at one London hospital alone all but fifteen were eliminated. Scores of makers and sellers of trunks, house agents, and owners of garages were interviewed. Places and people whose names ended in 'ford' received special attention. For weeks two hundred plain-clothes police were calling at hotels and lodging-houses along the south coast. The discovery of a minute sea parasite in the trunk caused the search to be extended to seafaring circles. Among the oddments which turned up and had to be investigated were a human skull, knives, and stains of varnish at first thought to be blood. Letters with suggestions and information, mostly worthless, poured in from all over Europe at the rate of hundreds a day. More than a thousand came from Germany. All this correspondence had to be sifted. It led to much vain work in the way of digging up gardens and ransacking empty bungalows. Sceptical Chief Constables were harried by persons claiming to be psychic, and the inevitable hoaxers added their mite to the trouble.

The cost of all this was enormous, and the work exhausting. A fleet of cars was hired, and extra staff engaged for clerical tasks. C.I.D. officers from Scotland Yard brought their families to Brighton; suites of hotel rooms were taken over, and a sort of battle headquarters was set up amid the *chinoiserie* of the Royal Pavilion. So huge an effort can seldom have produced results so disproportionately meagre. The plywood trunk was eventually traced to a big shop in Brighton, where by that time all recollection of the purchaser was lost; and this was all. Though the murderer, or so it was said, left one incriminating clue, no arrest was made. The victim's head and arms were never found, and she remains unidentified to this day. The cause of her death, and the motive behind it, can only be conjectured. Spilsbury was able to say that she had been neither shot nor strangled; the heart was not empty of blood, and he found no sign of what are called Tardieu spots —tiny capillary hæmorrhages due to raised blood-pressure. His otherwise negative findings support the probability that the woman was killed by a blow on the head. Her pregnancy was perhaps the motive. Who she was, where she came from, why her torso was found at Brighton and her legs at King's Cross—these are mysteries still.

In those days no passports were needed for short trips to France, and Chief Constable Wensley put forward the likely theory that the woman had come from the Continent, perhaps almost immediately before her death. It was a theory widely approved in Brighton, where, as the weeks went by and the patient, unobtrusive work of the police ceased to be news, it was hoped that the unpleasant incident would soon be forgotten altogether. Exactly a month, in fact, had passed since the plywood trunk was opened when a fresh discovery put Brighton once more in the headlines.

One of the first routine moves in the long investigation had been a house-to-house search of whole districts. When Kemp Street, a shabby little thoroughfare near the railway station, was so searched, one house, No. 52, was found empty and locked, and was left alone. It was a cheap lodging-house, and, it being holiday-time, owner and tenants were away. They began to come back soon after, but the police, who had enough on their hands, forgot to return. For reasons undisclosed the tenants left. The owner and his wife were so lazy and incurious that they did not enter the empty rooms. The outside of the house was about to be painted; the painters arrived, and put up a scaffolding, and almost at once, though the windows were closed, an offensive smell was detected coming from one of the rooms. This was reported to the police. It was now July 13; and after a delay of forty-eight hours the house was entered and searched. Another trunk was found—a large one, of black fibre, strapped and locked. Into it had been wedged the body of a woman, packed round with articles of clothing. A few naphthaline balls had done nothing to mitigate the pungent effects of decomposition. The owner and his wife, when asked how they had failed to notice these, explained that neither of them had any sense of smell. The vanished lodgers may have been normal in this respect, if equally incurious.

July 15 was a Sunday. Spilsbury, summoned from home, was at Brighton once more in the course of the morning. He performed a post-mortem on the body that afternoon, while the news spread among the week-end throng and the normal hosts of people taking their annual holiday. To those who live by letting lodgings it was depressing news. Brighton was getting altogether the wrong sort of reputation.

Spilsbury's card of the case is headed: "Shock—depressed fracture of the skull." For this time the body was complete, and undismembered. It was that of a woman whose age he estimated at forty—a very near calculation, since she was forty-two. She had been 5 feet 2 inches in height, with dark-brown hair bleached lighter, and was well nourished. Her head was much bruised, and she had been killed, in his own words, "by a violent blow or blows with a blunt object, e.g., head of hammer, causing a depressed fracture extending down to the base, with a short fissured fracture extending up from its upper edge." A piece of the skull, driven inward until it lay against the brain, was produced by Spilsbury at the trial which followed.

The woman wore a wedding-ring. Most of the clothing in the trunk was feminine, but there was also a man's jacket and overcoat. In the room were found a hammer and a tray from another trunk. (The tray was missing from the trunk figuring in what was now to be known as the Brighton Trunk Murder No. 1.) In a corner cupboard were smears of blood.

This time the victim was identified within twenty-four hours, and the police had then already named and described a man whom they wished to question. It was natural for the Press and public to connect this new crime with Trunk Murder No. 1, and a number of odd coincidences, some appearing to link the two cases, were now gradually disclosed. The dead woman was Violet Saunders, a divorcée and a professional dancer. She had adopted the ill-omened name of Kaye, which had a particularly sinister significance in Sussex, at the same time changing Violet to Violette. Since early in May she had been absent from the basement flat she occupied in Park Crescent, off the main Lewes road, and she was among the women listed as missing by the police during their investigations into Trunk Murder No. 1. A man with whom she had been living, and whom, indeed, she had been keeping out of her own immoral earnings, had been interrogated at Brighton Police Station as late as July 14. As he was able to bring proof that Violette Kaye was at least forty, while the cloakroom remains were those of a woman of about twenty-five, he was soon allowed to go.

He was now wanted again, and the more urgently because he was the last tenant of the room in Kemp Street in which the second trunk was found. He was known as Toni Mancini, and looked as Italian as his name. Not only, however, was he English, but his real name was England. Of the many others he used, most were Italian, but he was to be charged under the improbable alias of Jack Notyre. There were genuine Mancinis in the country at this time, one of them a well-known boxer. Another was to figure in the strangest coincidence of all those which cropped up in connexion with this case. Seven years afterwards Spilsbury was giving evidence at the Central Criminal Court against a second Antonio Mancini, accused of the murder of Harry Distleman, for which he was hanged.

The self-styled Toni Mancini, who became notorious under that name, and must be so called, was to be more fortunate. After leaving

Brighton Police Station on July 14 he made his way at once to London. The next day the hue and cry was out for him, and on the 18th he was recognized at Blackheath, and detained. Human nature was seen at its worst when he was brought back to Brighton: Market Street, where the Town Hall and police station stand, was packed with holiday-makers, men and girls, in swim-suits and beach pyjamas, jostling and hooting and hissing. Mancini came up before the magistrates on the 20th, and was charged with the murder of Violette Kaye.

These proceedings were carried on into August, Spilsbury giving evidence on the 15th of that month. When Mancini was committed for trial nothing had been said about Trunk Murder No. 1; whatever the public might think, the police took the view that they had two separate crimes on their hands. The investigation of the first had led to the discovery of the second. Chronologically, the latter came first; Violette Kaye had been dead a month when the torso in the plywood trunk was found; and the search for information about that unknown victim went on.

Mancini came up for trial before Mr Justice Branson at the Lewes Assizes in December. He was defended by Norman Birkett, who was briefed by a very astute solicitor, and who himself was to give a brilliant display of advocacy. Once more, and again at Lewes, the Crown relied very largely upon Spilsbury's evidence.

Mancini had told his story at the police court. Its outline was familiar. He had returned to the basement flat in Park Crescent on May 10 to find Violette Kaye dead. Other men visited her, at which times he would keep out of the way, and he supposed that one of them had killed her. But he feared the police would not believe this; he had a record, and his general mode of life was damning. Panic-stricken, he bought a trunk, put the body in it, and conveyed it to new quarters in Kemp Street.

At the trial Norman Birkett put forward an alternative defence. Roche Lynch, to whom the organs were sent for analysis, discovered traces of morphine. It was likely enough that such a woman as Violette Kaye was a drug addict, or at least took drugs, and in large doses, from time to time; under the influence of morphine she might have fallen down the area steps leading to her flat and fractured her skull, recovering sufficiently to reach her bedroom, where she died.

Before Spilsbury gave evidence on the third day of the trial much had been heard about Mancini's movements, and about statements alleged to have been made by him, before and after the discovery of Violette Kaye's body in Kemp Street. Chief Inspector Donaldson, of

Scotland Yard, under cross-examination by Birkett, was asked for details of the prisoner's convictions. This unusual request by the defence was designed to establish the fact that Mancini had never been known to use violence. His previous offences were petty thieving and loitering with intent. Spilsbury followed the chief inspector, taking into the witness-box a skull with which he demonstrated the position and nature of the dead woman's injuries. When he laid on the skull the fractured piece of bone which he had found lying against the brain Birkett sprang up to object. The defence had not been told of this exhibit, which had not been produced at the police-court proceedings. In cross-examining Spilsbury Birkett made the most of this tactical point before developing his argument of the fall down the area steps. At the head of these steps, which had an iron railing, was a stone brace, and at the foot a projecting stone window-ledge. On the assumption that a person affected by drink or drugs might trip over the brace, Spilsbury would not agree that the injuries he found were caused either by the railing or the window-ledge, still less by the flat paving of the area. They had been caused, he said, while the head was resting on some such hard surface, by a weapon like the double-headed hammer found with the fibre trunk in Kemp Street.

There were two controversial points here, affecting the alternative defence that Violette Kaye had been attacked by some one unknown. Mancini's story was that he had found her lying on her bed, not on the floor or any other hard surface. Then there was the hammer. At the police-court proceedings Spilsbury had stated that the broader end of this could have inflicted the injuries. He now thought that they were more likely to have been caused by the smaller end. Whatever made him change his opinion, Birkett did his best with the discrepancy.

The following questions and answers were among the last put to Spilsbury, with the conclusion of whose evidence the third day's hearing ended:

> Mr Birkett: "Are you really telling members of the jury that if some one fell down that flight and came upon the stone ledge he would not get a depressed fracture?"
>
> "He would not get this fracture."
>
> Mr Cassels (leading for the Crown): "If there had been a fall such as has been suggested in this case, would you expect to find injuries only to the head, and no injuries to other parts of the body?"
>
> "No. I should certainly expect to find bruises on other projecting parts."

Mr Justice Branson: "Is it, in your view, possible for this woman, having received the injury which you saw, and having gone through a period of unconsciousness, to recover sufficiently to walk to the bed or undress herself or do things of that sort?"

"It is possible to have happened after a depressed fracture, but in this case it is quite clear it had not happened."

Mancini, who was alternatively described as a waiter and a chef, was under examination and cross-examination for almost the whole of the fourth day. Norman Birkett made a very fine closing speech on his behalf, and the judge, in summing up, while giving due weight to Spilsbury's evidence, discredited that of several other of the Crown's witnesses; but the twelve Sussex citizens in the jury-box cannot have felt anything but disgust for what Birkett himself described as "a class of men and women belonging to an underworld that makes the mind reel." Mancini was a man of that class, and his story, in essentials, was one that had often been told before, and disbelieved. But the jury had not been convinced "beyond all reasonable doubt" that he had committed murder, and after debating for more than two hours they brought in a verdict of "Not guilty."

3

The murderers of Willie Starchfield and the unidentified victim of the first Brighton trunk crime are only two among a number who have made use of the amenities of the railway system. The less lucky include John Robinson and Patrick Mahon. It happened that while the Brighton case and its sequel were still very much in the news another body had to be disposed of, and it was not perhaps a coincidence that the new murderer's thoughts turned to railways. Cloakrooms were best left alone for the time being, and he seems to have had in mind a refinement of the technique used in the Starchfield case, which had shown that if human remains are left in a railway carriage it may prove impossible to say when they were put there. An improvement on this method would be to throw them out of the carriage window. Mahon got rid of some portions of Emily Kaye in this way; Crippen is thought to have thrown his wife's head over the side of a cross-Channel steamer, which is a sort of prolongation of a train. In the case now in question, something may have interfered with the murderer's plan, but in the result it was quite successful.

Spilsbury still had the Brighton trunk crimes in hand when he recorded details of two post-mortems later summarized on a whole batch of cards under the following headings: "(1) Examination of a pair of human legs and feet found under the seat of a railway carriage at Waterloo Station on Feb. 25, 1935. (2) Examination of human remains found in the canal at Brentford on March 19th." The details may be left to the imagination. The legs were those of a man, and the remains dredged a month later from the Grand Union Canal comprised a man's chest and upper abdomen, with the greater part of the neck and the arms down to the elbows. Dismemberment in both cases showed anatomical knowledge, and Spilsbury gave seven other reasons for concluding that legs and trunk belonged to the same body. It was that of a healthy man of about forty, with reddish hair and freckles, 5 feet 9 to 10 inches in height. He suffered from corns from tight-fitting shoes, and had not kept his feet very clean. There was no indication of the cause of death, which was probably a head injury. In the case of the torso, death had occurred more than three weeks before discovery, or round about the date when the legs, which had not begun to putrefy, were found at Waterloo.

The case had points that were suggestive, but baffling. The legs were wrapped in newspaper, with an outer wrapping of brown paper. The remains from the canal were in a sack. The train came from Hounslow on the loop line which crosses the canal at Brentford (where it is, in fact, the river Brent) a little way upstream from the spot where the sack was found. Spilsbury noted that the chest was severely crushed—"probably in canal by a barge." The craft could have dragged the bundle upstream from the neighbourhood of the railway bridge. It may well have been cast out of a carriage window there, as, perhaps, it was intended to cast the legs a month before, but the possibilities are very wide, since there is a continuous canal and river system to Brentford all the way from Llangollen, in Wales.

The dead man, like Rouse's victim, very probably belonged to the homeless and friendless class. Lacking head and hands, he was never traced. Neither was his murderer.

Many more such unidentified *disjecta membra* passed through Spilsbury's hands, discovered in trains and trunks and under floorboards, in rivers and ditches, or washed up by the sea, all that remained of nameless victims of murder, suicide, or accident. Sometimes identity could be reasonably conjectured. Many of these discoveries created a stir at the time, but are scarcely remembered now. There is no more impressive evidence of the demands made upon Spilsbury in such difficult cases, by coroners and police all over the country, than the way in which, again and again, a casual allusion to one of these forgotten mysteries will be found to have its complement among his cards. A reference, for example, in a book on crime to the case just considered is followed by a paragraph on what was called the "Torso Mystery" of 1938. Spilsbury's records for that year show that he was in this case too.

A Captain Butt had been missing from his home at Cheltenham for exactly a month when a male torso was caught in the net of some salmon fishermen in the river Severn, at a spot twelve miles from the town. Dredging produced two legs and two handless arms. In Spilsbury's opinion legs, arms, and trunk were all part of the same body, and this corresponded with the build and age of the missing man. Butt's shoes, for example, fitted the feet. The knees were arthritic, and Butt suffered from arthritis. Bruises and injuries on the back of the torso suggested to Spilsbury that the victim had been struck down by a motor vehicle.

Other circumstances left little doubt that the remains were those of the captain. Ten days after his disappearance a friend of his named Sullivan committed suicide. Butt's overcoat was found beneath the floor of Sullivan's cottage; Sullivan possessed an axe, and much of the dismemberment had been carried out with a similar weapon. The successful concealment of the head and hands, however, so common a feature in such cases, once more left a coroner's jury with no option but to return a verdict that there was insufficient evidence as to the identity of the body, and none as to the cause of death.

It has been remarked that among Spilsbury's friends at Scotland Yard Superintendent Cherrill probably saw more of him than any other. To some extent they worked on common ground. The case of some human flotsam washed ashore on the coast of Cornwall produced a notable example of what their skilled and patient co-operation could achieve. The remains were those of a woman, in a terribly fragmentary state. The legs were gone, and from the trunk and arms most of the flesh had rotted or been eaten away. The bare bones were so scarified by the action of sand that a local doctor thought the legs had been amputated. Spilsbury, nevertheless, was able to calculate the dead woman's height and weight, and to deduce from the hands, on which shreds of flesh remained, that she had never done heavy manual work. Cherrill, in his own province, was faced with another problem. What skin there was on the fingers was worn down as if filed, and no finger-prints could be obtained by ordinary methods. Cherrill performed the extremely delicate task of peeling off the rotting skin, revealing on the underside the pattern of ridged loops and whorls reversed. Faint though these were, he obtained recognizable prints.

In the meantime the usual thorough inquiries suggested that the body might be that of a woman known to have thrown herself from a ship. Her description tallied almost exactly as to height and weight with Spilsbury's estimate, and she had never done rough work with her hands. Relatives refused to say they could identify the remains, which in itself was scarcely surprising, and Cherrill travelled to the house in the north of England where the woman had occupied a room before she sailed. His journey served only to illustrate the least pleasing side of human nature. The relatives had forestalled him. One of them had observed that if they claimed to identify the body it would mean the expense of a funeral, but there was more to it than that—there was an insurance policy with a suicide clause—and when Cherrill examined the room where he hoped to compare his finger-prints he found that every inch of the floor and walls, the doors, cup-boards, and furniture, had been scrubbed and polished clean.

A notorious dismemberment case in 1936 found Spilsbury giving advice behind the scenes in an unofficial capacity. If the prosecution in a trial for murder did not require his services he could be retained or consulted by the defence, and he drew up a list of questions for counsel defending Buck Ruxton, the Parsee doctor who murdered his wife and maidservant at Lancaster and threw the all-but-unidentifiable remains into a ravine near Moffat, in Dumfriesshire. Professionally, Spilsbury must have regretted that they had been taken across the Border, for had they been found in England he would have been called in by the police as a matter of course, and the Scottish patho-logists who examined them were faced with problems after his own heart.

Chapter 5: SUBSTITUTION BY FIRE

In the early morning of the day after the Derby of 1930 the body of a young woman was found in a ditch at Epsom. A few hours later, in a car which he had not long learnt to drive, Spilsbury was making his way against the traffic still streaming from Epsom towards London. He performed a post-mortem on the body that afternoon. The cause of death was strangulation by a cord or rope.

The dead woman was identified as a waitress named Agnes Kesson. There was no clue to her murderer, and this fact, if Alfred Arthur Rouse is to be believed, led to another murder just five months later. "It was the Agnes Kesson case at Epsom in June," he wrote in a confession published after his execution, "which first set me thinking. It showed that it was possible to beat the police if you were careful enough."

Precept and practice are different things, and Rouse himself was not careful enough. He was, however, to make criminological history, for he was a man of ideas, and his novel method of getting out of difficulties of his own making, though unsuccessful, has since been imitated in this country and abroad.

Rouse, the son of a hosier, was born at Herne Hill, London, in 1894. When he was six years old his parents separated, and he was sent to live with an aunt. His youth was blameless and promising. He was intelligent, musical, clever with his hands, and a church-goer. By the time he was twenty he was holding a good position and felt himself able to marry. Before the wedding the First World War broke out, and Rouse at once enlisted in a Territorial battalion. His marriage took place towards the end of the year, and early in 1915 his unit went to France.

He served abroad for less than three months. His association with a French girl resulted in the birth of a child after his return to England. Such an episode was common enough, but with Rouse it was perhaps an indication of the weakness that was to be his undoing—the pursuit of women. On the other hand, this weakness may have been a symptom of the later degeneration of his character which seems to have been directly caused by injuries. At Givenchy, at the end of May 1915, a shell-burst wounded him in the head and thigh. For a long time his left leg was affected, but the most serious damage was to the left temporal region of the head, where a small operation had to be performed to remove splinters. Nearly three years later Rouse was complaining of dizziness, loss of memory, and pain during change of weather. He could not wear a hat, and neurosis retarded recovery of complete use of his injured leg. One medical report says: "His injury to the head is a strong factor in the case." The last report, however, in 1920, remarks: "Scar healed—no disability." Yet a disability was there; Rouse was a changed man.

In the meantime he had been discharged from the Army with a pension which rose to 40*s.* a week in 1919. It ceased in the following year, by which time, if Rouse had led a normal life, he would have been well on the way to earning a comfortable living. His wound had not impaired his intelligence and energy. By 1930, when he was employed as a commercial traveller by a Midland firm of brace and garter manufacturers, he was making about £500 a year. He had a car, the last of several, and he was buying a small house in the North London suburb of Finchley on the instalment system.

Unfortunately the instalment system entered into far too many aspects of his roving life. In addition to payments for his house and car, and his weekly allowance to his wife, which together accounted for half his income at its best, there was the upkeep of a child in Paris and of another (not his wife's) at home; at least two maintenance orders were out against him, and there were further commitments of this kind of which he must almost have lost count. Whether or no as a result of his head wound, Rouse's addiction to women had gone beyond all bounds. Several went through a form of marriage with him, and he had children all over Southern England, where his duties took him, and even farther afield. Miss Helena Normanton, who edited the Rouse trial in the "Notable British Trials" series, says that nearly eighty cases of seduction were traced to him. He remarked himself, in extenuation, that it takes two to make a bargain, and it is true that he found his dupes chiefly among ill-educated and credulous girls, of the class and type of Elsie Cameron, who were prepared to go far in pursuit of what they thought of as romance and hoped would better their position. Rouse always posed as a bachelor of means, with houses here and there and a public school and university background; and the poor fools believed him. There were one or two exceptions who should have known better, but he was in his way an attractive man, smart, with something of his boyish good looks, and a fluent and plausible, if boastful, talker. He could be kindly and attentive, and is said to have been sincerely fond of some of his many children. One, a boy, was being brought up by his long-suffering wife. Unable to have children of her own, Mrs Rouse sought in this way to satisfy what seems to have been her husband's genuine need of them. But towards the end of 1930, as more and more evidence of his infidelities came to her knowledge, she began to feel that she had stood enough, and there was talk of a separation.

Rouse by now had got himself into such a tangle that he could see no way out. His expenses were beyond his means, and his own peculiar brand of folly had involved him in a final imbroglio which threatened disaster. While one young girl was having her second baby by him in a London hospital, another, in Wales, was expecting her first; and she was not the friendless type upon whom he usually preyed. There is no stronger proof of Rouse's abnormality than the case of Ivy Jenkins. She was a probationer nurse, still in her teens, when he met her in London. In such a position as his any rational man, however profligate, would have taken warning as soon as he learnt something of her circumstances, for she came of a well-to-do family and had an affectionate father and brother capable of making things extremely unpleasant for her deceiver. Rouse persuaded her to pretend that they were married, and paid several visits to her home at Gelligaer, in Glamorganshire, in the rôle of her husband and in his own name. This was not enough; he was going to take her away early in November to have her child in the luxurious house he had bought and furnished for her at Kingston-on-Thames, and he further embroidered this fantasy by inviting her sister to come too. Rouse seems to have been as much in the grip of his inventions as of his passions; once he began to lie there was no end to it.

The journey to Richmond was actually fixed for November 6. When that date approached, however, Ivy Jenkins was seriously ill, and her father telegraphed to Rouse, asking him to come to Gelligaer. Rouse arrived on the evening of the 6th. But this was not at all what he had meant to do; as recently as the early hours of that morning he had no intention of going to Wales, or of ever seeing Ivy Jenkins again. He was then in a Northamptonshire lane, engaged in a chemical experiment from which, he hoped, he would emerge transmuted. It was to be the end of A. A. Rouse; another personality was to begin a new life.

2

The large village of Hardingstone lies a few miles south of Northampton, just to the east of the Northampton–Stony Stratford road, with which it is linked by a secondary road called Hardingstone Lane. A few minutes before 2 A.M. on November 6 the Hardingstone parish constable, Hedley Bailey, was wakened by his son. Young Bailey and his cousin, Alfred Brown, on their way home from a Bonfire Night dance at Northampton, had found a car burning in the Lane. Brown having gone on to rouse Police Constable Copping, within a short time all four were standing by the still-flaming wreck.

So intense was the heat that they had to stand some yards away, but a human shape could now be distinguished in the flames. While the younger Bailey telephoned to the police at Northampton buckets of water were fetched from Hardingstone, and the fire was soon put out. Since whoever was in the car was only too plainly beyond help, nothing was touched until Inspector Lawrence and a constable arrived in a police car from Northampton.

The inspector was in a difficulty. If he did the wrong thing it was because no suspicion of murder entered his mind. In the day-time Hardingstone Lane was quite a busy thoroughfare. It was on several bus routes. The charred body in the car was a horrible sight. The inspector decided to remove it, as soon as it could be handled, and to shift what was left of the car on to the wide strip of grass beside the road. This was done about five o'clock. The gruesome remains were taken to the Crown Inn at Hardingstone, and for more than an hour the wreckage of the car was left unguarded.

A worse mistake, on the part of trained policemen, was that no notes were made and no photographs taken while the body was still in the car. A great deal of trouble was caused, and doubts were left in many minds, because so important a part of the case that was to be built up depended on the recollections of the first witnesses on the scene of the crime.

Two of these, young Bailey and his cousin themselves, had a story which should have made any police officer think. They saw the glare from the burning car while they were walking down the main road from Northampton. As they were about to turn into Hardingstone Lane a man was climbing out of a ditch beyond the grass verge of the Lane itself. He wore a light raincoat, had no hat, and was carrying an attaché-case. As he walked towards the main road he passed the pair, and Bailey asked him what the blaze was. The man called back after he had gone by, "It looks as if somebody has got a bonfire up there." Puzzled by his behaviour, the young men glanced behind them, and observed the hatless stranger hesitating at the end of the Lane before they lost sight of him. It was a bright moonlit night, and they had seen his face clearly. When they met him again a few days later, in the Angel Lane Police Station at Northampton, they recognized him at once.

Fire had not touched the registration-plates of the car, and it was quickly traced. That same afternoon the Metropolitan Police were calling on Mrs Rouse. She had last seen her husband, she said, about one o'clock that morning, when he had called at his home for half an hour. She made a mistake of five hours in the time, and the details of this curious episode are obscure. Presumably accepting her story, the police took her to Northampton, but she did not see the body, which was quite unrecognizable. For a time, indeed, it was thought to be that of a woman.

The next news, which put a novel and startling complexion on the affair, came from Wales during the 7th, and resulted in detectives from Hammersmith Police Station waiting that evening at Hammersmith Bridge for the arrival of a motor-coach from Cardiff. A passenger, asked if he was Rouse, readily admitted his identity. "I am glad it is over," he said.

No doubt he was. A chance encounter, and his own subsequent actions, had thrown his plans hopelessly awry. The chemical experiment was a failure, and worse. It had to be explained away. But during the long drive from Cardiff, when, as he said, he could not sleep, he had at least had ample time to prepare his version of the tragedy in Hardingstone Lane; and a less conceited man might have felt that it would be difficult to disprove.[1]

To Detective-Sergeant Skelly he made a statement that evening. On Bonfire Night he was driving to Leicester to arrange some business with his firm, and to get money. The statement goes on:

> I picked the man up on the Great North Road; he asked me for a lift. He seemed a respectable man, and said he was going to the Midlands. I gave him a lift; it was just this side of St Albans. He got in, and I drove off, and after going some distance I lost my way. A policeman spoke to me about my lights. I did not know anything about the man, and I

[1] Nothing seems to have been said at his trial about a point which he should have been asked to explain. When arrested he had with him the attaché-case he had taken from the car in Hardingstone Lane. In it was the metal Army identity-disc issued to him sixteen years before. He had meant to leave this in the burning car, but forgot.

thought I saw his hand on my case, which was in the back of the car. I later became sleepy and could hardly keep awake. The engine started to spit, and I thought I was running out of petrol. I wanted to relieve myself, and said to the man, "There is some petrol in the can; you can empty it into the tank while I am gone"; and I lifted the bonnet and showed him where to put it in. He said, "What about a smoke?" I said, "I have given you all my cigarettes as it is." I then went some distance along the road, and had just got my trousers down when I noticed a big flame from behind. I pulled my trousers up quickly and ran towards the car, which was in flames. I saw the man was inside, and I tried to open the door, but I could not, as the car was then a mass of flames. I then began to tremble violently. I was all of a shake. I did not know what to do, and I ran as hard as I could along the road, where I saw the two men. I felt I was responsible for what had happened. I lost my head, and I didn't know what to do, and I really don't know what I have done since. . . .

At the end of this story, which was afterwards much elaborated—the passenger, for instance, was given a cigar—one word of truth came out. Shaken as he must have been by what he had just done, the meeting with young Bailey and Brown in the bright moonlight caused Rouse to lose his head completely. All his schemes were thrown aside. Instead of going to Scotland, as according to his confession he intended to do, he got a lift to London, called at his house soon after six o'clock, "because he did not want his wife to be upset," told her he would be back next day, and then made his way to Wales, and in Wales to Gelligaer, of all places. He was at Ivy Jenkins's home late that evening of the 6th. He had barely arrived when he was shown an evening paper with a photograph of his burnt car. So bemused were Rouse's wits at this time that he seems to have been genuinely surprised that an incinerated body in a car should be news with a capital 'N.' "I did not think there would be much fuss in the papers about the thing," he said. In the next morning's paper there were more details, including the name of the car's owner, and, what was worse, a reference to his wife. Before the Jenkins family could see this paragraph Ivy's 'husband' fled from Gelligaer back to London, where he found that news of his flight had preceded him.

In Rouse's confession, published after his execution, he tells what is probably the true story of the crime in Hardingstone Lane on Bonfire Night.

According to this, ever since he read of the unsolved mystery of Agnes Kesson's death on Derby Day he had been turning over in his mind ways and means, involving murder, of escaping from his difficulties. "I did not want to do murder just for the sake of it," he says.

Perhaps his original idea was murder for gain. Then came the more novel one of substitution, and some time in the late autumn, in the bar of a public house in Whetstone, near his home, he got into talk with a man of whom he says, "I thought he would suit the plan I had in mind." Rouse describes his victim as "a down-and-out—the sort of man no one would miss."

Rouse's plan fell into two parts. The first part was carefully thought out, and in some respects successfully executed. The second part does not seem to have been thought out at all. Granting that he was ill-balanced and even more egotistical and conceited than most murderers of his type, the mixture of foresight and folly of his actions is extraordinary. By that first week in November he had chosen his victim, and chosen him so well that to this day it is not known who he was. Such drifters will go anywhere on the chance of finding work, or picking up money. The bait of a free drive to the Midlands was enough for Rouse's new acquaintance. When, however, Rouse made this proposition, on the 2nd or 3rd of November, he himself was as usual short of ready money. On the morning of the 8th he would receive his weekly cheque for salary and expenses. Probably it would not have amounted to more than £10, but he could double this by asking, as he had asked before, for an advance on account of commission, which was paid monthly. To a man who intended to begin a new life under a new name the difference between £20 and almost empty pockets would seem to be of considerable importance. Yet what did Rouse do? He forwent his last opportunity of getting much-needed money in order to stage his murder on Guy Fawkes Night, because then, he says, "a fire would not be noticed so much."

This in itself was a fallacy. On Guy Fawkes Night people would be about late, and cheerfully interested in bonfires. On such a night—indeed, on any night—Rouse should have chosen some desolate spot, and an hour when every one would be asleep. For years he had been driving all over Southern England, and could have arranged conditions to fit the crime. He had taken some thought to this end, providing his victim with a bottle of whisky, so that the latter was soon in a drunken stupor, and might have been driven anywhere. But all precautions of this kind were thrown to the wind. Soon after half-past one in the morning he was setting about his grim task of throttling and burning on the outskirts of a large village, through which he had just passed, only a quarter of a mile from a main thoroughfare along which there was a good deal of traffic at night, within easy walking distance of a town of 90,000 inhabitants, and on the sole road connecting the two places. Many murderers have been caught through mischances they could not foresee; but Rouse was asking for trouble, and he got it.

3

A petrol fire can be a terrible thing. Tremendous heat is generated in a matter of seconds. Rouse's car had disintegrated into scrap metal, and though human flesh is tough, so much of the body found in the car had been burnt away that when Spilsbury examined the remains in the garage of the Crown at Hardingstone on November 10 he could conjecture the sex, medically speaking, only from a suspected fragment of the prostate gland. His case-card makes shocking reading when it is remembered that all this destruction was wrought in a very short time:

> Top of head and vault of skull completely destroyed. Brain exposed, shrunken and burned on top. Skin of face and ears destroyed. . . . Whole chest wall destroyed in front and front of heart and lungs exposed and partly burned. Skin of abdomen wall destroyed in front. . . . Forearms and hands completely destroyed and part of each upper arm; quite half, with charred bone projecting from stumps. Left foot completely destroyed; right foot separated and on running-board of car—extremity destroyed and toes missing. Greater part of legs below knees destroyed and thighs deeply burnt. . . .

Heat had literally burst the skull, but Spilsbury was able to ascertain that this had not been fractured by a blow. Certain muscles and organs were bright pink, and microscopical examination of mucus from the bronchial tubes showed fine particles of carbon. Spilsbury's conclusions were set out on his card as follows:

> Male. Height impossible to determine, but about Dr Shaw's estimate (5 feet 7 or 8 inches). Age from teeth, not much less than 21; probably about 30. Small features from size of jaw. Teeth neglected. Lungs pigmented—? coal miner. *Cause of Death*: fire in car and shock. No indication of poison. Period of survival very short.

This is all that is ever likely to be known about Rouse's victim, to whom Rouse himself never even gave a name. No very serious attempt was made to trace him—certainly nothing approaching the scale of the search in the first Brighton Trunk Murder four years later. The Northamptonshire police kept the case in their own hands, seeking the minimum of help from Scotland Yard, and their inquiries about missing men, and women, seem to have been limited to certain areas. A charred boot-heel was at first supposed to be a woman's; a later discovery of brace-buckles in the wreckage of the car, and of part of the fly of a pair of trousers protected by the bending of the left thigh against the stomach, confirmed Spilsbury's opinion as to sex.[1]

A wooden mallet, admittedly Rouse's, was found in the grass some fifteen yards from the burnt car. On it were three or four hairs. Rouse used the handle of the mallet to loosen the cap of his petrol-can. The presence of the hairs remains unexplained, and their nature uncertain; for though Dr Shaw, the Crown's other medical witness at the trial, declared that one of them was human, Spilsbury, who wrote on his card, "Appears to be human," would go no further in his evidence. "It has," he said, "the microscopic characteristics of a human hair. . . . That is as far as I think I can safely go." This, from Spilsbury, was cautious wording. Every one, nevertheless, including the judge, took it for granted that the hair was human. Mr Finnemore, Rouse's counsel, justly said that the mallet did not take the matter one step further; and the incident is chiefly of interest as a sidelight on the difficulties confronting the prosecution in preparing its case.

Fire had done its work so thoroughly, and Rouse's irrational actions were so confusing, that until his confession saw the light the motive for his crime, and the primary means he employed, could only be guessed at. He says he throttled his passenger into unconsciousness; Norman Birkett, who led for the Crown, knowing nothing of this, suggested that the victim was stunned with the mallet. At least one of the hairs on it, accordingly, had to be human. As for the motive, there had been hints of the true one at the police-court proceedings; when the case came before Mr Justice Talbot at the Northampton Winter Assizes quite as much was made of an insurance on the car, because there was a clause in the policy under which £1000 was payable in respect of the death, not only of the owner, but of a passenger. How Rouse himself, in the circumstances, could have claimed this

[1] The short-lived notion that Rouse's victim was a woman seems to have been revived, coupled with other surprising statements, in an unexpected quarter. Dr. Keith Simpson, who has appeared as Pathologist in the case for the Crown in a number of murder trials, writes in the first edition of his *Forensic Medicine*, published in 1947, as follows: "In 1930 a man named Rouse endeavoured to dispose of a woman he had murdered by setting fire to the body. In the rear compartment of a burnt-out car a body was found charred beyond recognition. The car was Rouse's, but the body was that of a woman, and post-mortem examination showed that she had been murdered by some blunt instrument such as a hammer. Such a weapon was, in fact, found in a ditch nearby. . . ."

money was never made clear. For tactical reasons, apparently, very little was said of the real springs of the tragedy—the accused's inextricable involvements with women; but he had already done himself much harm by silly bragging remarks about his "harem" which were reported in the Press. The prejudice caused by this publicity was one of the grounds on which his appeal was based.

A further cause of trouble for the prosecution, of which the defence made the most, and on which the judge passed some very severe strictures, was the laxity of the local police officers first on the spot. The Crown's chief expert witnesses were Spilsbury and Colonel Buckle, a fire assessor with much experience of burnt-out cars. The latter did not see the remains of Rouse's Morris Minor until they had been lying for a month at Angel Lane Police Station. In his evidence, nevertheless, and in an afterthought passed on to the prosecution and used in the cross-examination of Rouse, the colonel put forward a theory which was afterwards confirmed. It was that the petrol union joint was deliberately loosened, and the top of the carburettor perhaps removed; a trail of petrol was then led to the car from a can standing in the road, and ignited. This is exactly what Rouse, in his confession, says he did.

Spilsbury's contribution to the Crown's case fell into two parts. He had no difficulty in ascertaining the cause of death, shock from burns; but he could not assert, in so many words, that the unknown victim was unconscious before death, because no evidence of how unconsciousness might have been brought about survived the fire. He could only say that the position of the body when found indicated a state of unconsciousness, and the questions put to him by Norman Birkett in the second part of his evidence were designed to establish this theory. By the time he saw the body normal rigor had contracted the limbs; for the state of things existing at 2 A.M. on Bonfire Night he had to rely on the memories of the police and others present. Though these witnesses differed on minor points, they agreed on essentials. The body had been lying face downward across the front seats of the car, the head on the driver's seat, the right arm extended as though it had been resting on the scuttle-shaped backs of the seats, the left arm and left leg doubled under the trunk, the right leg stretched out through the gap where the near-side door had been. The hands and forearms, and the feet and lower legs, were burnt away. The seats had collapsed, and the charred debris of the fabric roof had fallen on the body, which was then in the condition described by Spilsbury as heat rigor or stiffening. This, in effect, owing to the rapidity with which the great heat was generated, contracting the muscles, fixed the body in the attitude it assumed immediately after death.

Asked by Norman Birkett what conclusions he drew from this attitude, Spilsbury said:

"I think it is consistent with the man either pitching forward or being thrown down, face downwards, on the seats of the car from the near-side door."

That door, in Spilsbury's opinion, had been open, and both the man's legs were stretched out through it; the left leg, being on the outer edge of the seats, was bent double under the trunk by heat stiffening, but the right leg, with less play, because it lay along the angle of the seats and the backs, was only slightly contracted, so that when the right foot was burnt off it fell on the running-board. Asked if he thought it possible that the man had made any movement after falling, or being thrown, across the seats, Spilsbury replied, "No, I think the stretching out of the right leg rules that out." In other words, the man had been unconscious, with his feet sticking out of the car, when the fire started.

The scrap of trouser-cloth, when first examined, still smelt of petrol, and Spilsbury made alternative suggestions to account for this. One was that liquid petrol was sprayed through the body of the car at the level of the seats in a very early stage of the fire, before the victim's left leg doubled up. (The petrol-tank in a Morris Minor of that date was behind the dashboard, and beneath it was the petrol union joint, found by Colonel Buckle, a month after the fire, to be a whole turn loose.) The piece of cloth being in the fork of the left leg, it was protected from air and flame when the leg contracted against the trunk.

"The only other explanation," Spilsbury went on, "is that the clothing had become soaked in petrol before the fire started."

It was the task of Mr Donald Finnemore, for the defence, to try to extract from Spilsbury some sort of admission that the man in the car might have been struggling to get out when he was overcome by the flames. By the time the car could be examined by the first witnesses on the scene its sides and doors had been completely burnt away; Mr Finnemore's argument was that after this occurred the victim, in his last agony, pushed his legs through the space where the door had been. Spilsbury would not agree that this was possible. "He would have been dead," he said, "long before that happened." He amplified this reply later. "I think he would have lost consciousness, if he had not died, before the fabric door had been burnt away. I do not think any voluntary movement could have thrust the foot through the opening."

A brief re-examination by Norman Birkett concluded with the following question and answer:

> "Assume that a man was trapped in the car and was in the doubled-up posture permitted by a space of 3 feet 4 inches, face downwards, buttocks up in order to get within that space, that that man dies fairly quickly, and that he remains there dead in this fierce heat until the door falls away. Would that account for the right foot being extended and the left not?
>
> "No, it would not, because, as he was dead, he could make no violent movement, and the effect of the intense heat would be to stiffen the contracted limbs in the position in which they already were, and not in any way extend them, even if the weight of the body itself did not prevent this. The fact that the right leg was extended beyond the door when the body was discovered points to the conclusion, in my view, that the door must have been open from the time when the body first assumed that position in the car. I can see no other explanation that would account for it."

The defence opened with Rouse in the witness-box. He was followed by two medical men and three expert engineers. Dr Hervey Wyatt, now Coroner for South London, said he did not think that very definite conclusions could be drawn from the position of the body when it was found. He agreed with Spilsbury that in such a fire death would ensue in about half a minute, during the latter part of which time the victim would be unconscious; but he did not agree that the available data proved unconsciousness throughout. The engineers, of whom one was a consultant and the others assessors, were called to say that there was nothing in the evidence inconsistent with an accidental fire. The consultant said that petrol union joints could be loosened by heat, and, if insufficiently tightened, by vibration; but when asked if it did not appear, from the evidence, that the cap of the carburettor had been taken off by hand he replied, "From what I saw it is probable. It is not probable that it could be blown off, and, if it has come off, somebody has taken it off." The two assessors maintained that the effect of great heat on a nut, such as the petrol union, was to loosen it, by distortion of the thread after expansion.

A car similar to Rouse's was at hand, for the jury to examine, but their view of the technical evidence was probably that of the judge, who said in his charge to them, "The defendant's experts are not able, any more than the prosecution's experts, to tell you with any certainty, or probably with any high degree of probability, how this fire actually arose." With regard to the medical evidence, however, it must have been clear to the jury that there was little real difference of opinion between the opposing witnesses. Spilsbury's views, as usual, were definite and lucidly expressed; Dr Hervey Wyatt's attitude is summed up in his answer to almost the last question put to him in cross-examination.

"What I am plainly suggesting," said Norman Birkett, "is that an unconscious man was thrown into that posture. Do you agree or do you not?"

"If the facts are as you say, yes."

Once more, in all probability, the witness most damaging to the accused was the accused himself. In a long, gruelling ordeal at the hands of Norman Birkett, Rouse's mixture of pert cocksureness and evasiveness, the unlikelihood of most of his story, and the long tale of his lies, made a bad impression. From the early hours of the trial the jury must have been waiting to hear him explain why he was hiding in a ditch when young Bailey and Brown turned into Hardingstone Lane on Bonfire Night. He could not have made matters worse by telling what was no doubt the truth—that he was dodging the lights of a car then coming down the main road from Northampton. He admitted that he was in a panic, and had lost his head, and the explanation might have passed. To deny, as he did, that he was in the ditch at all was silly. Bailey and Brown never varied their story from the beginning, and no one doubted it. The denial, and the whole of Rouse's behaviour at the time—his running *away* from Hardingstone, where he could have got help, his words about a bonfire, his hesitation at the main road, and his flight to London a few minutes later in a lorry—must have suggested very strongly to the jury that what threw him into a panic was not the "accident," but this unexpected encounter. Finally, like Seddon, Rouse did himself infinite harm by his callousness and his attempts to be clever in the witness-box. He scarcely pretended to have any feeling about the man burnt to death in his car. At the end of his cross-examination, when self-control was wearing thin, he made such answers as these:

"I should not throw a man. If I did a thing like that I should not throw him face downwards. I should think where I put him, I imagine."

"You would imagine what?"

"Hardly that I should throw him down like nothing. That is absurd."

"If you rendered him unconscious, would you have a delicacy about his posture?"

"No, but I think if I had been going to do as you suggest I should do a little more than that. I think I have a little more brains than that."

Rouse was in the witness-box for nearly the whole of the fourth day of the trial, which finished on the morning of the sixth day, when Mr Justice Talbot said of the case that it was a most exceptional one, adding, "I should think you would have to go a long way back in our legal history to find a case in which the facts bear any resemblance to these." The jury were an hour and a quarter in bringing in a verdict of guilty, but during that time they inspected the car and had lunch. It may seem a little hard that a man accused of a capital crime cannot know his fate until the jury has been fed. Rouse appealed; and a month later Sir Patrick Hastings, who led Mr Finnemore before the Court of Criminal Appeal, made a very interesting point which had not been raised at the trial. The judge had said that in his opinion no theory had been established as to motive which was even plausible. Patrick Hastings argued that in such a case, where the victim had not been identified, the prosecution should have to prove motive, and he quoted Chief Justice Cockburn to this effect. The other main ground of complaint was that evidence about Rouse's irregular mode of life had been aired at the police-court proceedings and widely reported in the Press, with headlines in which the word 'harem' was prominent. Though much of this evidence was withheld at the trial, it was then too late; the judge might say that no motive for the crime had been established, but the jury had read the papers.

The appeal, however, failed; but this was not the end. There was a strong feeling in some quarters that it should have succeeded, and Rouse's counsel addressed a Memorandum to the Home Secretary, setting out once more the grounds for a revision of the sentence. This failed, too, and Rouse was executed. More than a month later, after newspapers had printed his confession and a letter from his widow, a last echo of the controversy was heard in the House of Lords, when Lord Darling opened a debate on the question of publicity in sensational cases.

4

There are certain analogies between the cases of Alfred Rouse and Norman Thorne. Both ended in an atmosphere of some dissatisfaction, letters to counsel and to the papers, and appeals to the Home Secretary. Setting aside any antipathies which the accused may have brought upon themselves, it was the medical evidence that convicted them, and in both cases that evidence was Spilsbury's. For at the trial of Rouse once the jury had been told by the judge, what they must long have felt, that the engineers and assessors cancelled out, and that no one could say how the car caught fire, all they had to guide them were Spilsbury's deductions from the reported position of the body. As in the Thorne case, these deductions were matters of opinion, based on immense experience, but still theoretical, and they were challenged. The prosecution relied on them, as did the defence up to a point, but it put a different interpretation on the remainder. When, however, the judge remarked of the divergencies, taken together, "The whole of that is based on Sir Bernard Spilsbury's evidence?" Mr Finnemore agreed. Among the very few pencillings in Spilsbury's copy of the "Notable Trials" volume on the case is one against this passage, and it is tempting to think that he made it in irony, because by another coincidence, and not the least interesting, the Introduction to that volume is the work of the writer who edited a similar book, already quoted, on the Thorne trial.

For here, indeed, the resemblances between the two cases cease. It is a reasonable inference that they would have gone further had Rouse committed his crime a few years earlier, at or about the time of the Crowborough murder. There would then have been another outcry against Spilsbury's "infallibility," and the acceptance of his opinions as gospel. But since 1925 the case, as Plowden said, was altered. The tumult and the shouting had rather ignominiously died. There were no complaints about Spilsbury's evidence at the Northamptonshire Assizes. Before the Court of Criminal Appeal no more was said of it than had been said by Dr Hervey Wyatt at the trial. It was referred to only incidentally in the memorandum to the Home Secretary, on a technical point. As late as 1929 Miss Helena Normanton, in her Introduction to *The Trial of Norman Thorne*, was denouncing the state of things which permitted one man to dominate the courts. In 1931, when she devoted forty-five pages to Rouse, whom Spilsbury did so much to hang, the medical evidence is barely touched upon, and Spilsbury himself is not even mentioned by name. Yet in the two cases the medical evidence was of equal importance, and might be thought equally controversial. Spilsbury's replies to the leading questions put to him by Norman Birkett at Northampton recall in their tenor his examination by Curtis-Bennett at Lewes six years before, when so much indignation was aroused. Spilsbury's own position was as authoritative as ever, or more so. But this time no one grumbled—not even *The Law Journal*. There was no whisper of dissent. The case was indeed altered; but it is not easy to see why.

5

Since in the twenty years after Spilsbury had "practically retired" he was engaged on behalf of the Crown in upward of 130 cases of murder, quite often two or more of these overlapped, or were linked by some coincidence; and there are instances of a sort of neatness of arrangement which might be thought more common in drama than in life. If the case of poor Agnes Kesson, left dead under a hedge on Derby Day, serves as an introduction to the more spectacular crime in Hardingstone Lane, the Camden Town murder of 1933 comes as a tailpiece. It is not merely that Spilsbury was concerned in all three: the restless ghost of Rouse haunts the whole series too. He himself was inspired by the unsolved mystery of Agnes Kesson's death, and it can scarcely be doubted that his own *chef-d'œuvre* put ideas into the head of another man in difficulties. The torch, so to speak, was handed on; and by a last touch of the bizarre Rouse's imitator bore the grotesquely appropriate name of Furnace.

No more than a few lines can be given to this copyist, for Spilsbury came into the case only when it was over, and the copyist himself was dead. Furnace was a builder in a small way of business with a yard in Hawley Crescent, N.W.1, a short street joining Chalk Farm Road and Kentish Town Road just south of the Regent's Canal. By the end of 1932 he was in financial trouble, and he sought Rouse's way out. He did not have a car, but his office was a wooden hut in a yard full of the same inflammable material. In this hut, on the night of January 3, 1933, he shot a young friend named Spatchett, a rent-collector, took a considerable sum of money from his pockets, poured oil and paint over the furniture and body, and, having left a note suggesting that he himself had committed suicide, lighted a pyre which he hoped would consume the body beyond recognition. He then made his own way to Southend.

Though the fire was extinguished before all the dead man's clothing was destroyed, and though the murderer had forgotten, as others have done, that teeth are all but indestructible, for some time the police believed the corpse to be that of Furnace, and for twenty-four hours that the cause of death was burning. The coroner, Bentley Purchase, was dissatisfied with this assumption, because the body had been found sitting on a stool; he made a personal examination, and discovered a bullet-wound in the back. It was next established that the teeth were those of a much younger man; and by other evidence which survived the flames the corpse was identified as Spatchett's. In the ensuing hue and cry, lasting nearly a fortnight, the general public, as well as hundreds of police, took part. Furnace, posing as an invalid in lodgings at Southend, with nothing to do but read the papers—he is said to have got the idea of the method of concealment from a novel by Edgar Wallace—hastened the finish by writing a letter to a relative. He was tracked down and arrested on January 16.

Brought to Kentish Town Police Station, he made a statement on conventional lines. Spatchett had been shot by accident, and he, Furnace, had lost his head. For once this familiar form of apologia was not to be heard in a court of law. When arrested Furnace had been wearing his overcoat; the same evening, when in a cell at the police station, he asked for the coat, complaining of feeling cold. It was the one article of his clothing which had not been searched, and in the lining was a bottle of spirits of salts which he had bought in Southend. He died at St Pancras Hospital on the following morning—it is said in a small ward next to the mortuary where the body of Spatchett still lay.

Spilsbury performed the post-mortem, and his evidence at the St Pancras Coroner's Court closed the sequence of tragedies which seems to have been set in train when Agnes Kesson decided to go to Epsom for the Derby more than two years before.

Chapter 6: "CHILDREN AND YOUNG PERSONS"

Brutal violence to young children is so shocking to the feelings of all but the few degenerates or maniacs who indulge in it that it is distasteful to write of it at all. It would seem better left to those in whose province it really lies—the alienist, the psychologist, and the student of social conditions. On the other hand, the pathologist whose work is mainly in the coroners' courts becomes something of all three, and this is particularly true of Spilsbury, who was always looking beyond the physical data for any impelling diseases of the mind and their causes, and whose deepest feelings were moved by cruelty to the helpless. In a survey of his professional life something must be said about the painfully numerous cases of fatal brutality to children included in his records. By children is meant those of a few years of age and upward; upon the far more numerous cases of the newly-born and unwanted, found dead in boxes or under floorboards, in ditches and rivers, whose fate is at least understandable, there is happily no need to dwell.

A study of Spilsbury's case-cards, or of the records of any coroner's court, show that crimes against growing children fall roughly into three types: sexual attacks on girls, deaths from violent ill-treatment, such as beating, and those from neglect—that is, starvation or exposure. There are exceptional cases, which do not fall into any of these categories and are usually inexplicable; and Spilsbury's first recorded child murder (infanticide apart) was one of these. It was the case of Willie Starchfield, referred to in an earlier chapter of this book.

Willie Starchfield was five and a half. He was neither neglected nor otherwise habitually ill-treated, for Spilsbury's card describes the body as well-nourished, and a photograph of the unfortunate boy shows him dressed in the style associated with Little Lord Fauntleroy—velvet jacket and knickerbockers, with lace collar and cuffs. After he was found bruised and strangled in a railway carriage in January 1914 his father was charged with the murder, but was acquitted, the judge stopping the case. Mr and Mrs Starchfield lived apart, Willie being with the mother, but the result of the trial would seem to render inadmissible the theory of jealousy, the only conceivable motive for the crime. Even in those days Spilsbury was interested in the thymus, and he notes in this case that it was enlarged, producing the condition known as status lymphaticus. The very existence of this condition is now in dispute, but if it does exist it can never be a cause of death. Though a constitutional defect perhaps hastened Willie Starchfield's end, he was deliberately murdered.

That same year Spilsbury was giving evidence in a terrible case of a father and his thirteen-year-old daughter, and in a second trial at which a man was acquitted of a charge of shooting a girl of fifteen. Crimes against children, usually girls who were often under ten years of age, now occur periodically in his records, and in the summer of 1919 he was concerned in a notorious case which falls in the third of the categories mentioned above—killing by neglect. Other peculiarly shocking features throw a ghastly light on certain social conditions and outlook.

When that year opened a widower named Grant was living with Alice White, a married woman who called herself Mrs Grant, in a squalid cul-de-sac, Pembroke Place, in Kilburn. This pair between them, by their marriages and as a result of their irregular union, had had no fewer than seventeen children. Four or five were living, or, rather, existing, with them in Pembroke Place. On January 13 Constance Grant, aged fifteen, one of Grant's legitimate daughters and a mental deficient, was reported missing. Police inquiries failed to find a trace of her. Some months later the Grant family left Pembroke Place. Towards the end of July the next tenant of their rooms noticed an offensive smell in the kitchen. Taking up the floorboards, he found beneath what he thought at first was a large swede or turnip. It was, in fact, a human skull, and with it were other remains, forming a female skeleton.

These relics were so decomposed that neither the Divisional Police Surgeon nor Spilsbury could form any opinion of the cause of death. The capacity of the brain cavity, in Spilsbury's view, suggested mental deficiency. Blood had issued from chilblains on the toes, and the missing Constance Grant had suffered from chilblains.

The father was sought and found, but Alice Grant had by then left him. While he was in custody there was a new development—the charging of another and younger child, Ethel White, known as "Maggie," with an offence under the Burial Act. The story told by this poor little creature, who seems to have done her best to look after the other children in her dreadful home, was that a week after Constance's disappearance in January she found her sister lying dead in the coal-cellar. Frightened out of her wits, Maggie ran away. When she returned home some time later the body was gone. Her mother's threats induced her to hold her tongue. There was never, of course, any intention of punishing her for this; and while her case was under consideration Alice White was discovered, and, with Grant, was charged with manslaughter by neglect. The pair received heavy sentences.

The more dubious verdict of manslaughter sometimes returned when young girls have been murdered after criminal assault may be accounted for in part by the fact that the victims appear, and often pretend to be, older than they are. A typical case is that of Kathleen Baker, killed in 1927 at Oddington, near Islip, in Oxfordshire, by Frederick Boxall, a cowman. The body was exhumed a month after burial, and Spilsbury performed a second post-mortem. It was largely on his evidence that Boxall was convicted, but of manslaughter, not murder. He was sentenced to twelve years' penal servitude. He was only nineteen, and the girl's conduct and physical appearance may have led him to believe her older than her fifteen years. Throttling, the cause of death, is a very common feature of these cases, being often employed to stifle an outcry.

Spilsbury's records illustrate not only the frequency of crimes of this class, but their terrible sameness. It will be enough to take one more year, which found him concerned in several, before dealing separately with the notorious case which closed it, and then with three others that excited public interest in an equal degree some years later.

Neither of those with which 1931 opened are, in fact, strictly within the scope of this chapter, but for very different reasons both should be included. The first victim, Louise Maud Steele, was not a child, but a young woman of eighteen. The circumstances of her death, however, place it in the category covering most sexual offences against children, which are the work of degenerates, whose impulses render them for the time being insane. Miss Steele's murderer was a certified lunatic, and he behaved like one. On the morning of January 25 this poor girl's body was found on Blackheath, stripped of clothing except for one stocking, and mutilated in a manner only to be described in a medical text-book. She had been strangled by the neck-band of her frock, and of her other injuries, which fill four of Spilsbury's cards, some of the worst were inflicted after death. The man who killed her had been released from a mental home, presumably as cured, but his own family were so frightened of him that they would not have him in the house, and it was on their information that the police detained him on another charge before he could kill again. He was sent to Broadmoor.

The case of Gwendoline Molly Phillips, whose body was found on Exmoor two months later, deserves mention in this catalogue only because of its rare features. It was not, in Spilsbury's opinion, a case of murder or manslaughter. In September 1929, when Gwendoline Phillips was sixteen, she left the farm near Exford where she was employed to visit her aunt at Cutcombe, five miles away. Nothing was seen of her again until the end of March 1931, when a farmer who was burning rough grass on the moor discovered human remains in a patch of bog. Weather and animals had done their work, but the missing girl's spectacles and a hair-slide and buckle were identified. Hairs from the remains were matched with others on her hairbrush, which had been preserved. Spilsbury's conclusion was that the girl had probably tripped and fallen while running, suffocating in the bog before she could extricate herself.

In September of this year, 1931, a man named Salvage was sentenced to death for the murder of Ivy Godden, aged eleven, at Ashford, in Kent. The child died of shock from blows, her body being afterwards tied up in sacking and buried in a wood. Spilsbury's card records details of an unusual but familiarly revolting kind. He was performing another post-mortem on a dead girl that September, while Salvage was awaiting trial, and towards the end of the year was giving evidence in the case of Rex *v.* William Kell, a boy of eighteen accused of killing Madge Cleife, who was three years younger. It was another case of strangulation after criminal assault.

Less than three weeks before Christmas Spilsbury was called to Paddington mortuary to examine the body of another little girl of eleven named Vera Page.

2

The events connected with the murder of Vera Page occurred in that very mixed region of London which stretches north from Shepherd's Bush and Holland Park to Wormwood Scrubs and the Harrow Road. It is a region where the shabby-genteel merges into the slum, where the police used to patrol Notting Dale in pairs, and where, on the other hand, miles of mean streets are fringed along the south by avenues of trees and pleasant squares, expensive flats and large houses with drives, a colony of studios and the woodland of Holland House. It is one of the few hilly districts north of the Thames, with Campden

Hill and its water-tower standing up over against the similar sharp rise, topped by another landmark, the spire of St John the Evangelist, up which Montpelier Road climbs from Clarendon Road to Ladbroke Grove and Lansdowne and Stanley Crescents. Spilsbury had known the poorer part of this quarter well in his Paddington days, and it was to the more opulent fringe, at the better end of Clarendon Road, that he had been called in 1919 when Miles Seton was shot by Colonel Rutherford.

At the end of 1931 Vera Page was a pretty and attractive child of eleven, living with her parents in Notting Hill. On the evening of December 14 her father reported her missing. Having returned home from school at half-past four, she was at an aunt's house a quarter of an hour later, collecting two swimming certificates she had left there. She seems then to have walked about looking at the shops, brightly lighted and decorated for Christmas. Just before six she was seen close to her home, and again, as late as a quarter to seven, in Montpelier Road. She was carrying some papers, presumably the certificates, and swinging her red beret. She must then have been on her way home again. There was no further news of her until the morning of the 16th, when a milk roundsman found her body lying in some shrubs just inside the tradesman's entrance of No. 89 Addison Road.

Spilsbury was examining the body at Paddington mortuary a few hours later. Vera Page had been criminally assaulted and then strangled by hand. The body was superficially bruised, and after death a cord had been tied round the neck. In the crook of the right elbow was found a finger-stall covering a piece of lint stained by a suppurating wound and smelling strongly of ammonia. The size of the stall suggested that it was a man's. There was soot and coal-dust on the child's face and clothes, and her coat was spotted with candle-grease. Her beret and swimming certificates were missing. Though rain had fallen during the night of the 15th-16th, only the back of her coat, where it touched the soil, was damp, and other evidence made it plain that she had not been killed where she was found.

The coroner for the district was Ingleby Oddie. When he opened the inquest, which was not concluded until February, the first batch of over a thousand statements taken by the police had already covered a good deal of ground. The most important was that of a woman who lived in Stanley Crescent, at the top of Montpelier Road. At nine o'clock on the evening of the 15th she found a red beret and a piece of candle in her area. The beret had not been there a few hours earlier. As soon as this news came to hand Superintendent Cornish, who was in charge of the case, had telephoned to Spilsbury, and the pair went to Stanley Crescent, where they were joined by Chief Inspector (now Chief-Superintendent) Cherrill, the fingerprint expert. The Crescent is almost S-shaped, a narrow street of tall houses. From the area in question opened a disused coal-cellar and water-closet running under the pavement, and it seemed probable that one of these dark little chambers was the scene of the crime. But the actual sequence of events between the moment when Vera Page was seen climbing Montpelier Road to the church of St John the Evangelist, swinging her beret, and the discovery of her body half a mile away thirty-six hours later was still, as it remains to-day, very far from clear.

In Spilsbury's opinion she had been killed soon after she was seen in Montpelier Road at a quarter to seven on the 14th. From the state of the body, in which decomposition had begun, he concluded that for some time after death it had been in a warm place, such as an inhabited room. An external coal-cellar would not be warm in December. Yet the beret and the piece of candle had not appeared in the area until the evening of the 15th. With them were some scraps of torn cardboard, perhaps the certificates, which the woman of the house had thrown away. At that time the body of Vera Page was wherever it was being kept until the murderer could convey it to Addison Road early on the following morning, after the rain. It was conceivable that some whim took him back to the scene of his crime to toss the beret and the torn cardboard over the area railings. The candle-end need not have any significance.

All these streets lay in the prosperous fringe of the district, just north of Holland Park Avenue. They were lined by houses of the well-to-do, though some of those in Stanley Crescent let rooms and flats to lodgers. There were no shops, and the police station at the foot of Ladbroke Grove had been designed to preserve the amenities, and looked like a large private house. Stanley Crescent itself would be very dark on a December evening, and the whole of this quarter is secluded and quiet, though on the fringe of a main road, with its arc-lights and shops and traffic. On the south side of this dividing artery, which soon becomes Uxbridge Road, is Addison Road, another wide street of large houses, where the body was found. The Page family lived in the poorer northern part of the district, near Portobello Road. The murderer might live anywhere, but every indication pointed to his home being in the neighbourhood too.

The investigation went on, and hundreds more statements were taken, and when the last hearing of the adjourned inquest opened on

February 10 the coroner told the jury that important evidence would be heard. Spilsbury recapitulated his conclusions: Vera Page had been killed quite soon after she was last seen on the evening of December 14, her body had then been kept in a warm place for at least twenty-four hours, and it had been conveyed to Addison Road only a short time before it was discovered there. Marks made after death could have been caused by the body being flung over a man's shoulder during this removal, and it was perhaps to assist it that a cord had been tied loosely round the neck. Roche Lynch, who followed Spilsbury, gave the results of his analysis of the finger-stall and lint, of similar materials handed to him by the police, of various specimens of candle-grease, of the girl's clothing, and of the beret, which smelt of paraffin.

Among the next witnesses was a woman who stated that early in the morning of December 16 she saw a man wheeling a barrow along Holland Park Avenue towards Addison Road. On the barrow was a bundle done up in what looked like a red tablecloth.

The last witness called was Percy Orlando Rush, who was in a very anxious position. He was a married man living in Notting Hill, and he had known Vera Page. Just before her death he was wearing a finger-stall to protect a suppurating wound. The stall found with the body smelt of ammonia, and Rush was a launderer, who used ammonia in his work. The beret smelt of paraffin, and when he was first interviewed by the police, on the day after the discovery of the murder, they collected from his rooms a paraffin-soaked rag. He then had in his pocket a pyjama cord, and he possessed a red tablecloth and used candles.

Rush was questioned at length by Ingleby Oddie. He said that he discarded his finger-stall two days before the murder was committed. At the time when Vera Page was last seen he was miles away, having not long started to walk home from his place of work, a journey which took him two hours. He was at work all the next day, December 16, and after returning home did not go out again. It was in his favour that the results of Roche Lynch's analysis of the exhibits were in certain vital cases contradictory or inconclusive. Bandages and lint from Rush's home were not identical with those of the finger-stall found with the body. Comparisons of candle-grease proved indecisive. Finally, the woman who had seen the man with the barrow in Holland Park Avenue, which in the dark hours of an early winter morning was very well lighted, failed to identify Rush.

It was a case where circumstantial evidence had to be treated with the greatest care. In Notting Hill alone there were no doubt scores of people with injured fingers, and thousands who owned red tablecloths and used candles, paraffin, and ammonia. It does not seem to have been suggested that Rush possessed a barrow, or had access to any place other than his home where he could have taken the body and kept it concealed for more than a day. It must have seemed inconceivable that he would carry the corpse of a little girl through the streets to the house where his wife was waiting for him. The coroner pointed out the infinite possibilities of coincidence, and the jury took the minimum of time to return a verdict of murder against a person or persons unknown—a verdict which still stands as the last word on poor Vera Page.

3

Frederick Nodder is the only man who has in effect been tried twice in this country for the same murder. On January 10, 1937, he was charged by the Chief Constable of Newark with the whole of Section 56 of Offences against the Person Act, and at his first trial he was indicted upon nine counts under the Act—in short, he was charged with abduction by fraud of a little girl of ten, a crime which is a felony; but the judge and the jury had little doubt that he was guilty of a greater wickedness. It may have been this conviction, as well as failing health, that caused Mr Justice Swift to treat counsel and witnesses for the defence with a brusqueness and acerbity most unusual in a distinguished occupant of the Bench. In passing sentence the judge said:

"Frederick Nodder, you have been most properly, in my opinion, convicted by the jury of a dreadful crime. What you did with that little girl, what became of her, only you know. It may be that time will reveal the dreadful secret which you carry in your breast."

These were prophetic words. The judge was nearing the end of his life, but he lived to see the secret revealed, and Nodder brought from prison to be charged a second time, and this time with murder.

Nodder is a squalid figure of mystery. He was a motor mechanic, and is said to have served in the A.S.C. during the First World War. He was believed to be in his early forties when, in 1934, he came to live with a married couple named Grimes in Sheffield. He then called himself Hudson, but the Grimeses knew his real name. He was married, but had left his wife, and was at this time dodging a bastardy warrant. At the end of the summer of 1935 he left Sheffield for Newark with an introduction from Mrs Grimes to her sister, Mrs Tinsley, whose husband was a coal carter working in that town.

Still as Frederick Hudson, Nodder stayed for a few weeks with the Tinsleys, becoming very friendly with their children, who called him Uncle Fred. He then moved to East Retford, another Nottinghamshire town towards the Lincolnshire border, almost midway between Worksop and Gainsborough, and in June 1936 took a small semi-detached house called Peacehaven, a name never more inappropriate, in the village of Hayton, 3½ miles from Retford. He was now using his own name again. During this period he worked as a driver for haulage firms and the like, but because of dishonesty and drunkenness he seldom kept employment for long. While he was at East Retford and Hayton he was visited regularly by Mrs Grimes from Sheffield, at Hayton as often as once a week. He did not see anything of the Tinsley family at Newark from the time he left their house in 1935 until January 1937.

On the 5th of that month, at four o'clock, Mona Lilian Tinsley, a child of ten, left her school in Newark to walk home. About that hour a neighbour of the Tinsleys who had known Nodder when he was staying with them saw him loitering by the school gate. Half an hour later a schoolboy friend of Mona's, who also remembered Nodder, noticed the pair standing together at Newark bus station. Mona was not seen again alive by any of her family or friends except Nodder. A few last glimpses of her were obtained: by a bus conductor that afternoon, on the route from Newark to Retford, when Nodder was with her; by two men who saw the pair in Retford that evening; and by a maid in a house two doors from Peacehaven, who on the following morning caught sight of a little girl at Nodder's back door. From that moment Mona Tinsley disappeared.

The search for her had barely begun when Nodder, on the strength of his own statement, was charged on January 10 with abducting her. He said he had met the child by chance in Newark on the 5th, when she was on her way home from school. Her aunt at Sheffield, Mrs Grimes, had a baby boy then about nine months old whom she was bringing to Nodder's house at Hayton the next day, on one of her weekly visits. Mona wanted to see the baby, and her obliging 'Uncle Fred' carried her off with him to spend the night at Peacehaven. The distance from Newark to Hayton is over twenty miles. Nodder took no steps to inform the girl's parents of this odd proceeding, and left them equally in ignorance of what he said he did next day. On that morning, the 6th, he received a note from Mrs Grimes postponing her visit; whereupon, in his own words, he thought that his best plan would be to send Mona on to Sheffield with a letter to her aunt. The bastardy warrant being still out, he did not want to be seen in that city, and, having taken his little guest that evening as far as Worksop, he left her in the bus, which was going on to Sheffield—or so he thought. He never seemed sure about this. He then returned to East Retford and had several drinks before walking home. Outside Peacehaven the police were waiting for him. He told them that he had not seen Mona Tinsley for fifteen months. He was taken to Newark, and two days later produced the story outlined above.

It need hardly be said that Mrs Grimes had seen nothing of her niece. She and her husband began by denying that they knew where Nodder lived, though she had been seeing the latter regularly, and was engaged with him in some obscure business transaction involving lorries. She was to prove a most unsatisfactory witness at both trials. Even the Tinsleys seem to have been less helpful than was to be expected, and the relations between Nodder, a disgusting creature of filthy habits, and these two families in Sheffield and Newark are among the mysteries of the case.

No trace of Mona Tinsley was found at Peacehaven, with the possible exception of some childish scribbles. The house was in a revolting condition. Little doubt was felt, however, as to the poor child's fate, and while Nodder was awaiting trial scores of police and hundreds of people from the neighbourhood were combing the countryside. The district of which East Retford is the centre is flat and seamed with waterways—the river Idle, the Chesterfield Canal, a stream called the Ryton, and innumerable small drains and brooks. It is dotted with little woods and coppices, and Sherwood Forest is near at hand. The weather that winter was frightful: the rain poured down, every runlet was in flood, and the Idle, belying its name, was a torrent half a mile wide. With such conditions, in this type of country, it is not surprising that the army of searchers had found no clue to the missing child's fate when Nodder stood in the dock at the Birmingham Assizes in March. He did not leave it for the witness-box; no evidence was called for the defence; and on the second day of the trial he was sentenced to seven years' penal servitude for abduction by fraud—a further indication of the view which the judge, and, no doubt, the jury, took of the gravity of his offence.

Three months later the evidence so long sought in vain came to light. Time, in the words of Mr Justice Swift, revealed Nodder's dreadful secret. The river Idle, in its northward course to the Trent, runs through East Retford, passes within a mile of Hayton, and enters Yorkshire near the small town of Bawtry. Between Hayton and

Bawtry the river in its windings covers some ten miles. Along these windings, for half a year, Mona Tinsley's body had drifted through the weeds, until on June 6, a Sunday, it was seen floating by a party rowing downstream from Bawtry. It was almost completely clothed. That evening the child's father identified the remains. On the following morning, while Dr J. M. Webster, a Birmingham pathologist, was examining them in an outhouse near the river, Mona's coat and one of her Wellington boots were dredged up near the spot where her body was found.

It was not, however, until July 29, after an inquest had been opened and twice adjourned, that Nodder was brought from prison to Retford police station and charged with the murder. In the meantime, at the end of June, Spilsbury had travelled to Birmingham to inspect the sections taken from the body by Dr Webster and the microscopical specimens made from them. When Nodder's second trial came on in November, this time at the Nottingham Assizes before Mr Justice Macnaghten, the only new witnesses of importance were the medical men. The others, except for those concerned in the discovery of the body, had been heard before, and had nothing new to say. But that discovery, and the nature of the medical evidence, made all the difference between conjecture and certainty, between one indictment and another, between seven years' penal servitude and the execution shed at Lincoln Prison.

The second trial, like the first, lasted only two days. Webster and Spilsbury were in the witness-box towards the end of the first day. Almost at once Webster was asked by Mr R. E. A. Elwes, who, as at the first trial, appeared with Norman Birkett for the Crown, whether his attention had been drawn to any particular feature in the body when he first saw it within a few hours of its recovery from the river. Webster replied that he noticed a horizontal mark running round the neck. The body itself, through long immersion in water, had undergone the change known as adipocere formation, a chemical change in the tissues. From the advanced state of this slow process he concluded that the body had been in the water for five or six months. When the body was taken to East Retford for the post-mortem, and had been cleaned, he found that the mark on the neck did not quite go round; it did not meet at the back. It was not a natural fold, but was the result of a thin cord or string being tied about the neck before death. The dead child's tongue still bore the marks of teeth, indicating that it had been bitten at the time of death, or immediately before, and, in Webster's view, through the tongue being forced up by the pressure of the ligature on the throat. In other words, Mona Tinsley, who was quite healthy, had not died from natural causes or from drowning, but from strangulation. Decomposition, though retarded by the immersion of the body for months in cold water, made it impossible to determine whether she had also been the victim of a criminal assault.

Mr Maurice Healey, for the defence—he too had been at the first trial in the same capacity—tried to get Dr Webster to admit that the little girl might have caught the neck of her frock on a branch by the riverside, being throttled as she hung suspended before the branch broke and she fell into the water. The doctor would not commit himself; and in reply to Norman Birkett, who re-examined him, he said that in such a case the mark round the neck would tend to be oblique, whereas it was, in fact, horizontal.

This ingenious but far-fetched supposition was soon disposed of by Spilsbury, when he followed Webster. He agreed that the cause of death was strangulation, probably effected by a ligature being passed over the head and drawn backward from behind, so that it was not in contact with the extreme back of the neck. Asked by Norman Birkett what conclusions he drew from the indentations on the tongue, which were still visible when he examined Webster's specimens, he said that they would have passed away almost at once if the tongue had been bitten before Mona Tinsley died; they must have been caused at the moment of death, when the process of throttling forced the tongue between the teeth. As to the theory of accidental strangulation by the child's frock, Spilsbury said:

"Some part of the dress would make a pressure-mark corresponding to the upper margin of the article which was pressing on the neck. In the case of the clothing, from what I could see there was no narrow band along the upper part of the dress. The mark would be shallower and broader than the one found in this case."

Suspension, as from a branch, Spilsbury went on, was not strangulation. The body would be suspended by its own weight. In cases where the suspending ligature did not completely surround the neck it always dragged upward at the sides, leaving an oblique mark, not a horizontal one. Finally, the absence of any other bruises or marks on the body put the theory of suspension, in his own words, out of count altogether.

He confirmed Dr Webster's conclusions from the presence and condition of adipocere. There was nothing inconsistent with the body having been in the river since early in January. It must have been put into the water very soon after death, before the process of putrefaction began to develop; otherwise this would have continued to act with normal rapidity, and the body would have risen to the surface long before it did.

In a brief cross-examination Mr Healey suggested that Spilsbury found Dr Webster's evidence good only in parts, like the curate's egg. Spilsbury would not admit this; he did not think there was any part he did not agree with. He described the argument for death by suspension as very speculative.

There was only one witness for the defence. This time Nodder gave evidence. When Norman Birkett rose to cross-examine he had an easy task in showing up the absurdities of the prisoner's story. There was little Mr Healey could say in his final speech, except to suggest that if Mona Tinsley was murdered the crime was committed after January 6, when the accused was taken into custody, and that it took place not at Hayton, but in or near Worksop, where Nodder said he left the child in a bus, and through which town the little river Ryton flows to join the Idle just south of Bawtry. This point was to be raised again.

Mr Justice Macnaghten's summing-up presented two issues to the jury. Was Mona Tinsley murdered? Did they believe Nodder's story? As to the second, the judge left little doubt of his own opinion. Of the first, he said, "I think you may take it as absolutely certain that if there was any ground for challenging the medical testimony, if there was any ground whereby conclusions at which Dr Webster and Sir Bernard Spilsbury arrived could be disputed, testimony to that effect would have been offered to you." At the very end of his address he put these issues in other words. "On the first question, was the child murdered, you have the direct testimony of the doctors. On the second question, is the prisoner the person who murdered her, are the facts proved before you inconsistent with any other rational conclusion than that he *is* the person who committed this terrible deed?"

The jury had retired to consider their verdict when they were recalled to hear fresh evidence. The witness who found the body floating in the Idle on June 6 now said that a week or two earlier he and his sons, while boating on the Ryton near its junction with the larger river, saw a large sack awash on a mudbank. It gave off a very offensive smell. The implication that this story supported the Worksop theory was, however, rebutted by Dr Webster, who said that the retarded state of putrefaction of Mona Tinsley's body produced only a slight, musty odour. The jury withdrew again, and after a further absence of half an hour brought in a verdict of guilty.

Twice tried, Nodder twice appealed. The second appeal, like the first, was dismissed, and almost a year after his crime he was hanged.

4

Twelve months later, once more round about Christmas, Spilsbury was investigating two other crimes against young girls, the second of them exciting as much public interest as the unsolved murder of Vera Page, which it resembled in broad outline and in the unsatisfactory conclusion of the case.

The earlier crime belongs to the most shocking class of all, because of the ages of the victim and her murderer. Beryl Osborne was only four when she was gagged and assaulted in Hazellville Road, Holloway, by a boy of thirteen and a half, who then strangled her with a piece of rope and tied up the body. At his trial he was acquitted on the ground that he was too young to understand the gravity of his offence, and he was sent to an approved school. This was at the end of October 1938; in the following January Spilsbury was performing a post-mortem at Romford, in Essex, on the body of Pamela Coventry, aged nine and a half, which had been found in a ditch near Hornchurch.

Pamela had left her home in South Romford after lunch on the 18th to walk back to her school in Benhurst Avenue. Her stepmother watched her going along Southend Road towards a street called Coronation Drive, which leads to Benhurst Avenue past Elm Park Station on the District Railway. Two school-friends waited for her in vain at the corner of the Avenue. Somewhere on the way, less than a quarter of an hour's walk, the little girl had disappeared, in broad daylight. When she did not return to tea, and it was learnt that she had not reached the school, Mrs Coventry went to the police. The body was discovered early next morning.

It was naked, except for a cotton frock tied loosely round the neck, and doubled up, the knees being under the chin, tightly bound with black and green insulated wire and tarred string. Insulating tape covered the knots. Beneath the body was a rotting mattress. Rigor mortis was advanced, and there were the usual painful symptoms of strangulation, this time by hand. When Spilsbury began his examination, and straightened the limbs, the stub of a home-made cigarette fell out from between a thigh and the chest. He found a great number of small scratches and bruises on the head and body; a large bruise on the jaw was probably, he thought, caused by a blow, and another behind the left ear might be the result of a fall on a hard surface. The child had been criminally assaulted, and had evidently struggled with her assailant. She had died within an hour of her last meal, the dinner she had eaten at about one o'clock on the 18th.

It seemed certain that she had been decoyed into one of the houses she passed on her way to school—probably one of those in Coronation Drive. From this street it was only four or five minutes' walk to the spot where her body was found. Every house on her route was visited, and hundreds of people were questioned. During the ten days following the murder a few articles of her clothing came to hand; her Wellington boots were found in a continuation of Southend Road, and two metal buttons, with a piece of black insulated wire, wrapped in the issue of the *News Chronicle* for January 11, turned up near Elm Park Station. This parcel was held together by black insulation tape. Further search at the place where it was found produced Pamela's school badge. The insulated wire in the parcel was identical in composition with that used to bind up her body.

On January 28 police with a warrant searched a house in Coronation Drive. They brought away some tarred string and green insulated wire, copies of the *News Chronicle* for eight days in January, the 4th to the 12th inclusive, less the issue for the 11th, which was missing, and a raincoat on which were bloodspots. The child's nose had bled as a result of strangulation. On February 2 Leonard Richardson, who lived in the house, was arrested and charged with murder.

The case against Richardson rested in the main on the articles found in his possession, and exhibited at his trial at the Old Bailey; and their evidential value was very much on a par with that of the clues thought to be incriminating in the case of Vera Page. Thousands of people in the Romford area were using identical insulating wire and tape. It could not be proved that Pamela Coventry's blood and the spots on the prisoner's raincoat belonged to the same group. The missing issue of the *News Chronicle* was not in itself a strong point; and though Richardson rolled his own cigarettes, and used the same brands of tobacco and paper as those of the stub found with the body, the tobacco was a popular make, and sixty million cigarette-papers like his, it was pointed out, were in circulation at any one time. It was soon after hearing this piece of evidence that the jury, through the foreman, handed a note to the judge. They had heard enough, and the trial came to an early end with the acquittal and discharge of the accused. Richardson seems to have made a good impression, for he was congratulated by the foreman as he left the court.

5

The rarest class of murder, very fortunately—for it is the most terrifying to contemplate—is that apparently committed for the sake of killing by a person who by all accepted standards is perfectly sane. When the victim is an adult it may be suspected that an intelligible motive is there, though undiscovered. Like the song the Syrens sang, it may not be beyond all conjecture in such a case as that of Willie Starchfield, because his murderer is unknown. But the wholly negative circumstances which accompanied the deaths of two little girls in Buckinghamshire at the end of 1941 seems to present an insoluble problem. The impelling cause may have been some sexual aberration, but there is no evidence, medical or other, to support the theory. Spilsbury's post-mortem findings would appear, indeed, to put it out of court. On the police record of the man convicted of the murders was one charge of assaulting a woman; but this very common offence seems to bear no relation to the throttling and stabbing of children who were not otherwise abused or mishandled in any way. At the Court of Criminal Appeal the crimes were described as motiveless and causeless, and even in Spilsbury's records of forty years they are almost unique.

Among the documents in the case is a very brief summary of the facts, introducing Spilsbury's report, and it will be enough to quote this.

MURDER OF TWO CHILDREN AT PENN WOOD,
BUCKS, BETWEEN 19TH AND 22ND NOVEMBER, 1941

Two children were found murdered at Penn on 22nd November, 1941, after having been missing from home since 19th November.

Harold Hill, aged 26, a driver in 341 Battery, 86th Field Regiment Royal Artillery, formerly stationed at Penn, was found guilty of the murder and subsequently hanged.

The case was that Hill was the driver of an Army truck at Penn and was in the habit of giving rides to small children.

The children were Doreen Joyce Hearn, aged 8, and Kathleen Trendal, aged 6. They were missing from home from 4 P.M., 19th November, 1941, and after extensive search their bodies were found in a wood in the Penn district on 22nd November.

Sir Bernard Spilsbury performed the post mortem, and a copy of his report is as follows.

There is no need to give this report in full. Spilsbury summarizes his own findings at the end, in these words:

A comparison of the changes found in the two children show a number of points of resemblance.

In each case death was due to wounds in the neck which were chiefly stab wounds.

The same weapon may have been used in each case, the weapon having a blunt point and a rather blunt cutting edge.

In each case the child had been rendered unconscious by manual strangulation, before the injuries were inflicted, and they were probably unconscious when the injuries were inflicted.

The only indication of a possible struggle was a bruise at the back of the head of Doreen Hearn.

There was no indication of sexual interference in either case.

In other words, the murderer, who had the kindly habit of giving small children rides in his truck—kindly, it may be inferred, because in no instance was he charged with abusing their trust in him—suddenly decided to take two of them into a wood and stab them to death, first rendering them unconscious so that they should not feel the worst injuries. A very queer case.

6

Crimes of violence by the juvenile delinquent, or, more simply, the young lout (who is not always a boy), have become a commonplace in the new era which Spilsbury and his contemporaries lived to see, and with which he, for one, was in many ways out of sympathy. Mingled with the long tale of offences against children recorded in his cards are instances of crimes committed *by* children, because these too had fatal endings; but they are very rare, and, apart from such cases as that of the boy who murdered Beryl Osborne, they nearly all belong to a class which must always be exceptional—premeditated killing, usually for gain, by some precocious criminal still in his teens.

Spilsbury was not concerned in one of the best-known of these cases in recent times, the murder of Lady White by Jacoby. A case of much greater interest, the trial of John Donald Merrett in Edinburgh in 1926 for the murder of his mother, is dealt with in the next chapter. Jacoby, for that matter, though often described as a boy, was a youth of nineteen. But the cards for that year, 1922, include two other murders in this class. In April a seventeen-year-old footman strangled a District Messenger Boy, and Jacoby's crime in March had been preceded by an even more shocking affair, which was complicated by some unusual features.

Sarah Blake was a widow of fifty-five who managed the Crown and

Anchor Inn on Gallows Tree Common, midway between Henley and Pangbourne, in the Oxfordshire loop of the Thames. On the morning of Sunday, March 4, she was found dead in her kitchen, battered and hacked in a frightful manner. Spilsbury counted more than sixty wounds and bruises on her head, face, neck, hands, and forearms. The skull had been fractured in four places, and the neck was cut to the spine. The woman had been stunned by an early blow, but her murderer continued to rain others with a thick iron bar found beside the body, finishing his horrible work with a knife.

Mrs Blake had been seen alive at 6.30 the evening before. In Spilsbury's opinion she had been killed very soon after. There was a search for a cyclist seen near the inn that Saturday evening; local feeling was strongly aroused, and among the neighbours who came forward with information and offers of help was a boy of fifteen named Jack Hewett. About this time, however, there was a surfeit of sensational cases; three days after Mrs Blake's death Olive Young was murdered by Ronald True, and, with the Freda Kempton and Jacoby cases following, and the trial of Armstrong drawing near, the crime on Gallows Tree Common, in spite of this grimly appropriate name, did not attract the general notice it would have done in a month when headline homicide was less prevalent. Interest in it was revived when, on March 17, Robert Alfred Shepperd, detained at Reading for a minor offence, was released and immediately rearrested, charged on his own confession with the murder of Mrs Blake. But by the time Armstong was being tried at Hereford Shepperd was again a free man. His was one of the not uncommon cases of delusion or exhibitionism, and he could not have committed the crime to which he had confessed.

Confessions, however, were in the air; and now the unhappy parents of Jack Hewett, who, like Thorne, had been so anxious to help the police, heard him also admit to the murder at the Crown and Anchor. It was no delusion this time. The boy's case was one of the first in which the influence of "the pictures" was blamed in mitigation of a capital crime.

Mitigating circumstances of a far more compelling kind influenced a judge and jury fifteen years later, when a boy of sixteen, Henry Sidney Smith, was tried for the murder of his father. Sidney Joseph Smith—it is curious how often these first and last names go together—was a man of fifty-six who from being a carman in the employ of Carter Paterson rose to become licensee of two public houses, but then sank to the rôle of cellarman at a third at Lambeth, kept by his brother-in-law. A bully and a drunkard, violent when in drink, Smith made the lives of his wife and son almost unbearable. The climax to this domestic reign of terror came on the night of April 22, 1937, when, drunk as usual, Smith pursued his wife with foul language and his fist raised, and the boy, seizing a full milk-bottle, brought it down on his father's head. During the struggle that followed Mrs Smith ran out to call the neighbours. When she returned with help her husband lay dead or dying, and her son was standing over him with a kitchen knife.

At the Hackney mortuary next day Spilsbury found eight wounds on the head, and nine stabs on the chest and one arm. Four of these had reached the heart, and three the lungs. Young Henry Smith was committed for trial from the Bow Street Children's Court; but when, a month later, he appeared at the Old Bailey on the capital charge his acquittal on the grounds of age and provocation surprised no one.

To close a chapter on juvenile crime with the case of George Frederick Margerison is to run counter to Spilsbury's own opinion, repeatedly expressed. The case is of interest as one of the very rare instances, in forty years' work in coroners' courts, when that opinion was disregarded. Two juries, in fact, have put this boy's death on record as *felo-de-se*.

George Margerison was a few months younger than Henry Smith when in March 1926 he was found dead in a lane near Ribchester, in Lancashire. He had been shot in the right temple, the weapon, which lay beside him, being a .32 Mauser automatic. A verdict of suicide having been returned at the inquest, the boy's father, by a motion in the King's Bench Division of the High Court, secured an order for a second coroner's inquiry. On behalf of the family Spilsbury went to Ribchester in September, and a local doctor made a fresh examination of the body in his presence. At the new inquest Spilsbury said categorically, "By whatever means the boy came by his death it was not by suicide." He must have been a little astonished by the rebuff he received; for reasons that can only be conjectured the second jury ignored his evidence, and a second verdict of suicide was returned.

In writing up his case-card Spilsbury headed it "? Accident," and stated, without qualification, that in his view "the shooting was unexpected." He based that view on bloodstains on the dead boy's hat, and he was so dissatisfied with the result of the inquest that he took the hat away with him, and made a number of experiments with similar ones. Some time later he spoke of the case in public, heading his talk "A Hat from a Fatal Case of Shooting." He began

The black bowler hat which I am showing was obtained in the following circumstances. A normal, healthy boy, 16 years of age, was found dead on the ground in a quiet country lane. He had a bullet wound through the head; the bullet entered the right temple and emerged above and behind the left ear, its course being right to left and slightly backwards. There was no singeing of the hair, or blackening or tattooing of the skin round the entrance wound.

The automatic pistol, Spilsbury went on, lay on the ground on the left side of the body, near the left hand; one round had been fired, leaving five live cartridges in the magazine. Three more were found in one of the boy's pockets. His bowler hat lay brim downward near the weapon. In his upturned left palm was a partly smoked cigarette. The hat was spattered with tiny spots of blood distributed over the outer surface of the right side and extending forward to the front of the hat and downward within the curve of the brim. There were spots on the under surface of the brim, and larger bloodstains running forward and inward over the leather lining from right to left. Similar blood-spots, in which minute fragments of brain substance were visible, were found on the under surface of the brim on the left side.

The presence of blood on the hat showed that it was on the boy's head when he was shot. The entrance and exit wounds in the head must have been close to the under surface of the brim. A bullet passing through the cranial cavity produces a considerable rise of pressure during the very short time—perhaps $\frac{1}{500}$ of a second—that it takes to traverse the cavity. This rise of pressure causes the extensive fracturing sometimes found in shooting cases, and it may force blood and brain substance out of the entrance wound as the bullet passes through the brain.

"This, I believe," Spilsbury said,

> "is what happened in this case, and the blood mixed with the brain substance, which was forcibly ejected from the entrance wound, met the gases of discharge from the pistol, and was blown, in part as a fine spray, over the right side and front of the hat, curving round the edge of the brim to be deposited within it, in part in a mass producing the larger stains on the under surface of the brim and the leather lining in front, those on the lining indicating that the gases also raised the hat from the head.
>
> "The bloodstains on the under surface of the brim on the left side no doubt followed the bullet as it emerged from the head. This result from the passage of a bullet through the head has not been recorded previously as far as I can ascertain."

In conclusion, Spilsbury said that though the position of the entrance wound and the direction taken by the bullet suggested suicide,

> "the absence of scorching, blackening, and tattooing round the entrance wound, the fact that the hat was on the head at the time, and that the boy was holding a cigarette in his left hand when he pulled the trigger with his right hand—if he fired the weapon himself—are in my view contra-indications that it was a suicidal act."

If this characteristic piece of inductive reasoning ever came to the knowledge of young Margerison's parents it must have been some comfort to them to learn that, juries notwithstanding, the most eminent pathologist in the country continued to uphold his view, and theirs.

Chapter 7: MATRICIDE

MR WILLIAM ROUGHEAD closes his Introduction to *The Trial of John Donald Merrett*, edited by him for the "Notable British Trials" series, with the following words:

> But there is one question, touching the very marrow of the mystery, to which I should like to have had an answer: How did the accused propose to deal with the situation which his nefarious transactions had created? He had depleted his mother's bank accounts, dissipated her current income, despoiled her temporarily of a livelihood. Detection, imminent and inevitable, confronted him. He could not have counted upon a timely accident, or foreseen her suicide on the discovery of his guilt. What was he going to do about it? How was the plot to end?

This question must have been in the forefront of the minds of the six women and nine men of the jury which, on the seventh day of the trial in the High Court of Justiciary in the Parliament Square, Edinburgh, retired to deliberate upon the fate of John Donald Merrett. He was being tried, as Scots law allows, upon two very different charges taken together: (1) murder and (2) uttering—*i.e.*, presenting for payment—cheques which he knew to be forged. After an hour's absence the jury unanimously found the panel, otherwise the accused, guilty under the second charge; as to the first, that of shooting his mother, they returned by a majority a verdict of Not Proven. It will be recalled that Lord Alness, in alluding to this trial, over which he presided as Lord Justice Clerk, describes the finding of Not Proven, another peculiarity of Scottish law, as "unsatisfactory." Mr Roughead calls it "indefensible and invidious." But at least it means what it says.

For the full story of this remarkable case readers are referred to the volume mentioned above. Mr Roughead's Introduction is among the best things even he has done, and to paraphrase, however briefly, such a master of his subject seems almost presumptuous. But as one of the few trials in which it was possible to retain Spilsbury for the defence, something must be said about it here, and the more so because, to quote Mr Roughead again, "The crux of the case, as I see it, is the medical evidence."

Mrs Bertha Merrett was a woman of fifty-five, and her son, John Donald, was seventeen and a half, when the pair came to live in Edinburgh in January 1926. Mrs Merrett came of a prosperous Lancashire family, and had an income of £700 a year. Her son was born in New Zealand. Her husband deserted her, and she brought the boy to England in 1924, entering him at Malvern College, where he did well. He was to have gone to Oxford, but after he had been a year at the school his general conduct decided her to send him to Edinburgh University, which is non-resident. He could live at home with her in the Scottish capital, and be under her eye. After staying in rooms and at a boarding-house the two Merretts moved into a furnished flat at No. 31 Buckingham Terrace on March 10.

On March 17, a Wednesday, the daily maid who looked after the flat, a young married woman named Sutherland, arrived as usual at 9 A.M. Mrs Merrett and her son had finished breakfast in the only sitting-room, and, the table having been cleared, the former sat down at it to write letters. Behind her, on her right, was a bureau, its top opened. Young Merrett had taken a book to a chair in a recess near the door. This door was wide open. Mrs Sutherland was busy in the kitchen at the rear of the flat when, about 9.30, she heard a shot. Of what next happened she gave contradictory accounts. According to one, she saw, through the open door, Mrs Merrett falling from her chair, a pistol in her hand. Her final version, to which she adhered at the trial, was that after the shot she heard a scream and a thud; before she could collect her wits young Merrett came to the kitchen and said his mother had shot herself. Going with him to the sitting-room, or public room, as she called it, she found Mrs Merrett lying on the floor, bleeding from the head. Her chair was overturned. The pistol was then on top of the bureau. There was further contradictory evidence, including that of the police, as to whether the pistol, a small automatic, was ever on the bureau, or was discovered on the floor beside the body.

The whole affair, in fact, was very casually handled from the beginning. It was taken for granted that Mrs Merrett, who was still alive but unconscious, had attempted suicide. She was conveyed to the Royal Infirmary and placed in a barred ward, to all intents and purposes under arrest. There she lingered for a fortnight, at first conscious and able to talk rationally and to sign a cheque. She had no idea of what had happened, except that something like a pistol had gone off in her head; when asked, "Was there not a pistol there?" she replied, in astonishment, "No; was there?" She had been writing letters, and had just said to her son, who was standing by her, "Go away, Donald, and don't annoy me," when the explosion occurred. Donald Merrett agreed that she had used these words, but said he had gone back to the recess at the end of the room before the shot was fired. He told two stories about the pistol, which he had purchased, with fifty cartridges, a few days before the tragedy: first, that his mother knew of it, and took it from him, putting it in a small drawer of the bureau, and, later, that he did not think she knew he had it.

Of this young man's behaviour, during the last fortnight of his mother's life, Mr Roughead remarks that "it does seem to fall something short of what one should expect from an only and beloved son." Mrs Merrett had two married sisters, both of whom were abroad that March; Donald did not inform them of what had happened, though at the injured woman's request he telegraphed to a friend, Mrs Hill, at Brighton. He treated Mrs Hill in a very cavalier fashion when she arrived in Edinburgh. It was she who brought one of his aunts, Mrs Penn, hurrying back with her husband from the Riviera. Donald's normal activities, of which more will be said, included nightly visits to a Palais de Danse called the Dunedin; his mother was barely in the Infirmary when he was round at the Palais to take a girl-friend, one of the instructresses, to have tea at Queensferry. The pair were at a cinema that evening, sandwiching a brief call at the Infirmary in between these relaxations. A few days later the distressed son, who already had a motor-cycle, was ordering a new and more powerful one. He continued to go to the Palais, and to take his friend about, until, on April 1, Mrs Merrett died. She was never charged with attempted suicide, but the charge had been prepared

Nine months passed. By Mrs Merrett's will her whole estate was left in trust for her son until he reached the age of twenty-five. One of the two administrators was the Public Trustee, who, the other having renounced probate, acted alone. Mr and Mrs Penn took over the flat in Buckingham Terrace until it was due to be vacated in June. "It must," says Mr Roughead, "have been a strangely discomfortable household: the uncle and aunt, perplexed by the enigma of the mother's death; the nephew, who alone knew the answer; the maid, who had claimed to know and afterwards denied it." The uncle and aunt soon found other causes for worry in the nephew's conduct, though for some time they did not know the half of it. In April Donald borrowed money from them and went off to London "to consult a famous detective." With him went a male friend and two girls, one of whom, being under sixteen, was haled back to her home by the police. Donald himself was soon again in Edinburgh, penniless. Other misdemeanours were now coming to light; the police were in and out of the flat; and, the young prodigal having been examined by an alienist, and pronounced sound and sane, he was presently dispatched south again, to Disraeli's village of Hughenden, in Buckinghamshire, where it was felt that temptations would be fewer than in Edinburgh, and where, under a tutor, he could attack the studies which hitherto he had scarcely attempted to pursue.

For it was now known that after his first few weeks at Edinburgh University his class and his tutor, whose fees his mother paid, saw him no more. He would leave home each morning, his books under his arm, and amuse himself at the Palais de Danse or elsewhere until it was time to return. His mother's injury and death did not cause him to alter this routine, or to intermit his nocturnal visits to the Palais, which were effected with the help of a rope from his bedroom window. At the Palais he would "book out" his friend the instructress at a cost of 15*s*. for an afternoon or 30*s*. an evening. He took her about and bought her jewels, as well as the motor-cycle for himself. Aladdin did no better, for Donald's allowance was 10*s*. a week. On the day before Mrs Merrett was shot the Clydesdale Bank in Edinburgh notified her for the second time that she was overdrawn, and inquiries soon revealed the method by which the son had supplemented his allowance. His mother's principal account was with the Midland Bank at Boscombe, a suburb of Bournemouth; from this, and from the Clydesdale account, over £450 had been withdrawn during February and early March by means of twenty-nine cheques made out to J. D. Merrett. Forgery must have been suspected at once, and no doubt the Edinburgh police then began to put to themselves those questions propounded by Mr Roughead: if Mrs Merrett had not so conveniently died, what was the forger going to do about it? How was the plot to end?

2

To prove the forgery took time. Nemesis overtook young Merrett in November, in the form of a petition by the Procurator Fiscal of Midlothian, charging him with murder and uttering; he was arrested at Hughenden and taken to Edinburgh prison. His trial began on February 1, 1927.

Lord Alness was on the Bench; counsel for the Crown were the Lord Advocate and the Advocate-Depute; Mr Craigie Aitchison, K.C., led for the Panel. It was remarked of the latter, as he stood in the dock, a powerfully built young man six feet in height, that he looked much older than his eighteen years.

Five of the seven days' proceedings were taken up by the evidence for the Crown. It was impossible to keep the two charges against the accused tidily separate; after Mrs Sutherland had been severely questioned about her conflicting versions of the shooting, and a piper in the K.O.S.B.'s who ten months before was a policeman had artlessly displayed his lack of observation and faulty memory of what took place when he was called to the scene of the tragedy, the examination of Detective-Inspector Fleming raised the matter of the cheques. Two doctors from the Royal Infirmary followed, the second having been in charge of Mrs Merrett from within an hour of her admission until her death. It was elicited from these witnesses that neither saw any blackening or tattooing round her wound, as might be expected in a case of attempted suicide by shooting, when the weapon is held close to the head; but under cross-examination both admitted that there was much blood round the wound, which had to be removed with a swab soaked in water, and that in looking for powder-marks they did not use even a hand lens. The recollections of the second doctor of conversations with Mrs Merrett while she was his patient were, after the lapse of time, imperfect and confused. In reply to Mr Craigie Aitchison he said that her injury was always referred to as an accident, and that she had never repudiated the suggestion.

At the end of the third day the Crown called two more medical witnesses of heavier calibre, if the expression in this context is permissible—Professor Harvey Littlejohn and Professor John Glaister, respectively Professors of Forensic Medicine at Edinburgh and Glasgow Universities. They described a series of experiments made with the actual weapon employed, a .25 automatic of Spanish make holding six cartridges in the magazine. Shots were fired at ranges varying from point blank to nine inches into cards and into skin. There was much blackening and tattooing at the shorter ranges, a little at six inches, and at nine inches there was none at all. The piece of skin—there were curious rumours about how it was obtained—still showed blackening after having been soaked in water for nearly two months. Though the pistol was only four and a half inches long, Professor Littlejohn at first declared that in his view suicide was "inconceivable." He used the same word of the theory of accident, according to which Mrs Merrett had reached behind her for something from the bureau, overbalanced her chair, and, in falling, unwittingly snatched the pistol from a pigeon-hole. Pressed by Mr

Craigie Aitchison, the Professor qualified this opinion by saying, "If it can be proved to be a close discharge, then either suicide or accident is possible." He had no doubt, however, that it was not a close discharge. By a close discharge he meant one within three inches. He agreed that if there was a doubt as to whether the weapon was fired within that range, suicide or accident could not be excluded. The Professor's evidence, in short, after Mr Aitchison had done with him, had not advanced the Crown's case very far. Even to the lay mind Mr Aitchison's cross-examination is a masterpiece of persistence and skill.

If the crux of the case was the medical evidence the crux of the medical evidence was this question of powder-blackening and tattooing. The Lord Justice Clerk, speaking in his charge to the jury of the various arguments based on the wound, was to say, "I think you must take it that the case for the Crown on this matter depends on the absence of blackening, and in substance on nothing else." Because no such marking was detected with the naked eye after the wound had been cleaned, while experiments with cards and human skin seemed to show that tattooing, or penetration of the surface, could not be eradicated by washing, the prosecution maintained that the pistol could not have been held close to the head. The fact was glossed over that though the doctors who failed to find any blackening knew that Mrs Merrett was under a suspended charge of attempted suicide, they said nothing to contradict the idea. Even the defence neglected this point, and the judge, in summing up, only referred to it indirectly, when he reminded the jury that the case was accepted by all as one of suicide. A minor question was that of the course taken by the bullet, which was slightly upward from the wound in the right ear. Professor Glaister, when he followed Professor Littlejohn in the witness-box, spent most of his time there parrying another relentless cross-examination chiefly on these two points. Mr Craigie Aitchison complained of the witness's repeated hedging with the word "probable," and towards the end of the Professor's ordeal his replies give the impression of a man driven into a corner.

It was different with the remaining expert witnesses for the Crown—those called to give evidence on the financial side of the case, the second charge of uttering. They included two authorities on handwriting, one of these being Mr G. F. Gurrin. This name gave Mr Aitchison an opportunity which he was not the man to miss. In his only address to the jury, at the end of the evidence—in Scottish trials counsel do not make preliminary speeches—he referred to the case of

Adolf Beck. "I find it difficult in this case," he went on, "to get out of my mind this fact, that the name of the handwriting expert who led to the conviction of Adolf Beck was Gurrin—not the present Mr Gurrin. Out of respect to the present Mr Gurrin we refrained from asking what relationship he bore to the expert in the case of Adolf Beck." This might be thought hitting below the belt, but it was legitimate from counsel fighting for his client's life. It reminded the jury very forcibly that handwriting experts had been known to make disastrous mistakes. If it failed of effect it was because Mr Gurrin's conclusions from his study of the cheques now in question were supported in almost every detail by a second authority from Edinburgh, and by the general circumstances revealed by bank officials and the accused's own actions. Remarks by Mr Aitchison in his address to the jury suggest that he had not much hope of their acquitting Donald Merrett on the charge of uttering.

When the defence opened on the sixth day of the trial Merrett himself did not go into the witness-box. Those called on his behalf included official persons who testified that when Mrs Merrett died it was still taken for granted that she had committed suicide. Professor G. M. Robertson, an authority on mental diseases, was questioned about the effect of her injury on her mind. He said that though the brain itself had not been touched, the medical facts, as to which he was fully informed, indicated that the coverings of the brain were perforated. This must result in serious mental changes. Mrs Merrett would be in a state of what he called altered consciousness; while she might appear normal, her memory would be so affected that it was unsafe to draw inferences from anything she said during the last fortnight of her life. She might even have forgotten an impulse to commit suicide. Professor Robertson cited instances to support his conclusions.

The last two witnesses for the defence were Mr Robert Churchill, the gun expert, and Spilsbury. This pair had often appeared together in cases of shooting, and were to appear in many more in the future. Mr Churchill was already recognized as one of the highest authorities on firearms and the results of gunshot wounds. His evidence was therefore of great importance. In substance it was as follows:

Having carried out experiments in London with a weapon similar to that figuring in the case, he was present at Spilsbury's further experiments in Edinburgh with the actual pistol. The ammunition was the same as that bought by Donald Merrett, and came from the same shop. A .25 automatic cartridge contained two grains of flake smokeless powder, a very small charge. Flake powder, fired from a small pistol, would not really tattoo the skin, even at close range; the flakes would not penetrate, but merely adhere to the surface. Blackening from the discharge would be purely superficial, and easily removed by wiping with a damp cloth. He had no doubt of this. In these circumstances no inference as to distance could be drawn from the absence of blackening. He was quite clear about that, too.

From the direction of the wound, Mr Churchill said, it might have been suicidally inflicted or the result of an accident. He had experience of a case of a woman who had shot herself behind the right ear. There would probably be an instinctive movement of the head away from the muzzle, which would fully account for the course of the bullet after entry. With regard to the theory of accident, a similar wound could be reproduced by grasping the pistol with the thumb on the trigger-guard and the fingers at the butt. The automatic in question was in good working order; it was a cheap make, with a light pull. No reliance, said Mr Churchill, finally, was to be placed on such weapons, which might go off accidentally.

"The defence," says Mr Roughead at this point,

> reserved for the final round their heaviest weight. Fortunate, indeed, was the accused to secure the evidence of Sir Bernard Spilsbury. For a pannel to be able to call an expert of his calibre—of European fame, of the highest eminence in his profession, and of such unfailing fairness—was an advantage as unusual as it was inestimable.

By this time counsel and scientific witnesses for the defence had got to know one another very well. There had been a week of nightly conferences which must have recalled to Spilsbury the days when he worked with Muir, another Scot. With national thoroughness on national ground, the rigour of these meetings was unalleviated by such frivolities as refreshment. "There was not," says one of those who attended, "even anything to drink." But the Scottish brand of humour was not absent, and when on this sixth evening of the trial Spilsbury, in the witness-box, had given his qualifications Mr Craigie Aitchison began his examination with a little joke misheard by most of those in court: "Now, St Bernard . . ."

"I have applied my mind," Spilsbury himself began characteristically, "to the question of the possibility of drawing any certain conclusions as to whether the wound which resulted in Mrs Merrett's death was homicidal, suicidal, or accidental."

He went on to cite from his own knowledge, as Mr Churchill had done from his, a case of a suicide who shot himself behind the right ear. "So far as my experience goes," he added, "there is nothing in the site of the wound in the case of Mrs Merrett inconsistent with suicide."

Handed the pistol, he pointed out that it was an automatic weapon, light in weight and with a very short barrel, the muzzle projecting only one and a quarter inches beyond the finger on the trigger. It was thus easy to hold it in a position against the side of the head. Owing to the light weight there would be no strain on the hand or arm even if the pistol was held two inches away from the head. He agreed with a proposition put to Professor Littlejohn, that a considerable range of movement in the shoulder-joint was found in women, on account of the habit of putting up the hair.

Of the course taken by the bullet he said that slight inclination of the head would make all the difference, and that such a movement was to be expected in the case of all but very determined suicides. Most people, especially women, would dread the explosion. He concurred with Professor Littlejohn's view that an accident was possible, if not probable.

Then came his vital evidence on the question of powder-blackening. He said that in the circumstances—the bleeding, which would wash away some of the blackening, and the subsequent cleaning with a wet swab—he did not think that any sure conclusion could be drawn as to the distance from which the shot was fired. He then summarized the experiments made with Mr Churchill in London, and the later ones with the actual weapon in Edinburgh. He exhibited cards showing part of the blackening wiped off by a damp cloth. At two inches there was very little blackening. This was always less distinct on skin, because of the nature of the surface, and the moistness or greasiness of skin made it more easy to remove such markings. After wiping, a hand lens would be needed to detect any traces. The flakes of the smokeless powder used, unlike the particles of granulated powder, which penetrate the skin, were very easily removed, and left no trace.

Spilsbury reiterated his opinion that suicide was a possible explanation of what had occurred, and of the theory of accident he said, "From my own experience of accidental shooting one knows of extraordinary positions sometimes resulting from the accidental discharge of weapons, and in such a position as this an accidental discharge, I think, could never be entirely excluded. It might even be at a range greater than that which would produce local marks round the wound."

Questioned by Mr Aitchison about Mrs Merrett's mental condition after her injury and statements made by her not long before acute delirium developed, Spilsbury replied that any such statements should be accepted with great caution.

Nothing need be said of his cross-examination by the Lord Advocate. The latter failed to extract any qualification of Spilsbury's evidence-in-chief. A few questions from the bench closed his long occupation of the witness-box—only Professor Littlejohn had occupied it longer—his first appearance for the defence at a criminal trial, and the case for the defence itself.

The Lord Advocate rose at once to address the jury, for since the prisoner had not given evidence, his counsel had the last word before the summing-up. Mr Craigie Aitchison began his own speech in the course of the next morning, and in it he referred to Spilsbury in the eulogistic terms quoted by Lord Alness himself in the appreciation included in an earlier chapter. When the Lord Justice Clerk came to deliver his charge to the jury, and dealt with the conflict of opinion between the scientific witnesses, which he described as irreconcilable, he went out of his way, in a parenthesis, to stress the importance he attributed to Spilsbury's conclusions, to which, he said, "I should imagine you would be disposed to attach the very greatest weight." The summing-up was, on the whole, rather favourable to the accused on the charge of murder. On that of uttering it was more emphatically against him. The jury, as has been seen, followed the leads given them—as to the capital indictment by a majority, and unanimously as to the minor charge, a verdict which sent Donald Merrett to prison for twelve months.

If it was "an inestimable advantage" to a man accused of murder to have secured Spilsbury as an expert witness, young Merrett was no less fortunate in his advocate, of whose final speech, says Mr Roughead, "it is hard to write without hyperbole." The trial was conducted on all sides with great ability and remarkable fairness, for not even the judge alluded to the prisoner's absence from the witness-box. Mr Roughead, having remarked that by the provisions of the Criminal Evidence Act of 1898 the prosecution could not comment on this fact, goes on to say, "but we, to whom the provisions of the Act do not apply, may well wonder at the pannel's silence. If ever there was a case which called for such enlightenment, as he alone could give, surely it is this."

3

Three years and a month after the trial of Donald Merrett the second of the two most famous prosecutions for matricide in the last quarter of a century reached its culmination at the Lewes Assizes. Again the medical evidence, and again that of Spilsbury in particular, was all-important. Here, however, the points of resemblance between the two cases cease. Mrs Rosaline Fox and her son Sidney had nothing in common (except their relationship) with the Merretts. One tragedy took place in Midlothian, the other in Kent; the means of death, the procedure of the trials, the verdicts—all were different. And at Lewes, of course, Spilsbury was giving evidence in his everyday rôle of witness for the Crown.

Mrs Fox, who was sixty-three, was a Norfolk woman, born at Great Fransham, a small village which is a marketing centre for the upland district between Swaffham and East Dereham. The daughter of a farm-labourer, she married a signalman on the Great Eastern Railway, and had four children. It is said that the youngest, Sidney Harry, born in 1899, was the son of a railway porter with whom she lived after parting from her husband.

It cannot be pretended that Mrs Fox was an exemplary parent, but the influence upon her of her youngest, and apparently dearest, may have been a factor in her later decline into a common swindler. Sidney was in the hands of the police before he was twelve, and for the greater part of his adult life he was living on his wits. These could have been put to better purpose, for he had plenty of ability of a sort, and some charm of manner; but he belonged to that curious type which will take great pains, and run great risks, to avoid doing steady work. It would be interesting to know what men of this type, who must sometimes look ahead, think is going to become of them. Sidney Fox, for all his cleverness, never prospered; he was in prison several times; and when he died, at thirty-one, he and his mother had for some years been existing precariously by drifting from rooms and hotels to other rooms and hotels, usually without luggage and almost without money, leaving furtively and in debt when managements became too pressing. They were not entirely penniless: the eldest son having been killed in France in 1917, Mrs Fox drew a weekly pension of 10*s*., and Sidney himself, whose war record in England had been in the highest degree discreditable, nevertheless received 8*s*. a week for an ailment said to have been contracted in the service of his country. But these pittances went nowhere in the kind of life he and his mother chose to lead. A more dreary and nerve-racking one it is difficult to imagine. A pair of hares in a paper-chase, they left behind them a trail of bills and worthless cheques, and sooner or later the pursuit would catch up with them. Some time before the end Sidney Fox had perhaps decided to take drastic steps towards a new start.

In March 1928 he was sentenced to fifteen months imprisonment for stealing jewellery from a Mrs Morse, whose husband at this very time was about to institute proceedings for divorce, Fox himself being named as co-respondent. As Miss Tennyson Jesse puts it, he had been "outraging his own personal and peculiar morality in making love to the lady," for he was a homosexual, and proud of it. During this romance, when he and his mother were sharing a flat at Southsea with Mrs Morse, there was an escape of gas one night in the latter's bedroom. She roused herself just in time. Some rather sinister circumstances attended this incident; not only was the gas-tap out of use, and difficult to turn, but Fox had just induced Mrs Morse to insure her life for a large sum and then to make a will in his favour. It seems probable that he was trying his prentice hand at murder, as well as at a more tender, if to him uncongenial, pursuit. If this was so, the idea, having taken root, became a monstrously unnatural growth.

While Fox was serving his prison sentence his mother went to the workhouse, where, her health being poor—she suffered from paralysis agitans, among other things—she passed most of her time in the infirmary. Fox was released in March 1929, and the couple then resumed their normal life of fraud. On April 21 Mrs Fox made a will, leaving all she had to her son Sidney. As she had nothing to leave, except a small insurance dating back many years, arrears on which had recently been paid up, it is a fair assumption that she was being a party to some scheme, no doubt proposed by Sidney, by which they were both to benefit. It is only too likely that Sidney himself already had other views. On the 30th of the month he was taking out the first of a series of accident policies on his mother's life.

During the next six months the pair were on their travels, living on credit, by cashing cheques from stolen cheque-books, at times by pawning everything but the clothes they stood in. They even contrived to go to France on a pious pilgrimage to the grave of Sidney's eldest brother. Autumn came; and by way of hotels in London, Canterbury, and Folkestone they arrived on October 16 at the Metropole at Margate. Unpaid bills and cheques marked "No Account" were accumulating ever more thickly behind them. They had only a few shillings between them, and not even the brown-paper parcel which was their sole piece of luggage at Canterbury. The weather being cold, and Margate notoriously bracing, Mrs Fox wore both her stockinette dresses, one over the other.

Sidney Fox stayed at the Metropole rather more than a week, Mrs Fox not quite so long. Six days after their arrival, on October 22, he was in London, arranging for an extension until midnight on the following day of two insurances on his mother's life, one for £1000, the other for £2000. He had to borrow money to pay his fare back to Margate. Mrs Fox, who with all her faults loved and trusted this ruthless young egoist, happily had no suspicion, when she dined with him that evening at the hotel, that the very moment of her death was written on the policies in his pocket, and that it was drawing very near. Before midnight struck on the 23rd she may have had a few seconds of dreadful comprehension.

A little before that midnight there was an alarm of fire at the Metropole. The manager, arriving at the scene of it, saw Mrs Fox, wearing nothing but an undervest and apparently unconscious, being dragged from her bedroom, which was full of smoke. He helped to carry a badly burned armchair, still smouldering, into the corridor. Sidney Fox was there, having summoned help from the lounge downstairs. The police were called in, and two doctors, one of whom, Dr Austin, had prescribed a tonic for Mrs Fox three days before. He now found her beyond aid, and diagnosed the cause of death as shock and suffocation. The second medical man, Dr Nichol, did not dispute the conclusions of his colleague, who had been first on the spot. Dr Austin signed the death certificate, and at the inquest next day a verdict of death by misadventure was returned. Sidney Fox, on the strength of the insurance policies and the usual plausible lies, obtained advances totalling £40 from a local solicitor, and without paying the bill at the Metropole left Margate with the remains of his mother for Great Fransham, where on October 29 Rosaline Fox was buried. On the morning of the funeral her son was at Norwich, discussing his claim under one of the insurance policies with the local manager of the company concerned; and to that city he returned in the evening, putting up for a few more days of freedom at the last hotel he was to know. On November 2 he was taken into custody on a charge of unlawfully obtaining credit—he was an undischarged bankrupt—and haled back to Margate. Behind this almost venial charge far darker suspicions were taking shape. Within the week Scotland Yard was called in, and on the 9th Spilsbury and Chief-Inspector Hambrook were on their way to the churchyard at Great Fransham.

4

Spilsbury's card relating to Rosaline Fox, whose death had been certified as caused by shock and suffocation, is headed "Manual Strangulation." There was to be much argument at the trial because he alone of the medical witnesses saw the body while it was still well preserved. The coffin had been sealed with putty and was air-tight, and putrefactive changes were superficial. As soon as the organs and other parts removed by Spilsbury at the post-mortem became exposed to the air rapid decomposition set in, and one of the most important discoveries made by him, a bruise at the back of the larynx, was unrecognizable as such by the time the specimens reached his laboratory. He had gone to Great Fransham with an open mind; the circumstances of the case aroused grave suspicion, but Fox was still held only on charges of fraud, and it was thought that if murder had been committed the means employed was probably poison. It was chiefly this bruise, the size of a half-crown, in the loose tissue between the larynx and œsophagus, which convinced Spilsbury that Rosaline Fox died of manual strangulation.

Two months, in fact, went by before Sidney Fox was charged with the murder before the Margate magistrates and committed for trial. The case was transferred from Kent to the Sussex Assizes, and again history repeated itself in the County Hall at Lewes. Curtis-Bennett was there, with the Attorney-General, Sir William Jowett, for the Crown, and J. D. Cassels led for the defence; on the one side was the evidence of Spilsbury, who had performed the post-mortem immediately after the exhumation at Great Fransham, on the other that of two doctors who did not see the medical exhibits until three months later; and one of these doctors was Brontë. Among the medical points in dispute was whether a mark was a bruise or a post-mortem change. It was, in many respects, the Thorne case over again.

The trial opened before Mr Justice Rowlatt on March 12, 1930. The evidence of the fire at the Metropole was itself very damaging to the accused. An armchair had been badly burnt, and the carpet under it, but there was an unburnt strip of carpet between the chair and the gas-stove which was at first supposed to have caused the conflagration. By what accidental means could a flame have bridged that gap? Moreover, experiments made with the carpet by the chief of the Margate Fire Brigade proved that only some combustible, such as petrol, would burn it as it had been burned. In the hotel bedroom was a bottle of petrol, used by Sidney Fox to clean his only suit.

Equally damaging, as supplying motive, was the evidence of the insurance policies expiring at midnight on that 23rd of October. The background of the prosecution's case was filled in by hotel managers who had been defrauded, by the disproving of the accused's many and often silly lies about his mother's financial position and his own upbringing, and by the proof, which all this revealed, of the desperate situation to which this pair's long career of dishonesty had brought them. The law might deal leniently with an ailing woman of sixty-three, but it would be a different matter for Sidney Fox. The jury at Lewes knew nothing of his criminal record: they did not guess, when Chief-Inspector Hambrook was in the witness-box, that he had arrested Fox for forgery thirteen years before; but they must have felt certain that the latter's discreditable past went further back than his last few weeks of swindling in Kent, and that he had more to gain by his mother's death than relief from immediate difficulties. It is probable, in fact, that had things gone as he planned he intended to leave England for good.

Medical evidence for the prosecution began with that of the doctors called to the Metropole on the night of the fire. Mrs Fox had been lying across her bed, an odd position, when other guests at the hotel entered the smoke-filled room and carried her out; the body had been laid in another room before the two doctors arrived. Only Dr Austin made any sort of examination of it. Dr Nichol now said he was not satisfied with the cause of death; had the matter been in his hands he would have had a post-mortem. He had inspected the bedroom, and was puzzled by the gap between the burn in the carpet and the fireplace containing the gas-stove. These witnesses were in the box on the third day of the trial; it was not until the fifth day that Spilsbury began his evidence. He was preceded by Roche Lynch, who, at his request, had made tests for alcohol as well as for poison, and had found traces of the former. Sidney Fox had bought half a bottle of port for his mother a few hours before her death. If she drank a good deal of it, as the traces discovered some weeks after indicated, she was probably in a heavy sleep when her son's hands first went about her throat.

The defence in a trial for murder in this country is kept informed of the case it will have to answer, and this, moreover, has usually been developed at some length at preliminary proceedings in a lower court. Spilsbury, like most of the other witnesses now appearing at Lewes for the prosecution, had said all that he had to say two months earlier before the Margate magistrates. There were four crucial points in his evidence, as Fox's counsel knew—two negative and two positive. Examined by the Attorney-General, he now said that though Rosaline Fox had a slight disease of the heart, among other common symptoms of senile change, in addition to the paralysis agitans from which she had suffered, he found nothing to account for sudden death from heart failure or shock. Nor had she died from suffocation by smoke. He had examined the body, and made microscopical tests, for soot or carbon dioxide. His tests would have shown anything over 20 per cent. The lowest amount he had ever known to cause death was 45 per cent.—as a rule it was nearer 70 per cent. He found no traces at all. In his own words, the effects of the fire in the room could be eliminated.

He then produced a model of the human mouth, showing part of the air passages, the jaw, and the tongue. After explaining where he had looked for soot on the lining of the passages he pointed out the spot, at the back of the larynx, where he had found a large, recent bruise. In his opinion it was caused by some mechanical violence, a breaking or tearing of small blood-vessels. "It was then," he said, "that I had the first indication of the conclusions to which I finally came, that death was due to strangulation."

He also found, by making transverse cuts across the tongue, a bruise invisible to the naked eye midway between the tip and the back. Mrs Fox had false teeth, which after her death were found in the bedroom basin; the bruise was probably caused by the back teeth during the act of strangulation. He could not account for it in any other way. After mentioning further conditions very characteristic of death by this means Spilsbury answered a final question from the Attorney-General by saying that, having weighed all the facts, he could come to no other conclusion than that Mrs Fox had died of strangulation by hand, probably while asleep and before the fire started—certainly before there was any appreciable amount of smoke in the room.

Mr Cassels, in cross-examination, did not press the question of soot in the air-passages. If Spilsbury said there was no soot it could be taken that there was none; nor was the defence based on the theory that Mrs Fox died of asphyxiation. The bruise on the larynx, which had vanished in corruption before any second person except the Chief Constable of Norfolk could see it, was a very different matter. But here Cassels ran up against Spilsbury's most positive mood. "It was a bruise, and nothing else. There are no two opinions about it." Having, in fact (as Spilsbury himself very well knew), two medical witnesses who would say that it was not a bruise, but a mark of putrefaction, counsel abandoned this point for the moment, and raised that of a tiny bone in the larynx called the hyoid, which in old people becomes brittle and easily broken. Spilsbury agreed that though the dead woman's hyoid was intact, he had broken it by a little pressure; but he added that he had with him notes of six cases of manual strangulation, the victims being of various ages up to fifty-six, and in only one was the hyoid fractured. When the theory of the defence was indicated by questions about the effect on an elderly person's heart of sudden exertion, such as getting out of bed in a panic, he replied that paralysis agitans, by slowing down the power of movement, was actually a protection against sudden death from this cause.

The last witness for the prosecution, Dr Henry Weir, a pathologist and authority on diseases of the heart, in substance supported Spilsbury's opinions. Dr Weir summed up his views in reply to a final question in re-examination: "In my opinion death was due to heart failure due to partial strangulation, to commencing strangulation. In other words, that the strangulation in itself did not cause death, but brought on heart failure." The marks on the larynx and tongue, which he had seen on Spilsbury's microscopical slides, must have been caused by violence.

Sidney Fox gave evidence on his own behalf—a well-dressed young man, too cool and confident, with drooping left eyelid like Neville Heath's, and a voice described as "the acquired-genteel type." He made a terrible slip while being cross-examined. Mrs Fox's bedroom at the Metropole had two doors. Both were closed when the rescuers arrived. Fox was asked by the Attorney-General why, after opening the door communicating with his own room and being driven back by smoke, he closed the door again, and then, on his way to summon help, closed his own outer door and passed that of his mother's room without opening it. "So that the smoke," was his reply, "should not spread into the hotel." Here was the truth; he could not be sure that he had killed his mother, and she must be left to suffocate as long as possible. It is not known, in fact, how long the fire had been burning before he ran downstairs.

Fox's long tale of lies, like those of so many others in his position, was mercilessly exposed. He was in the witness-box for most of the seventh day of the trial; and in the evening another Sydney, this time a Sydney Smith, Professor of Forensic Medicine in Edinburgh University—he would have been an appropriate witness in an earlier trial for matricide—was called to dispute Spilsbury's conclusions. He was followed, the next day, by Brontë.

It is said of this trial, as it is so often said of others, that it involved a direct conflict of medical evidence. That form of words is seldom strictly correct, because the evidence on which medical witnesses for the prosecution and the defence respectively base their opinions is seldom the same. In the nature of things, the pathologist called in for the Crown is first in the field—sometimes, as in this and in the Thorne case, by several months. He sees symptoms, like the bruise on Mrs Fox's larynx and the mark of the cord round Elsie Cameron's neck, which disappear or alter very rapidly. Both Professor Smith and Brontë were faced with this difficulty—precisely as Brontë himself (as he was now reminded) had been faced with it in this same court five years before almost to a day. Both did their best to convince the jury that Spilsbury did not know the difference between post-mortem discolouration and a bruise. Brontë was, as usual, rather pugnacious. He was compelled, however, to admit the weakness of his position—the weakness inherent in all such cases—when he said of the bruise, "It was not there when I saw the larynx. I cannot say what Sir Bernard Spilsbury saw." That was the trouble; and the contention of Brontë and Professor Smith that Rosaline Fox died of heart failure accelerated by shock was vitiated by the fact that Spilsbury had seen something which, through no fault of their own, they could not see.

There was never much hope for Sidney Fox, though in his conceit he may not have realized this until the end. He must have realized it then, for he is one of the very few convicted murderers who, since the foundation of the Court of Criminal Appeal, have not appealed to it.

Chapter 8: "THESE VILE GUNS"

THE earliest of Spilsbury's cases of murder by shooting to excite much public interest was the killing of Jacob Dickey by Alexander Mason in May 1923. Poor Dickey had posthumous fame thrust upon him because he was the first taxi-driver to be murdered; but as the story unfolded, and long after it was officially closed, less irrational reasons kept interest and concern alive. These had nothing to do with the medical evidence, and though Spilsbury performed the post-mortem on Dickey's body, he was not a witness at the trial. From his point of view the case was adequately epitomized in the six lines he gave it on his card:

> Prisoner took taxi intending to attack and rob the taximan. He fired at deceased's head and deceased did not appear to have been shot but turned and attacked him. He then got deceased's head between his (prisoner's) knees and fired at his head and shoulders. Fired seven shots.

Except for Dickey himself, those concerned in the affair were on the whole a despicable set of people, and it was very largely because the most despicable was called as a witness for the Crown that subsequent trouble arose. There is an analogy here with the later case of Podmore. Moreover, in contrast with that case, the police investigation into Dickey's murder left, for once, a good deal to be desired.

Alexander Mason was a Scot, aged twenty-two, who described himself as a cabinet-maker. He must soon have abandoned this profession; in January 1922 he and James (or "Eddie") Vivian, an American criminal well known to the Metropolitan Police, were convicted in London of housebreaking. Vivian received the heavier sentence because he was carrying a revolver. As soon as Mason was due for release he was taken to Glasgow and given another term of imprisonment for robbing his grandfather. He was free at last on Saturday, May 5, 1923, and the next day he returned to London, paying his fare with £2 which Vivian sent him in the guise of an uncle. He went straight to the room in Pimlico where Vivian was living with (and on) a prostitute named Hettie Colquhoun. There was no question of cabinet-making; two days later the pair, who were almost out of money, were scouting in Norwood for a suitable house to burgle.

The following day was Wednesday, May the 9th. That evening Jacob Dickey was in his cab in the rank outside the Trocadero Restaurant in Shaftesbury Avenue. At a quarter to ten some people in Acre Lane, Brixton, a thoroughfare running into Brixton Hill, saw two men struggling together in a side-street called Baytree Road. Shots were heard; one of the pair then ran off, while the other, who was Dickey, staggered to the street corner, where he collapsed and died. With his last breath he warned the startled witnesses to keep away because his murderer had a revolver.

His cab was standing in Baytree Road, both doors swinging open. Near it, on the ground, were lying a gold-mounted ebony stick, a a right-hand suède glove, a jemmy, and the weapon itself—a seven-chambered American revolver, an unusual make. Six empty cartridges (not seven, as Spilsbury says on his card) and one loaded were in the chambers. Dickey had been shot four times, a bullet through his neck opening the left carotid artery. The other wounds were not serious. He was slightly bruised about the face, knees, and knuckles.

Immediately after the shooting two women in a house in Acre Lane were disturbed by a man in their back garden who frightened them into allowing him to pass through the house to the street. In a neighbouring garden was found the suède glove for the other hand. Footprints suggested that the murderer had crossed a number of gardens and walls in making his escape. This cross-country flight was to raise an important question later in the case.

The gold-headed cane being soon identified as belonging to Eddie Vivian, who had also been known to carry firearms; he was promptly picked up. His story set the police looking for Mason. The latter was detained in the Strand, taken to Brixton, and charged with the murder. Vivian told his story at the police-court proceedings, and again at the inquest, and on neither occasion was it challenged by Mason, who, perhaps unfortunately for himself, reserved his defence. He had asked for legal aid, under the Poor Prisoners Act, and at the police-court had been warned that as the law then stood he could not get it at that stage unless he gave evidence, but the magistrate then went on to advise him to say nothing without the advice of a solicitor or counsel. Mason was in a cleft stick; by taking this well-meant advice he forfeited the moral advantage of denying at once the accusation made against him by his worthless friend. When he did deny it, at his trial, it was too late.

Vivian, worthless though he was, was the Crown's chief witness. By his account, he told Mason, at the latter's request, how to obtain a revolver, and lent him the stick and gloves, but knew nothing more about the affair until Mason returned to Pimlico, dishevelled and bloodstained, saying that he had made "a terrible mess of things." Mason's belated version of the crime was that Vivian had been with him that night and had shot Dickey, the pair escaping together, though by different routes, over the garden walls. Only one fugitive was seen, and there were other very weak points in this story, and at least one provable lie. Mason had a bad time at the hands of Muir, who led for the prosecution; but he had one piece of luck, a serious slip remaining undiscovered until some time later. The judge, Rigby Swift, had no doubt that he was guilty, and the jury came to the same conclusion in seventeen minutes.

Mason's appeal was dismissed; but he was not to hang. As in Podmore's case, there was strong feeling about the tainted character of the evidence against him. His youth and deceptively ingenuous looks roused sympathy, and it was realized that he had handicapped himself by accepting the advice to reserve his defence at the police-court. The fact that both doors of Dickey's cab were open lent some support to the assumption that there were two passengers. Mason's counsel, A. C. Fox-Davies, was a very brilliant man who not only combined Chancery and criminal practice, but also wrote novels and a monumental work on heraldry, but his style of advocacy irritated the judge. Swift, for whatever reason, was in one of his harsher moods, and his summing-up, though strictly fair, was dead against the prisoner. He did, indeed, comment severely on some of the police work, in particular the production of a plan based upon an Ordnance map of the Acre Lane district which, though sworn to as accurate, was out of date and misleading. Sixty thousand people signed a petition for a reprieve, and, whether or no this influenced the Home Secretary, the death sentence was commuted to one of penal servitude for life. Mason was released after serving fourteen years of it. He died during the Second World War, serving as a seaman in a torpedoed merchantman.

As has been said, in one respect he was lucky. The story of how his life was saved by a thunderstorm has often been told. Muir visited the scene of the crime, as he almost always did in such cases, but on account of the storm he saw it only from a car. After the trial he went to Baytree Road again, and realized that Vivian could not have escaped by the route Mason swore he had taken. The way was blocked by garages built since the production of the map put in evidence.

There was a further singular development some years later. Like Spilsbury, the officer nominally in charge of the case, Superintendent Carlin, was not called as a witness at the trial. In 1927, when he had retired, the superintendent published his memoirs, and in dealing with the murder of Dickey made two remarkable statements. Vivian had sworn that the revolver was never in his possession; he only told Mason how to procure it. Carlin now said that Vivian admitted to him that he himself handed it over to his friend. Secondly, Mason's request for a revolver was alleged to have been made in a letter from Glasgow, which Vivian said he had destroyed. Carlin asserted that he had somehow "secured" this letter, and that it merely asked for money.

These statements, if true, not only discredited the Crown's chief witness, a poor one at the best, but raised some very unpleasant doubts about the whole conduct of the case. It has been charitably assumed that Mr Carlin, who died soon after the publication of his book, wrote it when in poor health and from memory.

In this atmosphere of uncertainty and mishandling lies the real interest of a case which is otherwise out of the common because Spilsbury, after being called in at the start, had nothing more to do with it.

In a country where, as Caroline of Brunswick observed, "*on a diablement peur de la corde*," murder by shooting is seldom premeditated by the sane. The method is so noisy that as a rule it gives the murderer less time for escape than any other. With a few exceptions, even criminals who carry firearms, like Mason and his friend Vivian, only shoot from panic or to clear a way. Until two world wars flooded England with revolvers and automatics there were far more shooting cases in rural districts, where shotguns are common, than in London and other large towns; and even in the country, in the hundred years since James Blomfield Rush tried to pistol an entire household, killing two and wounding two more, premeditated murders by this means have been very rare.

On the other hand, it is fatally easy to pick up and fire a pistol or gun in the heat of temper, or when resisting an attack; and firearms are a dreadful temptation to the homicidal insane. In Spilsbury's long list of shooting fatalities, which includes every kind, murders by demented men or women predominate.

These crimes seem peculiarly tragic because the motive, to a rational mind, is usually so trifling. Sometimes there is no apparent motive at all. Some form of jealousy is at the back of most of them—jealousy of a wife or a husband or a lover, occasionally of a father or mother. The Rutherford case, already told, is typical. Even more senseless, for no third party appears to have been involved, was a murder and suicide which took Spilsbury to Hampstead some twelve years later. Margery Cotterill was only twenty-two when she was shot by her husband in the house of her father, Gerald Lawrence the actor, in July 1930. Mrs Cotterill, who was also on the stage, had married in opposition to her family's wishes. Eardley Cotterill, her husband, was a gramophone engineer whose work often took him abroad. He seems to have been deeply in love with his wife, but her early affection for him did not last, and though there was no open breach, the pair had seen little of one another for a year when Cotterill returned from a visit to Albania, went to the house in Ornan Road, and after a quarrel with his wife shot her four times with a five-chambered revolver and put the last bullet in his own head.

A rural tragedy of the kind poetically associated with Shropshire occurred in the neighbouring county of Hereford in January 1932, and entailed for Spilsbury an exhausting journey in bitter weather. Arriving at Ross-on-Wye at 2.45 P.M., he performed a post-mortem on the body of Benjamin Parry, aged thirty-one, gave evidence at the inquest, and left again for London at 7.20. Parry, a servant at a house called Hunter's Hall, in the village of Lea, died of a gunshot wound in the neck. Mrs Edith May Dampier, his mistress—it was believed in a double sense—said that Parry had shot himself, and he was found sitting in an armchair with the gun between his knees. Spilsbury, however, said that the wound could not have been self-inflicted, and, this opinion being confirmed by Mr Churchill, the gunsmith, Mrs Dampier was arrested. At her trial on a charge of shooting Parry she was found guilty, but unfit to plead.

In these early 1930's Spilsbury was concerned in a number of notorious shooting cases, including one of the few premeditated murders in this class which have remained unsolved, and a fashionable *cause célèbre* in London. The most shocking affair of all, the slaughter of a whole family in Kent, was the result of what seems to have been a sudden fit of homicidal mania in a young man, outwardly sane, who unfortunately had a weapon to hand.

Early in June 1932 Mrs Swift, a woman of sixty-five who managed Ye Olde Sportsman Inn at Seasalter, near Whitstable, arranged an outing with her daughter, Mrs Stemp, who was in the same line of business at Wadhurst. Mrs Stemp's daughter of fifteen was also of the party. In Mrs Swift's car they drove to King's Wood, not far from

Ashford, and picnicked there, at the edge of the trees close to Challock Cross Roads. At this time there was wandering about the wood, with terrible thoughts seething in his suddenly disordered brain, a private of the Buffs named James Thomas Collins. He had come from the musketry school at Hythe, where he was on a course, and he had contrived to bring his rifle with him. His aimless roving brought him upon the party of three, picnicking under the trees, and he shot them all. Mrs Swift died with a sandwich in her hand. The madman took the body of the girl, Peggie, to the car and drove off, startling all who witnessed this demented transit by his wild demeanour. He jettisoned the dead girl at some distance from King's Wood, and left the car at a garage. His murderous mania had spent itself. He menaced some of the army of searchers who later found him hiding in another wood, but he did not fire again.

Though it means looking ahead, some account of the terrible coincidence of 1940 should follow here. In that year there was a second massacre by shooting in the same county. Again Spilsbury went down into Kent—this time to the County Hospital at Pembury, near Tunbridge Wells—to examine the bodies of another trio of women. Mrs Dorothy Fisher and her daughter had been shot dead in a cottage in the village of Matfield. Their housekeeper, Miss Charlotte Saunders, was lying in a wood near by. No weapon was found. Broken crockery in the cottage, when pieced together, showed that tea had been laid for four, and a single woman's glove of white hogskin suggested that there had indeed been a visitor. Spilsbury's post-mortem settled this question, and disposed of the theory originally held (as in the case of Messiter) that Miss Saunders had been killed by a blow on the head. Each of the cards is headed "Shock due to shot-gun injuries. Murder."

The extraordinary family history behind this multiple crime is a warning against mixing the oil and water of regular and irregular unions. Before the outbreak of the Second World War Mr and Mrs Walter Fisher were living with their two daughters at Twickenham. In the common phrase, they had drifted apart. Apparently without any serious thought of divorce, each took a lover. Mrs Fisher's was a Dane, a vague figure who hovers on the outskirts of the case. Mr Fisher's fancy turned to a young widow, Mrs Florence Iris Ouida Ransom, for some reason known as Julia, who had a farm at Piddington, near Bicester, in Oxfordshire. Both the Dane and Mrs Ransom were frequent visitors at the Twickenham house; and when Fisher took a cottage at Matfield, in Kent, and spent week-ends there with his Julia, to all appearance the latter remained on friendly terms with his wife.

When the elder Miss Fisher married she may have been glad to be free of this singular *ménage*. At the outbreak of war the younger daughter, Freda, was nineteen, and her mother forty-seven. The household now broke up: Fisher retired to the farm near Bicester with Mrs Ransom, coming up to his business in London every day, and a little later, in March 1940, Mrs Fisher and the girl went to live at Crittenden, as the Matfield cottage was named. Miss Saunders, a woman of fifty, joined them as housekeeper. If absence did not make the heart grow fonder the show of tolerance and good feeling all round was kept up, and Fisher paid several visits to his wife and daughter.

In July the invasion barges for "Operation Sea-lion" were being assembled at the Channel ports, and the preliminary phase of the Battle of Britain began. There were air battles over Kent. Down in quieter Oxfordshire Mrs Ransom was managing the farm. She now called herself Mrs Fisher. A Mrs Guilford and her son Fred were imported to help about the place, it being concealed from Fisher that they were, in fact, Mrs Ransom's mother and brother.

There is another proverb about absence, to the effect that it inflames violent passions. Mrs Ransom was a woman of unbalanced mind, who in the past had been a patient at hospitals and mental homes. No doubt she was always jealous of Mrs Fisher, though this feeling was also concealed. Brooding over the situation, she may have become suspicious of Fisher's visits to Matfield. She did not know what went on there. On July 8, having asked Fred Guilford to show her how his gun worked, she borrowed it to shoot rabbits. The next morning she was seen, wearing her white hogskin gloves, on the train which left Bicester for Paddington at 8.56. There was a less positive identification of her at Tonbridge in the afternoon. She was back at the farm that night. When Guilford asked for his gun she was reluctant to return it, though she said she was scared of the weapon, and had not used it. She had thrown away the dozen cartridges he had given her.

It was on that day, the 9th, that the triple murder at Matfield took place. After the inquest on the 13th Mrs Ransom was arrested. Statements by Spilsbury and Churchill, the gun expert, had been read. Mrs Fisher had been shot twice in the back, and her daughter three times, also in the back. Miss Saunders had died instantly from a single shot fired close to her head.

Mrs Ransom was tried at the Old Bailey on November 8, before Mr Justice Tucker. The trial had been postponed in order that the prisoner could be kept under medical observation. She herself said that her mind was a blank about all the events of July 9: she did not know what she had been doing. The judge, in his summing-up, remarked that the prosecution relied very largely on the glove found in the cottage. Mrs Ransom was convicted; but in the following month she was pronounced insane, and sent to Broadmoor.

This was an extremely deliberate crime. It would seem, from the presence of the fourth tea-cup, that Mrs Ransom had invited herself to the cottage, which was on the telephone. A friendly tea-party was of a piece with the curious manner in which the Fisher family had long conducted its amatory affairs. The borrowed weapon was an ordinary shot-gun, single-barrelled and a single-loader; it was heavy, with a stiff pull, and very unlikely, in Mr Churchill's opinion, to go off accidentally. The cartridges fitted tightly, and were difficult to extract. How Mrs Ransom contrived to shoot both Mrs Fisher and her daughter in the back will never be known; having done so, she loaded and unloaded three more times to make certain. The circumstances of Miss Saunders's death are equally obscure. The murderess remembered to collect the used cartridge-cases, which were never found. Neither were the six unused, and her reluctance to return the gun suggests that she had suicide—or another murder—in her disordered mind. Had she been as careful about retrieving her glove she might be free to-day.

3

In the first week of October 1931 Spilsbury was at Oxford, combining lectures with conferences in connexion with the trial of Henry Seymour, Mrs Kempson's murderer, which was to open on the 20th. On the 5th he received a call for help from Superintendent Hambrook, of the C.I.D., who was at the Coverdale Kennels, Tarrant Keynston, near Blandford, in Dorset. Spilsbury left Oxford that afternoon, fitted in a post-mortem at Holborn on the way, and arrived at Blandford about eleven o'clock in the evening. At 11.30 he began his examination of the body of Edward George Welham, who had died in hospital on the 2nd of shot-gun injuries inflicted the day before.

It must have seemed that fatality pursued the Coverdale Kennels. They were the hobby of a Christchurch business man interested in sporting dogs, who established them in 1929 and put in as first manager and trainer William Steer. A few months later Steer was found shot in a badger-hole, a 12-bore gun by his side. His death was accepted as accidental. He was succeeded by Welham, a young bachelor of twenty-four. On the morning of October 1, 1931, Welham in turn was discovered lying shot on the floor of his office, a room formed by running up partitions in the middle of a long Army hut used for the kennels. One of his guns, a 16-bore, was beneath him. A single charge had torn through his shoulder and entered his neck and head. He had fallen on his back, and when shot appeared to have been sitting or standing at a knee-hole desk under the office window.

Dr Kenneth Wilson, who examined the body next day at Blandford Hospital, did not know that a piece of evidence suggestive of suicide had been removed before the police reached the kennels; but even if he had not made a study of shot-wounds it is unlikely that he would have been misled by it. It was obvious to him that Welham had been shot in the back, at a range of several feet, and could not have contrived to inflict such a wound himself. At the inquest, which opened on the 3rd, this testimony led to the Chief Constable of Dorset calling in Scotland Yard.

Spilsbury's examination confirmed Dr Wilson's opinion. The charge of shot had spread considerably, for there were two separate areas of injuries, 3½ inches apart, and that on the neck and head measured 6 inches by 8. The wounds passed obliquely upward. Spilsbury refers to experiments made by him and Mr Hambrook, and later by a Dorchester gunsmith, Mr Allen Jeffrey.

> Body placed in sitting posture and shoulders bent forward as much as possible. The largest ragged wound at back of head was 2 ft. 11 in. above table, and the lower wounds in shoulder area were 1 ft. 9½ in. above table.
>
> I saw a board traversed by shot holes which was removed from wall of room in which deceased was found shot. I also saw a board which had been the target at which the sporting gun was fired at different ranges.

His "Conclusions" follow:

> All injuries caused by single discharge which had caught shoulder obliquely from below upwards, causing superficial injuries, the main effects being in head; the fissured fracture was ass effect of discharge in left side of head. From direction of shot holes in wall, weapon was horizontal when fired. Deceased must have had his back to weapon, and must have been bending forward over table at side of which his body was found. The lateral spread of shot at back of shoulder was rather more than 3 inches. Experiments with weapon therefore indicate discharge from several feet at least. Wounds therefore could not have been self-inflicted.

In fact, Mr Jeffrey's experiment proved from the spread of the shot that the gun had been fired into Welham's back at a range of more than 12 feet. The door of the office and the desk under the window were in line, and the distance between them was 13 feet. In Mr Hambrook's words: "Welham was shot by some person who stood in the doorway and thrust the muzzle of the gun slightly through the opening."

Spilsbury having left, on his way back to London and Oxford, the superintendent continued an investigation the difficulties of which were to be increased by the attitude of Welham's neighbours. The dead man had been well liked, but the people of Tarrant Keynston were determined to ignore the evidence of murder. It was a plain case of accident or suicide, and further inquiries were hampered by a conspiracy of silence. No one knew anything. So pronounced was this hostility, of which Mr Hambrook says, "I cannot very well deal with it in print," that a most unusual course was taken by the rector of the parish, who from the pulpit asked his parishioners to help the police —in other words, not to obstruct them.

Only a small group of persons was in close contact with Welham during his working hours—a young assistant named Frederick Deamen, Mary Hathaway, the kennel-maid, and her parents and brother. Welham lodged with this family. Miss Hathaway did not come to the kennels until the afternoon; the story told by Deamen, who was there as usual on the morning of the shooting, was that shortly before ten o'clock Welham sent him to look for a blind spaniel to which the young trainer was much attached. When about 120 yards from the hut Deamen heard a shot, but thought nothing of it. Having retrieved the spaniel, which had wandered some distance, he returned to the kennels to find his employer lying in a pool of blood. He ran at once to the Hathaways' cottage, which was less than a quarter of a mile away, and Thomas Hathaway, the father, a man of sixty, came back with him, followed after a few minutes by Mary Hathaway and her brother. It was the girl who noticed that Welham's jacket, which he usually kept fastened, was unbuttoned, and that his wallet was sticking half out of the inside pocket.

The next to arrive was the police constable stationed in the village. Like everybody else, he knew a good deal about shot-guns, and, his first impression being that it was a case of suicide, he looked about for the means by which Welham had reached the trigger of the long-barrelled weapon while holding the muzzle to the back of his head. It was usual, as the officer remarked, to find a stick or string in such a case. To this prophetic observation Deamen and Hathaway replied that they had moved nothing.

The case bristled with interesting features. The kennels stood in a small plot of land bounded by a road and the little river Tarrant.

Attached to them were 600 acres of shooting, and quite close to the building was Ashley Wood, in which Steer had been found shot. A kale field across the road was a favourite hunting-ground of the blind spaniel, and here Deamen heard the dog barking just before the sound of the explosion in the hut reached him.

It was plain that the murder itself had been premeditated. Welham had two guns, the 16-bore and a 12-bore. They were kept in the hut, in a cupboard beside his desk. The younger Hathaway stated that on the evening before the tragedy he cleaned both guns, at Welham's request, after which the pair went out shooting with the 12-bore. This was replaced in the cupboard beside the 16-bore, which was clean and unloaded. The next morning, as usual, Welham went to the kennels before breakfast, for which he returned to the Hathaways' house at eight o'clock. It is Superintendent Hambrook's belief that during this absence the murderer entered the hut and took the gun. He must then have withdrawn to cover, of which there was plenty near at hand. Perhaps he merely hid behind a corner of the hut until Welham came back.

If, however, he came and went twice unseen he must have owed as much to luck as to timing. The door of the office faced the road, but while Welham was away at breakfast Deamen was somewhere on the other side of the thin partition, cleaning the kennels. Though the blind spaniel crossed the road to the kale field almost every morning, it could scarcely be foreseen that Welham, on his return, would decide to go shooting and send Deamen to fetch the dog. (Incidentally, had Welham then opened the cupboard door he could have seen that the 16-bore was missing.) As soon as Deamen was out of sight behind a hedge, though little more than a hundred yards away, the murderer came out from his hiding-place and fired into Welham's back from the door of the office. If he could not see Deamen he could hear him calling for the dog. He had time to thrust the gun beneath the dying man's shoulders, and to take the wallet from the jacket pocket. A pound note was found in the wallet, but it was learnt that Welham should have been carrying about £10. It was literally a matter of seconds for the murderer, and he left untouched another £9 in the desk.

Such, at least, is one reconstruction of the murder. The facts remain unknown, or undisclosed. Superintendent Hambrook, necessarily cautious, says, "I think I know who committed the crime." The evidence, however, was insufficient to justify a charge. He could discover no other motive but the money in Welham's possession, and though a few pounds seems miserably disproportionate to the careful planning, the brutality of the crime itself, and the risks involved, murder has been done for less.

The superintendent was barely back at Scotland Yard, with his case in the unsatisfactory state in which it remains to-day, when he learnt of another instance of the obstruction from which he had already suffered. That it was well-meant was small comfort to him. Thomas Hathaway confessed that he had lied to the local policeman. Something *had* been moved from the hut. When Hathaway entered, with Deamen, he saw leaning against some sacks a long stick of hazel, from which a string trailed across the floor to the trigger of the gun. The string had come away from the trigger, and Hathaway, instantly thinking of suicide, and of the added distress this act would cause to Welham's mother and family, seized an opportunity to slip the cord from the stick and pocket it. Of all this, apparently, Deamen knew nothing.

Fortunately, the stick was left in the office, and Hathaway kept the string. When conscience moved Hathaway to admit what he had done Superintendent Hambrook went down to Dorset again. Experiments showed that the gun could not have been fired, in the way it must have been fired, by any such device. The discovery was further proof of premeditation. But it came too late to be of any help to the superintendent in proving his case.

Andrew Lang used to say that in his youth there were still people in Argyll who knew the secret of the Appin murder of 1752, when Campbell of Glenure was shot, as described in *Kidnapped*. Clannishness, as Mr Hambrook found to his cost, is not peculiar to Scotland, nor is oral tradition; and Dorset folk, a hundred years hence, recalling among themselves a story handed down from father to son, may be naming the murderer of Edward Welham.

4

A fortnight before Private Collins went berserk with a rifle in Kent a sensation on a different social stratum had burst upon a delighted London. On the morning of May 21 the police were summoned, not for the first time, to No. 21 Williams Mews, off Lowndes Square, which runs south from Knightsbridge near Sloane Street. The mews, like so many in London, had in course of time justified the origin of its name: coachman's quarters were changed into maisonettes, and garages became lounges. In No. 21 lived Mrs Elvira Dolores Barney; and here, in the early hours of that morning, a young man named William Thomas Scott Stephen had been shot in the lung, a wound of which he died within ten minutes.

Mrs Barney, who was separated from her husband, was the daughter of very rich parents: her father, Sir John Mullens, had been Government Broker, and lived in Belgrave Square. She was twenty-seven, and would inevitably have been described as beautiful had she been the reverse, just as everything about her little two-floored dwelling was called luxurious. Photographs of her published by the Press showed a handsome young woman, but this was not the Mrs Barney of 1932. The sort of life she led had coarsened her looks, and she was growing stout. She might have been ten years older than her age, and Sir Patrick Hastings, who defended her at her trial, says of her that she was "a melancholy and somewhat depressing figure."

This degradation is important, for she must have been aware of it, and no doubt it made her the more possessive and jealous of the worthless young man who had become her lover, and who, in spite of the powerful attraction of her money, showed a tendency to wander after fresher charms. Scott Stephen was only twenty-four, but his father had already cut off his allowance, and even his mother had closed her purse to him. He was without occupation, unless hanging on the fringe of what was called the Smart Set can be so described, and his only home was in Williams Mews. He and Mrs Barney talked of marriage, if she could get a divorce, and as his family had more or less washed their hands of him, their discouragement of this final folly may have been as much for her sake as for his.

Mrs Barney drank too much, and, Stephen being what he was, their relationship was an unhappy alternation of passion and violent quarrels, which were the talk of the mews. Ten days before Stephen's death, according to one story, Mrs Barney had leaned out her bedroom window with little or nothing on and fired a revolver at him. If she did her aim was poor. Stephen, having nowhere else to go, was said to have spent the rest of the night in a van standing in the mews.

On the evening of the 30th Mrs Barney, like Hans Breitmann, gave a party. It was the last of many which had often kept her neighbours awake into the small hours. One had ended in the police being summoned to quell the noise. They were called another time by Mrs Barney herself, who wanted Stephen ejected. On the 30th about a score of people were there, but the party ended early. Mrs Barney and Stephen drove to the Café de Paris, and then to the Blue Angel Club in Dean Street, while quiet settled down on Williams Mews. It was broken soon after 4 A.M. by the familiar sounds of a quarrel at No. 21. Mrs Barney was heard screaming that she would shoot some one, and one or more shots followed.

Inured to this sort of thing, Williams Mews did nothing about it, though it heard further outcries, now uttered in fright and anguish. It was Mrs Barney who called a doctor by telephone at a quarter to five. He arrived to find her partially sobered but hysterical, and the body of Scott Stephen lying on the upper landing near the bathroom door. A small revolver was beside him.

The police having come once more, Detective-Inspector Winter took charge, and Spilsbury, at Verulam Buildings, was called out of bed. Constables were counting glasses and gin bottles, and the inspector, surveying the depressing scene by the merciless early light while he tried to get a coherent statement from Mrs Barney, must have been wondering to himself, "Vere ish dot barty now?" Some members of it were to prove very shy. It was perhaps one of them who rang up within an hour or two of the calamity to say that he had heard that something had happened, and wanted news. He would give no name, nor did he accept a cordial invitation to come round and explain who he was and how he knew that anything had happened.

In this sort of pocket pandemonium, with large men tramping all over the little house, a gaping crowd outside, and Mrs Barney still hysterical, often abusive, sometimes violent, and sometimes reverting tragically to childhood and calling wildly for her mother, Spilsbury was on his knees by the body on the narrow landing. Stephen had been shot at close quarters in the chest, the bullet passing through his lung and coming to rest against a fractured rib. The flow of blood downward from the wound indicated that he had been standing when shot and had remained erect for a few minutes. He had coughed up blood and slightly spattered the passage wall. His clothes were not scorched, and there were no powder-stains on his hands. The revolver beside him was a five-chambered .32 of American make. It had been fully loaded. A fact to be useful to Mrs Barney was that though there were two spent cases, between them was a live cartridge.

Other features were to emerge which went some way to support her story, which she never varied. The revolver was hers; on the night of the party she threatened to shoot herself, as she had pretended to do before, and while Stephen was trying to keep the weapon from her, and she struggled with him, it went off. Until he died he kept repeating, "It is not your fault." Largely, however, as a result of the findings of Spilsbury and Mr Churchill, the authority on firearms, on June 3 Mrs Barney was arrested on the capital charge. Her trial began at the Old Bailey a month later, the judge being Travers Humphreys. Sir Percival Clarke led for the Crown, and Patrick Hastings for the defence.

The behaviour of the crowd of smartly dressed women who packed the court, among them friends of the accused, from whom they had received kindness and hospitality, did much to arouse feelings of sympathy for Mrs Barney. It recalled the trial of George Joseph Smith, and Hastings made the most of it. His conduct of the case was a brilliant piece of advocacy. Though nominally on the defensive, he attacked from the start. He was well supported by his client. A month in prison had, temporarily at least, recalled Mrs Barney to her senses, and she made a good witness.

Some of those for the prosecution, on the other hand, fared badly under cross-examination, and Hastings was only really afraid of two —Spilsbury and Churchill. His appreciation of Spilsbury, in connexion with this case, has been quoted elsewhere, with his story of how the latter was ordered out of court for the first time for many years. Hastings having asked that all witnesses should be made to leave, it is significant to find the judge inquiring if he included Spilsbury. Hastings said he would prefer him to go with the rest. When Spilsbury returned, to give his own evidence, it was, says Hastings, "rather damaging." So was that of Churchill. "Both cast doubts on the prisoner's version."

Churchill, who was called first, said that the revolver used was one of the safest types made. The hammer could not be cocked by hand; a long pull on the trigger was needed to raise the internal hammer and revolve the drum. He had experimented with a similar weapon, and when aiming at his coat lapel had great difficulty in pulling the trigger, the guard of which admitted only one finger.

Spilsbury followed. He had heard, at the police-court, Mrs Barney's account of the struggle for the revolver. His opinion, based on the position and direction of the wound, and the distance, some three inches, from which the shot must have been fired, was that such an accident as she described was very improbable, even if Stephen was holding the pistol by the butt, with his finger on the trigger. Held in this way, and twisted towards him, it was unlikely that the muzzle would be so far from his clothes as to fail to scorch them. On the other hand, if Mrs Barney gripped the butt, and Stephen the short barrel, after the discharge the latter's hand would have shown traces of powder-blackening. In short, either there was no struggle, or at the moment of firing the two were standing apart, and since suicide was not suggested, Mrs Barney must have fired the shot.

Cross-examination of Spilsbury was always a thankless task, and Hastings now took the unusual course of not attempting it. He asked three questions only. First, what tests had Spilsbury made to confirm his argument that the bullet had travelled horizontally? Spilsbury replied that his tests had been carried out on a skeleton. One of Stephen's ribs was fractured by the bullet, and Hastings next inquired if it was not a fact that the relative position of human bones varied slightly from case to case. Spilsbury agreed that this was so. Asked finally if the best test of the line of flight would not be a post-mortem examination, he agreed to this also. Being Spilsbury, he was content with "Yes." Hastings had now done with him, and it was left to the judge to extract the further answer that he had, in fact, performed the post-mortem. Hastings knew this perfectly well. Travers Humphreys saw to it that every one else knew it too.

Question and answer had lasted less than a minute. A recent newspaper article, by the hand which made such a hash of Spilsbury's evidence at the trial of Podmore, describes the episode as follows:

> Spilsbury was subjected to the most gruelling cross-examination any expert witness has ever undergone in a murder trial. And as he left the box, two hot, angry patches suffused his smoothly shaven cheeks, evidence of the merciless handling he had received from Sir Patrick.

Journalism of this type is easy game, but such a complete travesty of the facts goes beyond accepted limits. It does as much disservice to Patrick Hastings, whose decision not to cross-examine was an astute tactical move, as to Spilsbury himself.

The tactical move was made possible because Hastings had other cards in his hands. A good deal had been made of two points which seemed to tell heavily against his client—the earlier shooting from her bedroom window and the assertions of several witnesses that at least two shots had been fired on the night of May 30/31. As to the former incident, Mrs Barney denied firing from the window. It was one of the occasions on which she had threatened suicide, and to frighten Stephen, who had ended a too familiar scene by walking out, she fired into the wall. As some corroboration of this story, there was a bullet-hole in the wall, and the most careful examination of the ground outside failed to find a bullet or any mark of one. A flash said to have been seen may have been an instance of association of ideas, often misleading and dangerous in courts of law, for the same or another witness spoke of smoke issuing from the revolver. The cartridges used were charged with smokeless powder.

The defence further contended that this shot accounted for one of the spent cases found in the revolver. The position of the second spent case, separated from the other by a live round, became therefore of importance. Had Mrs Barney fired twice at Stephen she would have fired successive rounds. Confident witnesses who had heard more than one shot became less confident when cross-examined. When Hastings came to the words said to have been uttered by Mrs Barney, "I will shoot you," he argued very plausibly that this was another case of imagination aiding memory, and that what she had really cried out was, "I will shoot"—meaning that she would shoot herself. It was brought out in evidence that Stephen had said he was afraid of her committing suicide in one of these hysterical tantrums.

It was not only the newspapers which fostered the impression that the people of Sybaris scarcely lived as luxuriously as Mrs Barney in her converted coachman's quarters in a mews; Sir Percival Clarke described these as "extravagantly furnished," though at least one room was not furnished at all. Hastings, in his final speech, was justifiably scathing about exaggerations which created prejudice among the censorious and less well-to-do. A trial for murder is no occasion for flippancy, and the point was not made that such people should have been disillusioned by the revelations of the life led by Mrs Barney and her circle. What with quarrels, hang-overs, revolvers, and a quite remarkable amount of talk about suicide, the Bright Young Things appeared to take their pleasures sadly.

No hint of what the judge thought was allowed to emerge in his charge to the jury, which Hastings describes as "absolutely dispassionate and scrupulously fair." Travers Humphreys paid a well-deserved compliment to the "remarkable forensic effort" of the leading counsel for the defence. If the jury took two hours to make up their minds, the evidence they had heard was very nicely balanced, and they had been given a choice of three verdicts—murder, manslaughter, and acquittal. They chose the last.

Mrs Barney, as if determined to make her life a moral tale, resumed her old habits, and died in Paris a few years later.

5

The choice put before the jury in her case is typical of trials for murder by shooting, in which (when insanity is not an issue) the possibility of manslaughter or accident is more often present in the minds of jurymen than in any other class of capital case. Scientific evidence, even that of such authorities as Spilsbury and Churchill, carries less than its usual weight when a firearm is the weapon employed. There are almost always other confusing factors, including, as often as not, a struggle. The trial of John Donald Merrett is exceptional, for here everything hung upon the scientific evidence called in formidable strength by both sides; nevertheless (or because this evidence seemed to cancel out) the jury was unable to agree. Manslaughter being out of the question and suicide most improbable, it fell back upon the peculiar verdict of "Not Proven." (It may be suggested that if this way out was available to English juries they would most often take it in cases of shooting.) Of nearly two hundred trials for murder in which Spilsbury was called as a witness for the Crown, only a handful ended in an acquittal; and they are almost all shooting cases. In a number of others a charge of murder by shooting was reduced to manslaughter.

This was the upshot of the Casserley case, which made news in the spring of 1938. In the interim between the acquittal of Mrs Barney and the trial of Edward Chaplin for killing Percy Casserley, Spilsbury helped to investigate a murder of which something should be said, because it has features which seem without parallel. It is not strictly a shooting case; but before the victim was strangled and flung into a water-tank she had been shot. Spilsbury had to decide what she had died of.

On November 25, 1934, her body was recovered from the water-tank by the Brighton police after two men had reported hearing shots and screams near East Brighton Golf Course, which extends across the Downs between Preston and Moulscombe. She was identified as Edith Drew-Bear, a cinema attendant, aged twenty-one. Spilsbury carried out the post-mortem two days later. Miss Drew-Bear had been shot five times in the back and head, but none of these wounds was fatal; the bullets were only of .22 calibre, and had slight penetration. Nor had she been drowned. The cause of death was strangulation, after the shooting, by means of a silk scarf knotted tightly under her chin.

Percy Charles Anderson, the thoroughgoing young degenerate who killed her, had in his pocket when arrested a bottle of irritant poison, a mixture of ammonia chloride and zinc chloride; in his rooms were bullets identical with those which had wounded Miss Drew-Bear, together with other cartridges, a home-made pistol, a sheathed knife, a loaded stick, and the empty container of a second pistol called "The Walden Safety Revolver." This was a twelve-chambered weapon firing .22 ammunition. Presumably the one used against Anderson's victim, it was never found. Though its ammunition had small penetrative power, the shock of the wounds inflicted on Edith Drew-Bear would have been enough, in Spilsbury's opinion, to render her unconscious.

The owner of this collection of weapons and poison admitted having been with the young woman on the day of her death. After a quarrel with her, and a swim in the sea to cool himself off, his mind, like Mrs Ransom's, became conveniently blank; and at his trial at the Lewes Assizes in the following March insanity was pleaded. The murder was not unfairly described as maniacal, and Spilsbury, when cross-examined, agreed that a maniacal attack was one showing a complete lack of reason. He added, however, in reply to the Lord Chief Justice, that the use of the word 'maniacal' in such a case did not mean that the attacker suffered from mania. In a summing-up in which Lord Hewart referred to Spilsbury as "that wonderful witness, so fair, so clear," he made it plain that 'maniacal,' like 'safety,' could have more than one meaning. Anderson was convicted. After he had been executed at Wandsworth Spilsbury performed the post-mortem.

If Spilsbury's evidence at the trial of Mrs Barney was considered damaging, what he had to say at that of Edward Royal Chaplin, six years later, must at one time have seemed conclusive. Again, however, the uncertainties so often inherent in shooting cases were strikingly demonstrated. Norman Birkett, for the defence, made the most of them, and though his client did not go free, the conviction was for manslaughter, not the murder of which Chaplin was accused.

Percy Casserley, a man of fifty-eight, had been a director of a brewing firm until a few months before his death. He and his wife, who was more than twenty years the younger, lived in very comfortable circumstances in a modern detached house in Wimbledon. Casserley was a heavy drinker, apt to be quarrelsome and violent when in his cups, and a habit of keeping a loaded revolver at hand was to hasten his end. On March 22, 1938, he returned home from the last of several visits to what was described as a nursing home for nervous complaints. Late on the following evening Mrs Casserley ran to a neighbour with the news that while she was out some one had broken into the house and injured her husband. Casserley was lying on the floor of the lounge, shot through the head. He died soon after the police came.

The Casserleys had some good table silver, and cups and goblets from a sideboard were laid out on the dining-room carpet. With them was a heavy torch, dented and bloodstained. The only thing missing, however, was Percy Casserley's revolver. He had been hit about the head as well as shot, and first appearances suggested that, having disturbed a thief at work, he had run to the lounge for this weapon; the intruder had followed him, clubbed him with the torch, and in the course of a struggle wrenched the revolver from him. This theory entailed a number of improbabilities, but, in the words of a Press report, "All the resources of Scotland Yard were called on in the widespread hunt for the gunman-burglar."

Spilsbury, though one of these resources, did not see the body until the 25th, some thirty-six hours after the crime. On the previous day, while he was busy with post-mortems at St Pancras, Marylebone, and Paddington, his friend Dr Gardner, from Weybridge, performed the first autopsy on Casserley. Already the theory of the gunman-burglar, if the police ever seriously held it, had been abandoned. The Casserleys' maid having talked freely, Mrs Casserley and Edward Chaplin, a builder's foreman, had come under suspicion.

The two were about the same age. During Casserley's absences at the home for nervous complaints Chaplin had stayed at the Wimbledon house, and Mrs Casserley at Chaplin's flat. She was about to become the mother of his child, and her husband refused to divorce her. These and other circumstances, among them the absence of any sign that the house had been broken into, put a different complexion on the evidence of the silver on the dining-room floor. Chaplin having made a statement, he was taken into custody. On the 29th of the month he took the police to the place where he had hidden the missing revolver. Spilsbury's post-mortem report appearing to throw doubt on Chaplin's story, the latter was charged with the murder of Casserley. Mrs Casserley was also put under arrest, as accessory after the fact; but on account of her state of health she was allowed to remain with friends, and later to go into a nursing home.

Chaplin's version of what had happened on the evening of March 23 was that he had gone to see Casserley to have a frank discussion of the situation. When he said he was the father of Mrs Casserley's child Casserley became abusive and attacked him. As the two men struggled together up and down the lounge Chaplin, in self-defence, hit out with the torch he had with him. Casserley, being in a blind rage, further injured himself by blundering into the furniture and falling. He then went to a bureau and took out the revolver; attempting to wrest this from him, Chaplin forced his hand upward, and the weapon went off. Mrs Casserley then appeared on the scene, and while her husband was breathing his last the evidence of breaking and entering was hastily improvised.

Spilsbury's reconstruction of events was different. It was the result of two visits to the house. Casserley had been struck three violent blows on the top and back of the head, causing lacerated wounds.

There were abrasions and bruises on his face, bruises on his back, and others on his hands and forearms, caused as he tried to protect himself. A trail of blood spots suggested that while in a dazed condition he had fallen over the back of a chair, but such a fall could not have produced any of his injuries. At some time after he received these he was shot twice. One bullet went through the skin at the back of the neck, and had been fired from a distance of at least six inches; the second and fatal bullet-wound was just in front of the left ear, the revolver muzzle having been pressed close to the skin, which was blackened. This bullet passed through the brain, and was found by Dr Gardner between the brain and the right wall of the skull.

A significant discovery was made by Mr Churchill when he examined the revolver. Owing to a defect in the mechanism it had to be hand-fed.

Chaplin and Mrs Casserley having been committed for trial at the end of April, an application for separate trials was granted by Mr Justice Humphreys, who was to preside at both. That of Chaplin began on the 25th. During Spilsbury's evidence Norman Birkett, who led for the defence, objected to the witness's use of the word 'attack.' "It is not in his province to speak of attack; it is a matter which is being investigated." "What phrase," asked the judge, "do you suggest he should use? Somebody who hit him?" Birkett rejoined that the whole point of the defence was that there was no attack by Chaplin, whereupon Travers Humphreys, in his dry voice, proposed the phrase, "The individual who caused the injury." "I think it is splitting hairs," said Spilsbury.

So, in a sense, it was, but the defence had to do everything in its power to impress upon the jury that Casserley was the aggressor. Birkett seized every opportunity to do this, and to emphasize features undoubtedly in favour of the accused. Casserley was a wronged man, violent when in drink, jumpy and more than usually irascible when deprived of it, as he had been in the nursing home. Most important point of all, the revolver was his, and there was no proof that Chaplin knew where it was kept. Skilful advocacy drove home the element of doubt so common in shooting cases, and the jury gave the prisoner the benefit of it. He was, however, sentenced to twelve years' penal servitude for manslaughter.

As accessory after the fact, Mrs Casserley received a sentence of eleven days, and was immediately released.

Chapter 9: QUEER CASES AND ODD ENDS

Masochistic practices were old when Clement VI denounced the Order of Flagellants in the fourteenth century, the Catholic Church having a very good idea of what impelled men, in the name of religion, to walk naked in procession through the streets, flogging each other until the blood ran. Some of these practices entail risks worse than blood-letting. In January 1935 Mr Justice Atkin was reading a paper to the Medico-Legal Society on "Murder from the Point of View of the Psychiatrist," in the course of which he said:

> In masochism the man or woman derives sex gratification from physical discomfort or pain and moral humiliation. Sir Bernard Spilsbury has called attention recently to accidental deaths in men due to this cause, and considers it possible that some cases of suspected murder may be due to masochistic practices.

Spilsbury had experience of several of these rare cases. Two led to charges of murder, and in a third there was natural suspicion of foul play until his testimony established the facts. All these three cases involved that common type of masochism in which a person ties himself up, or causes another to tie him up. In two of them, by an odd chance, the victims bore the same name.

Towards the end of May 1923 Drummer James Frederick Ellis, of the Leicestershire Regiment, stationed at Aldershot, was reported absent without leave. Ellis was twenty-one, and a native of Hull, as was his friend Lance-Corporal Dearnley, the two having joined the Army together. Dearnley, on being questioned after Ellis's disappearance, said that the latter had talked of emigrating to Australia. Ellis, however, was no farther away than the Long Valley, where on September 26 his body was found under some gorse-bushes in a patch of marshy ground. The circumstances were so puzzling that a month later Spilsbury was asked by the Hampshire police to examine the remains.

He found the body to be reduced to a skeleton, except for portions of the lower limbs, which were clothed in tight-fitting garments—

trousers, puttees, and boots. The head had come away from the trunk. Before death Ellis had been tied up very thoroughly with drum-cord, and his head enveloped in an Army coat strapped over nostrils and mouth by a webbing belt. The lower jaw was still held in place by a handkerchief and a piece of cloth tied behind the neck. Another piece of cloth was rolled up between the jaws. As vermin and moisture destroyed the flesh, and damp contracted the twenty feet of stout cord with which the body was trussed like a chicken, breastbone and ribs and vertebræ were crushed and fractured. The cause of death was suffocation, probably within ten minutes of Ellis being tied up.

"He could not have trussed himself up," Spilsbury wrote in conclusion.

> The ligature round the mouth must have been tight, and with the rolled-up cloth he would be securely gagged. The belt also must have been tight. This could not have been done by the deceased. He would have been unable to call out or talk.

In the meantime Lance-Corporal Dearnley, questioned again, had second thoughts. He described a game of Indians and Cowboys, in which he tied up Ellis at the latter's request. When he last saw his friend, who had boasted that he would be the first back in camp, the drummer was trying to free himself. Spilsbury's testimony at the inquest disposed of most of this story; it seems probable that Ellis did ask to be tied up, perhaps not for the first time, but when the thing was done he was incapable of movement and already being choked to death. Further evidence came to hand of a quarrel between the two friends over a girl, to whom, after Ellis was reported missing, Dearnley was alleged to have said, "He is dead, and only a mile away." The lance-corporal was arrested on a coroner's warrant, and in November stood his trial for murder at the Winchester Assizes, where Spilsbury again gave evidence. The result was a conviction; Dearnley's appeal was dismissed, and a last-minute petition for a reprieve failed also. But the case was not yet over.

The day after the petition was rejected Dearnley's execution was postponed. There had been questions in the House of Commons, and the Home Secretary now announced that the inquiry was to be reopened. Doubts may have been thrown on the story told by the young woman in the case, and it is certain that Spilsbury made his own opinion clear—namely, that the tying-up was an act of masochism performed at Ellis's wish. Whatever Dearnley's intentions, it is a feature of such cases that these perverts will go to great lengths in being tortured, or in torturing themselves, as the next instance to be considered illustrates. The upshot of this strange affair was that the death sentence on Dearnley was commuted to one of penal servitude for life.

When Drummer Ellis died a namesake of his was a schoolboy of twelve. It would be of interest to know whether Francis Charles John Ellis read of the tying-up case in the Long Valley. He liked to bind other boys for fun, using reef knots, and is said to have tied himself up in such a way that he had difficulty in getting free without help. In 1931 he was twenty, in his first year at Cambridge, where he was studying archæology and anthropology and learning Arabic, proposing to take up scientific excavation as a career. Early on a February morning his gyp found him dead, bound and gagged, in his rooms in college. Spilsbury examined the body that afternoon. Fully clothed except for jacket and shoes, it had been lying face downward on some chair cushions near the door. The wrists were tied behind the back with a handkerchief, the limbs and trunk trussed tightly with every variety of ligature—more handkerchiefs, a kitchen cloth, electric flex, a leather strap, and—recalling the case of the dead drummer—puttees and a webbing belt. Many of the knots used were reef knots. Like James Ellis, Francis Ellis was gagged, with a handkerchief wrapped round a sponge. His whole head was tied up in other handkerchiefs knotted over neck-ties, soft collars, and a bath flannel. Like the drummer, he had died of suffocation, but the cause was not the gag or the head coverings; he could have breathed through his nose. Spilsbury explained how in his opinion death had come about.

> "Ellis gagged himself and tied himself up. Bows at the back of the head would facilitate removal. The tying of the wrists was his last act. When completely tied up he would be unable to bend and must have fallen backwards, bruising his elbows and then rolling over on to his left side. He could easily be smothered by the cushions, especially if stunned by the fall. There is no indication that any other person took part in the tying up or had anything to do with his death."

There were naturally those who would not believe this explanation. The police suspected suicide. There was talk of murder. The case had some peculiar features, apart from the most peculiar of all, the tying-up itself; overnight Ellis had sported his oak, but when the gyp arrived in the morning the outer door was unlocked, and the room was in darkness. The dead youth might have unlocked the door before he began to bind himself, but this last process, it was thought, would have been impossible without a light. For this and other reasons a well-known medical man declared at the inquest that both accident and suicide were ruled out. Spilsbury agreed that the switching off of the light was a strange feature. He did not exclude the possibility of suicide, but the indications pointed far more to accidental death. He explained to the coroner what he believed to have happened: Ellis tied himself up in a standing position, because he had to reach the various articles used in a certain order; he placed cushions on the floor to break the fall which was almost inevitable once he was rigidly bound, and when the fall occurred he was smothered by them. Spilsbury's views prevailed, and a verdict of accidental death was returned.

Eleven years later Spilsbury added to his records a case at Hampton, on the Thames. A boy of fifteen was found suffocated in his bedroom, half suspended in a kneeling position by a rope tied round his neck over a pair of flannel trousers and then hitched to a bedpost. The case-card is headed: "Hanging in attempt to stimulate sexual appetite. Asphyxia."

Such perverted practices among adolescents and young men, who often grow out of them, only make news in the Press on the very rare occasions when they end fatally; it is otherwise when they are carried on in after-years and lead to unsavoury divorce proceedings. Perversion of a different kind figured in the case of Rex *v.* A. J. Peake in 1939, when divorce was preceded by a charge of murder. The details on Spilsbury's card are unprintable. In the last years of his life he was to be consulted by the defence in another trial for murder arising out of a remarkable tying-up case in the West Country. This will be dealt with in its turn.

2

When Spilsbury was a three-year-old boy at Leamington a curious discovery was made in a London street intimately associated with the profession he was to follow. Half a century later, at a meeting of the Medico-Legal Society, he was among those who discussed a paper read by Dr P. B. Burgin on the Harley Street mystery of 1880.

In 1879 the tenants of a house in that respectable thoroughfare—or, at least, their servants—began to be troubled by an unpleasant smell in the cellars. Drains were relaid, but the smell persisted. Some of the cellars extended under the street pavement; and in one of these, though not until June 1880, the butler and a footman discovered the body of a woman, greatly decomposed, forced head downward into a large barrel. It was estimated that the body had been in the barrel for at least two years, but why the discovery was not made earlier does not appear. The woman's age was put at between forty and forty-five. She had been stabbed in the left breast, apparently after death, for there had been little bleeding, and at some time the body had been buried in or covered with chloride of lime.

The occupants of the house had been in possession for nearly twenty years. They were accustomed to go away in the autumn, taking the domestic staff with them, the house being then left in charge of a caretaker and his wife. This couple denied ever noticing a smell in the cellars. In the autumn of 1878 they had seen the barrel; before that year, it appears, it was not there. The cellar in which it stood was used only for rubbish. Vague and contradictory evidence by servants throws light on the domestic economy of large, well-to-do households in the Victorian era. The master and mistress knew and cared little or nothing about what went on in the basement; the staff, in that dark warren, did very much what it liked. It was no one's business to inspect an underground cavern used as a rubbish-dump. The difficulties in the circumstances of tracing the history of a decomposed body which had been concealed no one knew when or how proved insuperable; and the verdict at the inquest was that of murder against some person or persons unknown.

Dr Burgin having finished his paper, the learned audience may have smiled when Spilsbury opened the discussion by observing that the association of dead bodies with Harley Street naturally suggested criminal abortion. A doctor who engaged in such practices and found himself with a corpse on his hands, would be faced with the problem confronting so many murderers—how to dispose of it. The stab in the breast, if a post-mortem wound, was probably an attempt to divert attention from the real cause of death, should the body be discovered too soon. The use of chloride of lime in mistake for quicklime showed lack of chemical knowledge. Such an error, indeed, often committed by laymen, and the assumption that absence of bleeding after a deep stab would not arouse suspicion, suggests that the murderer in this case fell somewhat below the standard to be expected of a Harley Street physician; but this unsolved mystery of 1880 leaves much good stuff for the imagination to play with—the dim street of tall houses, the brass plates glimmering in the flicker of gas-lamps, and, through the autumn midnight, some fashionable doctor conveying the body of his victim (and the barrel?) to its penultimate resting-place in a neighbour's cellar.

The tale is told here because, a few years after that meeting of the Medico-Legal Society, Spilsbury was to be actively concerned in the mystery of another body discovered in a cellar. The case has serio-comic features, especially as related by ex-Superintendent Robert Fabian, who was first summoned to the scene, and who tells the story again in a recently published book of reminiscences.

In June 1935 Mr Fabian was at Kennington Road Police Station when "a trembling voice" asked for the C.I.D. It was the manager of the Equestrian Public House, in St George's Circus, who had found a mummified body in a cellar beneath the saloon bar, and wanted to know what he was to do with it. Mr Fabian's first instinct was to reply, "Try it in the beer," but, suppressing his sense of humour, he said he would be along at once. The cellar in question was a large one, triangular in shape, with a recess at one end. Coal was stored in it, and it was also used as a dumping-ground for broken or unwanted furniture and other odds and ends. The cellarman, having been told to tidy it up, began by moving a large bundle, apparently of old carpets tied with electric flex, which stood upright in the recess. Cutting the flex, he found under more wrappings of curtains and oil-cloth what nowadays would be called a dehydrated corpse, the brown skin like parchment, the flesh perished, and the bones standing out. It was so light and stiff that it was easily held erect with one hand. The head, which was fractured, had come apart from the neck. The body was clearly that of an old man, but the face was unrecognizable, and there was no clue to his identity.

The usual specialists summoned from Scotland Yard were accompanied by Spilsbury, who in his thorough way afterwards filled no fewer than four cards with a summary of his examination. Routine police work, in the meantime, discovered who the victim was, and how he came to be wrapped up like a package for the post. He was a man of eighty—yet another Ellis—who had been missing for nearly a year. Well-known in the public houses of the district, he had fallen asleep one afternoon in the bar of the Equestrian. It was after closing time when the barman noticed the old man and roused him; only half awake, Ellis made for the street door, and accidentally opened that leading to the cellar, the floor of which was 9½ feet below. He crashed down the steep steps and broke his neck. Some time later the barman went down for coal and found the body. He was alone in the house; he had once been in some small trouble with the police; and he now fell into a panic. He swathed the body in its cocoon of curtains and the rest and propped it in the corner. That evening he gave notice, and the next day disappeared.

Such was his story when he was run to earth, and Spilsbury's findings bore it out. Ellis was a healthy man for an octogenarian, but the shock of a fall down the cellar steps, to say nothing of a fractured skull and other injuries, might have caused instant death. The injuries were consistent with a fall. Mummification was brought about by the combination of sudden death, a fairly rapid cooling of the body in the cellar, and its being rolled up in an air-tight bundle. The barman, who pleaded guilty at the Old Bailey to concealment of the body in order to prevent an inquest, was sentenced to three days' imprisonment, which meant immediate release.

3

In the following year a far more tragic case—for at eighty a man cannot have much longer to live—found Spilsbury following up damning evidence against an accused with one of his rare public expressions of personal feeling. Edward Lloyd, aged thirty-six, stood charged with the murder of his wife. Lizzie Lloyd had been undergoing skin-grafting by Sir Harold Gillies at the L.C.C. Hospital in Shepherd's Bush. After her husband had come from Wales to see her she was found with her throat cut, and in a dying condition. A razor was beneath her body. Lloyd, who was still in the hospital, had a superficial cut on his own throat. He admitted bringing the razor with him, but at first said that his wife had inflicted her dreadful wound herself. Later he agreed that this story must be untrue; his wife would never have done such a thing, and therefore he must have killed her, but he could remember nothing about it.

Spilsbury's evidence left no doubt that Mrs Lloyd, who had been in hospital for six months, could not possibly have cut her throat in such a determined manner. But at the Old Bailey, before Mr Justice Charles, he went on to say:

> "This poor woman had a good deal of deformity of the face. There was a solid tube of skin stretched from her left cheek down to her left shoulder. . . . She had a built-up nose in casing, it was rather bulbous. She had also, on one side, a false lip. . . . Her appearance would probably have been repulsive to any ordinary person. It might have given the defendant a serious shock. It is quite likely that the difference in her appearance was startling to him if he had not seen her for six and a half months. . . . Such an effect would be greater upon him if he had been working hard, had been suffering from insomnia, and had recently had influenza. The impression conveyed . . . might have been that she was in a dreadful state."

Lloyd had, in fact, suffered from insomnia and influenza. He had been under great mental strain, and letters to Mrs Lloyd hinted at suicide if she did not soon return. Wounded in both legs during the First World War, he was discharged from the Army with an excellent character, and he was devoted to his wife. Before and during the proceedings against him, which were conducted with great fairness, he was under medical observation. Spilsbury's unsolicited description of the terrible sight that awaited him when he first saw his wife after a parting of six months drove home to the jury an impression already formed of an unbalanced state of mind; and Lloyd was pronounced unfit to plead. This was a plain case for the compassion too often indiscriminately shown towards the individual who kills another.

Few withers would be wrung were a corporation or limited company accused of conspiracy to murder. In England, at any rate, this happy event has yet to happen, but such impersonal bodies can be indicted for manslaughter, and in 1926 Spilsbury was partly instrumental in clearing the name of a well-known firm charged, under the Offences against the Person Act, with "setting a man-trap calculated to destroy human life upon the trespasser or other person coming into contact with it." Messrs Cory Brothers, having suffered from pilferage of coal at their property at Ogmore Vale, at Bridgend, in Glamorganshire, surrounded it with a wire fence charged with an electric current. A young collier named Brynmor John, out ratting in a drizzle with some friends, slipped while running and fell face down on a sheet of corrugated zinc near the fence, the bottom strand of which he grasped in an attempt to break his fall. He could not withdraw his hand from the wire; a friend who tried to pull him away by his damp clothing received a slight shock. John must have been dead before the friend ran to the power station to have the current cut off.

Relatives instituted a prosecution for manslaughter. Marshall Hall was briefed for the company; it was one of his last cases, and at Bridgend Police Court, for the last time, he cross-examined Spilsbury and Willcox. He died before the trial came on, and Norman Birkett conducted the successful defence at the Cardiff Assizes. Spilsbury, though a witness for the prosecution, must have influenced the issue by the extreme fairness of his evidence. He agreed with Willcox that it was an exceptional occurrence for a current of so low a voltage to cause the death of a healthy young man of eighteen. It was brought out that John and his friends, alarmed by something, were running away, and the point was made, to which Spilsbury agreed, that in the young collier's agitated state of mind a slight shock might have an effect out of proportion to the actual current used. Spilsbury summed up the whole argument for misadventure on his case-card:

> It was drizzling, with rain at times. All exposed surfaces would be wet. The current entered by the hand which grasped the wire, and probably left by the other hand which probably contacted the zinc sheet when he fell. The contact was not merely momentary. Mental state of the deceased; shock unexpected; deceased was already alarmed and was running away. . . .

The case of the poacher, Waudby, who died of a shot-gun injury after an affray with a farmer, is included here, instead of in the chapter on shooting cases, because it was another occasion on which Spilsbury's evidence, with that of Churchill, confuted some very hard lying and cleared the name of an innocent man. In the early spring of 1933 Waudby and four others, all from Hull, were encountered on a poaching expedition by a farmer named Rose, of Gibraltar Farm, near Beverley. Rose, who was carrying a double-barrelled 12-bore, fired a shot over their heads, whereupon all five fell upon him and knocked him down, kicking him as he lay on the ground. In the struggle the second barrel of the gun was discharged, Waudby receiving the shot in his left thigh, the wound from which he subsequently died.

His companions swore as one man that the farmer fired the second shot while on his feet, and at a distance of several yards. The Chief Constable of the East Riding had good reasons for doubting this story, among them the facts that the stock of the gun was broken off, and that the whole weapon was muddy; and at his request Spilsbury and Churchill went down to Beverley. At the adjourned inquest the testimony of this pair, who so often worked in harmony together, completely confirmed the farmer's version of the affair, which was that while he was on the ground Waudby tried to wrest the gun from him, seizing it by the muzzle. On Spilsbury's card his "Conclusions" run:

> As the bone was 1 inch in diameter at the site of fracture, and as the whole charge struck the bone squarely, none of the shot even glancing off the side, the whole charge must have struck the bone within an area of $\frac{3}{4}$-inch diameter. The shot therefore could not have begun to spread. It was a very near discharge, confirmed by small size of hole in clothing, less than 1 inch. No blackening or scorching of clothing; not touching. Lower edge of skin wound much lower than fracture, from about 45 degrees from the horizontal, but the wound was stretched by muscle injury; angle was probably not greater than 30 degrees. Injury not inflicted while firer was standing. Could have been inflicted if stock end of weapon was on the ground and the barrel raised to an angle of 30 degrees with the ground.

Churchill's examination of the gun showed that the barrels were much worn. The spread of shot from them would be more irregular and scattered than from new barrels. Had they been new the spread at the distance of a yard would have been $1\frac{1}{4}$ inch from the right barrel, and $1\frac{1}{8}$ from the left. The gun expert agreed that such a wound could not have been produced if the two men were standing face to face, but only if one or the other were on the ground, or if Waudby gripped the barrels with his left hand while kicking with his left foot.

The four hardy perjurers should have given more thought to their story. They can hardly have foreseen, however, the standard of deductive reasoning that was to blow it sky-high.

It was during this summer that reports appeared in the Press of the recovery of the body of Lord Kitchener, who was presumed to have gone down in H.M.S. *Hampshire* while on a voyage to Russia in 1916. Mr (now Sir) Norman Kendal, then Deputy Assistant Commissioner (C.I.D.) at Scotland Yard, was at the Oval one afternoon, watching Rhodes, in his forty-ninth year, take altogether six Australian wickets for 79 in the final Test Match, when he was called away by Superintendent Wensley to an undertaker's parlour in Waterloo Road. On a bier lighted by candles stood a coffin said to contain the Field-Marshal's body. A Mr Frank Power alleged that he had found the coffin in a lonely grave on the coast of Norway, and had shipped it to England. Power, who was known under other names, had disappeared, and the Admiralty stated that no one from the *Hampshire*, which was torpedoed off the Shetlands, had reached Norway, alive or dead. Mr Kendal had the coffin taken to Scotland Yard, where it was opened in the presence of Ingleby Oddie, the coroner for Central London, who authorized the seizure. Spilsbury was also there, but no one supposed his services would be needed. Nor were they; there was nothing in the coffin but pitch.

4

Of the three cards chosen to close this chapter, one is selected because the story attached to it has a certain macabre humour. A man hanged himself from the roof of a tall building on the boundary of two London coroners' districts. He gave himself far too long a drop, and his head was torn off. The body fell to the pavement within the limit of one coroner's jurisdiction; the head rolled down the street, and was found by a police constable several yards inside the second coroner's area. Which official was responsible for the inquest? Neither particularly wanted the missing portion. In the end the coroner who had the head contrived to pass the buck, so to speak, to his colleague.

The second card concerns a case which had a really humorous sequel. It records the post-mortem on the body of Ernest Percival Key, an elderly jeweller who was murdered in his Surbiton shop on Christmas Eve 1938. William Butler was convicted of the crime and duly hanged. This was one of the cases in which Spilsbury was associated with his friend Dr Eric Gardner, who, as County Pathologist for Surrey, was first on the scene of the murder, a back room lower than the adjoining one, from which it was reached by two steps. When Spilsbury arrived he paused on the first step. "Ah," he said. "A knife murder." The blood had not splashed the walls, as would have been the case had a bar or bludgeon been used. The murderer had left behind him his bowler hat, and from its size and some hairs found in it Gardner had already been able to give the police useful indications of its owner's appearance. His deductions were written up in a London newspaper in an exaggerated style, and an even more garbled story, based on this report, presently appeared in a Berlin daily. The most hard-headed Germans can be taken in by a suggestion of the occult; and now Scotland Yard received a letter from the *Reichkriminalpolizeiamt* asking for information about "the clairvoyant, Erich Gardner," whose magic arts enabled him, by looking at a hat, to solve a murder case.

The third card emphasizes a point just made—how ubiquitously the figure of Spilsbury intrudes upon every aspect of the medico-legal scene for almost half a century. He is found in the background of cases better known for their purely legal side. Some, like his post-mortem nearly twenty years ago on the body of Mrs Henderson, the first wife of one of Haigh's victims, have been recalled from oblivion by events occurring or reported since his death. This book was nearly finished when there was news in the papers that A. J. Maundy Gregory had died in Paris as far back as 1940. Gregory was charged in 1933 with an offence under the Honours (Prevention of Abuses) Act. He was fined and sent to prison for two months, but to the profound disappointment of every one except possibly a few of the recently ennobled, there were no scandalous revelations. While Gregory was in prison, however, Spilsbury went down to Bisham, in Berkshire, for the exhumation of Mrs Edith Marion Rosse, who had died in the previous September in Gregory's house in Hyde Park Terrace. The cause of death was given as cerebral hæmorrhage and chronic Bright's Disease. Gregory went to much trouble to have her buried in the damp churchyard of Bisham, on the Thames opposite Marlow. By a will scrawled during her last illness on a menu-card she had left him £18,000.

Spilsbury noted on his card that the churchyard had been flooded during the winter. There was water in the coffin, and the body was much decomposed. The microscope revealed no evidence of hæmorrhage or Bright's Disease, or of any other. Analysis by Roche Lynch found no trace of poison. At the inquest, held at Paddington, the coroner, Ingleby Oddie, remarked that he did not wish to emphasize the fact that certain drugs decomposed when buried in waterlogged soil. In the circumstances no charge could be brought.

Chapter 10: LONDON NIGHT LIFE: THE 1930's

SPILSBURY's records furnish a comprehensive cross-section of the deeps of London night life for more than a generation. From Dorothy Balsden's death at the hands of Alabaster in 1912 to the multiple murders of Frederick Cummins in 1942, everything is there —dubious night clubs and restaurants, pimps, prostitutes and perverts, Chinese drug-peddlers selling opium and cocaine, the prowling criminals from outside this specialized underworld who make it a hunting-ground, and the killers of women who find in it their easiest prey. It is a dreary tale of the pursuit of women, drink, and drugs, ending in murder or suicide, and few of the scores of cases in which Spilsbury was concerned are of much interest except to the sexual psychologist and the morbid.

The latter revelled in such a tragedy as that of Freda Kempton, who was only twenty-one when she took her life in her lodgings in Westbourne Grove early in 1922. Here were all the elements of romance—youth, beauty, blighted love, bright lights and champagne, and even a sinister Chinaman and Mrs Meyrick. With its echoes of the recent death of Billie Carleton, the actress, it was a crime reporter's dream, and columns were written about its wretched ending. Far more effective is Spilsbury's summary on his card, where drama was merely incidental.

> *History.* Occupation—Dancing Mistress. Died in her lodgings on March 6th from convulsions. Rosa Steinberg (a witness): 'Knew deceased for 2 months. About 4 weeks ago we were in a night club, when deceased was introduced to a Chinaman, "Billy," who had a restaurant in Regent Street. She went outside with Billy. Came back in 5 minutes. Mouth twitching. She said: "I have been drugged." She added: "When I used to take cocaine about a month ago, my mouth used to twitch." About a month previous to this deceased showed me 13 packets of cocaine. On another occasion after she had gone to the Chinese restaurant to see Billy she showed me a tiny blue bottle full of powder which she said was cocaine. On the day before her death we went to the Chinese restaurant with Billy, where he gave her a small coloured bottle containing powder.

She afterwards asked Billy whether one could die by sniffing cocaine. He said, "No, but by putting it in water." We afterwards went home in a taxi. She was very depressed. On that occasion she said she would put cocaine into water and drink it. I told her not to be so silly.'

They were back at the night club—it was Mrs Meyrick's notorious "43"—and at the Chinese restaurant the next evening. Poor Freda Kempton, whose lover had abandoned her for another woman, had not long before been a witness at the inquest on a friend who committed suicide. She kept talking about this, and that night she drank cocaine in water. Webster's analysis found nearly 7 grains in the organs.

The Chinaman "Billy," who denied that he had ever seen cocaine, was known to the police and the underworld as Brilliant Chang, or "The Cocaine Millionaire." He was believed to use as innocent accomplices laundry-women who brought the drug ashore from ships in dock concealed in dirty linen. Before he opened his restaurant at 104 Regent Street, Chang had been a general merchant and an Admiralty contractor. The police are perhaps more sophisticated than the Navy, but with all their knowledge they could prove nothing against him. They had, however, the last word: they got him deported.

The 1930's are particularly rich in notorious cases from the seamy side of life in the West End. Spilsbury was engaged in most of them, beginning with the murder of Nora Upchurch in the autumn of 1931. A dreadful feature, among others only too familiar, links Frederick Field, who stood his trial for the crime, with another Frederick, surnamed Murphy, with Robert Dixon, and perhaps with Thomas Thorn, already referred to, who at this time was in Broadmoor. All four were to be tried a second time within these ten years for a second murder; against all four, at one or the other of their trials, Spilsbury gave evidence; and the three first-named at least, though legally and medically sane, belonged to the abnormal type whose lusts impel them to murder women.

Nora Upchurch was only twenty when she was killed. Sometimes described as a dancer, she was known as Norma Laverick in her real profession, for the purposes of which she had a flat near Shaftesbury Avenue as well as the rooms which were her home in Pimlico. She seems to have been a kindly and likable creature, as are so many of these unfortunate women whose lives end tragically; the men involved in such cases are almost uniformly detestable. Nora Upchurch's body was discovered on the morning of October 2, when a sign-fitter's manager and one of his workmen entered some empty premises in Shaftesbury Avenue. In the dim light the manager saw a figure on the floor and tapped it with his umbrella, saying, "Another of these wax models." Frederick Field, the workman, if two of his several statements are to be believed, knew better.

Nora Upchurch had been strangled, and in Spilsbury's opinion had probably died on September 29, when she was last seen at her rooms in Pimlico. Field at once came under suspicion because of an improbable story about a key to the empty premises which had been in his possession, and which was now missing. At the adjourned inquest at the end of November, however, an open verdict left him still a free man. In the meantime he had made a bargain with a newspaper that should he be charged with the murder the costs of his defence would be met in return for an exclusive statement. This sort of thing had been done before, and though the need did not then arise, Field bore the proposal in mind.

A year and a half went by, and the crime in Shaftesbury Avenue remained, as far as the public knew, unsolved. Field went into the Royal Air Force. In July 1933 he called to see the news editor who had bargained with him eighteen months before. He made a statement which was taken down by reporters. More than six hours later the newspaper got in touch with Scotland Yard, and at ten o'clock that evening Field was brought to Marlborough Street Police Station, where he confessed to the murder of Nora Upchurch.

Whatever the police might suspect, this confession did not tally with the facts. Field said he throttled the girl with his hands, whereas Spilsbury found that she had been strangled by the belt of her dress. There was evidence that she had been afraid of some unknown man, who could hardly be Field, and it soon became clear that whether the latter was guilty or innocent the purpose of his confession was to get money from the newspaper. He retracted it, in fact, on his committal for trial, saying that he had confessed in order to prove his innocence; at the Old Bailey he pleaded Not Guilty, and Mr Justice Swift stopped the case. Of the course taken by the newspaper concerned, the judge said:

> "Anything more disgraceful I have never heard. A man goes to a newspaper office and says, 'I am confessing that I have been guilty of murder.' The newspaper representatives thereupon take him about the country, photographing him, and for hours refrain from communicating with the police as every decent and respectable citizen ought to do as soon as he hears that a crime has been committed. . . . I warn newspapermen of these proclivities, that if they do this sort of thing, they are likely to find themselves very seriously dealt with."

When Superintendent Cornish, who handled this case, described Field as a woman-killer, he was writing after 1936. In that year, having been arrested as a deserter from the R.A.F., Field a second time volunteered a confession of murder. The victim was Mrs Beatrice Vilna Sutton, a prostitute who had been found strangled in her flat at Clapham the day before. Again Field tried the technique which had once been successful; before coming up for trial he withdrew his confession. This time, however, he had confessed too much, and he was convicted and hanged.

There can be little doubt that he was in the direct line of descent from Jack the Ripper and Neil Cream, though, like most later practitioners, who have usually been ignorant men, his method was strangulation. This type of crime is difficult to prevent or punish both because of the abnormal motive, and of the mode of life of the victims most often chosen; but circumstances, chief among them the increased efficiency of the police, have rendered it, if not less common, at least less wholesale than in its heyday. It was the conditions of a war, as much as the advent after half a century of another murderer on a monstrous scale, that made possible in 1942 a few days' panic recalling those of 1888 and the early 1890's, when the Ripper and Cream were terrorizing whole districts. Throughout the more civilized 1930's, however, the prowling woman killer was horribly active in London. A dozen victims could be named, and in eight cases Spilsbury was called in. Within four years the murders of four women of the streets, all strangled and all but one living in Soho, swelled the list of unsolved crimes. Rightly or wrongly, rumour attributed them to some known hand, especially if that hand had already struck more than once. Field, it has been mentioned, had his peers. Frederick Murphy, acquitted on a charge of murder in 1929, was convicted and hanged at a second time of asking in 1937. The woman in each case was strangled, and Spilsbury was the Crown's medical witness at the second trial. In 1939 Robert Dixon, charged under the name of Stephenson with a similar crime, had just begun a ten years' sentence for manslaughter when he was again put in the dock, accused of murdering another woman by the favourite means, strangulation, in 1927. Again the charge was reduced to manslaughter, but this time Dixon got sixteen years. Spilsbury performed both post-mortems, and gave evidence at both trials.

The foreign element among these poor victims, as well as their trade, is revealed in such nicknames as French Marie, French Fifi, and French Paulette. Their way of life, it has been said, rendered them easy prey;

how easy can be seen in the case of Dora Alicia Lloyd, one of the unsolved cases of these years. Her murder was heard, and her murderer described, but he was never caught. Spilsbury was called to her rooms in Maida Vale in February 1932. Like so many more, she had been strangled by hand. The people in the house, accustomed to pay no heed to men who came and went, had heard a taxi drive up late the night before. A man was seen to get out, and there was a knock at the front door. Presently the lodger who had the room above Dora Lloyd's was disturbed by muffled screams and gurgles and thumps below. Then the front door banged, and footsteps walked away. The lodger stayed in bed.

On the day that Frederick Murphy heard his appeal dismissed the President of the Court, Mr Justice Swift, delivered a similar judgment in the case of Leslie George Stone, convicted of murdering Ruby Keen. Though the background of this crime was the evening life of Leighton Buzzard, not the night haunts of London, it ran true to the type just dealt with, and certain peculiar features which lift it out of the commonplace caused not only Spilsbury, but Scotland Yard as well, to be instantly called in, and the trial of the accused to be removed from Bedford Assizes to the Old Bailey.

Ruby Keen, a good-looking girl of twenty-three who worked in a factory at Dunstable, was about to be married to a police officer in the Bedfordshire Constabulary. When in her own free time he was on duty she saw no harm in going out with other young men, among them being another police constable and Leslie Stone. Early on the morning of April 12 she was found dead in a lane near her home. She had been strangled, and almost all her clothing had been ripped off her body. Spilsbury's opinion was that she had been knocked down by a blow on the chin and then strangled with the scarf she was wearing. She had not been assaulted; her assailant, discovering that she was dead, had then run away.

The local police were faced with an awkward situation. Among the possible suspects was a member of the force, and a second constable, as the dead girl's fiancé, was closely concerned in the case. It was for these reasons that Scotland Yard was so promptly called in. Chief Inspector Barker, who eight years before had arrested Frederick Browne, one of the murderers of Police Constable Gutteridge, went down to Leighton Buzzard, and within a few days Leslie Stone, who had already made a statement, was under arrest. Quick work on the spot was followed by more in the laboratory; traces of sand on the trousers of Stone's new suit, though he had attempted to clean them, were identical with soil taken from the ill-named Lovers Lane, where Ruby Keen was killed, and where the imprint of a knee was found. A minute piece of green silk taken from Stone's jacket was similar to the material of her dress. Only on the last morning of the trial did Stone give his account of what had happened in Lovers Lane. It did not explain how the girl's clothing came to be torn from her body, and in other respects bore the familiar stamp of the afterthought. Stone was convicted, and his execution took place on Friday, August 13.

Before his trial began the two police officers involved in the case had left the force. Ruby Keen's fiancé was asked to resign; his colleague was dismissed.

2

Spilsbury's most sensational cases in this *genre* in the 1930's came at opposite ends of the social scale. Some account has been given in an earlier chapter of the shooting of Thomas Scott Stephen in the spring of 1932, and of the subsequent trial of Mrs Barney. The Max Kassell case followed nearly four years later.

At the end of January 1936, at ten o'clock one morning, the body of a man was found under a hedge in Cell Barns Lane, on the southern outskirts of St Albans. Though the neighbourhood has become almost suburban, the man's flashy clothes, pointed, polished shoes, and manicured hands would have looked rather out of place there; and, in fact, Soho was in the picture again. And not only Soho; in the cosmopolitan background of the case, which stretched from Riga to Montreal and Buenos Aires, were such characters as Charles Hainsuk, once "Jo the Terror" of the Paris underworld, and Alexandre Stavisky.

Chief Inspector Sharpe, of Scotland Yard, was at Cell Barns Lane within an hour of the discovery, and he was followed by Spilsbury, who saw the body on the spot. The man had been shot six times, in the chest, back, and side. Two of the wounds were dangerous, if not fatal, but the immediate cause of death was hæmorrhage. The man's face, which was scarred with old injuries, had been battered by a fist. Spilsbury extracted four of the bullets; afterwards describing the scene, the chief inspector said, "Sir Bernard is so coldly efficient and business-like. How different to dear old Brontë!"

Spilsbury put the time of death at between 3 A.M. and 6 A.M. that morning. It was plain that the man had not been shot where he was found. There was nothing on him to show who he was, except a heavy signet ring of gold and blue enamel marked with an M or W. A published description, however, soon resulted in identification by relatives;

he was Max Kessell Allard, known also as Max Kassell and Red Max, a Latvian by birth and nearly sixty years of age. With this information, and news from Little Newport Street, Soho, where on the night of the crime there had been the noise of a quarrel, followed by shots and the breaking of a window, the police had pieced together the circumstances of the murder within a few days. But the other actors had already fled to Paris.

The foreign names and background, the subsequent trial in Paris, the evidence of the now ancient "Jo the Terror," and the mention of Stavisky lent melodramatic colour to what Chief Inspector Sharpe has described as a small-time crime. The murder was the result of a quarrel over £25. Max Kassell, as he is best known, had been a dealer in drugs and the exploitation of women all his life. At the time of his death he owed the £25 to Suzanne Bertron, who lived in the house in Little Newport Street with an old accomplice in Kassell's numberless infamies, George Lacroix, otherwise Marcel Vernon. A maidservant, Marcelle Aubin, was also in the top-floor flat that night, and it was she who told the story of the murder to the police. Kassell, having been decoyed to the house, was shot while the two women sat listening in Suzanne Bertron's bedroom. He broke the window in an attempt to summon help, and lived for some time with six bullets in his body, but he was dead when a car came in the early morning, and Lacroix and the driver carried him downstairs and then drove to Cell Barns Lane. The women tried to remove all traces of the murder from the sitting-room, which, with its chocolate-coloured wallpaper, its fringed silk tablecloth, its prints of old masters, and the calendar of a Paris firm hanging by the china animals on the mantelpiece was a corner of that lower-bourgeois France from which Suzanne Bertron came. They washed away bloodstains and burnt the dead man's hat and the lace window curtain. They collected five cartridge-cases, and on Lacroix's return from that grim journey into Hertfordshire the sixth was found in the armchair in which Kassell had died. A new pane was put in the window, but there were pieces of glass outside and traces of blood on the carpet when the police came to the flat after the tenants had fled. Terrorized by their friends, Marcelle Aubin died some time later while on her way to France.

The French police were only too pleased to arrest Lacroix and Suzanne Bertron; they wanted them so badly that they refused to extradite them. Held on other charges, the pair were tried for the murder in Paris. Spilsbury was subpœna'd as a witness, but the trial clashed with another of his cases, the death of Mrs Sarah Alice Scott at the hands of her son Douglas, who was afterwards sentenced to ten years' penal servitude for manslaughter.

It came out that Kassell, who in London had carried on some sort of a business in jewellery, chiefly earned his living by finding husbands for foreign women who wanted to come to England, letting furnished flats for immoral purposes, and sending girls to the Argentine. In view of this record it may have appeared to the logical French mind that the world was well rid of him; Suzanne Bertron was acquitted, and it was on the other charges that Lacroix was sentenced to ten years on Devil's Island.

3

When the 1930's began Spilsbury was at the height of his power and prestige, and the next ten years were the busiest of his life. He was still talking of retiring, but no one could be found to take his place. He was still accumulating material for the text-book on pathology which he was going to write, but he never found the leisure to begin it. He was performing a thousand post-mortems a year, making his own notes and filling in every form himself, and his habit of taking infinite pains had not weakened with age. When he was not travelling, or at some coroner's court, or giving evidence at a trial, he was working in his small laboratory at University College, or in the smaller one he had fitted up in his rooms in Verulam Buildings. His family at Marlborough Hill scarcely saw him except during occasional week-ends there or in the West Country he loved, or in the summer-holiday season, when even he relaxed for a few weeks.

The family was growing up. During this decade the second son, Peter, was studying for his medical degree. He had taken up rowing at Oxford, and afterwards rowed for Leander. Evelyn, the daughter, was at work, and the youngest son, Richard, was still at school, where he annoyed his father by taking no interest in the O.T.C. Alan, the eldest of the four children, was always delicate, but in his twenties he began to take some of the routine laboratory tasks off Spilsbury's hands, acting as secretary and keeping the records.

In 1936 Spilsbury had one of his rare illnesses, and the newspapers made front-page headlines of it. He underwent a minor operation for an infected arm, caused, it was thought, by post-mortem-room poisoning. That year he flew for the first time in his life, to perform a post-mortem in the Channel Islands. Twelve months later, in April 1937, a post-mortem at Kensington links Spilsbury with a crime, committed after his death, that was to have features as dreadful and sensational as any in his own unrivalled experience. The wife of a young doctor named Archibald Henderson died suddenly at a hotel in Gloucester Road. The verdict at the inquest, after Spilsbury had given evidence, was death from natural causes. Dr Henderson, to whom the dead woman left a considerable fortune, afterwards married again, and he and his second wife were to be among the victims of George Haigh, who, on his own confession, disposed of the bodies in an acid bath.

In 1932, when the Nazi Party won its victory at the polls in Germany, and the name of Hitler began to overshadow Europe, died Spilsbury's old adversary, Robert Brontë, at the relatively early age of fifty-two. In this event there is to be seen something symbolical in Spilsbury's own career. With Brontë, another age he had known was passing, the age between the wars, uncertain and anxious, but happier than anything he and his contemporaries were to know after. In the following year Hitler became Reich Chancellor, and for the second time within a generation the world was heading for disaster.

Part Five

THE LAST PHASE: 1939–47

Chapter 1: DOMESTIC TRAGEDY

SPILSBURY was in his sixty-third year when the Second World War began. He had never been more busy, but he appeared to be in good health. No man of his age could expect to face once more the conditions of wartime, as they are to-day, with the resilience of middle life; but it is probable that he did not yet realize that years of overwork had left him few reserves against the added strain, and none capable of resisting the mental and physical shock of the domestic tragedies which were soon to overwhelm him.

For some time he had been relieved of a part of the drudgery he had chosen to impose upon himself by the company in his laboratory at University College of his eldest son, Alan. Peter, the second son, was about to qualify as a doctor, and Richard was at Oxford. Evelyn had married a few years before. Spilsbury himself was spending more and more of what with another man would have been leisure studying specimens and writing notes for his book in the chambers in Verulam Buildings, but the family headquarters was still at Marlborough Hill, and his two sisters, both unmarried, had for some time been living near by in Hampstead. Only his younger brother, Leonard, an engineer, was out of the country, in Scandinavia, where events were to compel him to remain.

Great Britain declared war on Germany on a Sunday, two days after partridge-shooting, and also gunfire in Poland, had begun. Spilsbury was at the Battersea Coroner's Court on the Monday, and was busier next morning at St Pancras, and autopsies at these two mortuaries, with occasional excursions to Hackney (which is under the same coronership as St Pancras), carried him through the rest of that beautiful autumn. What remained of 1939 was, for him, equally uneventful, though a post-mortem at Hackney, just before Christmas, on the body of Arthur Haberfield, whose throat had been cut, had a sequel at the Old Bailey in the following year, when Sidney Charles Pitcher, on trial for murder, was found insane.

Towards the end of the ominous lull between the overrunning of Poland and the invasion of Denmark and Norway, London was startled by a political assassination. Sir Michael O'Dwyer had been Governor of the Punjab at the time of the Amritsar riots in 1919, and had fully endorsed the methods by which General Dyer quelled the disturbance, though these methods caused the ruin of that officer's career. On March 13, 1940, two days before those Ides celebrated for another political murder, Sir Michael was one of a distinguished company at a joint meeting at Caxton Hall of the East India Association and the Royal Central Asiatic Society. As the meeting was breaking up a Sikh named Udham Singh fired all six rounds of a .45 Smith and Wesson revolver into a group on the platform of whom O'Dwyer was one. The latter was shot twice in the back, and killed instantly, one bullet passing through the heart and right lung, and the second through the kidneys. Lord Zetland, Secretary of State for India, who had been in the chair, was slightly injured, as were Lord Lamington and Sir Louis Dane. Udham Singh, who gave the improbable name of Mohammed Singh Azad, and who spoke English, asked as he was being searched whether Lord Zetland was dead, adding that he ought to be.

During the three months between Spilsbury's post-mortem on Sir Michael's body and the trial of Udham Singh at the Old Bailey early in June many things happened. The storm having burst over Scandinavia, Holland and Belgium soon went the way of Denmark and Norway, and when the trial opened the German armies were sweeping through France, and nearly a thousand little ships were ferrying to safety the last of the British and French forces penned about Dunkirk. At this time, all over England, the staffs of empty or half-empty hospitals were still waiting for the tens of thousands of wounded which, on the analogy of 1914–18, had been expected to fill them. The rest of the medical profession not in the services was taking the strain of double and treble work, with inevitable casualties among the older members. One of these was Spilsbury.

In the middle of May he collapsed while at work at the mortuary table. He was suffering from a slight stroke, and had to rest for some weeks. Here was a plain warning to alter his way of life, but he was the last man to heed it. He even insisted on leaving his sick-room to give evidence at the trial of Udham Singh, when his appearance shocked those so long familiar with his brisk walk and erect carriage and the fresh complexion which perhaps only fellow-doctors associated with dangerously high blood pressure. Pale and stooping, he was allowed to answer a few essential questions from the well of the court, and he was not cross-examined.

Yet he was at work again before the end of that month, and photographs taken soon after show him looking very much his old self. Except for the gap of five or six weeks in his sequence of cards, there is nothing in these records to suggest that 1940 was not a normal year. Of his cases in the second half of it he preserved the notes of more than three hundred, among them being the post-mortem on the body of Sir Michael O'Dwyer's murderer, executed on the last day of July.

Another gap, of one day, September 16, would pass unnoticed by those who did not know that 1940 was a terrible year for Spilsbury.

2

With the beginning in August of the daylight bombing of London the domestic life of the Spilsbury family, as of so many more, was suddenly and finally disrupted. The house in Marlborough Hill was closed. The street backs on to the cuttings and tunnels of what was then the L.N.E.R., and the neighbourhood was to suffer badly when night bombing started, No. 32 itself being damaged by blast. After this it was sold. Of the four young Spilsburys, Peter was now a qualified medical man and house surgeon at St Thomas's Hospital. While he went into rooms in that district Alan, from lodgings in Cricklewood, still came daily to his father's laboratory in Gower Street. Richard was in the Army, and Evelyn was driving an ambulance. Spilsbury himself remained at Verulam Buildings, going about his work in his Armstrong-Siddeley AGN 250, which had succeeded his pre-war Morris, and allowed liberties with dimmed traffic lights and one-way streets which might have meant endorsements and fines for the owner of a car less well known to the Metropolitan Police. He would never have become a good driver within the meaning of the Highway Code, but he seems never to have been involved in an accident until two years before his death, when, after colliding with a pony trap, he appeared at Odiham Police Court, charged with dangerous driving, and was fined £10 and costs.

Two days after that memorable evening of September 7, when the taller buildings of London were reddened by the fires of Stepney and the Docks, St Thomas's Hospital was bombed for the first time. Four nights later, on the 13th, two more blocks were hit. At 8.30 P.M. on the 15th it was the turn of the medical outpatients' block and College House. There were no casualties among the patients, but two house surgeons and a nurse were killed. One of the house surgeons was Peter Spilsbury.

In the confusion after the bombing the news was not sent to

Spilsbury, or it went astray, and he was left to learn it in a peculiarly tragic manner. When he went to work as usual the next morning he had two cases waiting for him at the Westminster Coroner's Court. Having performed the post-mortems, he gave evidence in the first case, and while waiting for the second to begin sat in court going through letters which had come for him that morning. As he read one he was seen to be on the verge of collapse. It was from a friend, condoling with him on the death of his son. No name was mentioned; Spilsbury had already seen Alan that day, but until inquiries had been made from the court he did not know whether it was Peter or Richard who had been killed.

Though there is no record of those two Westminster post-mortems, there are three cards for the following day, the 17th, when Spilsbury was again at work at Hackney. But he was a changed man. It is agreed by all who knew him that he never recovered from the shock of Peter's death, conveyed to him as it was in circumstances which aggravated the blow. From that day, as more than one has put it, "he began to fail." His tall figure became a little bent; he was more silent, more withdrawn into himself. But there was no apparent failure of energy. He threw himself into his work with more concentration than ever, as his records for the rest of that year show. His cards alone for the remaining three and a half months total 150. Work can be both a tyranny and an anodyne; it had become both.

Christmas passed, and January 1941, and in February a bomb hit Verulam Buildings. Spilsbury's chambers were damaged, but he would not leave them. In March the tall, barrack-like block was hit again, and now he had to go. He joined his eldest sister, Constance, in Frognal, a long road that climbs steeply to Hampstead Heath past University College School, at which, in its Gower Street days, he had spent a few terms half a century before.

But grief and troubles were accumulating. Since the still more distant years at Leamington the children of the restless James Spilsbury had always been deeply attached to one another, and a sorrow the more poignant because it ensued so soon after the loss of Peter was the death of Constance Spilsbury herself, which occurred almost exactly a year after her brother joined her at Hampstead. Yet another blow, to him in some ways the saddest of all, was to come.

Chapter 2: MASS MURDER AND MAD MURDER

It is a relief to turn away for a time from the tale of misfortunes which, in the last and most vulnerable years of his life, fell crushingly upon a great and lovable man. These misfortunes were unsuspected by the tens of thousands of people, many of them facing tragedies of their own, who knew Spilsbury only by name and reputation. To the public he was still the figure he had been for a generation—the incomparable witness and solver of mysteries, an outstanding personality in the criminal courts, a walking legend. Nor was the public wrong; there was as yet no perceptible change in the side they saw or read of, no diminution of skill and patience and authority, and if "Spilsbury in the Box" made fewer and smaller headlines than in old days, violent death was much more common, and private murder was almost crowded out of the papers by news that might affect any household in the land. When murder did occur—at least in the London area—as often as ever Spilsbury was among the earliest on the scene, and a predominant figure in whatever proceedings might follow. His only concession to altered circumstances, which included the hardships of wartime, was that he avoided long journeys. After his illness in the spring of 1940 he is not often found travelling far out of London, though when he had barely emerged from convalescence he went to Pembury, in Kent, to perform the post-mortems on the three victims of Mrs Ransom, whose crimes are dealt with in an earlier chapter. At the later police-court proceedings his reports were read.

In October he went as far as Ventnor, in the Isle of Wight, on another shooting case, the murder of Frank Cave, a man of sixty-five, by Mabel Lucy Attrill, whose weapon, like Mrs Ransom's, was a shot-gun. A third murder by shooting, in London in December, belonged to a class that was to become increasingly common with the growth of armed forces in the country. For killing a man named Sholman with a rifle James McCallum, a lance-corporal of the Canadian Military Police, was sentenced to penal servitude for life.

Including the trial of Udham Singh, Spilsbury was concerned in ten cases of murder that year. Of another dozen in 1941 one took him to Chichester and a second to Dover. The murder of Lilian Welch, a member of the A.T.S., near Chichester in February was marked by peculiar circumstances and extreme brutality. William Flack, of the Royal Corps of Signals, a man with a record of violence, deliberately drove the wheel of a heavy lorry over her head. In the same month, at Westminster, Spilsbury was examining the body of Harry Distleman, aged thirty-six, dead of a stab-wound under the left armpit which severed the axillary artery and the accompanying vein—the stroke of a practised user of the knife. The case recalled old memories, for the murderer was Antonio Mancini, a name known throughout the country at the time of the Brighton murders seven years before, when it was the alias adopted by John England, or Notyre.

Two cards dated April 18 are filled with details of head-wounds inflicted on George Ambridge, a man of fifty-six, of whose murder at Willesden James O'Connor was convicted and William Redhead acquitted. The death sentence on O'Connor was commuted to penal servitude for life. Among Spilsbury's other homicidal cases of that year one was remarkable for the use by the murderer, Lionel Watson, a bakelite moulder, of prussic acid, with which he poisoned Phyllis Crocker and her two-year old daughter. A crime of a type only too common, which remained unsolved, though rumour was soon to link it with the sensations of February 1942, was the killing of Maple Church, a girl of nineteen, whose body was found in October in a bombed building in Hampstead Road.

The records preserved of another very full year in coroners' courts, almost all in London, reflect little more than did those of 1914–18 of the conditions of wartime, aggravated though these conditions were. Air-raids account for only a handful of cases. There is once more an apparent increase in the proportion of suicides. That limitations of diet had not yet cured the English of the habit of gobbling their food is suggested by two cases of asphyxia. A middle-aged man died because a mass of meat five inches long became wedged in his larynx, and a young woman came to the same end through trying to swallow a whole rasher of bacon, rind and all. And in August, after carrying out post-mortems in almost every imaginable locale, Spilsbury had a new experience when he performed one in the Tower of London, where a British subject named Jakobs was shot as a spy. One of the firing-squad appears to have fired high, his bullet entering the head, but there were seven wounds in the target area over the heart.

2

The year 1942, which opened with new military disasters, but was to end with El Alamein and the landings in North Africa, will always be criminologically famous for a series of murders unparalleled since Jack the Ripper terrorized Whitechapel. Most of the victims plied the same dangerous trade as that of the Ripper's, but belonged to the more prosperous half-world of the West End. Spilsbury justly described some of the injuries characteristic of these crimes as "frightful," and only the swift sequence of events, including the apprehension of the murderer within a week of his first killing, stayed a panic that might have equalled that of 1888.

On the morning of February 9 the body of a woman was found in a surface air-raid shelter in Montagu Place, between Edgware Road and Baker Street. She had been strangled. Her handbag was missing, but she was identified next day as Miss Evelyn Margaret Hamilton, a school-teacher aged forty. She was on her way from the South of England to her home in Newcastle. Her presence in the district where she was killed, and the circumstances leading to her death, remain unexplained. It is possible that in the black-out her murderer conveyed the body from elsewhere.

Within thirty-six hours of this discovery a younger woman, Evelyn Oatley, described as married and at one time an actress, was found with her throat cut in a room in Wardour Street. She was lying naked on the bed, and was otherwise shockingly maltreated, among the weapons which the murderer left behind being a tin-opener. Spilsbury's examination of the body showed that she had been throttled into unconsciousness before she was killed.

This murder came to light on the 11th, and on the night of the 13th there was news of two more. Mr Jouannet, the manager of a hotel, returning to his flat in Sussex Gardens, near Paddington, in the same Edgware Road district as Montagu Place, discovered his wife dead in conditions which in many respects resembled the murder of Evelyn Oatley. Mrs Jouannet, who helped in the management of the hotel, used, for other purposes, the name of Doris Robson; by a coincidence her home, like Miss Hamilton's, was Newcastle. About the same time the police were called to a house in Gosfield Street, between Broadcasting House and the Middlesex Hospital, where they found the fourth victim of the series, Mrs Margaret Florence Lowe. Spilsbury, called in to all four cases, said that Mrs Lowe had died only an hour or two before Mrs Jouannet. Both had been strangled.

For a few days, over a considerable area of London, to the danger and gloom of the black-out, the strain of war, and the continuing tale of bad news—Singapore fell at the time of these murders—a real terror was added. Women were afraid to go out alone, and rumours of new crimes spread through Paddington and Soho. Nor were they all rumours; during these days four other women reported to the police that they had been attacked in the darkness by a man who tried to strangle them. It was natural that two unsolved crimes of a similar type, just four months old and occurring near together in time and place in the same north-western region of London—the murders of Maple Church, in Hampstead Road, and of Mrs Humphries in Gloucester Crescent—should be attributed by popular belief to the sadistic strangler now abroad.

Thanks to the energetic work of the C.I.D., the terror was short-lived. On February 16, only three days after the last murders, Frederick Cummins, a leading aircraftman and air cadet, was detained on suspicion, to be charged on the following day with the murders of Evelyn Oatley, Mrs Lowe, and Mrs Jouannet. On the 20th he was further charged with attacking Mrs Greta Heywood near the Haymarket on the night of the 12th, and on the 12th of March with a similar attack on Mrs Kathleen King, or Mulcahy, at Paddington. Finally, on March 27, he was accused of the first of his known crimes, the murder of Miss Hamilton, and committed for trial.

Cummins, who was twenty-eight, was a sexual maniac, but in other ways he was sane enough. His murders were committed partly for gain. He robbed all his victims, and Evelyn Oatley's cigarette-case was found in his room. Among the clues which led to his speedy downfall were the prints of his left little finger on the tin-opener found in Wardour Street, and of his left thumb on a mirror there. Soon after his trial opened at the Old Bailey on April 25 Superintendent Cherrill was giving evidence about the print of the little finger when he noticed that the wrong photograph had been handed to the jury. Though of the same finger, it was not the print in the case then being tried, that of Evelyn Oatley. It came from one of the other murders. The jury was discharged, and a new trial, before a fresh jury, began two days later.

Cummins having been convicted of Miss Oatley's murder, and his appeal dismissed, he was hanged on June 25, less than five months after his multiple crimes were committed. Spilsbury performed the post-mortem on the body after execution.

3

This autopsy was Spilsbury's third that year in these circumstances, and he was to perform six more in 1942. Seven took place at Wandsworth, and two at Pentonville. In 1943 he performed another eight after judicial hangings. Since executions in public were put a stop to they have been conducted under increasingly strict conditions, and until Spilsbury's day it was almost unknown for the subsequent post-mortems to be performed by anyone but the prison doctor. One or two London coroners, however, took to calling him in on such occasions when his services were available. His interest in the effects of judicial hanging, on humanitarian grounds, was well-known, and his realization that the cervical spine should be broken at a more or less constant level led, as has been seen, to a modification of existing practice in the case of the drop. In his later years he was more and more often called in to these post-mortems when his other work permitted.

He was again at Wandsworth less than a fortnight after the hanging of Frederick Cummins, but there is no indication on his case-card that the story of Alphonse-Louis-Eugène Timmermann, executed on July 7, falls into a different category from the rest. It is in accordance with a custom adopted in these later years, not for security reasons, that Spilsbury ends his notes with the formula "No history."

Timmermann was a Belgian, aged thirty-seven. Arriving in England from Lisbon that summer in a British ship full of refugees, he told circumstantial tales of the adventures and hardships of a journey across occupied France and a hostile Spain to freedom. He wished to join the Belgian merchant fleet then sailing from British ports. His papers from the Belgian consulate in Portugal appeared to be in order, and up to a point he had been well coached; but, as so often happened, German *Grundlichkeit*, or thoroughness, was marred by an elementary blunder. In Timmermann's wallet were a small square of cotton-wool, some orange-sticks, and an envelope containing Pyramidon powder, things which he could have acquired in England. They are the tools for invisible writing, and they hanged him. Being a very short man, weighing only 120 lb., he was given a long drop—nearly 9 feet.

Spilsbury was concerned in another spy case, full details of which cannot be told. The story begins like that of Timmermann and many more, with the landing in England of a man who alleged that he had escaped from occupied Europe to serve in the armed forces organized by his legitimate Government, then functioning in London. Suspicions were aroused, and the man was seized and questioned by that Government's intelligence service. He was perhaps treated with some severity, and, after confessing that he was a German, and had been sending information by radio, he collapsed. He died that night in the cellar in which he was confined. The irregularity of these proceedings was only one among several reasons for keeping them quiet. Certain British authorities (not the police) having been consulted, a coroner was informed, who at once removed the body and got in touch with Spilsbury. The circumstances were explained to the latter, and testimony at the subsequent inquest, including Spilsbury's, though adequate, was so limited that no information that could be of use to the enemy was disclosed.

Of the nine murder investigations in which Spilsbury was engaged in 1942 five were shooting cases. Excluding the last, which remains unsolved—the death of G. W. Gardiner in Kilburn in December from a bullet through the neck—the series ended as it began, with a case at least in one respect unparalleled.

At the outbreak of war Reginald Sidney Buckfield was a labourer living at Houghton, near Mansfield, in Nottinghamshire. He was a married man with three children. Enlisting in 1940, he saw service in Africa. In October 1942 he was roaming about the northern part of Kent, absent without leave from his unit, an anti-aircraft battery stationed at Gravesend, and maintaining himself by working for farmers. On the morning of the 10th of that month he was stopped by a police constable in Gravesend Road, on the outskirts of Strood, and, having admitted that he was an absentee, was taken to the police station at Rochester, which forms, with Strood and Chatham, one large town. There his uniform was taken for examination, his fingerprints were taken, and a hair was pulled from his head. He remarked that there was something fishy about this: a man did not have his fingerprints taken and his hair pulled out for being an absentee. "It seems funny," he added; "every time I make a break there is either a break or a murder, and I have already been interrogated for two." Later, to the Chief Constable of Rochester, he said that he had been interrogated for three murders. His treatment might seem fishy, but murder had not been mentioned; he was detained as an absentee, pending the arrival of a military escort to remove him.

He was, in fact, suspected of murdering Mrs Ellen Symes, who had been stabbed in the neck on the evening of the 9th in Brompton Farm Road, a turning off Gravesend Road. She was pushing her son of four in a perambulator, and the child told the police that a soldier had attacked his mother, but he could not, of course, give evidence in court. (There is an analogy here with an undisclosed feature of the Rouse case.) Mrs Symes, who was expecting another child, was able to push the perambulator almost to her own house in Brompton Farm Road before she collapsed and died.

During the first day that Buckfield was in a cell at Rochester police station he was busy writing. When the military escort came for him on the 13th he handed a dozen sheets of paper to a detective, saying, "Read them very, very carefully. You'll find them very interesting." This was no more than the truth. The prisoner had been writing a story, entitled "The Mystery of the Brompton Road Murders, by Gunner Buckfield." Told largely in dialogue by Buckfield himself, under his nickname of Smiler, for he was always smiling, it was unfinished, but it revealed knowledge of the circumstances of Mrs Symes' death which should have been unknown to him on the day when he said he wrote it, October 10. Only nicknames and abbreviations were used, such as "Pop" and "Bert," none of which, except Buckfield's own, had any connexion with the case, and there was a mysterious Stranger towards whom suspicion was obviously supposed to be directed. "Bert," however, who was made to be jealous of his wife, had points of resemblance to Mr Symes.

In possession of this singular document, probably the only one of its kind, and also of a bone-handled table-knife, found in a garden near the scene of the crime, which several witnesses identified as Buckfield's, the police went on collecting more evidence until November 9, when the prisoner was charged with the murder. He was tried at the Old Bailey before Mr Justice Hallett on January 20, 1943. Spilsbury, who had conducted the post-mortem on the body of Mrs Symes and had examined the knife, was the third witness called by the prosecution. He had not much to say, except that the blow must have been delivered with a good deal of force, for the point of the weapon had gone a quarter of an inch into the bone of the spine, and that the knife exhibited could have inflicted such a wound. Under cross-examination he denied that the murderer must necessarily have got his clothing bloodstained.

The attempt of the defence to build up an alibi for the accused came to nothing. Buckfield's explanation of the damning title he had given his work of fiction was that he was thinking of Brompton Road in London. An illiterate man, but not without intelligence, he had convicted himself, like so many more, by trying to be clever. His behaviour, however—he smiled at everything and everybody—

suggested strongly that his intelligence was deranged; and, the jury having brought in a verdict of guilty, the judge, in passing sentence of death, observed that, as was usual, investigation would be made as to whether there was any medical explanation of the act. Buckfield was reprieved, and sent to Broadmoor.

Chapter 3: THE TYRANNY OF WORK

WHEN Spilsbury joined his sister at a private hotel in Frognal in March 1941 he had no intention of remaining there for long. For a still busy man, liable to be called out to travel considerable distances at any hour, Hampstead had all the disadvantages of St John's Wood, and he expected soon to find other quarters as centrally situated as his chambers in Verulam Buildings. The events of the past year, however, had no doubt sapped his energies more profoundly than at first he realized. To do anything beyond his accustomed round had become an effort. He does not seem to have made a serious attempt to find a new home for himself before the illness and death of Constance Spilsbury in the following spring still further taxed resources gravely weakened by failing health and the yet greater shock of his son's death; and from now onward—that is, from March 1942—he appears to have resigned himself to a mode of life markedly at variance with the habits of the individualist he had been, and, indeed, remained.

He gained benefits to which these habits had made him unaccustomed. His wife was out of London; one son was in the Army, and the other too delicate to do more for his father than help him with clerical work in his laboratory. His daughter, whom he saw constantly, could not then make a home for him. In Hampstead, for the first time for years, and when he most needed attention, he was relieved of the necessity of looking after himself. How little, however, a novel environment caused him to change the habits of a lifetime is shown in many instances. To the day of his death there were guests at the hotel who did not know who he was. They saw him only at breakfast, reading the paper or writing his notes; after that he would walk downhill to the garage in Finchley Road where he kept his car and go off on his round of post-mortems at various coroners' courts, or perhaps to assist the police in a case of murder. Any spare hours were spent as usual in the laboratory in the Department of Pharmacology in the University College buildings in Gower Street, where, after the students and staff were evacuated, he was often the only person at work. He had dinner at one or the other of his clubs—latterly, as a rule, at the United Universities. During the six years he lived at the hotel he dined there only three times.

Even less than usual was seen of him at week-ends, which he spent with friends, often enjoying the one relaxation left to him—listening to Sunday-afternoon concerts broadcast by the B.B.C. In the summer, when he could spare the time, he would go away from Friday to Monday with Alan or some other member of his family to that West of England where almost all his holidays were spent. At this time he was lecturing at the hospital at Godalming, and in the long evenings of double summer-time Dr Gardner used to drive him there. The pair would then dine at the Talbot at Ripley, or at some other country inn which had a flower-garden, and afterwards spend a quiet hour among the colour and scent of the flowers which Spilsbury loved, but which he never had time to cultivate.

Always uncommunicative on personal matters, he now went about his work more than ever absorbed in it, or in his thoughts, carrying his habit of reticence so far that many of his friends among the police knew nothing of the change in his mode of life, and supposed the proprietress of the hotel, who took telephone calls for him, to be his secretary. His friends, watching with concern the gradual but marked decline of his health and energy, more than once urged him to consult some fellow medical man. But Spilsbury knew all about his health—by now, indeed, too much.

When in his early days at the hotel he was once or twice asked for medical advice he always replied that he was not a general practitioner. He had not lost his very personal sense of humour, and hypochondriacal fellow-guests would be somewhat taken aback by his addendum that when they were dead he would cut them up and tell them what was the matter. He had a small bedroom, No. 5, on the second floor. It looked down on to the steep street, lined here with tall, inconvenient red-brick houses, just above the point where it turns sharply to fall to Finchley Road. In this room, simply furnished, with a divan bed and a small writing-table, he spent his nights for six years—sleeping, when he could sleep, and, when he could not, filling in post-mortem forms and writing his notes. During the heavy bombing raids he would join the other guests in a back sitting-room on the ground floor, bringing his cards and notebooks with him, and behaving with his usual unruffled calm. Bombs fell on either side of the hotel, but it escaped serious damage. Almost his only visitors were his family. Alan was constantly there, and Richard whenever he was on leave. It was a queer life for such a man as Spilsbury, at once a public figure and a recluse, but with his kindliness and capacity for getting on with every one, his equability of temper, and the self-sufficiency which had always made such small demands on others, he appeared to adapt himself to it from the first. In fact, it was a long time since the places where he slept or ate his meals had played any important part in his life. That was lived within himself, and in his work. Faced with this detachment, few of those who now saw him daily can have guessed, if they did not know, what he had been through—still less the fears he had already begun to feel for the future.

2

Of the post-mortems he performed in 1943 Spilsbury preserved case-cards of more than three hundred. This and the following year are the last of which such records approach completeness. Except for perhaps half a dozen, these autopsies were performed in London, a very high proportion at St Pancras, where Spilsbury's old friend Bentley Purchase, for many years Coroner for the Northern District, had since 1940 been giving him more and more work locally, to spare him the fatigue of journeys farther afield. The eight post-mortems conducted after executions, again mostly at Wandsworth, included that on the body of F. J. Winter, Spilsbury's third spy. One more judicial hanging in 1944 closes a series going back to the execution of Mahon, twenty years earlier. Uniform among the non-medical features of these cases is the description of the deceased as well nourished, whether or no they partook of the proverbial last hearty breakfast.

Only one of Spilsbury's half-dozen capital cases that year took him out of London. Chichester was again the scene of a murder by a soldier, and the description of the terrible knife-wounds inflicted on a girl of twenty-two by Charles Raymond, a French-Canadian, fills nearly five cards. But though Spilsbury played no part in the early stages of a later case of murder at Portsmouth, he intervened decisively at the end.

On November 29, Mrs Robinson, the proprietress of the John Barleycorn public house in Commercial Road, Portsmouth, was found dead in her bedroom. In addition to head injuries, her throat "bore marks which gave unmistakable evidence of strangulation by hand. The injuries were consistent with strangulation by the application and tightening of a right hand from in front." This description is quoted from an article on the case contributed to the *Police Journal* by Dr Keith Simpson, who examined Mrs Robinson's body after Scotland Yard had been called in. He also found scratches on the throat apparently made by two finger-nails. Mrs Robinson was an elderly woman, and the motive of the crime was robbery, £450 having been stolen.

Three weeks later the police detained a man named Harold Loughans, who was alleged to have been heard to say, "I did the murder in Hampshire fourteen days ago." His right hand was deformed, but it was found by Keith Simpson to span very closely the distances between the finger-marks on Mrs Robinson's throat, and on December 21 Loughans was charged with the murder. When the case came up for trial at the Winchester Assizes in March 1944, the jury was unable to agree. A fresh trial began at the Old Bailey on the 22nd of the month. The defence had by now sought the help of Spilsbury. It was obvious to him, as soon as he had examined the accused man's right hand and arm, that Loughans was incapable of exerting any pressure whatever with those fingers. Several years before he had got the hand caught in some machinery; in wrenching it out he pulled away all the muscles of the arm, and though after his injuries were healed his fingers were saved, they could be bent in any direction, and were quite useless—so useless, in Spilsbury's opinion, that they had not even the power to leave a scratch. At the second trial this evidence was conclusive, and Loughans was acquitted. It is not uncommon for innocent men to boast of committing murder, though why they do so is a mystery; and Loughans was far from a model character, for within two months of his release he was given a five years' sentence for housebreaking.

With the end of Hitler in the following year Spilsbury was told that he might be required to identify the Führer's body. At a meeting of the Medico-Legal Society he said that Hitler had abnormally long thumbs, especially the right one. In 1945 he also examined three pieces of leather brought from Buchenwald concentration camp. One had been made into a knife-case; another, which was tattooed, came from a lamp-shade. The tattooing, Spilsbury said, proved that this specimen was human skin, as, in his opinion, were the others.

3

The tyranny of work is tolerable when it is an end in itself, as long as there is yet some mirage of achievement in view, and while another delusion endures—that it is possible to stop. It becomes a tragedy when an ageing and ailing man has still to drive himself to earn a living and to provide for others. There is no discharge in that war. No one can say when Spilsbury first faced the truth that time was running desperately short, that his great powers might soon begin to fail him, that a lifetime of unselfish labours had brought him within sight of comparative poverty, and that the book he had lived with was indeed a mirage, and would never be begun. He never talked about this, but there is indirect evidence that by the early 1940's—probably after his stroke—the fear of the future was upon him.

He suffered from arthritis, but the only really serious thing the matter with him, and the cause of the stroke, was an internal complaint which could probably have been cured by an operation. His friends urged him to have one, but he always made light of the matter. His real reason, for he once admitted it, was the fear that during an illness and convalescence others might step into his place and deprive him, when his health was restored, of work which had become a financial necessity. It was not in his nature to realize that though no man is indispensable, some are all but irreplaceable, and that of such he was one. If he could have regained normal health all the work he could do would have been thrust upon him. By compelling himself to struggle on against growing infirmities he brought about the conditions he dreaded. The work was there, but others stepped in to do much of it because he was no longer physically capable of doing it himself.

The final tragedy was to come. He was devoted to his delicate eldest son. The two were together every day in the Gower Street laboratory, yet when Alan fell ill in November 1945 his father had not realized that he was ailing. In three days the young man was dead, of galloping consumption.

Chapter 4: THE LAST CASES—CORNOCK AND ANTIQUIS

IF, towards the very end, Spilsbury seemed to those who knew him best a shadow of his former self, even the shadow was a formidable one. In his last year a newspaper reference to his name could influence the issue in a trial for murder. At the Bristol Assizes Mrs Cecil Cornock was in the dock, accused of murdering her husband in December 1946. The case was one which brought to light masochistic practices by the dead man similar to those indulged in, also with fatal results, by the two young Ellises. Mrs Cornock's solicitor, Mr R. Addington Ingle, says of it:

> On the last day of the trial the *Daily Mail* published an article headed "Spilsbury advises the Defence," and while, at that stage of the proceedings, all evidence had been called, there is no doubt at all in my own mind that the mere fact that this article appeared, indicating that Spilsbury was interested in the matter, had a very substantial psychological effect on the minds of the jury, and I feel largely contributed to the successful termination of the case from Mrs Cornock's point of view.

Mr Ingle was writing to forward a statement by Dr Charles Gibson, Lecturer in Forensic Medicine at Bristol University and Surgeon to the Bath City Police. Dr Gibson first met Spilsbury at an inquest in 1937 His statement tells more fully how, ten years later, the shadow of a great name could still reach from London to Bristol.

> At Bristol in December 1946 Cecil George Cornock was found drowned in his bath under extremely suspicious circumstances. At the time of his death there were in the house his wife, their ten-year-old son, and a crippled man who was a friend of Mrs Cornock's. Circumstances pointing to foul play were:
>
> 1. The deceased was found at post-mortem examination to be a perfectly healthy man.
> 2. There were multiple injuries to his head and limbs.
> 3. There were marks round his wrist and ankles where he had clearly been recently bound by cords.
> 4. A large number of letters of an affectionate character were found to have been mutually exchanged between Mrs Cornock and the cripple.

5. A period of nearly two hours had elapsed between the wife finding her husband submerged in his bath and any attempt being made to summon aid from doctor, ambulance, or police.

Mrs Cornock having been charged with the murder, Dr Gibson was called in to assist the defence. The Crown's case was that Cornock had been tied in his bath with cords round his wrists and ankles, that he had been struck six blows on the head with a large toy boat weighing a pound and a half, and that, having been thus stunned, he was pushed under the bath-water and drowned. There was no dispute about the cause of death, which was drowning, but the defence challenged all the other medical theories of the Crown pathologists.

Cornock was a sexual pervert of the type that desires the infliction of physical pain upon himself by others. He would insist upon being beaten while tightly bound to the tripod of an electric boiler. The defence was that he had been indulging in these practices just before he went to his bath, and Dr Gibson proved by experiments on himself that marks of a cord tied round a wrist would be noticeable several hours after the cord had been removed.

The main issue, he points out, was the interpretation of the various injuries, particularly those on the head. Police photographs showed these to be black, and pathologists described them as "abrasions with bruising." There was not the slightest break in the skin of the skull, and in contrast with the apparent severity of the injuries, as seen in the photographs, microscopic slides of sections of the actual wounds showed very little bruising. Dr Gibson's view was that violent blows from such an implement as the toy boat would cause considerable bruising—that is, spilling of blood—in the scalp tissues.

"I felt," he goes on,

> that the explanation of the small amount of bruising was that the head, and, indeed, the whole body, had been subjected to a number of unavoidable bumps when Mrs Cornock and the cripple were struggling to get this six-foot unconscious wet man out of the bath. They also half carried, half dragged him from the tiny bathroom across a passage into a bedroom where the wife tried to resuscitate her drowned husband by artificial respiration.
>
> At this stage I felt I must have confirmation, criticism, or rejection of my theories before I could put them before an Assize Court. I felt that this help could be of value only if it were given by the highest and most experienced authority. I remembered the friendly help and courtesy shown me ten years previously by Sir Bernard Spilsbury. It was nevertheless with some trepidation that I wrote to ask if I could come to see him. I had neither the claim of being an old friend, nor an old student of his.

Sir Bernard replied at once saying that he would be delighted to help me and putting a whole afternoon at my disposal.

He gave me a most cordial reception in his laboratory on the 5th of February, 1947. I was rather struck with the toll which the past ten years had taken of him physically, and he looked considerably older than his seventy years. Mentally, however, his powers seemed to be unchanged, and his grasp of a rather complicated story was completely sure.

Dr Gibson describes how Spilsbury asked for the prosecution's evidence in detail, as it had been given in the magistrates' court, making notes and putting a very occasional question. Then he made a careful study of the police photographs of Cornock's body, and tested the effect of blows by the duplicate model boat made by Dr Gibson for demonstration. He then settled down to a most minute examination of Dr Gibson's microscopic slides.

"The time seemed endless," the statement continues,

while I waited for his verdict on them. At last he looked up and said, "There is no bruising at all in these sections of the skull." I pointed out one small area where there was a little spilt blood, and, having looked at it again, Sir Bernard said, "That is minimal bruising, and could not possibly be caused by a heavy blow from the boat."

Discussing the case at length, and listening to his visitor's reconstruction of events, Spilsbury said that he wanted more proof of some of the points, and that it must be visible proof, to convince a jury. At the same time he was already firmly of the opinion that the prosecution's theory was totally wrong. Puzzled by the discrepancy between the appearance of bruising on the photographs and the absence of it in the microscopic sections, he finally suggested that Dr Gibson should find out what type of photographic plates had been used.

Dr Gibson returned to Bath greatly encouraged. A fortnight later he was in London again, spending another afternoon with Spilsbury. The police photographs, he had learnt, were taken on orthochromatic plates which made a red colour appear as a dark black. The apparent bruises were, in fact, abrasions which could easily have been caused without the use of violence. Armed with this information, he found Spilsbury, who said that he had been giving the case much thought, prepared to agree whole-heartedly with his original reconstruction.

At the request of Mrs Cornock's solicitors Dr Gibson afterwards invited Spilsbury to give evidence for the defence, but the latter replied that the strain of a four-day murder trial away from London was more than his physique would stand. He had, however, done all that was needed. He had given his immense experience and his encouragement to the defence, and at almost the last minute a newspaper heading added the weight of his name.

"I shall always remember with gratitude," Dr Gibson concludes,

> the enormous moral support which Sir Bernard gave me. The trial lasted a full four days, and I could feel his presence with me throughout. Some people have regarded him as a man who liked the limelight, but in my view that was not true. He gave me who had no claim on him the most patient help and kindly encouragement in this case in which he was not going to figure. I feel sure that when Mrs Cornock was found "Not Guilty" Sir Bernard regarded himself as rewarded for having been instrumental again in bringing justice to pass, as he had done so many hundreds of times before.
>
> I never saw him again, but not long after I mourned the passing of a great gentleman and a brilliant medical jurist.

2

Alec de Antiquis was a man of thirty-one, the father of six children, the owner of a prosperous little motor-cycle repair shop in South London, and a one-time corporal instructor in the Home Guard. He was shot dead in broad daylight by one of three young ruffians escaping from a jeweller's shop which they had raided. Three years before, the brother of one of his murderers—all three carried firearms, and were equally guilty—had been sentenced to eight years' penal servitude for manslaughter in the case of Captain Binney, who, like de Antiquis, had tried to stop some escaping shop-breakers. It should cause surprise and disgust that any sympathy can be felt for irreclaimable blackguards who start as what are called juvenile delinquents, graduate at Borstal, and become habitual criminals of the most dangerous type; but while poor Alec de Antiquis, who was doing his duty as a citizen, got a bullet through his head and was forgotten, letters poured into the office of the Home Secretary protesting against the execution of his murderers. However, Mrs de Antiquis got a medal from the police. They have no illusions about these things.

They certainly had none about Harry Jenkins, who had two convictions before he was twenty for assaulting policemen, breaking the jaw of one of them. Christopher James Geraghty had twice escaped from Borstal, where, as he said, "the idea of going straight is laughed at," and where, again in his own words, he learnt to be vicious and took pride in being the terror of the others. In April 1947 this pair, with friends of the same kidney, had recently carried out an armed robbery in Bayswater. One of the friends having disappeared with the proceeds, Jenkins and Geraghty were in need of money. With a younger boy, Terence Rolt, who was only seventeen, they planned a raid on a jeweller's shop at the corner of Tottenham Street and Charlotte Street, not far from the scene of Voisin's murder thirty years before. At lunch-time on April 29 they drove up in a stolen car, handkerchiefs tied round their faces, bludgeoned two old men in the shop and fired at one of them, and were then driven out by assistants who came running from a back room. The stolen car was jammed by a lorry which had backed in front of it during the melée, and the trio, revolvers in hand, ran down the street, making for Tottenham Court Road. Alec de Antiquis, riding along Charlotte Street on his motor-cycle, switched off his engine and ran his heavy machine in the path of the fugitives. One of them—it was Geraghty—shot him through the head. At least one other passer-by, George Grimshaw, a surveyor, attempted to stop the murderers, but was thrown to the ground and severely kicked. With the streets full of shoppers and people going to lunch, the three got away.

The officer whose turn of duty put him in charge of the case—he was deputizing for Chief Superintendent Barratt—was Superintendent Robert Fabian. Descriptions of the three criminals were contradictory and of little help. There were no fingerprints, and no clues in the abandoned car, which had been stolen only a few minutes before the crime. Two revolver bullets, one from the head of de Antiquis and one from the wall of the shop, came from different weapons. Nearly three days went by before information from a taxi-driver sent Fabian and his men to Brook House, a block of offices in Tottenham Court Road. In a disused office on the top floor, where two of the murderers had hidden for a time, were found a raincoat, a cap, a pair of gloves, and a scarf folded into a triangle, its ends knotted. The ticket of a firm of multiple tailors inside the lining of the raincoat led Fabian, after routine inquiries, to the home of the Jenkins family in Bermondsey. The end was now in sight. Harry Jenkins would say nothing, but Geraghty betrayed the boy Rolt, and Rolt told the rest of the story.

Before any one of the three was charged two revolvers were found in the Thames mud at Wapping. One was the weapon with which Antiquis was shot; the second had been fired in the jeweller's shop. Firearms were, indeed, being jettisoned all over London. The atrocious circumstances of the murder caused a stir even in the criminal world; and no one disapproved more strongly of the methods used than quiet, respectable craftsmen who regarded burglary or housebreaking as a business like any other, tried to provide for their wives and children against rainy days, and played the game with the police.

At the Old Bailey, in July, Jenkins and Geraghty were sentenced to death. Rolt, being too young for the death penalty, though old enough to commit robbery under arms, was sentenced to be detained for a recommended period of not less than five years. Appeals and sentimental petitions having failed, the older pair—Jenkins was twenty-three, and Geraghty twenty-one—were very properly hanged.

Spilsbury had been called in the day after the shooting. In this, his last big case, he was once more associated with old friends. The coroner for the district was Bentley Purchase. Fabian, a young man as superintendents go, was well known to them both. He was with Spilsbury when the latter examined the body of Alec de Antiquis, and he was shocked by what, to him, was a marked and sudden declension of sureness and perception that had become legendary. Not long before, Dr Gibson had been impressed by Spilsbury's grasp both of the detail and the broad outline of a case. Now Spilsbury was sadly puzzled, looking for the exit wound of the bullet, which remained in the dead man's head. It fell out during the examination, and Fabian handed it to him, reminding him that he had found it. But Spilsbury knew that he had not found it. For a moment his powers had lapsed, and he may have been aware of other lapses.

Chapter 5: THE FINAL POST-MORTEM

DURING the last year of the War, and the beginning of what was to follow it, it was obvious to Spilsbury's few close friends that the decline of his general health and mental alertness, first noticeable after his stroke in 1940, was becoming ever more marked. On medical questions, until the very end, his conclusions were as unassailable as ever; but the process of arriving at them was slowing down. In other matters he who would never make a decision until reflection assured him that it was the right one now put off making it because his mind was tired. Such mechanical work as writing reports and filling in forms, which from deep-rooted habit he could not delegate to others, suffered with the rest, and this in spite of what very few people knew, that he had more time for writing. The insomnia caused by his complaint was growing worse.

To strangers and the undiscerning he did not seem much altered. He now habitually wore glasses; his hair was whiter; but normally he kept his fresh colouring, and, with the plumpness of figure and face which blurred the once clear-cut features, he looked more than ever like a benevolent agriculturist, as may be seen in a photograph taken as late as the time of the Antiquis case. He is leaving the Old Bailey at a brisk walk, as neatly dressed as ever, and a rather wary look from behind the glasses may be due to the fact that he had seen the photographer. He never abated his dislike of being photographed.

He was still lecturing at the Royal Free Hospital and at St Thomas's. Otherwise his days were spent as they had been spent for forty years, at coroners' courts, where work at the post-mortem table was becoming more difficult as arthritis began to cripple his hands. Nothing would induce him to modify his methods, though it was a serious matter to him that the number of autopsies he now got through in a week might at one time have been accomplished in a day. This work was his livelihood, but he could not scamp it to earn a few more guineas. So far as he allowed them, his friends did everything to spare him worry and fatigue, and in his last years his income was derived almost wholly from St Pancras and its connected court at Hackney, where Bentley

Purchase saw to it that he was kept too busy to have time for exhausting journeys to more distant courts. Every morning Spilsbury would arrive at the little building among the tombs and flower-beds of old St Pancras churchyard, bringing the completed post-mortem forms of the previous day's work. This was an old habit; he never posted these forms—or only once. Now, however, he would ask if there was anything for him to do.

The steep climb up Frognal from the garage in Finchley Road put a strain upon his overworked heart, and he was glad to sit in the hall of the hotel before starting up the stairs to the second floor. In the winter he suffered from bronchitis and heavy colds. He was growing more absent-minded, and he seems never to have understood such new, irritating worries as the rationing of clothes, food, and petrol.

No one, however, was less given to self-pity, and these last years were not all drabness. Injected into the routine that made life simpler—work, lunch, more work, and then dinner at his club—were the luncheon parties with his daughter and her young friends in the rather curious *milieu* of the station restaurant at Euston. There was always music; there were visits, though becoming rarer, to the West Country, to Minehead or the Luttrell Arms at Dunster; and there was Oxford, his affection for which Spilsbury never lost. The War over, Richard was back there, at Magdalen, his father's college, for the last two years of his interrupted classical studies. Spilsbury went to see him several times, and in May of 1946 was there for Eights Week with a little party consisting of Evelyn, Ernest Goddard, the family lawyer and friend, and Mrs Goddard. They lunched in Eastgate, drove to Magdalen and the river, and dined at the Lambert Arms at Aston Rowant on the way home. If these renewed glimpses of the streets and spires amid which, half a century before, he had spent three happy years, recalled memories of a leave-taking scarcely noticed and soon forgotten, it may have given the most modest of men pleasure to be recognized and cheered on the tow-path.

2

One of the holidays at Minehead, taken shortly before Alan's death in 1945, had lasted longer than usual. A second slight stroke compelled Spilsbury to rest. He is thought to have had a third stroke towards the end of 1947, while alone in his bedroom at the hotel in Hampstead. No medical man living can have known more than he about thrombosis and embolism—his filing cabinets contained records of thousands of cases—or about the cause of these strokes in his own case. Nor can he have had any illusions about the ultimate result, if no cure was attempted, of the consequent insomnia, or, at least, inability, in an increasing degree, to snatch more than short periods of sleep. Two of his friends, in different words, have described that result. One, a fellow-pathologist, has said that of about a thousand cases of suicide that have come within his experience 75 per cent. were due to lack of sleep. The other, to whom fell the distressing task of inquiring into the death of the man he had first seen and admired thirty-seven years before, at the trial of Crippen, said in his summing-up, "This was not the Bernard Spilsbury we knew."

In a man habitually so reserved no one detected the imperceptible change, and it came unrecognized, as it always must, by the sufferer himself. Not even Spilsbury can have known when the inevitable happened, and the balance of an exceptionally equable and well-regulated mind was first disturbed. It remained, however, in some respects so orderly and logical that it is now possible to say that round about such and such a time insomnia, and pain, and worry, definitely took charge.

For many years it had been Spilsbury's custom to order his post-mortem forms in bundles of five hundred. His last order in 1947 was for only a hundred. He began to work through these, and it seems certain that from then onward the final steps were being as methodically planned.

Midway in December he was coming to the end of the forms, and he wrote a letter to Dr Eric Gardner, then in Switzerland. He said that by the time the letter reached his friend, "it would be all over." He would not linger on to be a burden to others. By the same post Dr Gardner received the English papers, in which was the news that it was indeed all over.

On December 17 Spilsbury had left his hotel after breakfast as usual. He took out his car, drove to the St Pancras Coroner's Court, and from there to Hampstead, where he performed a post-mortem. He lunched at his customary table at Euston. In the meantime the proprietress of the hotel, going round the bedrooms after he had left, noticed that his front-door key, which he always carried on his key-ring, was lying on his dressing-table. When in the afternoon he came back, saying that he had forgotten something, he had to ring to be let in; but he did not take the key.

He drove down the hill to the garage in Finchley Road, where he told the staff that he would like to give them their Christmas boxes, as he would not be using his car again before Christmas. A little later he was at his laboratory in University College, destroying papers and notebooks, and writing his last post-mortem report for his friend Purchase. He used his last form, and walked out to catch the 5.30 post, the first and last time he was to use the post for this purpose.

He dined early at his club, as usual by himself. He exchanged a few words with members, and on going out handed to the hall porter the key of his private cupboard. He would not be needing it, he said, in the new year.

About 7.30 he was again in his laboratory in Gower Street. This is a little room with a window at the narrow end overlooking the courtyard. His bench was under the window, with on one side of it a sink, racks of test-tubes, and another bench on which stood Bunsen burners. On a table were his cabinets of case-cards. Since Alan's death he had allowed no one to touch anything in this room, and latterly papers and dust had accumulated. No one who saw Spilsbury in his last days, dressed as carefully as ever, could have guessed that he was too wearied to carry his old fastidiousness further, and that he was now working in conditions that at one time he could not have endured.

At ten minutes past eight that evening a colleague on the university staff returned for some purpose to his own room. Passing the door of Spilsbury's laboratory, he saw a light in the fanlight over the door, and he smelt gas. Spilsbury's poor sense of smell was well known, and, the door being locked, and no answer being received to knocking, a watchman was fetched with the pass-key. When the door was opened it was clear that what had happened was no accident.

Among those first informed was Bentley Purchase. He arrived to find artificial respiration still being tried, and on the official form the time of the death of his old friend was given as ten minutes past nine. But all had been over long before that.

Dr R. H. D. Short, who performed the post-mortem, gave as the primary cause of death coronary thrombosis; the secondary cause was carbon monoxide poisoning.

Spilsbury's remains were cremated at Golders Green. Some who were there, though they had scarcely known him outside professional occasions, came not only to show respect for a great man, but because of the affection they had come to feel for him.

3

The opinions held of Bernard Spilsbury by those who knew him as a man and as a pathologist have been cited in the course of this book. These memories, and a legendary name, are his monument; he left no other, or only an example. A list of his appointments, and of the various bodies and committees on which he was invited to sit, would merely indicate that he was, in the words of the *British Medical Journal*, "one of the most distinguished figures in forensic medicine." Such a list—and it is a long one—gives no hint of his lasting influence on the science of pathology and on medical jurisprudence. He found the former still an empirical science, and left it a precise one, and forensically, it has been said, he raised the giving of professional medical evidence from a suspect and controversial status to an honourable and exact plane.

No layman, in any case, can express views, were more needed, on his professional achievements. To live for many months, however, as it were in his company, is to gain a very decided impression of his character. This is doubly the right word, for he was born in an age, and of a stock, which attached great value to character as a human quality. He lived on into another age, among the marked characteristics of which appear to be self-pity, envy, and hatred; but he himself remained unchanged and unaffected. No man—and in his later years he suffered more than most—can ever have been less touched by bitterness. Fame did not alter him, and its rewards interested him not at all. Truth was what he most cared about, and after that to help, and to be kind; and if he had spent his whole life in general practice in the country, as was once his ambition, he would have been just as great a man.

INDEX